Theorising the Responsibility to Protect

One of the most important developments in world politics in the last decade has been the spread of the idea that state sovereignty comes with responsibilities as well as privileges, and that there exists a global responsibility to protect people threatened by mass atrocities. The principle of the 'Responsibility to Protect' is an acknowledgment by all who live in zones of safety of a duty of care towards those trapped in zones of danger. In this book, Thakur and Maley argue that this principle has not been discussed sufficiently in the context of international and political theory, in particular in terms of the nature and foundations of political and international order and the strength and legitimacy of the state. This book brings together a range of specialist authors to discuss the different ways in which the Responsibility to Protect can be theorised, using case studies to locate the idea within wider traditions of moral responsibilities in international relations.

Ramesh Thakur is director of the Centre for Non-Proliferation and Disarmament at the Australian National University. Formerly assistant secretary-general of the United Nations, he is editor-in-chief of *Global Governance* and a member of the Editorial Board of *Global Responsibility to Protect*. Among his many books are *The United Nations, Peace and Security: From Collective Security to the Responsibility to Protect* (Cambridge, 2006) and *The Responsibility to Protect: Norms, Laws and the Use of Force in International Politics*.

William Maley is professor of diplomacy in the Asia-Pacific College of Diplomacy at The Australian National University, and a member of the Editorial Board of *Global Responsibility to Protect*. He has co-edited *The Soviet Withdrawal from Afghanistan* (Cambridge, 1989) and *Russia in Search of Its Future* (Cambridge, 1995).

Theorising the Responsibility to Protect

Edited by

Ramesh Thakur and William Maley

 CAMBRIDGE
UNIVERSITY PRESS

CAMBRIDGE
UNIVERSITY PRESS

University Printing House, Cambridge CB2 8BS, United Kingdom

Cambridge University Press is part of the University of Cambridge.

It furthers the University's mission by disseminating knowledge in the pursuit of education, learning and research at the highest international levels of excellence.

www.cambridge.org
Information on this title: www.cambridge.org/9781107621947

© Cambridge University Press 2015

First published 2015

Printed in the United Kingdom by Clays, St Ives plc

A catalogue record for this publication is available from the British Library

Library of Congress Cataloguing in Publication data
Theorising the responsibility to protect / edited by Ramesh Thakur, William Maley.
    pages   cm
ISBN 978-1-107-04107-3 (hardback) –
ISBN 978-1-107-62194-7 (paperback)
1. Responsibility to protect (International law)
2. Humanitarian intervention.   I. Thakur, Ramesh Chandra, 1948–
II. Maley, William, 1957–
JZ6369.T47   2015
327.1–dc23

                                                    2015007315

ISBN 978-1-107-04107-3 Hardback
ISBN 978-1-107-62194-7 Paperback

Contents

Figures

Notes on contributors

Editors

Ramesh Thakur is director of the Centre for Non-Proliferation and Nuclear Disarmament in the Crawford School of Public Policy at the Australian National University. Formerly assistant secretary-general of the United Nations, he was a commissioner of the International Commission on Intervention and State Sovereignty and is a member of the editorial board of *Global Responsibility to Protect* and *Global Governance* and editor-in-chief of *Global Governance*. His many books include such titles as *The United Nations, Peace and Security: From Collective Security to the Responsibility to Protect* (Cambridge, 2006).

William Maley is professor of diplomacy at the Asia-Pacific College of Diplomacy at the Australian National University and a member of the editorial board of *Global Responsibility to Protect*. He was a participant in the June 2001 New Delhi Roundtable of the International Commission on Intervention and State Sovereignty and has co-edited *The Soviet Withdrawal from Afghanistan* (Cambridge, 1989) and *Russia in Search of Its Future* (Cambridge, 1995).

Other contributors

Amitav Acharya is UNESCO chair in Transnational Challenges and Governance and chair of the ASEAN Studies Center at the American University in Washington DC, author of *Whose Ideas Matter? Agency and Power in Asian Regionalism* and a member of the editorial board of *Global Responsibility to Protect*.

Alex J. Bellamy is professor of Peace and Conflict Studies at The University of Queensland, director of the Asia Pacific Centre for the Responsibility to Protect and non-resident senior adviser at the International Peace Institute. His recent books include *The Responsibility* *to Protect: A Defense, Providing Peacekeepers* (which he co-edited) and *Massacres and Morality: Mass Killing in an Age of Civilian Immunity.*

Mats Berdal is professor of Security and Development in the Department of War Studies at King's College London. He was formerly director of dtudies at the International Institute for Strategic Studies (IISS). He is the author of *Building Peace after War* and co-editor of *Political Economy of Statebuilding: Power after Peace.*

Michael Byers is Canada research chair in Global Politics and International Law at the University of British Columbia, and author of *Custom, Power and the Power of Rules: International Relations and Customary International Law* (Cambridge, 1999).

Jean-Marc Coicaud is professor of Law and Global Affairs, and director of the Division of Global Affairs at Rutgers University. He is also a global ethics fellow with the Carnegie Council for Ethics in International Affairs. He is author of *Politics and Legitimacy: A Contribution to the Study of Political Right and Political Responsibility* (Cambridge, 2002) and co-editor of *Fault Lines of International Legitimacy* (Cambridge, 2010).

Tim Dunne is executive dean of the Faculty of Humanities and Social Sciences and professor of International Relations at The University of Queensland, where he is also a senior researcher at the Asia Pacific Centre for the Responsibility to Protect. He is a widely published author, having written and edited ten books and over fifty articles and chapters.

Gareth Evans is chancellor of the Australian National University and president emeritus of the International Crisis Group. He was Australian foreign minister from 1988 to 1996 and was co-chair of the International Commission on Intervention and State Sovereignty.

Jonathan Graubart is director of the International Security and Conflict Resolution Program, chair of the Fred J. Hansen Institute for Peace Studies and professor of Political Science at San Diego State University. He specialises in international relations, international law and human rights. Graubart received his PhD in Political Science at the University of Wisconsin-Madison in 2002 and is the author of *Legalizing Transnational Activism: The Struggle to Gain Social Change From NAFTA's Citizen Petitions.*

Susan Harris Rimmer is fellow at the Asia-Pacific College of Diplomacy at the Australian National University, and an Australian Research Council future fellow. She was previously the manager of Advocacy and Development Practice at the Australian Council for

International Development (ACFID), and she has worked for the UN High Commissioner for Refugees, the National Council of Churches and the Australian Parliamentary Library. She is the author of *Gender and Transitional Justice: The Women of Timor Leste*.

Siddharth Mallavarapu is associate professor and chair of the Department of International Relations at the South Asian University, New Delhi, and the author of *Banning the Bomb: The Politics of Norm Creation*. He recently co-edited *International Relations: Perspectives for the Global South*.

Edward Newman is Professor of International Security at the University of Leeds and was previously Director of Studies on Conflict and Security in the Peace and Governance Program of the United Nations University in Tokyo. He is editor of the journal *Civil Wars* and author of *A Crisis of Global Institutions? Multilateralism and International Security* and *The UN Secretary-General from the Cold War to the New Era*.

Jacinta O'Hagan is fellow in International Relations at the Australian National University and author of *Conceptions of the West in International Relations Thought: From Oswald Spengler to Edward Said*.

Charles Sampford is director of the Institute for Ethics, Governance and Law at Griffith University, where he was Foundation Dean of Law. He is author of *Retrospectivity and the Rule of Law* and *The Disorder of Law: A Critique of Legal Theory*.

Abiodun Williams is president of The Hague Institute for Global Justice and was previously vice president of the Center for Conflict Analysis and Prevention at the United States Institute for Peace in Washington DC. He also served as director of the Strategic Planning Unit at the Executive Office of the United Nations Secretary General, and he is author of *Preventing War: The United Nations and Macedonia* and *Many Voices: Multilateral Negotiations in the World Arena*.

Part I

Context

1 Introduction: theorising global responsibilities

Ramesh Thakur and William Maley

One of the most important developments in world politics in the last decade has been the spread of the twin ideas that state sovereignty comes with responsibilities – both domestic and international – as well as privileges, and that there exists a global responsibility to protect people threatened by mass atrocity crimes. The 2001 report of the International Commission on Intervention and State Sovereignty entitled *The Responsibility to Protect* put these ideas into active circulation, and United Nations resolutions in 2005 on the sixtieth anniversary of the establishment of the United Nations gave the idea further substance. More recently, the justification of NATO action in Libya on the strength of Security Council Resolutions 1970 and 1973, which made explicit reference to the principle of the Responsibility to Protect, has put this particular notion at the centre of discussion of some of the most challenging political dilemmas of our times. As international leaders struggle to find ways to deal with mounting political violence in Syria and more recently with the emergence of the self-styled 'Islamic State in Iraq and Syria', the idea of the Responsibility to Protect, now increasingly labelled simply R2P, is never far below the surface.

These concrete political developments have helped to generate a substantial scholarly literature concerned with the genesis of the idea of the Responsibility to Protect, and with the way in which it has been refined through multilateral deliberation. Through mainstream as well as dedicated journals such as *Global Responsibility to Protect*, researchers have sought to explore the ambit of the Responsibility to Protect doctrine, discussing, for example, whether it can properly be applied in circumstances where a population is threatened by the ravages of natural disaster. Nonetheless, in a real sense the doctrine remains under-theorised, or at least only weakly related to existing bodies of theory concerned with the nature and foundations of political and international order. Its implications for ideas about the appropriate scope, strength and legitimacy of the state have received relatively little attention. The aim of this collection is to help to fill this gap.

First, however, it is necessary to set the scene by exploring the context within which the idea of a responsibility to protect took shape. One key element of this context was a critical weakness in the normative framework determining how states should relate to each other and to international organisations. This weakness arose because of the unsatisfactory nature of ideas about 'humanitarian intervention' that had found their way into circulation. The other key element was a sequence of events in which ordinary people were brutalised in ghastly ways in various parts of the world. While the Holocaust had already provided an unprecedentedly horrific example of mass murder on an industrial scale, there had been hopes in the aftermath of the Second World War that the new architecture of the United Nations, the development and anathematisation of the idea of genocide and the capacity of media to expose horrendous acts of cruelty would put a stop to such events. Yet they persisted, and in the post-Cold War period, developments such as ethnic cleansing in the Balkans, and above all the Rwandan genocide of April–June 1994, made it a matter of urgency to find a better way of protecting the vulnerable.

The problem of humanitarian intervention

The use of the vocabulary of humanitarianism to justify political measures – up to and including the use of force – is hardly a novel development.[1] It is relatively straightforward to identify specific impulses in different contexts that one might class as 'humane': the activities of the Knights Hospitaller from the eleventh century, the enactment by the English Parliament of the *Statute of Charitable Uses* of 1601, the Abolitionist activities of figures as diverse as William Wilberforce and John Brown and the establishment of the Red Cross in 1863 all come to mind. The genesis of these impulses was often to be found in religion, and, in this sense, they were not particularly a product of the rationalism and individualism associated with the Enlightenment. Unfortunately, the claim to be acting on humanitarian grounds was open to being used in other ways. The grimmest example of this was provided by Germany in the 1930s, where Berlin frequently sought to justify the expansionism of Germany by reference to alleged infractions of the rights and freedoms of ethnic Germans living in other countries such as Czechoslovakia and Poland.

---

[1] See Nicholas J. Wheeler, *Saving Strangers: Humanitarian Intervention in International Society* (Oxford: Oxford University Press, 2000); Ramesh Thakur, 'Humanitarian Intervention', in Thomas G. Weiss and Sam Daws, eds, *The Oxford Handbook on the United Nations* (Oxford: Oxford University Press, 2007), pp. 387–403.

While earlier conflicts had certainly attracted attention in terms of their humanitarian implications,[2] and statesmen in the 1920s had sought to outlaw war as an instrument of policy,[3] in the aftermath of the Second World War, a new framework of norms and rules was developed to deal with the use of force in international relations, a framework centred on the Charter of the new United Nations. At one level, the framework was a simple one. Article 2.4 provided that 'all Members shall refrain in their international relations from the threat or use of force against the territorial integrity or political independence of any state, or in any other manner inconsistent with the Purposes of the United Nations'. Article 51 provided *inter alia* that 'nothing in the present Charter shall impair the inherent right of individual or collective self-defence if an armed attack occurs against a Member of the United Nations, until the Security Council has taken measures necessary to maintain international peace and security'. Article 39 sought to head off unilateral impulses by stating that 'the Security Council shall determine the existence of any threat to the peace, breach of the peace, or act of aggression and shall make recommendations, or decide what measures shall be taken in accordance with Articles 41 and 42, to maintain or restore international peace and security'. Article 41 provided that 'the Security Council may decide what measures not involving the use of armed force are to be employed to give effect to its decisions', and, critically, Article 42 provided that 'should the Security Council consider that measures provided for in Article 41 would be inadequate or have proved to be inadequate, it may take such action by air, sea, or land forces as may be necessary to maintain or restore international peace and security. Such action may include demonstrations, blockade, and other operations by air, sea, or land forces of Members of the United Nations.'[4]

As can be seen, the United Nations Charter codified both the law and the new normative consensus. One crucial problem, however, remained. When the Charter was being drafted, its authors were haunted by the knowledge that the League of Nations that had been established in 1920 had proven impotent in dealing with the challenges of the 1930s because

---

[2] See Martha Finnemore, *The Purpose of Intervention: Changing Beliefs about the Use of Force* (Ithaca: Cornell University Press, 2003), pp. 58–66; Gary J. Bass, *Freedom's Battle: The Origins of Humanitarian Intervention* (New York: Alfred A. Knopf, 2008).

[3] See William Maley, 'Norms as frames for institutions: The Pact of Paris, Nuremberg and the international rule of law', in Charles Sampford and Ramesh Thakur, eds, *Institutional Supports for the International Rule of Law* (New York: Routledge, 2015), pp. 116–131, at pp. 119–121.

[4] For a detailed discussion of these provisions' operation, see Ramesh Thakur, *The United Nations, Peace and Security: From Collective Security to the Responsibility to Protect* (Cambridge: Cambridge University Press, 2006).

its membership was far from universal, and there were no particular costs for states that chose to abandon their membership. Ensuring the widest possible subscription to the new international organisation and the norms that it was setting out to foster was therefore of crucial importance. Yet at the same time, there was no prospect whatever that the great powers would relinquish their own security to the dictates of an untested multilateral organisation. For this reason, the Charter granted permanent membership of the Security Council to five states – the United States, the United Kingdom, the Soviet Union, France and China – and with it, the power to veto any non-procedural resolutions. When the Cold War broke out, leading to decades of tension between United States and the Soviet Union, the Security Council became one of the theatres for their confrontation, and a degree of paralysis afflicted the Council, at least when issues of concern to the two superpowers, the United States and the Soviet Union, were potentially on the agenda.

The possibility that the Council could prove impotent – either because of a stand-off between the superpowers or by virtue of a simple lack of interest in some remote part of the world – raised the question of what should be done when some horror seemed to require action, but action could not be justified by reference to self-defence or to explicit Security Council authorisation. An answer came with the idea of 'humanitarian intervention', which might be morally justifiable even if legally indefensible. Different scholars offered somewhat varying definitions. Jennifer M. Welsh, for example, explicitly defined humanitarian intervention as 'coercive interference in the internal affairs of the state, involving the use of armed force, with the purposes of addressing massive human rights violations or preventing widespread human suffering'.[5] Adam Roberts, on the other hand, defined it as 'coercive action by one or more states involving the use of armed force in another state without the consent of its authorities, and with the purpose of preventing widespread suffering or death among the inhabitants'.[6] Various examples of state behaviour were from time to time cited as examples of humanitarian intervention, including the Indian intervention in East Pakistan in December 1971, the Vietnamese invasion of Cambodia in December 1978 that resulted in the displacement of the genocidal Khmer Rouge regime and the Tanzanian overthrow of the Amin regime in Uganda in April 1979.

---

[5] Jennifer M. Welsh, 'Introduction', in Jennifer M. Welsh, ed, *Humanitarian Intervention and International Relations* (Oxford: Oxford University Press, 2004), p. 3. In 2013 Welsh succeeded Edward Luck as the special adviser to the UN secretary-general on R2P.

[6] Quoted in Thomas G. Weiss, *Humanitarian Intervention: Ideas in Action* (Cambridge: Polity Press, 2007), p. 5.

Yet while a number of observers welcome the consequences of these specific actions, many at the same time voiced very considerable unease about the principles involved. A wide range of criticisms surfaced. One related to sincerity of purpose. Did Vietnam *really* invade Cambodia on the basis of humanitarian motives, or did such claimed motives simply provide convenient cover for an intervention carried out for quite different purposes? Another related to consistency, and to the fear that the doctrine of humanitarian intervention would simply magnify asymmetries of power in the international system, with states that had long seen themselves as meeting some standard of 'civilisation'[7] becoming moral policemen for younger states only recently freed from colonial domination, and acting with considerable hypocrisy to boot. Yet another criticism drew on the ethics of consequences to suggest that humanitarian intervention provided no guarantee that the 'beneficiaries' would ultimately be better off than if no intervention had occurred. None of these objections was trivial, and in large parts of the world they undermined any claim to legitimacy that humanitarian intervention might have sought.

Theory and practice

Despite these inadequacies in the concept of humanitarian intervention, it did seem in some ways to fill a need. At the beginning of the 1990s, specifically following the ejection of Iraqi forces from Kuwait in early 1991 pursuant to UN Security Council Resolution 678, President George H. W. Bush's envisioning of a 'new world order' struck something of a chord for those who had hoped to see the day when the Cold War paralysis of the Security Council would be surmounted and the Council might begin to function more as its architects had intended. Alas, this was not how things worked out. The first half of the new decade was dominated (or perhaps stained) by a number of developments that seemed to create anew the need for some morally defensible form of international action to shelter the vulnerable. With the attention of the wider world focused on the holding of the first multiracial elections in South Africa, extremists in Rwanda embarked on the genocidal slaughter of those they conceived to be enemies.[8] And, as Yugoslavia disintegrated, Bosnia-Herzegovina became the theatre for hideous exercises in 'ethnic

---

[7] See Gerrit W. Gong, *The Standard of 'Civilization' in International Society* (Oxford: Oxford University Press, 1984); Brett Bowden, *The Empire of Civilization: The Evolution of an Imperial Idea* (Chicago: University of Chicago Press, 2009).

[8] See Roméo Dallaire, *Shake Hands with the Devil: The Failure of Humanity in Rwanda* (Toronto: Random House, 2003); Samantha Power, *A Problem from Hell: America and the Age of Genocide* (New York: Basic Books, 2002).

cleansing',[9] and the United Nations itself was comprehensively humiliated by the massacre of men and boys in Srebrenica in July 1995.[10] Yet there were distinct and chilling differences between the two cases. The crisis in Bosnia, a European state, became a major preoccupation for the Security Council and for Western capitals. The Rwandan genocide, by contrast, was not an event about which key Western capitals wanted to know, and it was only through the determined efforts of figures such as UN Force Commander General Roméo Dallaire of Canada and UN Security Council President Colin Keating of New Zealand that it attracted attention at all. The killing of Africans seemed to weigh very differently in the moral calculus of key Western leaders than did the killing or displacement of people in Europe who looked rather like them. NATO's February–June 1999 intervention in Kosovo without Security Council authorisation added to this impression.[11]

The combination of problems crying out for attention and a doctrinal response, the weaknesses of which seemed to undermine its legitimacy, set the scene for conceptual innovation. Two other factors, however, also proved to be of critical importance. One was the commitment of the Canadian government to promote the informed discussion of alternative approaches. Lloyd Axworthy, Canada's foreign minister from 1996 to 2000, was a dynamic advocate of innovative approaches to complex international challenges, and on 14 September 2000 he launched the International Commission on Intervention and State Sovereignty, the Advisory Board of which he subsequently chaired. Canada provided and mobilised the material support which was necessary for a commission of this kind to be able to operate. The other factor was the fortuitous assembling of Commission members: a remarkable mix of scholars and practitioners, while the choice of Gareth Evans and Mohamed Sahnoun as co-chairs was particularly inspired. Given the complexity and sensitivity of the issues involved, the Commission's members performed quite remarkably in producing a consensus report that broke ground both practically and theoretically. The historian Sir Martin Gilbert has described the idea of the responsibility to protect as 'the most significant adjustment to national sovereignty in 360 years'.[12] One reason why this

---

[9] See David Rieff, *Slaughterhouse: Bosnia and the Failure of the West* (New York: Touchstone, 1996).

[10] See *Report of the Secretary-General Pursuant to General Assembly Resolution 53/35: The Fall of Srebrenica*, Document A/54/549 (New York: United Nations, 15 November 1999).

[11] For reflections on this case, see Albrecht Schnabel and Ramesh Thakur, eds, *Kosovo and the Challenge of Humanitarian Intervention: Selective Indignation, Collective Action, and International Citizenship* (Tokyo: United Nations University Press, 2000).

[12] Martin Gilbert, 'The Terrible 20th Century', *The Globe and Mail* (Toronto), 31 January 2007.

could be the case is that the work of the Commission's members did not cease when it presented its report. On the contrary, a number of the members of the Commission have been active contributors to ongoing debates about the evolution of the idea of a responsibility to protect, not simply as 'keepers of the flame', but as sources of further innovative thinking.[13]

Theorising R2P

The title of this volume is *Theorising the Responsibility to Protect*, but, given the multiple understandings of theory, it is important to clarify some of the ways in which theory and theoretical reflection might illuminate a doctrine of this kind and enhance an understanding of the ways in which it might contribute normatively to international relations. R2P is not a positive social science theory of the kind that might be used to attempt to predict the course of specific political events. Theories of this kind have a venerable history in international thinking, ranging from older ideas about power balancing as a source of political stability to much more recent theories about liberal or democratic domestic political arrangements as bases for peace.[14] Those who wish to theorise the responsibility to protect will need to focus their attention on a quite different set of theoretical issues. Fortunately, there are a number which cry out for attention, and which contributors to this book take up in different ways.

A first and very important set of issues relates to conceptual clarification. This has two dimensions at least. A doctrine such as R2P is formulated in the words and sentences of a natural language. There is abundant scope for clarifying exactly what these words and sentences actually connote. Words can be ambiguous in their meaning, or susceptible to multiple interpretations by different audiences. As the R2P doctrine has passed through different sets of hands, it has on a number of occasions been refined and clarified, sometimes in ways that augment its prospects of securing a wider degree of support. This has consequences. Anne Orford, for example, has pointed out that the 'vocabulary of

---

[13] For their reflections on what makes international commissions and high-level panels successful, see Gareth Evans, 'Commission Diplomacy', in Andrew F. Cooper, Jorge Heine and Ramesh Thakur, eds, *The Oxford Handbook of Modern Diplomacy* (Oxford: Oxford University Press, 2013), pp. 278–302; Ramesh Thakur, 'High-Level Panels', in Jacob Cogan, Ian Hurd and Ian Johnstone, eds, *The Oxford Handbook of International Organizations* (Oxford: Oxford University Press, forthcoming).

[14] See Richard Little, *The Balance of Power in International Relations: Metaphors, Myths and Models* (Cambridge: Cambridge University Press, 2007); Michael W. Doyle, *Liberal Peace: Selected Essays* (New York: Routledge, 2011).

"responsibility" works here as a language for conferring authority and allocating powers rather than as a language for imposing binding obligations and commanding obedience'.[15] Another dimension of conceptual clarification, which remains largely unexplored, relates to the challenges of moving from English as the language in which R2P was originally formulated into other languages which may not be endowed with exact equivalents of some of the key terms that figure in the 2001 report of the International Commission on Intervention and State Sovereignty, or in subsequent documents formulated within the UN system such as the 2005 World Summit Outcome.[16] For example, there is no particular reason to assume that the two key words 'protect' and 'responsibility' have direct equivalents in all languages, and it may be necessary to draw on semantic theory in order to be able to explain to different audiences what these English terms mean.[17]

A second set of issues is related to the elaboration of normative justifications for R2P. The R2P doctrine is fundamentally normative. It is offered as a set of proposals about what should be done in certain circumstances, namely those in which vulnerable people are faced by the threat of mass atrocity crime. It is directed at shaping the behaviour of actors who might be called upon to engage in preventative action, or in reacting, or in rebuilding. But if it is to carry weight, it cannot simply be because it was articulated in 2001 by an eminent group of scholars and practitioners. Something else is required, and what this 'something else' might be is a matter that can be illuminated from a range of theoretical perspectives, whether based on deontological or consequentialist ethics, or some logic of the institutional structure of the international system, or the normative implications of some particular political philosophy.

A third set of issues is concerned with the relationship of R2P to wider social phenomena. The R2P doctrine began its life as a set of ideas, but at maturity it may be more important as a behaviour-shaping norm in an environment in which many other norms are also to be found. The theorising that is involved here relates to wider discussions about what Jon Elster once called the 'cement of society'[18] – only in this case, it is perhaps international society rather than a single community that is the focus of our attention.

[15] Anne Orford, *International Authority and the Responsibility to Protect* (Cambridge: Cambridge University Press, 2011), p. 26.

[16] See *World Summit Outcome*, Document A/RES/60/1 (New York: United Nations, 24 October 2005), paragraphs 138–139.

[17] See Anna Wierzbicka, *Imprisoned in English: The Hazards of English as a Default Language* (New York: Oxford University Press, 2014).

[18] Jon Elster, *The Cement of Society: A Study of Social Order* (Cambridge: Cambridge University Press, 1989).

The structure of the book

The chapters that make up this book take up a number of these issues, but they have not been assembled with a view to promoting any particular agenda, let alone R2P as a principle or norm. As readers will see, some sharply divergent perspectives are to be found in its pages. This is not surprising, for the criteria for selection of contributors are grounded in their having distinctive voices, rather than in their willingness to sing as part of a choir.

The book opens with a section on context, and specifically with an overview by Gareth Evans of the circumstances in which the idea of a responsibility to protect came to be articulated and the international political environment in which it continues to evolve. He notes the way in which the report of the International Commission changed the course of debate by re-characterising the right to intervene as the responsibility to protect; by broadening the range of actors within the frame of discussion; by expanding the focus of discussion to include prevention and rebuilding, as well as reaction by force; and by clarifying the range of operating principles that should be used to shape decision-making at critical points when the threat of mass atrocity crime had to be confronted. He concludes with a comprehensive overview of developments in the decade since the report was published, recognising that the practical implementation of R2P remains a work in progress.

Further context is provided in chapters by Charles Sampford and Ramesh Thakur, and Amitav Acharya. Sampford and Thakur investigate philosophical shifts in the understanding of sovereignty, with the Enlightenment producing a shift in the relationship between sovereign and subject comparable to Ludwig Feuerbach's 'suggested reversal of the relationship between man and God', and the report of the International Commission performing 'another Feuerbachian inversion to turn the right of other states to intervene into the Responsibility to Protect'. They note the strength of an emotional and functional commitment to sovereignty in the developing world, highlight some concrete challenges to the Westphalian image of the state as the 'ultimate authority and power' and conclude that 'once people have secured their sovereign rights through the establishment of even a half-decent democracy, no one else can trump those sovereign rights'.

Amitav Acharya links debates about R2P to wider questions about the origins and diffusion of norms in international affairs. He addresses this by locating it within a wider discussion of whose norms matter. He contrasts an approach to norm diffusion characterised by what he calls 'moral cosmopolitanism', emphasising the critical role of mainly Western norm entrepreneurs, with a more general framework based on the concept of 'norm circulation' which sees norm creation as a two-way process in which 'global norms offered by transnational moral actors are contested and localised to fit the cognitive priors of local actors (localisation), while this local feedback is repatriated back to the wider global context along with other locally constructed norms', helping 'to modify and possibly defend and strengthen, the global norm in question (subsidiarity)'.

The next section of the book explores links between R2P, normative theory and global governance. Tim Dunne surveys conceptions of world order, which he sees as both 'a place where there are flows of ideas and materiality on a global scale and an institutional design that embodies shared values and purposes'. He explores in detail the distinction between pluralist and solidarist conceptions, and argues that in 'the construction of the secondary institution of R2P, we see how the tension between solidarist values and pluralist institutions is being played out'. He contests the perspective that would characterise R2P simply as solidarist, and notes that pluralism is not doctrinally opposed to humanitarian intervention. For Dunne, pluralism may lend important support to R2P's quest to modify world order.

Michael Byers examines R2P in the context of ideas about the nature of international law, specifically investigating the extent to which it has become part of that body of international law dealing with the use of force by states. He provides a comprehensive overview of both the use (or non-use) of force in the post-Cold War period, embracing Somalia, Bosnia, Rwanda and Kosovo, and then traces developments since the report of the International Commission that might be seen as shaping the emergence of the R2P norm as a part of international law. He concludes that R2P, 'insofar as it concerns the use of force, is now limited to being part of the context of Security Council decision-making', but goes on to suggest that it is reshaping the environment within which assistance to non-state actors is contemplated, and that, more broadly, the effects of such normative innovation may be felt first at the margins rather than at the core of established ways of doing things.

Edward Newman is centrally concerned with the multilateral dimension of R2P. Multilateral action on R2P, he argues, 'is inherently legitimate *because* it is conducted through established multilateral channels, and most importantly the UN. R2P is therefore anchored to a Westphalian, pluralist conception of international society and existing norms of world order.' Nonetheless, he sees fundamental problems with the principle, related in part to 'the inherent difficulties of international collective action'. He anticipates that the implementation of R2P is likely to remain 'inconsistent, controversial, and contested'.

Abiodun Williams investigates the relationship between global governance and R2P. 'Global governance', he writes, 'is vital to the development of R2P, which in turn provides the foundation that allows global governance to sustain itself'. He sees global governance as 'a diverse collection of multilevel and multisectoral authorities aimed at structuring the behaviour and interaction of state and non-state actors'. It faces a number of challenges, which Williams identifies under the headings of state dominance, compliance and institutional proliferation. He argues that R2P's development is 'inextricably linked with the public face of global governance, the United Nations', which in turn generates a need for institutional reform and enhanced coordination in both the UN system and at national levels.

Jean-Marc Coicaud examines R2P in the light of recent international crises. He notes a range of fundamental principles at the core of international law, and makes the point that there can be competition or tension between them, as, for example, one may find between non-intervention and the sovereign equality of states on the one hand, and self-determination and respect for human rights on the other. He goes on to discuss R2P in the light of experiences in Syria, Ukraine and Gaza. The Ukrainian crisis, he argues, shows how the idea of R2P can be hijacked, in this case by Russia, whereas the Gaza crisis demonstrates how difficult it can be to find a middle ground between the Israeli and Palestinian sides. He concludes that R2P is, on its own, 'not sufficient to solve the problems it seeks to address'.

Alex J. Bellamy traces the important connections between R2P and the 'just war' tradition. He argues against treating principles as a checklist to be ticked off, instead arguing that they make up a holistic framework that can guide moral reasoning or debate. He sees just war thinking as embodying substantive, prudential and procedural criteria for the taking of action, and strongly defends the UN Charter as providing an institutional framework for decision-making, arguing that 'morality is better served by a system that subjects moral claims about the use of force to external scrutiny'.

Jonathan Graubart provides a challenging critique of the wisdom of legitimating what he calls 'another category of military intervention'. Drawing on the critical concept paper circulated by 2009 UN General Assembly President Miguel d'Escoto Brockmann, he elaborates what he sees as an 'underlying pluralist–anti-imperialist critique' of R2P, and, taking the Libyan case as an example, argues that 'a deepening of R2P's norm on military intervention will, on the one hand, present a powerful and malleable rationale for justifying the use of force while, on the other, presenting limited operational constraints'. He favours eliminating any military intervention component from R2P.

The final section of the book takes up several issues relating to R2P and wider international social purposes. Mats Berdal discusses the relationship between United Nations peacekeeping and the Responsibility to Protect, a relationship he describes as intimate, complex and paradoxical. He examines the evolution of UN peacekeeping, noting that peacekeepers were witnesses to some of the shocking events that proved to be the stimulus to the articulation of the R2P doctrine. He then takes up the issue of civilian protection as part of UN mandates and missions, noting the problematic consequences of conflating R2P with civilian protection in peacekeeping. He concludes by exploring a number of complications of peacekeeping, most notably the mismatch between expectations held by desperate people on the ground, and what can realistically be achieved by under-resourced missions, with an aversion to casualties driven by the domestic priorities of troop-contributing states.

William Maley takes up the issue of how distinct but parallel norms can affect each other. R2P has taken shape in a context in which a range of other norms of humanitarian import can be found, most importantly those embodied in international humanitarian law and those providing for protection for refugees. Examining the content of and the enforcement mechanisms for these norms, Maley argues that they relate to R2P in different ways. The criminalisation of war crimes in international humanitarian law provides micro foundations for the macro responses that R2P may require. By contrast, there is a risk that political leaders seeking to wash their hands of domestically unpopular responsibilities towards refugees at their borders may seek to exploit the R2P norm in order to undermine their specific normative obligations towards refugees. The dangers of such unintended consequences need to be highlighted by scholars and norm entrepreneurs, and more broadly it is important to be vigilant in ensuring that protective norms are sustained.

Susan Harris Rimmer addresses the issue of gender. She shows how the evolution of the R2P norm has been influenced by the parallel women, peace and security agenda that has recently been receiving attention not just from scholars but in the Security Council as well, but argues that on the whole the relationship has been 'overlooked or undercooked'. Specifically, she notes that there have been diverse responses to R2P from women, with female leaders of international humanitarian agencies on the whole taking a positive view, as have women political leaders, but with civil society activists more inclined to see R2P either as a product of a process that was itself gendered, or as a pathway to military intervention of a kind that they disapprove of in general. Harris Rimmer notes that in the recognition of gender, there have been varying degrees of progress as different issues relating to R2P have come up, and concludes that there is a need to 'include the participation of more and diverse women in shaping its ambitious vision for the future'.

Jacinta O'Hagan addresses the question of whether the Responsibility to Protect is a Western idea. She notes at the outset that 'the West' is a fluid and amorphous concept, but accepts that there are powerful links 'between Western history and political thought, and conceptions of sovereign responsibility'. She discusses the cultural politics of sovereignty and responsibility, making the point that the idea that there is a duty on political authority to protect subjects or citizens is one that 'spans many societies and cultures'. She goes on to discuss the cultural politics of R2P, arguing that it is built on commitments to institutions and norms that have been 'widely endorsed' by both Western and non-Western states; notes that non-Western approaches to R2P have not been homogeneous; and concludes that the debate now is not about whether R2P should be embraced but about how it should be interpreted.

Finally, Siddharth Mallavarapu argues that discussion of R2P needs to be located in wider discussions related to contending logics of intervention, race and international politics, and the complexities of altruism. Drawing on Third World Approaches to International Law (TWAIL) sensibilities, in his view, 'it is important to ensure that greater agency be attributed to local populations', and he goes on to argue that 'agency also needs to be understood here as crediting them with intelligence to figure out what might work best for their own political systems in crisis situations. Western intervention or doctrines like R2P cannot serve as a panacea to deeper structural problems which an unequal international order itself has in various ways perpetuated.'

2   The evolution of the Responsibility to Protect: from concept and principle to actionable norm

Gareth Evans

In its conception, birth and growth to maturity – and what may be now its mid-life crisis – the Responsibility to Protect (R2P) has been, at least in the eyes of its progenitors, much less about theorising than action. The focus from the outset was on practical impact. Our perception was that whatever else went wrong in the conduct of international relations, the world could no longer afford to mishandle its collective response to genocide and other mass atrocity crimes. We saw a new conceptual framework for addressing these issues, built on sound legal and philosophical foundations, as a crucially necessary ingredient. But the point of crafting it was above all political – to energise effective collective action by generating a new consensus reflex among international policymakers and those who influenced them to view man-made human rights catastrophes, when any such new case arose, as everybody's business, not nobody's.

Challenge

Achieving such a new consensus was a huge challenge.[1] It is almost impossible to overstate the extent to which there had been an absence of consensus on these issues in the past. In pre-modern – including biblical – times, mass atrocities seem to have been a matter of indifference to everyone but the victims. With the emergence of the modern system of nation states in the seventeenth century, that indifference simply became institutionalised: sovereign states did not interfere in each other's internal affairs. Certainly, there were instances in the nineteenth century of

---

[1] This and the following three sections draw substantially on earlier publications by the author, especially Gareth Evans, *The Responsibility to Protect: Ending Mass Atrocity Crimes Once and for All* (Washington DC: Brookings Institution Press, 2008), Part I; Gareth Evans, 'The Responsibility to Protect: Ending Mass Atrocity Crimes Once and for All', *Irish Studies in International Affairs* 20 (2009), pp. 7–13; Gareth Evans, 'Lessons and Challenges' in Jared Genser and Irwin Cotler, eds, *The Responsibility to Protect: The Promise of Stopping Mass Atrocities in Our Time* (New York: Oxford University Press, 2012), pp. 375–391.

European states intervening in various corners of the Ottoman Empire to protect Christian minorities at risk; however, there was no generally accepted principle in law, morality or state practice to challenge the core notion that it was no one's business but their own if states murdered or forcibly displaced large numbers of their own citizens, or allowed atrocity crimes to be committed by one group against another on their soil.

Even after the Second World War, with the awful experience of Hitler's Holocaust; the recognition of individual and group human rights in the UN Charter and, more grandly, in the Universal Declaration of Human Rights; the recognition by the Nuremberg Tribunal Charter in 1945 of the concept of 'crimes against humanity'; and the signing of the Genocide Convention in 1948, things did not fundamentally change. The over-whelming preoccupation of those who founded the UN was not, in fact, human rights, but the problem of states waging aggressive war against each other. What actually captured the mood of the time, and the mood that prevailed right through the Cold War years, was, more than any of the human rights provisions, Article 2.7 of the UN Charter: 'nothing con-tained in the present Charter shall authorise the United Nations to inter-vene in matters which are essentially within the domestic jurisdiction of any state'.

The state of mind that even mass atrocity crimes like those of the Cambodian killing fields were just not the rest of the world's business prevailed throughout the UN's first half-century of existence. Vietnam's invasion, which stopped the Khmer Rouge in its tracks, was universally attacked, not applauded, while Tanzania had to justify its overthrow of Uganda's Idi Amin by invoking 'self-defence', not any larger human rights justification.

With the arrival of the 1990s and the end of the Cold War, the prevailing complacent assumptions about non-intervention at last came under challenge as never before. The quintessential peace and security problem – before the 11 September 2001 attacks on the United States came along to change the focus to terrorism – became not interstate war, but civil war and internal violence perpetrated on a massive scale. With the break-up of various Cold War state structures and the removal of some superpower constraints, conscience-shocking situations repeatedly arose, above all in the former Yugoslavia and Africa.

But old habits of non-intervention died very hard. Even when situa-tions cried out for some kind of response and the international commu-nity did react through the UN, such actions were too often erratic, incomplete or counter-productive, as in the debacle of Somalia in 1993, the catastrophe of Rwandan genocide in 1994 and the almost unbelievable default in Srebrenica, Bosnia, just a year later, in 1995. Then the killing and ethnic cleansing started all over again in Kosovo in 1999. Not everyone, but certainly most people and governments, accepted quite rapidly that external military intervention was the only way to stop it; but again the Security Council failed to act in the face of a threatened veto by Russia. The action that needed to be taken was eventually performed by a coalition of the willing but in a way that, given that the coalition bypassed the Security Council, challenged the integrity of the whole international security system (just as the invasion of Iraq did four years later, in far less defensible circumstances).

Throughout the decade of the 1990s a fierce and bitter argument raged, with trenches dug deep on both sides. On the one hand, there were supporters of 'humanitarian intervention': the doctrine that there was a 'right to intervene' militarily, against the will of the government of the country in question, in these cases. Its most influential advocate was the French doctor, non-governmental organisation leader (co-founder of both *Médecins Sans Frontières* and the breakaway *Médecins du Monde*) and government minister, Bernard Kouchner. The doctrine was not new: 'humanitarian intervention' terminology had been first used – in more or less its modern sense of military force deployed across borders to protect civilians at risk – as early as 1840,[2] and it has been the subject of perennial discussion in international law literature since the early twentieth century. But Kouchner gave it a new lease of life by inventing and popularising the expression '*droit d'ingérence*', the 'right to intervene' (or, by extension, '*droit d'ingérence humanitaire*'),[3] which had a real resonance in the new circumstances of the post-Cold War world when both the need and the opportunity to take protective action repeatedly arose.

On the other hand, there were defenders of the traditional prerogatives of state sovereignty who made the familiar case that internal events were none of the rest of the world's business. It was very much a North–South debate, with the many new states born out of decolonisation being very proud of their newly won sovereignty, very conscious of their fragility, all too conscious of the way in which they had been on the receiving end in the past of not very benign interventions from the imperial and colonial powers and not very keen to acknowledge the right of such powers to

---

[2] See sources cited in International Commission on Intervention and State Sovereignty (ICISS), *The Responsibility to Protect: Research, Bibliography, Background* (Ottawa: International Development Research Centre, 2001), pp. 16–17.

[3] See Mario Bettati and Bernard Kouchner, eds, *Le devoir d'ingérence* (Paris: Denöel, 1987), p. 300.

intervene again, whatever the circumstances. Hardly anyone talked about prevention or less extreme forms of engagement and intervention, and there was no system of international criminal justice to which anyone could resort. The options were 'send in the marines' or do nothing.

This was the environment which drove UN Secretary-General Kofi Annan to make his despairing and heartfelt plea to the General Assembly in his 2000 *Millennium Report*: 'if humanitarian intervention is indeed an unacceptable assault on sovereignty, how should we respond to a Rwanda, to a Srebrenica – to gross and systematic violations of human rights that offend every precept of our common humanity?'

Conception 2001–2005

It was in response to this challenge that the idea of 'the responsibility to protect' was conceived. In September 2000 the Canadian Government, on the initiative of Foreign Minister Lloyd Axworthy, appointed the International Commission on Intervention and State Sovereignty (ICISS), co-chaired by the present author and the distinguished Algerian diplomat and UN Africa adviser Mohamed Sahnoun (and including Ramesh Thakur, one of the co-editors of this volume, as an influential member), tasked to wrestle with the whole range of questions – legal, moral, operational and political – rolled up in this debate, to consult with the widest possible range of opinion around the world and to bring back a report that would help the secretary-general and everyone else find some new common ground. Just over a year later, in December 2001, the Commission published its 90-page report and 400-page supplementary volume of research essays, bibliography and background material under the title *The Responsibility to Protect*.[4]

In trying to craft a new conceptual approach to the problem of mass atrocity crimes, the Commission was conscious of a number of other more or less contemporaneous efforts – apart from Kouchner's *droit d'ingérence* – that were being made to try to forge intellectual consensus. First, there was the UK prime minister, Tony Blair, who sought to articulate, in a 1994 Chicago speech defending the NATO air strikes on Kosovo, a 'doctrine of international community', based on a 'subtle blend of mutual self-interest and moral purpose'. But the criteria he offered for military intervention were a muddled mixture of conceptual, evidentiary

---

[4] International Commission on Intervention and State Sovereignty (ICISS), *The Responsibility to Protect* (Ottawa: International Development Research Centre, 2001). Both the Report and the Supplementary Volume are accessible at www.globalr2p.org.

and political considerations, and his perspective was national rather than international, and wholly reactive rather than preventive. Like Kouchner before him, Blair knew how to rally the North, but his doctrine fell on very deaf ears in the South.

Then there was the idea of 'human security', which came to prominence in 1994 with the launch of the UNDP's 1994 *Human Development Report*, with its subtitle *New Dimensions of Human Security*, and seemed an innovative attempt to bridge the gap between the prevailing perspectives in the North and South. However, so many different issues and themes nestled comfortably under its wings that it was difficult to extract any prescriptions about how to deal with any of them other than to look at problems in a 'people first' way. In the present context, it lacked any kind of operational utility.

Much more immediately relevant was the concept of 'sovereignty as responsibility' as articulated by the distinguished scholar and former Sudanese diplomat Francis Deng as the representative of the UN secretary-general on Internally Displaced Persons (IDP) along with his Brookings Institution colleagues, particularly Roberta Cohen.[5] Conceptualising sovereignty this way – not just in terms of the traditional preoccupation with control of territory – gained traction from all the post-Second World War institutional developments associated with the establishment of the United Nations, whose human rights instruments did involve the voluntary acceptance, at least in principle, of internal sovereignty-limiting obligations.

Then there was Secretary-General Annan's own attempt to resolve the conceptual impasse at the heart of the sovereignty–intervention debate by arguing that there was not just one kind of sovereignty in play here but two: that *national* sovereignty had to be weighed and balanced against *individual* sovereignty, as recognised in the international human rights instruments.[6] But the general response, shared by the Commission, was that this approach did not so much resolve the dilemma of intervention as simply restate it.

Yet another development (although this had greater resonance during the later stages of the evolution of R2P, in particular its embrace by the UN in 2005, than in its original conception by ICISS) was within the newly emerging African Union (AU), whose founders were showing a much greater willingness than the Organisation of African Unity, which the AU grew out of and formally replaced in 2002, to accept that state

[5] Most comprehensively in Francis Deng et.al., *Sovereignty as Responsibility: Conflict Management in Africa* (Washington DC: Brookings Institution Press, 1996).
[6] Kofi Annan, 'Two Concepts of Sovereignty', *The Economist*, 18 September 1999, pp. 49–50.

sovereignty had limits. Its Constitutive Act, the text of which had been agreed in 2000, recognised 'the right of the Union to intervene in a Member State pursuant to a decision of the Assembly in respect of grave circumstances, namely war crimes, genocide and crimes against humanity'.

A final strand in the mix was the emergence in the UN from 1999 onwards of a formalised set of principles and strategies addressing the protection of civilians in armed conflict (POC), which recognised the need, along with many other forms of protection, to ensure that in conflict situations non-combatants were not the victims of atrocity crimes.[7] Probably its most important practical application in the present context has been in widening the scope of military peacekeeping mandates to ensure that there is capacity to deal forcefully with those who are violently disruptive – and to ensure in particular that there will be no more debacles in the future like that of Srebrenica in 1995, when 8,000 men and boys were taken from under the unprotesting noses of UN peacekeepers and led to their slaughter. What POC did not address, however, were mass atrocity crimes occurring other than in times of armed conflict, as with Cambodia in the mid-1970s and Rwanda in 1994. For ICISS, these one-sided violence situations (of which, in subsequent years, further major examples have been Kenya in 2008, and both Libya and Syria in their early stages) remained a central challenge.

These efforts to set international thinking on a new path had all broken new ground in various ways, but none of them developed any real political traction in generating new consensus about how to respond to the situations that had so troubled and divided the international community during the 1990s. That was essentially the achievement of the ICISS report, which did change the course of the debate in four main ways.

Its first innovation was presentational: re-characterising the 'the right to intervene' as 'the responsibility to protect', and in the process restating the issue as not being about the 'right' of any states, particularly large and powerful ones, to throw their weight around militarily, but rather the 'responsibility' of all states to act to protect their own and other peoples at risk of suffering from mass atrocity crimes. The Commission's hope was that this new language would enable entrenched opponents to find new ground on which to more constructively engage: with a new script, actors have to change their lines, and think afresh about what the issues in the

---

[7] The key initiating document here was the first report by the secretary-general to the UN Security Council on the *Protection of Civilians in Armed Conflict*, Report S/1999/957, 8 September 1999.

play really are. Our model in this respect was the Brundtland Commission, which had earlier introduced the concept of 'sustainable development' to bridge the huge gap which then existed between developers and environmentalists.

The second move was to broaden the range of actors in the frame. Whereas 'the right to intervene' focused just on international actors able and willing to apply military force, the new R2P formulation spread the responsibility. It started by recognising and insisting upon the responsibility of each sovereign state itself to protect its people from harm; it moved from there to the responsibility of other states to assist them if they were having difficulty and were willing to be assisted; and only then – if a state was manifestly failing, as a result of either incapacity or ill-will, to protect its own people – shifted to the responsibility of the wider international community to respond more robustly.

Third, the Commission insisted on dramatically broadening the range of responses. Whereas humanitarian intervention focused one-dimensionally on military reaction, R2P involves multiple elements in the response continuum: preventive action, both long and short term; reaction when prevention fails; and post-crisis rebuilding aimed again at prevention, this time of recurrence of the harm in question. The 'reaction' element, moreover, was itself a nuanced continuum, beginning with persuasion, moving from there to non-military forms of coercion of varying degrees of intensity (such as sanctions or the threat of international criminal prosecution), and only as an absolute last resort – after multiple criteria were satisfied – contemplating coercive military force.

Finally, ICISS sought to clarify the principles which should govern that last, hard choice – recognising that however much one might strive to avoid resorting to military coercion, in some cases that might still be the only credible option. So when was it right to fight? The initial criterion was *legality*, where the task was seen as not to find alternatives to the clear legal authority of the Security Council, but rather to make it work better, so there was less chance of it being bypassed. But that needed to be supplemented by five criteria of *legitimacy*, designed as a set of benchmarks which, while they might not guarantee consensus in any particular case, would hopefully make its achievement much more likely: seriousness of the harm being threatened (which would need to involve large-scale loss of life or ethnic cleansing to prima facie justify something as extreme as military action); the motivation or primary purpose of the proposed military action; whether there were reasonably available peaceful alternatives; the proportionality of the response; and the balance of consequences (whether more good than harm would be achieved by the intervention).

Birth 2005

Many good ideas, in international relations as elsewhere, are stillborn. As numerous blue-ribbon commissions and panels have discovered over the years, it is one thing to labour mightily and produce what looks like a major new contribution to some policy debate, but quite another to get any policymaker to take any notice of it. The ICISS report looked headed for that fate, and more rapidly than most of its kind, when it was published in the immediate aftermath of 9/11, in December 2001, at a time when international attention became far more preoccupied with terrorism than the internal human rights catastrophes which had consumed so much attention during the 1990s.

But a constituency for its ideas slowly began to build in the context of the lead-up to the UN's Sixtieth Anniversary World Summit in September 2005, which was aimed at fundamentally rethinking the organisation's contemporary role and relevance. And at that summit, just four years after the first articulation of the concept – a mere blink of an eye in the history of world ideas – 'the responsibility to protect' was unanimously adopted by more than 150 heads of state and government sitting as the UN General Assembly.

The critical link between the ICISS report and the real birth of R2P at the 2005 World Summit was the work of the UN secretary-general's High-Level Panel on Threats, Challenges and Change, of which the present author had the good fortune to be a member. As part of its 2004 report, *A More Secure World: Our Shared Responsibility*, it endorsed what it described as 'the emerging norm that there is a collective international responsibility to protect, exercisable by the Security Council authorising military intervention as a last resort, in the event of genocide and other large-scale killing, ethnic cleansing or serious violations of humanitarian law which sovereign governments have proved powerless or unwilling to prevent'.[8] The support that mattered most – fairly passive though it was at the time – for the future of this recommendation was probably that from the Chinese member, former Vice Premier and Foreign Minister Qian Qichen. Without his immense prestige in Beijing being in play, it is difficult to believe that, given the traditional strength of its concerns about non-intervention, China would have been quite as relaxed on this issue as it proved to be at the World Summit.

---

[8] High-Level Panel on Threats, Challenges and Change, *A More Secure World: Our Shared Responsibility* (New York: United Nations, 2004), p. 106: accessible at www.un.org /secureworld.

The crucial next step was for the High-Level Panel's recommendations to be picked up in the secretary-general's own report to the Summit, designed to bring together in a single coherent whole all the credible UN reform proposals in circulation. In his eighty-eight-page report, *In Larger Freedom: Towards Development, Security and Human Rights for All*, published in early 2005, Kofi Annan duly obliged, saying that 'while I am well aware of the sensitivities involved in this issue ... I believe that we must embrace the responsibility to protect, and, when necessary, we must act on it'.[9]

When the world's heads of state and government finally convened in New York, it was after intense months of in-house wrangling in New York about nearly every one of his sixty or so recommendations. The atmosphere was not helped by the late arrival on the scene of the famously ideological and combative new US ambassador, John Bolton, with some 700 spoiling amendments designed to throw the whole painfully evolving negotiating process into chaos. In the event, while the whole Summit proved to be a major disappointment to all those who had hoped it would result in a major overhaul of the UN system and global policy, with very little of substance agreed on anything, the secretary-general's recommendation that the concept of R2P be endorsed (although not his proposals for agreed criteria to govern the use of force) survived almost unscathed. That this happened was anything but inevitable. A fierce rearguard action was fought almost to the last by a small group of developing countries, joined by Russia, who basically refused to concede any kind of limitation on the full and untrammelled exercise of state sovereignty, however irresponsible that exercise might be. What carried the day in the end was persistent advocacy by sub-Saharan African countries, led by South Africa, supplemented by a clear – and historically quite significant – embrace of limited-sovereignty principles by the key Latin American countries.[10]

The language in which the 2005 World Summit endorsed the concept appeared as paragraphs 138 and 139 of its Outcome document:[11]

[9] Kofi Annan, *In Larger Freedom: Towards Development, Security and Human Rights for All*, Document A/59/2005 (New York: United Nations, 2005), paragraph 135: available at www.un.org/largerfreedom.

[10] For an account of the debate, see Alex J. Bellamy, 'Whither the Responsibility to Protect? Humanitarian Intervention and the 2005 World Summit', *Ethics and International Affairs* 20 (June 2006), pp. 143–169.

[11] *World Summit Outcome*, Document A/RES/60/1 (New York: United Nations, 24 October 2005), available at www.un.org/summit2005/docments.html.

RESPONSIBILITY TO PROTECT POPULATIONS FROM GENOCIDE, WAR CRIMES, ETHNIC CLEANSING AND CRIMES AGAINST HUMANITY

138. Each individual State has the responsibility to protect its populations from genocide, war crimes, ethnic cleansing and crimes against humanity. This responsibility entails the prevention of such crimes, including their incitement, through appropriate and necessary means. We accept that responsibility and will act in accordance with it. The international community should, as appropriate, encourage and help States to exercise this responsibility and support the United Nations in establishing an early warning capability.

139. The international community, through the United Nations, also has the responsibility to use appropriate diplomatic, humanitarian and other peaceful means, in accordance with Chapters VI and VIII of the Charter, to help to protect populations from genocide, war crimes, ethnic cleansing and crimes against humanity. In this context, we are prepared to take collective action, in a timely and decisive manner, through the Security Council, in accordance with the Charter, including Chapter VII, on a case-by-case basis and in cooperation with relevant regional organisations as appropriate, should peaceful means be inadequate and national authorities are manifestly failing to protect their populations from genocide, war crimes, ethnic cleansing and crimes against humanity. We stress the need for the General Assembly to continue consideration of the responsibility to protect populations from genocide, war crimes, ethnic cleansing and crimes against humanity and its implications, bearing in mind the principles of the Charter and international law. We also intend to commit ourselves, as necessary and appropriate, to helping States build capacity to protect their populations from genocide, war crimes, ethnic cleansing and crimes against humanity and to assisting those which are under stress before crises and conflicts break out.

Whatever its impact in the world of policymaking and action – and that story, which for this author remains very much the main point of focus, is continued in the next section – this UN resolution has certainly made an impact in the scholarly world. A major parallel debate has been waged – and in many areas still continues, as later chapters within this volume make clear – about such issues as the nature and distinctiveness of R2P as compared with related concepts; the significance of the differences in its formulation as between the ICISS report and the General Assembly resolution; its status as a 'norm', 'emerging norm' or something less than that; the extent to which it is built entirely on existing international law obligations or seeks to create new ones; and how it fits within post-colonial and other discourses, and so on. The present author has addressed many of these matters elsewhere,[12] and this is not the occasion to rehearse them all again, but it may be useful to respond again quickly to some of the more tenacious academic criticisms which have accompanied R2P's evolution. If academic debate is not grounded in reality, parallel debate can all too readily occupy a parallel universe.

The oft-repeated argument that R2P is simply 'old militarism in a new bottle' is one that has no *conceptual* credibility, whether in its original ICISS formulation or subsequent UN clothes. The whole point of the enterprise was to move away from the one-dimensional military preoccupations of 'humanitarian intervention', to focus on preventive strategies and to emphasise the importance of reactive strategies which do not involve the use of coercive force. Whether the argument has *practical* credibility depends on how the new norm is actually applied by governments. But while it is certainly the case (as will be discussed below in the context of the debate over the Libya intervention) that more agreement is needed on the criteria for undertaking military intervention, it is hard to find any evidence that R2P has encouraged the irresponsibly trigger-happy: if anything, states have been far more comfortable with its non-military dimensions.

The argument that R2P is 'old doctrine in a new bottle' has been quite persistent, especially the suggestion that the real doctrinal heavy-lifting had already been accomplished with the emergence in the literature, if not of mainstream political discourse, of 'sovereignty as responsibility'. ICISS commissioners have always acknowledged that this was one important strand in their thinking, and very much part of the total concept as it emerged. But it was only one part – addressing sovereign states' treatment of their own people, not what others should do to help or intervene if they failed in that responsibility. No one had previously used the phrase 'the responsibility to protect' as an organising or

---

[12] See, for example, Evans, *The Responsibility to Protect* (2008), pp. 56–71; Gareth Evans, 'Response to Reviews by Michael Barnett, Chris Brown and Robert Jackson', *Global Responsibility to Protect* 2 (2010), pp. 320–327; Gareth Evans, 'Ethnopolitical Conflict: When Is It Right to Intervene?', *Ethnopolitics* 10:1 (2011), pp. 115–123; Gareth Evans and Ramesh Thakur, 'Correspondence: Humanitarian Intervention and the Responsibility to Protect', *International Security* 37:4 (2013), pp. 199–207.

energising principle of general application, and no other formulation has been able to attract anything like the consensus around R2P.

The argument that R2P has been a 'good idea diluted' has, surprisingly, continued to linger. It is the case that in the process of transformation from ICISS report to UN resolution language – a process which has continued to some extent with the further articulation of the issues in a series of well-received annual reports to the General Assembly by the secretary-general from 2009 onwards – the scope of the R2P concept was in one important respect narrowed, and in another major respect presentationally refined. But the notion that these changes have undermined the effectiveness of the original concept is not accepted by the present author or any other member of the Commission.

The 'narrowing' that took place in paragraphs 138 and 139 was in order to create a much more precise definition of the threshold for the application of the doctrine – in terms of the occurrence or anticipation of 'four crimes' ('genocide, war crimes, ethnic cleansing and crimes against humanity'). The ICISS report, while essentially focusing on that same group of mass atrocity crimes, had used a broader and more ambiguous formulation – 'a population suffering serious harm, as a result of internal war, insurgency, repression or state failure' – which made some states nervous about potential overreach. Narrowing and deepening the relevant language – the product of the World Summit bargaining process – made for a stronger, not weaker, R2P.

The major presentational refinement that has taken place during R2P's evolution has been the characterisation of the relevant responsibilities in terms of 'three pillars'. This was implicit in paragraphs 138 and 139 of the 2005 Outcome document, and in fact in the Commission's report before it, but was made explicit in the secretary-general's 2009 report. Pillar One is the responsibility of each state to protect its own population from the atrocity crimes in question; Pillar Two is the responsibility of others to assist it to do so; and Pillar Three is the responsibility of the wider international community to respond in a 'timely and decisive' fashion and by all appropriate means (not excluding coercive military action, in accordance with the UN Charter) if this becomes necessary because the state in question is 'manifestly failing' to protect its people. Characterising the different responsibilities in this way has in fact proved extremely helpful in practice in getting the great majority of states to understand and accept what is involved, and has given the doctrine greater political force and effect than it would have otherwise have had.

Some commentators have made far too much of the distinction between the three pillars approach and that in the original ICISS report, which primarily describes the responsibilities in question as being to 'prevent', 'react' and 'rebuild'. The point is simply that these are alternative ways of organising and presenting exactly the same material. A homely metaphor might help make the point. Think of a cake with three layers – labelled, respectively, from the bottom up, 'prevention', 'reaction' and 'rebuilding' – which is then sliced vertically into three big wedges, labelled, respectively, Pillars One, Two and Three. The state itself has the responsibility under Pillar One to perform all three roles of prevention, reaction and rebuilding, as circumstances require; as does any state assisting it under Pillar Two; and as does the wider international community when playing an even more activist role under Pillar Three.

There is another continuing debate as to R2P's normative status, fuelled by a lack of real clarity in the literature as to what international 'norms' actually are, and a tendency for international relations scholars and lawyers to talk past each other on this subject. This writer does not argue that R2P could be properly described in 2005 as a new rule of customary international law, or can be now. The obligations of states not to themselves perpetrate atrocity crimes is well-embedded in substantive international human rights and humanitarian law, but this is not the case for Pillars Two and Three of R2P: their responsibility to assist, or engage more robustly, with other states when the latter are, through incapacity or ill-will, not doing what they should. Such a legal obligation may evolve over time, but that will depend on how comprehensively these dimensions of R2P are implemented and applied in practice, as well as recognised in principle, in the years ahead. But it is strongly arguable that R2P, with the weight behind it of a unanimous General Assembly resolution at head-of-state and government level, and many subsequent international applications and affirmations, can already be properly described as a new international norm: a new standard of behaviour, and a new guide to behaviour, for every state.

Growth to maturity 2005–2011

With the 2005 UN General Assembly resolution, R2P was finally, officially, born. Moreover, within a year of that decision, it had been affirmed in a Security Council resolution.[13] The world seemed well on its way, at last, to seeing the end, once and for all, of mass atrocity crimes: the murder, torture, rape, starvation, expulsion and destruction of property and life opportunities of others for no other reason than their race,

---

[13] UNSCR 1674, 28 April 2006.

ethnicity, religion, nationality, class or ideology. The British historian Sir Martin Gilbert described the whole R2P enterprise as 'the most signifi-cant adjustment to sovereignty in 360 years'.[14]

But words on UN paper are one thing, implementation something else. It took three more years of often torturous argument about R2P's scope and limits before the new norm first showed its bite in 2008 in Kenya, and another three before it seemed to have finally come of age with its application by the UN Security Council in the critical cases of Côte d'Ivoire and Libya in 2011. There were, in the meantime, political rear-guard actions to fight off, conceptual challenges to resolve and practical institutional changes to make, and all of this took time.

The first major political challenge to the 2005 resolution by those who had never really accepted it came with the debate in the UN General Assembly on the occasion of the first secretary-general's report on R2P in 2009. But it became apparent, by the conclusion of that debate, that out of the entire UN membership, there were only four states who wanted to go so far as to overturn the whole 2005 consensus: Nicaragua, Venezuela, Cuba and Sudan. And since then, in subsequent annual debates, even after the implementation of the Security Council's mandate in Libya drew wide criticism from mid-2011 onwards, opposition voices have been even more muted.

It is true that there has been more visible enthusiasm expressed, in many state contributions, for the general obligations involved in Pillars One and Two, than there has been for the more challenging demands of Pillar Three – and also true that there is widespread recognition that there is always likely to be disagreement about how best to respond to a catastrophically deteriorating situation. However, none of this translated into any continuing challenge to the notion that timely and decisive collective action may indeed be necessary where a state is manifestly failing to meet its responsibility to protect its own people. As Secretary-General Ban Ki-moon put it in 2011: 'It is a sign of progress that that our debates are now about how, not whether, to implement the Responsibility to Protect. No government questions the principle.'[15]

As to conceptual issues, a good deal of often confused debate continued among policymakers for some years after 2005 as to what are, and are not, 'R2P situations'. But most of these issues now seem to be resolved. It is now generally understood, and accepted, that R2P is about the

---

[14] Martin Gilbert, 'The Terrible 20th Century', *Globe and Mail* (Toronto), 31 January 2007.
[15] UN Press Release SG/SM/13838, 23 September 2011. For full accounts of the General Assembly debates from 2009 onwards, see, variously, the websites of the International Coalition for the Responsibility to Protect www.responsibilitytoprotect.org and the Global Centre for the Responsibility to Protect www.globalr2p.org.

'four crimes' – not human security, human rights violations or conflict situations in a general sense, however much its language might be thought to lend itself to these situations; nor is it about the wider international community's responsibility to respond to natural disasters or other humanitarian catastrophes, unless some element of criminal responsibility comes into the picture. To conceive of it otherwise is to dilute its impact as a catalyst and energiser for responding to mass atrocity crime situations which were so often ignored in the past.

Moreover, it is now generally acknowledged that for R2P to justify any kind of serious coercive response there has to be some scale and contemporaneity about the atrocity crimes committed or feared. Saddam Hussein was a serial human rights violator whose behaviour in persecuting political opponents amply justified condemnation and sanctions, but if his genocidal assaults on Kurds in the late 1980s and southern Shiites in the early 1990s could be regarded as justification for the most extreme form of R2P reaction – military invasion – over ten years later, then there would have been ample justification for a military assault on Robert Mugabe based on his genocidal behaviour in Matabeleland in the 1980s: and down that path lies the abandonment of any prospect of international consensus on hard cases in the future.

As successive situations have arisen and been debated, more and more consensus is evident on its conceptual scope and limits. So far at least as policymakers are concerned – some academics remain more difficult to persuade – it would now be generally agreed, in the view of this author, that, to take a range of controversial cases, the coalition invasion of Iraq in 2003 and Russia's invasion of Georgia in 2008 were not justified in R2P terms (despite the views of Tony Blair and Vladimir Putin, respectively); that the Burma/Myanmar cyclone in 2008, after which the military regime badly dragged its feet for a time in allowing international assistance, was not an R2P case (contrary to the views of the then French Foreign Minister Kouchner), but could have been if the generals' behaviour had continued long enough, which in the event it did not, to be characterisable as so recklessly indifferent to human life as to amount to a crime against humanity; that Somalia and the Congo for many years, Darfur certainly in 2003–2004, although more ambiguously since, and Sri Lanka in the horrific final military confrontation in 2009 between government forces and Tamil Tigers, in which so many civilians perished, have been properly characterised as R2P cases; and that post-election Kenya in early 2008 was an absolutely clear-cut case of an exploding situation being widely, and properly, characterised in R2P terms (and at the same time an important demonstration that an effective R2P response could take a diplomatic rather than coercive military form).

By 2011, there was little or no dissent from the proposition that the situation in Côte d'Ivoire in 2011 – in which (as more or less simultaneously with Libya) the Security Council both invoked R2P and authorised coercive military action – was a clear R2P case, although complicated by other legitimate agendas running simultaneously, with regional-organisation action to enforce a democratic election outcome and a UN mandate extending to force protection rather than just civilian protection. Nor was there any significant disagreement, at least at the outset, that Libya in early 2011 was a textbook case for the application of the R2P principle.

Further evidence of the growth to maturity of R2P in the years since 2005 lies in the institutional efforts that have been made to develop the preparedness – diplomatic, civilian, military and legal – to deal with future situations of mass atrocity crimes. The UN Joint Office – bringing together the secretary-general's Special Advisers on the Prevention of Genocide and on R2P – is, after several years of frustrating prevarication, up and running and making its voice increasingly heard. Within key national governments and regional organisations, 'focal points' are gradually being established with officials whose day job it is to worry about early warning and response to new situations as they arise, and to energise the appropriate action throughout their respective systems.[16] And although we seem not much closer than ever to establishing effective military rapid reaction forces on a standby basis, let alone any standing international forces of the kind that have long been argued for, key militaries are devoting serious time and attention now to debating and putting in place new force configuration arrangements, doctrine, rules of engagement and training to run what are now being understood as a separate category of activity to both traditional war-fighting and peacekeeping, located on the spectrum between them and being increasingly described as 'Mass Atrocity Response Operations'.

An important parallel institutional development, not directly attributable to R2P but contributing enormously to the new norm's actionable effectiveness, has been the rapid development of international criminal

---

[16] A particular initiative of Australia, Costa Rica, Denmark and Ghana to establish a global network of such focal points has seen some 40 states sign up as of September 2014. Although in some cases cosmetics need to be matched by more substance, the reality is that from Uruguay to the United States, from the DRC to Cote d'Ivoire, from Lithuania to New Zealand, there is a large and growing group of states building a real community of commitment.

law institutions: specialist national courts established with international assistance, such as the Special Courts for Sierra Leone and Cambodia; specialist tribunals to deal with war crimes committed in specific conflicts, in particular for the former Yugoslavia and Rwanda; and, most importantly, the International Criminal Court (ICC), established as a permanent court by the Rome Statute of 1998 to hear cases of genocide, crimes against humanity and war crimes, with no time limitation on its ability to prosecute.

Mid-life crisis 2011–2014[17]

The maturing of R2P was widely seen to have been complete with its invocation, and robust and effective application, by the Security Council in the cases of Côte d'Ivoire and Libya in early 2011, two real-world, real-time situations in which atrocities were occurring on the ground and feared likely to occur on a greater scale if strong action was not taken. But subsequent developments have also raised the question as to whether, instead of setting new benchmarks for its further acceptance and application in future, these cases would prove to be the high-water mark from which the tide would now permanently recede.

In Côte d'Ivoire the intervention was brought quickly to a successful conclusion: it was at the time largely uncontroversial and has remained so. The Libyan intervention was also relatively uncontroversial at the outset, but – unhappily – did not remain so for very long. In February 2011, Colonel Muammar Gaddafi's forces responded to the initial peaceful protests against the excesses of his regime, inspired by the Arab Spring revolutions in Tunisia and Egypt, by massacring at least several hundred of his own people. That led to the unanimous UN Security Council Resolution 1970 of 26 February, which specifically invoked 'the Libyan authorities' responsibility to protect its population', condemned its violence against civilians, demanded that this stop and sought to concentrate Gaddafi's mind by applying targeted sanctions, an arms embargo and the threat of ICC prosecution for crimes against humanity.

Then, as it became apparent that Gaddafi was not only ignoring that resolution but planning a major assault on Benghazi in which 'no mercy or pity' would be shown to perceived opponents, armed or otherwise – his reference to 'cockroaches' having a special resonance for those who

---

[17] This section draws on Gareth Evans, 'Responding to Atrocities: The New Geopolitics of Intervention', in Stockholm International Peace Research Institute, *SIPRI Yearbook 2012* (Oxford: Oxford University Press, 2012), pp. 15–39.

remembered how Tutsis were being described before the 1994 genocide in Rwanda – the Security Council followed up with Resolution 1973 of 17 March 2011, also invoking R2P, which, by majority vote with no veto or other dissenting voices (although there were abstentions from Brazil, China, Germany, India and Russia) explicitly authorised 'all necessary measures', that is military intervention by member states, 'to protect civilians and civilian populated areas under threat of attack'. Acting under this authorisation, NATO-led forces took immediate action, and the feared massacres did not eventuate. If the Security Council had acted equally decisively and robustly in the 1990s, most of the 8,000 murdered in Srebrenica and 800,000 in Rwanda might still be alive today.

But as subsequent weeks and months wore on, the Western-led coercive military intervention – which finally concluded only with the capture of Gaddafi and comprehensive defeat of his forces in October 2011 – came under fierce attack by the 'BRICS' countries (Brazil, Russia, India, China and South Africa) for exceeding its narrow civilian protection mandate and being content with nothing less than regime change. This continuing dispute and all the distrust it engendered had a major impact on the Security Council's response to Syria, where the one-sided violence by the regime was by mid-2011 manifestly worse even than that which had triggered the Libyan intervention. In the face of vetoes from Russia and China, and continuing unhappiness by the other BRICS members, the Council found itself for many months unable to agree even on a formal condemnatory statement, let alone more robust measures such as sanctions, an arms embargo or the threat of ICC prosecution.

Part of the reason for the paralysis over Syria, as compared with the speedy and effective response to Libya, is that the geopolitics of the Syrian crisis were very different, with potentially explosive regional sectarian divisions, no Arab League unanimity in favour of tough action, a long Russian commitment to the Assad regime and a strong Syrian army, which meant that any conceivable intervention would be difficult and bloody. But recriminations by the other BRICS as well – all of whom were on the Security Council at the relevant time – were crucial to the explanation.

Their complaints with regard to Libya were not about the initial military response – destroying Libyan air force infrastructure and air attacks on the ground forces advancing on Benghazi – but what came after: that the interveners, in their determination to achieve regime change, rejected ceasefire offers that may have been serious, struck fleeing personnel that posed no immediate risk to civilians and locations that had no obvious military significance (like the compound in which some of Gaddafi's relatives were killed) and, more generally, comprehensively supported the rebel side in what rapidly became a civil war, ignoring the very explicit arms embargo in the process.

The Western P3 (that is the Security Council permanent members the United States, the United Kingdom and France) do not lack some answers to these charges. If civilians were to be protected house-to-house in areas like Tripoli under Gaddafi's direct control, they say, that could only be by overturning his whole regime. If one side was taken in a civil war, it was because one-sided regime killing sometimes leads (as now in Syria) to civilians acquiring arms to fight back and recruiting army defectors. Military operations cannot be micromanaged with a '1,000-mile screwdriver'. And a more limited 'monitor and swoop' concept of operations would have led to a longer and messier conflict, one that would be politically impossible to sustain in the United States and Europe and likely to have produced many more civilian casualties.

And yet... These arguments all have some force, but the P3 resisted debate on them at any stage in the Security Council itself, and other Council members were never given sufficient information to enable them to be evaluated. Perhaps not all the BRICS are to be believed when they say that, had better process been followed, more common ground could have been achieved, but they can be when they say they feel bruised by the P3's dismissiveness during the Libyan campaign – and that those bruises will have to heal before any consensus can be expected on tough responses to such situations in the future.

Future

Just as any celebration about the triumph of the R2P principle would have been premature after the Libyan resolutions in early 2011, so is it too early to despair now about its future. There are three reasons for believing that the whole R2P project has not been irreversibly tarnished, and that, even for the hardest cases, Security Council consensus in the future is not unimaginable

The first is that there is effectively universal consensus on basic R2P principles. Whatever the difficulties being experienced in the Security Council, the underlying norm is in remarkably good shape in the wider international community. The best evidence of this, as already noted,[18]

---

[18] See text at note 15 above. For an account of the most recent debate, see 'Summary of the Sixth Informal Interactive Dialogue of the UN General Assembly on the Responsibility to Protect, held on 8 September 2014', Global Centre for the Responsibility to Protect,

is in the annual debates on R2P in the General Assembly, even in the aftermath of the strong disagreements over Libya. No state is now heard to disagree that every sovereign state has the responsibility, to the best of its ability, to protect its own peoples from genocide, ethnic cleansing and other major crimes against humanity and war crimes. No state disagrees that others have the responsibility, to the best of their own ability, to assist it to do so. And no state seriously continues to challenge the principle that the wider international community should respond with timely and decisive collective action when a state is manifestly failing to meet its responsibility to protect its own people.

Second, the Security Council itself continues to endorse the principle and use its language. For all the continuing neuralgia about the Libyan intervention and the impact of that in turn on Syria, the Council had, since its March 2011 decisions on Cote d'Ivoire and Libya, by August 2014 endorsed not only nine presidential statements, but nineteen other resolutions directly referring to R2P, including measures to confront the threat of mass atrocities in Yemen, Libya, Mali, Sudan, South Sudan and the Central African Republic, and resolutions both on the humanitarian response to the situation in Syria and recommitting to the fight against genocide on the twentieth anniversary of Rwanda.[19] There were just four Security Council resolutions prior to Libya using specific R2P language, but there have been nineteen since. While none of these have authorised a Libyan-style military intervention, together they do confirm that the rumours of R2P's death in the Security Council have been greatly exaggerated. The kind of commitment that has been shown in supporting robust peacekeeping operations in Mali and the Central African Republic in particular is very different to the kind of indifference which characterised the reaction to Rwanda and so many other cases before it.

Third, for all the division and paralysis over Libya and Syria, it is possible to see the beginning of a new dynamic in the Security Council that would enable the consensus that matters most – how to react in the Council on the hardest of cases – to be re-created in the future. The ice was broken in this respect by Brazil in late 2011 with its proposal that that the idea be accepted of *supplementing* R2P, not replacing it, with a complementary set of principles and procedures which it has labelled 'responsibility while protecting',

New York: accessible at www.globalr2p.org/media/files/summary-of-the-r2p-dialogue -2014.pdf.

[19] See 'R2P References in United Nations Security Council Resolutions and Presidential Statements', Global Centre for the Responsibility to Protect, New York, September 2014: accessible at www.globalr2p.org/media/files/unsc-resolutions-and-statements -with-r2p-table-as-of-august-2014–1.pdf.

or RWP.[20] There were two core elements of the proposal: first, there should be a set of prudential criteria fully debated and taken into account before the Security Council mandated any use of military force; and second, there should be some kind of enhanced monitoring and review processes which would enable such mandates to be seriously debated by all Council members during their implementation phase, with a view to ensuring so far as possible that consensus is maintained throughout the course of an operation. While the response of the P3 to the Brazilian proposal has so far remained highly sceptical, it has become increasingly clear that if a breakthrough is to be achieved – with un-vetoed majorities once again being possible in the Council in support of Chapter VII-based interventions in extreme cases – they are going to have to be more accommodating. The incentive to do so may be that that there have been intriguing signs that the two BRICS countries that matter most in this context because of their veto-wielding powers, China and Russia, may be interested in pursuing these ideas further.

In Beijing in October 2013, the foreign ministry's think tank, the China Institute of International Studies, brought together specialist scholars and practitioners from China and the other BRICS countries (Brazil, Russia, India and South Africa) together with a handful of Western specialists, including the present author and Ramesh Thakur, for a two-day meeting to discuss R2P. Strong support was expressed around the table for the principle of 'responsible protection' (RP), which had been floated by the Chinese scholar Ruan Zongze in a 2012 journal article,[21] which explicitly referred to and built upon the Brazilian RWP proposal, and which evidently had been the subject of much internal discussion since in Chinese policymaking circles. In the same month, the Diplomatic Academy of the Russian Ministry of Foreign Affairs, apparently on the initiative of Foreign Minister Sergei Lavrov himself, hosted a one-day meeting on R2P, evidently the first of its kind, attended by senior ministry officials and Russian academics and a handful of Western specialists. While less focused than the Beijing event, there was again much attention paid to RWP and the Chinese RP concept, and an emerging sense from the

---

[20] The RWP idea was first mentioned by President Dilma Rousseff in her speech to the General Assembly on 25 September 2011, then followed up by Foreign Minister Antonio Patriota in a speech read to the Security Council on 9 November 2011, and spelt out in a concept paper circulated on 11 November 2011 as A/66/551 – S/2011/701. In more recent iterations, Brazilian spokespersons have focused on the two core elements mentioned (see, for example, Permanent Representative Maria Luiza Ribeiro Viotti's statement in the interactive debate on 5 September 2012: www.globalr2p. org/media/files /brazil-statement-2012.pdf) but have not been playing an active role in advancing them.

[21] Ruan Zongze. 'Responsible Protection: Building a Safer World', CIIS, June 2012: accessible at www.ciis.org.cn/english/2012–06/15/content_5090912.htm.

meeting that Russia needed to align itself with those views. Of course, with the subsequent explosion of concern about Russia's behaviour in Ukraine – combined with the cynicism that is bound to be generated, in an R2P context, by Moscow's claim to be acting in Crimea to protect its Russian nationals and language-speakers (albeit there was no crude reliance on R2P as such as occurred in Georgia in 2008) – the atmosphere in the Security Council will not be conducive, in the immediately foreseeable future, to winning consensus in a big-principles debate on anything to do with state sovereignty and the proper scope and limits of coercive intervention. However, the seeds for future constructive discussion have been sown.

There are bound to be acute frustrations and disappointments and occasions for despair along the way, but that should not for a moment lead us to conclude that the whole R2P enterprise has been misconceived. There is, effectively, universal consensus now about its basic principles, and disagreement only about how they are to be applied in the hardest of cases. Given the nature of the issues involved, it is hardly unexpected that such disagreements will continue to arise, and certainly to be assumed that only in the most extreme and exceptional cases will coercive military intervention be authorised by the Security Council.

What is much better understood now by policymakers around the world – even if they do not always act accordingly – is that if the Security Council does not find a way of genuinely cooperating to resolve these cases, working within the nuanced and multidimensional framework of the R2P principle, the alternative is a return to the bad old days of Rwanda, Srebrenica and Kosovo. And that means either total, disastrous inaction in the face of mass atrocity crimes, or action being taken to stop them without authorisation by the Security Council, in defiance of the UN Charter and every principle of a rule-based international order. There is room for optimism that the enormous progress made over the last decade will continue; but there is no doubt that the completely effective practical implementation of R2P is going to be work in progress for some time yet.

3   From the right to persecute to the
Responsibility to Protect: Feuerbachian
inversions of rights and responsibilities
in state–citizen relations

Charles Sampford and Ramesh Thakur

The Responsibility to Protect, commonly shortened to R2P, is widely
seen as a quintessentially post-Westphalian, liberal, internationalist
norm. As such, it is alternately the poster-boy and whipping-boy of the
supporters and detractors of liberal internationalism. However, its relationship with Westphalian statehood is a little more complex. R2P owes it
origins to a major push by UN Secretary-General Kofi Annan, scarred by
the atrocities in Rwanda in 1994 and Srebrenica in 1995 that happened
on his watch as the under-secretary-general for peacekeeping, to forge a
new normative consensus on when and how the international community
should prevent and stop such tragedies. In his first report on R2P in
2009, his successor, Ban Ki-moon, reframed R2P in the metaphor of
three pillars. Pillar One was defined as 'the enduring responsibility of the
State to protect its populations, whether nationals or not, from genocide,
war crimes, ethnic cleansing and crimes against humanity, and from their
incitement'. Pillar Two was described as 'the commitment of the international community to assist States in meeting those obligations'. Pillar
Three was defined as 'the responsibility of Member States to respond
collectively in a timely and decisive manner when a State is manifestly
failing to provide ... protection'.[1] While primacy was to be given to
peaceful means, should they prove inadequate to ensure protection, the
international community should use more robust action: 'no strategy for
fulfilling the responsibility to protect would be complete without the
possibility of collective enforcement measures, including through sanctions or coercive military action in extreme cases'.[2]

---

[1] Ban Ki-moon, Implementing the Responsibility to Protect. Report of the Secretary-
General, Document A/63/677 (New York: United Nations, 12 January 2009), pp. 8–9,
paragraph 11(a, b and c).
[2] Ibid., p. 25, paragraph 56.

38

The first pillar of R2P thus provides the core justification for sovereigns claims to rule and the basis of the social contract that Hobbes posited for their subjects. However, the security of their subjects was doubly undermined: first by the fraudulent nature of the claims of many sovereigns to protect their subjects, and secondly because the successful repression of civilians was one of the most common ways of establishing sovereignty and the basis of sovereign legitimacy. Seventeenth-century 'R2P' was more likely to be the 'right to persecute' than a responsibility to protect.

The Enlightenment turned the relationship between sovereign and subject on its head in an inversion that Sampford has likened to Feurbach's suggested reversal of the relationship between man and God.[3] While justifying democracy and human rights within democratic sovereign states, the Enlightenment raised questions about what democracies should do to states that trampled on rather than recognised the rights of their citizens – and about the putative right of humanitarian intervention. Unfortunately, however, this new right was as liable to abuse as the claims of sovereigns to protect them. The Report of the International Commission on Intervention and State Sovereignty (ICISS) performed another Feuerbachian inversion to turn the right of other states to intervene into the Responsibility to Protect.[4]

In *The Structure of Scientific Revolutions*, Thomas S. Kuhn outlined the process by which a dominant paradigm in science is replaced by a new paradigm. Normal science is concerned with solving puzzles within a particular framework. However, in the course of ongoing research, anomalies are uncovered, reflecting an empirical variance with the dominant theory that suggests deficiencies in the existing paradigm. This generates auxiliary hypotheses within the dominant paradigm to explain the anomalies. But if there comes a point where the old paradigm proves unable to accommodate the anomalies, the pressure grows for a new paradigm to emerge. At this point 'the anomalous has become the expected'.[5] In this chapter, we argue that a similar 'structure of philosophical revolution' occurred to flip the understandings, expectations, limitations and exercise of state sovereignty as the dominant paradigm of the contemporary world order. Accumulating anomalies and 'pockets

---

[3] Charles Sampford, 'Professions without Borders: Global Ethics and the International Rule of Law', Public Lecture, Queensland University of Technology, 19 August 2009.
[4] International Commission on Intervention and State Sovereignty (ICISS), *The Responsibility to Protect* (Ottawa: International Development Research Centre, 2001).
[5] Thomas S. Kuhn, *The Structure of Scientific Revolutions* (Chicago: University of Chicago Press, 1962), p. 53.

of apparent disorder', or 'gaps' in common parlance (and sometimes 'disconnects' in more contemporary usage), were reconciled by reformulating sovereignty as state responsibility and citizen rights.

The Feurbachian analogy

Emphasising Kuhn highlights the gradual drip of evidence on an inadequate theory leading to a permanent inversion in which support for the old theory withers quite rapidly. This essay examines an alternative analogy to Kuhn's portrayal of scientific revolutions typified by the Copernican inversion of the Ptolemaic image of earth as the centre of the heavens. Emphasising Feurbach highlights the dramatic philosophical insight which leads some to completely orient their view but which leaves others still holding on to the previous view as a matter of faith. The Enlightenment inversion of sovereign–subject relationships and the subsequent inversion of the right to intervene to the Responsibility to Protect display elements of each. One could distinguish between the two analogies in that matters or religion cannot be undermined by facts in a way that 'scientific' theories can. The Feurbachian analogy is the more apt of the two metaphors also because of the clear, if (for understandable political reasons) unacknowledged, philosophical antecedents of R2P in the Christian tradition's just war theory (as discussed by Alex Bellamy Chapter 10 in this volume).

Ludwig Andreas von Feuerbach (1804–1872) was a German philosopher who is acknowledged as an intellectual bridge in the development of dialectical materialism from Friedrich Hegel to Karl Marx. An atheist, he pondered the relationship between God and man. Christians imagine that God created man in his own image. Feuerbach suggested that it was at least as likely that man created God in his own image. R2P represents just such a Feuerbachian reversal of the way rulers and ruled relate to each other. Enlightenment *philosophes* suggested a similar inversion for sovereignty. Before the Enlightenment, 'subjects' had to demonstrate their allegiance and loyalty to their 'sovereign'. The *philosophes* proclaimed that 'governments' had to justify their existence to 'citizens' who chose them. Once the reversal of the relationship was suggested in this 'great leap forward', it was very hard to go back to the pre-Enlightenment way of looking at things. Indeed, it became as broadly popular with civilians as Westphalian sovereignty was with some authoritarian states. This approach led, in the increasingly large number of democracies, to the new basis of sovereign legitimacy in domestic law and political theory – the acquiescence, then consent, then the active choice of the governed. It also had a profound impact on the way in which the ruler's right to use force was conceived and justified, initially with respect to subjects within territorial jurisdictions but eventually also with respect to the international use of force in the jurisdictions of other sovereigns.

The Westphalian protection racket

The use of force both within domestic and foreign jurisdictions, no matter how benevolent, enlightened and impartial in intent, has empirical consequences. In particular, it shapes the domestic and international struggle for power and helps to determine the outcome of political contests. This is why it is inherently controversial, contentious and contested. Rulers have long claimed that the protection of their subjects is the first duty of the sovereign's primary responsibility of the relevant sovereign states – an idea that is grounded in the long-standing attempts by rulers to legitimise their regimes based on the claim that they protected their people. While there were other claims to legitimacy, including the claim to be anointed by God (or, more directly, to be a God), this is always, at least, a supplementary claim of those who justify the power they wield.

Of course, with every grant of power comes the possibility of abuse. What happens if the rulers do not live up to their claims and it is not such a good deal for their subjects? What if they cannot or will not protect their subjects? Worse still, what if they become a threat to the very people whose defence is the core of their *raison d'être*?[6] There is a special obloquy for those who are entrusted with power for the benefit of another and use it against them – doctors who murder patients, parents who abuse their children, teachers who brainwash rather than educate their pupils, and priests who prey on children for whose moral enlightenment they are responsible. It is common for the law to treat such abuse of power as aggravating the offence. Some sovereigns turn out to be a greater threat to their peoples than the real or imagined enemies against whom they claim to protect their people from, and are rarely punished at all. Even when they kill thousands, prison doors do not generally open for them. Indeed, the doors that do open for them are those of the palace at home, the embassy abroad and the private jet in between – as well as the doors to bankers who lend the tyrant money to buy the plane and the palace and

---

[6] Locke's repudiation of Hobbes puts it quite nicely: 'This is to think, that men are so foolish, that they take care to avoid what mischiefs may be done them by *pole-cats*, or *foxes;* but are content, nay, think it safety, to be devoured by *lions*'. John Locke, *Two Treatises of Government*, Thomas Ira Cook and Robert Filmer, eds (New York: Hafner Press, [1690] 1947), II: 93.

to pay for the persecution of civilians.[7] And after it is all over, the citizens will have the responsibility to repay this 'sovereign debt'.

Why is this tolerated? Why don't other states intervene to protect citizens from the tyrants who oppress them? The answer lies in the wars of religion culminating in the Thirty Years War (1618–1648) which involved frequent interventions, purportedly to protect co-religionists from persecution. Because such interventions were generally undertaken for other reasons, the plight of those to be protected often worsened and the intervening forces added to that plight. Indeed, the 1648 Treaty of Westphalia can be seen as based on the view that the consequences of intervention were so bad that it was better to let the tyrant do what tyrants do, and the principle of non-intervention was born in the presumption of the lesser evil. It was seen as better to have refugees streaming over the border out of the tyranny than to have troops going the other way to stop it. Hence the characterisation of the Treaty of Westphalia as 'a tyrant's charter' – written of the tyrants, by the tyrants and for the tyrants.[8]

Despite the claims of sovereigns to protect their peoples, the Westphalian concept of sovereignty and sovereign legitimacy is effectively predicated on its opposite. Sovereignty is based on control of territory. This concept had a number of different formulations – most notably Hans Kelsen's formulation that the regime had to be 'by and large effective'.[9] The effectiveness is initially established by the 'prior successful use of force'[10] to gain effective control against a previous sovereign. It is maintained by a continued perceived willingness and capacity to use that force against anyone who would seek to similarly supplant them. The main threat was traditionally other tyrants or groups demanding religious or other freedoms. Members of such groups are not protected from attack but subject to it. If people did not like the sovereign or what was done in his or her name, then it was necessary for the sovereign to impose his will and demonstrate his authority by massacring groups of subjects and gruesomely executing their leaders. Rather than giving way to the wishes

---

[7] An example of black humour in a similar vein: you kill one person, you get sent to trial for murder; kill ten, you get sent to a mental asylum; kill 10,000, you are invited to Geneva for UN peace talks.

[8] With apologies to the United Dutch Provinces, the only signatory clearly not a tyranny, and to Abraham Lincoln and his Gettysburg address.

[9] Hans Kelsen, *Pure Theory of Law*, trans. Max Knight (Berkeley: UCLA Press, (1960) [1967]).

[10] See Charles Sampford, 'Sovereignty and Intervention', Plenary Paper, *World Congress of Legal and Social Philosophy*, New York, June 1999; later published in Burton Leiser and Tom Campbell, eds, *Human Rights in Philosophy and Practice* (London: Ashgate 2001), Ch. 16.

of the people, sovereigns saw it as their duty to enforce their will and demonstrate their sovereignty. Their *raison d'être* was not the rights of citizens but the preservation of the dynasty and its authority.[11] Where the criterion of sovereignty was the prior successful use of force, human rights violations did not so much undermine sovereign legitimacy as prove and reassert it.

One may conclude that, despite traditional claims of sovereigns to protect their people, the heart of Westphalian sovereignty undermined it. The authoritarian states that were emerging during the century of Westphalia and those that followed were not so much concerned with protection of civilians but protection *from* civilians, and used their claimed monopoly of legitimate force against them.[12] If one were to formulate an R2P principle for Westphalian states, they would be more likely to refer to a right, indeed a responsibility, to use force against any of their people who disagreed with them (or were just insufficiently supportive). This was an assertion and exercise of power not in the name of citizens, but over them. For some of the more religiously minded, it might be seen as the 'responsibility to persecute'. For those who just 'did it because they could', it became a 'right to persecute' that was recognised, if sometimes reluctantly, by other sovereign states.

This idea has been embraced by tyrants the world over. This is not an 'eastern' or 'Asian' value. It is a Western idea that has been picked up with obscene alacrity, sometimes displacing contrary traditions rooted in local conceptions of the proper relationship of duties and rights binding sovereigns and subjects. It has demonstrated its appeal to tyrants of countries large and small from all regions, religions, cultures, languages and climates. The tyrant's rule based in terror does not discriminate on grounds of race, religion, or gender, but is an equal opportunity offender and that is why it needs a universal norm to prohibit and end it.

Sovereign legitimacy – domestic and international

As we have seen, in 1648 legitimacy in both domestic and international law and political theory was based on the effectiveness of the sovereign's

---

[11] If they claimed higher purposes and external responsibilities, these were likely to be connected with religion rather than human rights. Sovereigns might purport to be more concerned about the afterlife of their subjects than their present life – to the extent that some thoughtfully burned heretics.

[12] Although Max Weber did not refer to the 'monopoly of legitimate force' until 250 years later, the seventeenth-century rulers were very much concerned to establish such a monopoly against their 'over-mighty subjects'. See Max Weber, 'Politics as a Vocation', Gordon Wells and John Dreymanis, eds, *Complete Writing on Academic and Political Vocations* (New York: Algora Press, [1919] 2001).

rule. Within some European states, it was challenged almost immediately and within thirty years concepts of sovereignty in domestic and international law started to diverge. John Locke argued that sovereigns were *entrusted* with power. If they abused that trust and became a threat to their people, the latter had a right to revolt. That was a pretty inefficient form of regime change and the right to revolt against governments who did not protect their citizens became a right to choose the government that best reflected their interests and values. The political system was held to embody, articulate and facilitate the achievement of the social purposes of a community. This shift was part of the Enlightenment's great leap forward in which a variety of governance values (liberty, equality, fraternity, democracy, human rights and the rule of law) were demanded and partly secured in the United States, United Kingdom, and a growing number of European countries.

International law, however, has continued to recognise states and governments on the basis of who exercises effective political control over discrete territories. Even when a democratically elected government is overturned by a *coup d'état*, the ambassadors of the new regime are accredited by foreign powers and are allowed to take that country's seat at the United Nations and other international forums. In the last century, India and Vietnam were censured by the UN community for their interventions in Bangladesh and Cambodia respectively which rid the world of regimes that had carried out large-scale brutal massacres. This glaring inconsistency caused considerable tension and great soul searching within democratic states and led to the tentative and controversial claim that there was an emerging norm of humanitarian intervention.

Some of the most thoughtful soul searching was carried out in response to challenges acknowledged and articulated by Annan. In his annual address to the UN General Assembly in 1999 he challenged the international community to devise principles governing the exercise of sovereignty and the conditions under which 'humanitarian intervention', as it was then called, could be justified. In the inaugural Ministerial Conference of the Community of Democracies, Annan proposed that 'wherever democracy has taken root, it will not be reversed'. ICISS responded to the first challenge in 2001 and a Council on Foreign Relations Task Force responded to the second challenge in 2002.[13]

These responses have stimulated rather than resolved debate between traditional state sovereignty based on power and popular sovereignty

---

[13] International Commission on Intervention and State Sovereignty (ICISS), *Responsibility to Protect*; Independent Task Force Sponsored by the Council on Foreign Relations, Threats to Democracy: Prevention and Response (Council on Foreign Relations, Washington, 2003). Thakur was a member of the first and Sampford of the second.

based on the active choice of the governed. The revival of pre-twentieth-century ideas of intervention faced a lot of hostility that not only cited Westphalian norms but also the sorry history of interventions that helped stimulate it. One of the problems was that this was formulated as a right of states rather than civilians. One of the great achievements of ICISS was to effect a 'Feuerbachian inversion' on the 'right to intervene'. The relevant rights belonged to human beings. States had responsibilities to protect them – with the primary responsibility being of the state in which they reside and contingent responsibility on other states. It is radical because it denies tyrants the right to do what tyrants have always done and for which international law rewarded them. Accordingly, we see R2P not as a Western attempt to interfere in other people's problems, but as a global attempt to deal with a Western problem at the heart of the Westphalian system that some would-be tyrants were, unfortunately, deeply attracted to. But it was also a legitimate concern of others who fear not only selfishly motivated interventions disguised in the language of humanitarian concerns, but also a breakdown of the very principle on which the present world order resting on a system of independent and autonomous states is organised.

Developing countries and sovereignty

One of the legitimate concerns was that the new enthusiasm for intervention might be directed at developing countries soon after they had wrested sovereignty back from their colonial overlords. The continued silencing of non-Western voices in the Western discourse on the historical memories and changing notions of sovereignty is at once rather surprising and deeply disrespectful of their experience. Thus a recent article points out that non-intervention in one another's internal affairs was only a twentieth-century attribute of sovereignty and that indeed the right to intervene – for example, to protect co-religionists under threat by a ruler from a different denomination – predates non-intervention as an *attribute* of sovereignty.[14] Of the 106 references cited in the article, just four are recognisably non-Westerners by name, of whom one is Japanese: so only three might have some colonised-country background. Even Francis Deng, the intellectual godfather of sovereignty as responsibility, doesn't rate a mention.

Are scholars from countries that were once European colonies likely to forget or overlook the brutal historical fact that their nations were

[14] Luke Glanville, 'The Myth of "Traditional" Sovereignty', *International Studies Quarterly* 57:1 (2013), pp. 79–90.

invaded, conquered, annexed and ruled by the European powers through the height of the Westphalian order of traditional sovereignty? It is simply not possible to understand the strength of their visceral reactions to the so-called right to humanitarian intervention without grasping how the colonial experience is deeply internalised in their collective consciousness and continues to scar their memories. Their post-1945 elevation of non-intervention as a peremptory norm from which no derogation is permitted and their abiding attachment to the new norm rest on this memory. R2P never would have gained such rapid uptake and traction had ICISS not conducted its extensive outreach exercise, which comprised listening to and then reflecting the voices heard in its final report.[15]

The input of historical trauma of the colonised societies makes them deeply suspicious of various concepts of suspended sovereignty,[16] inter-rupted sovereignty,[17] and, most significantly, conditional sovereignty.[18] Western countries had justified invading them because of their supposed backwardness and newly unacceptable practices (such as the slave trade, which Western countries had dominated a few decades before). Were they now to be invaded because they were practising milder forms of the human rights abuses perfected by Western nations?

Developing countries fear that in some sections of the West today, the view has gained ground that anyone *but* the legitimate authorities can use force. As already noted, the doctrines of sovereign equality and non-interference are distinctively European in origin and construct. In the era of decolonisation, the sovereign equality of states and the correlative norm of non-intervention received their most emphatic affirmation from the newly independent states. Ironically, while aspects of sovereignty were being progressively pooled, if not superseded, in the construction of the increasingly borderless European Union (EU), some of its most passionate defenders were to be found among developing countries. That said, the United States is second to none in the jealous defence of national sovereignty against international encroachments. Its 'sovereign-tists' have launched three lines of attack: that the emerging international legal order is vague and illegitimately intrusive on domestic affairs; that the international lawmaking process is unaccountable and the resulting

---

[15] See Ramesh Thakur, 'Intervention, Sovereignty and the Responsibility to Protect: Experiences from ICISS', *Security Dialogue* 33:3 (2002), pp. 323–340.

[16] Alexandros Yannis, 'The Concept of Suspended Sovereignty in International Law', *European Journal of International Law* 13:5 (2002), pp. 1037–1052.

[17] For example of trusteeships, see Simon Chesterman, *You, the People: The United Nations, Transitional Administration, and State-Building* (Oxford: Oxford University Press, 2004); Richard Caplan, *International Governance of War-Torn Territories: Rule and Reconstruction* (Oxford: Oxford University Press, 2005).

[18] ICISS, *Responsibility to Protect.*

law unenforceable; and that Washington can opt out of international regimes as a matter of power, legal right and constitutional duty.[19]

At one level, the developing countries' attachment to sovereignty is deeply emotional. The most important clue to understanding their concerns is the history of Europe's encounter with Arabs, Africans and Asians. The relentless march of colonialism and imperialism is never based on anything so vulgar as commercial and geopolitical calculations: land and wealth grabs. No, it is always driven by a lofty purpose. The deployment of moral arguments to justify imperialist actions in Iraq in 2003, for example, had a direct structural counterpart in the British annexation of the Indian kingdom of Awadh (Oudh in its anglicised version) in the first half of the nineteenth century. The structure of justification makes use of a specific set of techniques for the mobilisation of democratic consent and international support – through political representatives, the press and the interested and attentive public – of decisions taken in pursuit of national interests by an elite group of policymakers.

Tracing its origins to John Locke and John Stuart Mill, Chatterjee locates it in the paternalistic belief that people and nations who are morally handicapped or in a state of moral infancy deserve a benevolent despot who will protect and look after them.[20]

What is remarkable is how many of the same arguments, including the evangelical fervour, the axiomatic assumption of the mantle of civilisation, the fig-leaf of legalism, the intelligence reports, the forgeries and subterfuges and the hard-headed calculations of national interest, remain exactly the same at the beginning of the 21st century ... the liberal evangelical creed of taking democracy and human rights to backward cultures is still a potent ideological drive, and ... the instrumental use of that ideological rhetoric for realist imperialist ends is entirely available, as we have seen in Iraq.[21]

Many African and Asian countries achieved independence on the back of extensive and protracted nationalist struggles. The parties and leaders at the forefront of the fight for independence helped to establish the new states and shape and guide the founding principles of their foreign policies. The anti-colonial impulse in their worldview was instilled in the countries' foreign policies and survives as a powerful sentiment in the corporate memory of the elites. All too often, developing-country views

---

[19] Peter J. Spiro, 'The New Sovereigntists', *Foreign Affairs* 79:6 (2000), pp. 9–15.
[20] Partha Chatterjee, 'Empire after Globalisation', *Economic and Political Weekly* 39:37 (11 September 2004), p. 4158.
[21] Ibid., p. 4163.

either fail to get a respectful hearing at all in Western policy and scholarly discourse, or are patronisingly dismissed.[22]

At another level, the commitment to sovereignty is functional. State sovereignty is the bedrock principle of the contemporary international system that provides order and stability. The most important task on the agenda of the international community therefore should be not to weaken states nor to undermine the doctrine of state sovereignty, but to strengthen the institutions of state and make them legitimate and empowering of people, and respectful and protective of their rights.[23] In the words of Kofi Annan, 'one of the great challenges of the new millennium is to ensure that all States are strong enough to meet the many challenges they face'.[24]

The debate over R2P is not and ought not to be a North–South issue. But it can be turned into one either because of wilful – and sometimes self-serving – obstinacy on the part of key emerging countries,[25] or because of calculated neglect of their legitimate concerns by a declining West. Many non-Western societies have a historical tradition of reciprocal rights and obligations that define the terms of engagement of sovereigns and their subjects. Contrary to what many developing-country governments might claim, R2P is rooted as firmly in their own indigenous values and traditions as in abstract notions of sovereignty derived from European thought and practice. As argued by ICISS co-chair Mohamed Sahnoun, in many ways R2P is a distinctly African contribution to global human rights.[26]

Asia has its own rich traditions that vest sovereigns with responsibility for the lives and welfare of their subjects, while circumscribing the

---

[22] Ramesh Thakur, *Towards a Less Imperfect State of the World: The Gulf between North and South* (Berlin: Friedrich Ebert Stiftung, Dialogue on Globalization Briefing Paper 4, April 2008).

[23] See Simon Chesterman, Michael Ignatieff and Ramesh Thakur, eds, *Making States Work: State Failure and the Crisis of Governance* (Tokyo: United Nations University Press, 2005).

[24] Kofi A. Annan, *In Larger Freedom: Towards Development, Security and Human Rights for All*. Report of the Secretary-General, Document A/59/2005 (New York: United Nations, 21 March 2005), paragraph 19.

[25] Ramesh Thakur, 'R2P after Libya and Syria: Engaging Emerging Powers', *The Washington Quarterly* 36:2 (2013), pp. 61–76.

[26] Mohamed Sahnoun, 'Africa: Uphold Continent's Contribution to Human Rights, Urges Top Diplomat', *allAfrica.com*, 21 July 2009 (www.allafrica.com/stories /printable/200907210549.html). For another African perspective that also strongly supports R2P, see Samuel Atuobi, 'The Responsibility to Protect: The Time to Act Is Now', *KAIPTC Policy Brief* No. 1 (Accra: Kofi Annan International Peacekeeping Training Centre, July 2009). In Chapter 4 in this volume, Amitav Acharya develops this argument still further to make the strongest claim yet that R2P should be considered an African norm export that has been elevated to the global level.

sovereign's exercise of power with the majesty of law that stands above the agents of the state. Many traditional Asian cultures stress the symbiotic link between duties owed by kings to subjects and loyalty of citizens to sovereigns, a point made by civil society representatives who accordingly conclude that, far from abridging, R2P *enhances* sovereignty.[27] In India, Ashoka, the great Mauryan emperor (third century BC), inscribed the following message on a rock edict: 'this is my rule: government by the law, administration according to the law, gratification of my subjects under the law, and protection through the law'.[28] Modern India's constitution imposes an R2P-type responsibility on governments in its chapters on fundamental rights and directive principles of state policy.[29]

This is not to deny that the concern that R2P may be abused to justify self-interested invasions should be fully acknowledged and addressed. The thoroughly Western Westphalian principle of non-intervention was generated by direct experience of the consequences of abuse. The ICISS report acknowledged this risk – a risk that materialised almost immediately when Commissioner Michael Ignatieff used it to justify the invasion of Iraq.[30] There are several ways of limiting the risk of abuse:[31] reaffirming the Westphalian formula because of the sorry track record of intervention, narrowing the scope, highlighting some of the ICISS moves underlining the centrality of Pillar One, and emphasising that the rights belong to those being persecuted rather than those going to their aid.

Concrete challenges

However, it would be a major mistake to treat sovereignty as mainly a function of the law and practice of state intervention. The Westphalian image of a state as the ultimate authority and power is also challenged by the realities of the twenty-first century. One set of challenges relates to recognising the power dynamics in an international system where the only superpower, the United States, has considerable power, which it

---

[27] World Federalist Movement, *Global Consultative Roundtables on the Responsibility to Protect: Civil Society Perspectives and Recommendations for Action, Interim Report* (New York: WFM, January 2009), p. 8: 'At almost every roundtable, civil society emphasised how R2P principles already resonate with pre-existing cultural values'.

[28] Quoted in Stanley Wolpert, *A New History of India* (New York: Oxford University Press, 1977), pp. 66–67.

[29] Ramesh Thakur, 'The Responsibility to Protect Revisited', *Daily Yomiuri*, 12 April 2007.

[30] Michael Ignatieff, 'Why Are We in Iraq?' *New York Times*, 7 September 2003 (www.nytimes.com/2003/09/07/magazine/why-are-we-in-iraq-and-liberia-and-afghanistan.html?pagewanted=all&src=pm).

[31] See Charles Sampford, 'A Tale of Two Norms', in Angus Francis, Vesselin Popovski and Charles Sampford, eds, *The Norms of Protection* (Tokyo: UN University Press, 2012).

has been able to exercise virtually unchecked until very recently. However, probably more fundamental are the set of challenges from the rise and recognition of new actors playing significant roles and wielding significant power, including transnational corporations (several of which are wealthier than all but the top ten states), the United Nations itself,[32] international agencies like the World Bank and the International Monetary Fund (IMF) imposing aid conditionality, indigenous peoples, international NGOs and powerful individuals.[33] Indeed, individuals have become objects of international law as bearers of duties since the Nuremberg trials, and subjects of international law as holders of rights under human rights instruments and some treaties.[34]

A third set of challenges comes from the apparent inability of some states to maintain the internal order and control that is central to sovereignty. Accordingly, state breakups and state failure may mean the end of viable central public authority and control so that the rights of citizens cannot be met and interstate relationships cannot be meaningfully pursued. A fourth set of challenges lies in the formal end of professed indifference to the internal governance of other states and the attempts to formulate norms for such internal governance that are intended to be enforced. Some argue for an emerging right of democratic governance[35] – at least where democracy has been established.[36] This highlights the disjunction already noted between International Relations and International Law conceptions of sovereignty as the prior successful use of force, and the internal conceptions of popular sovereignty that now dominate a majority of nations.

Of course, the consequences of transferring domestic and internal approaches to sovereign legitimacy to international relations would be so profound that there is a natural hesitation in linking international legitimacy to domestic democratic legitimacy. Nevertheless, there is clear movement in this direction with some states joining bodies – for

---

[32] See Ramesh Thakur, 'Multilateral Diplomacy and the United Nations: Global Governance Venue or Actor?', James P. Muldoon, Jr., JoAnn Fagot Aviel, Richard Reitano and Earl Sullivan, eds, *The New Dynamics of Multilateralism: Diplomacy, International Organizations, and Global Governance* (Boulder: Westview, 2011), pp. 249–265.

[33] Daphne Josselin and William Wallace, eds, *Non-State Actors in World Politics* (London: Palgrave, 2001).

[34] Ronald A. Brand, 'Sovereignty: The State, the Individual, and the International Legal System in the Twenty-First Century', *Hastings International and Comparative Law Review* 25 (2002), pp. 279–295.

[35] Thomas M. Franck, 'The Emerging Right to Democratic Governance', *American Journal of International Law* 86:1 (1992), pp. 46–91.

[36] Kofi A. Annan, *We, the Peoples: The United Nations in the 21st Century*. Millennium Report of the Secretary-General (New York: United Nations, 2000).

example, the European Union and the African Union – that impose obligations concerning internal governance. While armed intervention is still relatively rare to enforce internal standards of governance and respect for human rights, there are increasing attempts to generate formal mechanisms for protecting human rights, from the UN Human Rights Council to the European Court of Human Rights, which can give binding orders to sovereign states. In addition, aid and trade can be tied to what is considered to be acceptable internal behaviour of states.

A fifth set of challenges is based on the fact that many issues cannot be dealt with within traditional boundaries; for example, environmental and health problems such as AIDS, SARS and avian flu. The most pervasive set of challenges arises from the movement of people, ideas and goods. International communications weaken a state's control over its own people and more people are on the move, reducing loyalty to the state. For some, the participation in economic success, not coercive power or legal authority, becomes the primary source of identity. Commerce is boundary-less while the state's authority and ability to use its laws and coercive power stops at its borders as the most lucrative business of all, the 400 billion dollar trade in illicit drugs and human smuggling, grows exponentially. Transnational criminals use weak or failed states as bases and safe havens as well as sources to fund their operations.[37] While police officials in pursuit of a suspect must halt at a border, money launderers cross with ease and transfer millions of dollars all over the globe instantaneously. As the state weakens economically, so does any real threat to use its coercive power and its system of the rule of law to compel other states to follow its pattern. Instead, chimerical wars on drugs are launched at the same time as anti-terrorist wars unleash new sources for those same illicit drugs.

Many of these challenges are mutually reinforcing and produce contradictory behaviour. Countries that provide legal protection to refugees in flight from persecution also interdict refugees and prevent them from arriving on their shores. Radical Islamist rebels who would be captured or killed on a state's own territory are supplied arms in their fight against Arab dictators. The threats to sovereign states themselves heighten the debate over the conception of sovereignty. Accordingly, the sovereignty of states unwilling or unable to fulfil certain basic standards of human

---

[37] Jessica Stern, *The Ultimate Terrorists* (Cambridge, MA: Harvard University Press, 1999); Mark Galeotti, *Cross-Border Crime in the Former Soviet Union* (Durham: Durham University Press, 1995); Jorge Heine and Ramesh Thakur, eds, *The Dark Side of Globalization* (Tokyo: UN University Press, 2011).

rights may be jeopardised,[38] while their actions may threaten the security of other states, for example by generating refugees or exporting environmental hazards.[39]

As states are weakened economically and become weaker sources of identity, individuals and groups may look to other ethnic and religious identities – either within states (for example, in the Balkans) or across states (for example, ideas of a new Islamic 'caliphate'). This is particularly likely for those excluded from, or alienated by, the international market economy. And as some states are weakened, the ability of more powerful states to intervene is increased – and the costs of doing so are considerably reduced. Where the power differential is limited, intervention is extremely costly and would rarely be exercised merely for the benefit of oppressed peoples – in which case interventions would only be undertaken where it significantly advanced the interests of the interveners. If there is a huge disparity in power, the costs might be sufficiently low for leaders to act for the benefit of those to be protected. However, there is a natural scepticism that powerful nations engaging in intervention might still only do so if it advanced their own interests and that the protection of other peoples might be at best a secondary goal that is not actively secured, and at worse an excuse for action that worsens their condition.

The United Nations: an organisation of, by and for sovereign states?

As previously outlined, the Treaty of Westphalia was a tyrant's charter in which the prior successful use of internal force justified the continuing use of internal force for any purpose that the sovereign sought fit. In many ways, the United Nations continues this tradition as the chief agent of the system of states for exercising international authority in their name. For countries emerging from colonial bondage into independence, who soon after the UN's establishment constituted the majority in the organisation, UN membership was the final symbol of independent sovereign statehood and thus the seal of acceptance into the community of nations. The United Nations also became the principal international forum for collaborative action in the shared pursuit of the three goals of state-building, nation-building and economic development. The United Nations was

---

[38] Simon Chesterman, *Just War or Just Peace: Humanitarian Intervention and International Law* (Oxford: Oxford University Press, 2001).

[39] Howard Adelman; and Gil Loescher, *Refugee Movements and International Security*. Adelphi Paper 268 (London: Brassey's, 1992); Ramesh Thakur, 'Threats without Enemies, Security without Borders: Environmental Security in East Asia', *Journal of East Asian Studies* 1:2 (August 2001), pp. 161–189.

therefore the main arena for the jealous protection, not the casual abrogation, of state sovereignty.

The United Nations is an organisation dedicated to the territorial integrity, political independence and national sovereignty of its member states and the maintenance of international peace and security on that basis. But the overwhelming majority of today's armed conflicts are internal, not interstate. Moreover, the proportion of civilians killed by the direct violence of war, and from conflict-related starvation and disease, increased over the course of the last century. This presented the organisation with a major problem: how to reconcile its foundational principle of member states' sovereignty with the primary mandate to maintain international peace and security and the equally compelling mission to promote the interests and welfare of 'we, the peoples of the United Nations'. Annan discussed the dilemma in the conceptual language of two notions of sovereignty, one vesting in the state, the second in the people.[40]

The UN Charter is itself an example of an international obligation voluntarily accepted by member states. On the one hand, in granting membership to the United Nations, the international community welcomes the signatory state as a responsible member of the community of nations. On the other hand, by signing the Charter the state accepts the responsibilities of membership flowing from that signature. There is a de facto redefinition from sovereignty as right of exclusivity to sovereignty as responsibility in both internal functions and external duties.

While the UN Charter and subsequent treaties embrace human rights, Article 2(7) of the Charter prohibits the United Nations from intervening in 'matters that are essentially within the domestic jurisdiction' of any member state. Yet by the very fact of signing the Charter a country accepts collective obligations and international scrutiny. The restrictions of Article 2(7) can be set aside when the Security Council decides to act under the collective enforcement measures of Chapter VII to meet threats to or breaches of international peace and security. The scope of what constitute such threats and breaches has steadily widened to include such matters as HIV/AIDS, terrorism and atrocity crimes. In any case, Article 2(7) is about matters 'essentially' within domestic jurisdiction. This immediately implies that the issue is subject to judgement, which may differ from one competent authority to another and may undergo evolutionary change over time. Moreover, as shown in Somalia in the early 1990s, the collapse of state authority means that there is no

<hr>

[40] Kofi A. Annan, 'Two Concepts of Sovereignty', *The Economist*, 18 September 1999, pp. 49–50.

functioning government to fulfil an essential condition of sovereignty, and that the violence, instability and disorder can spill over from that failed state to others. This is why the Security Council dealt with Somalia under the coercive clauses of Chapter VII rather than the consensual Chapter VI. Applying this argument more broadly, some analysts have questioned just how many of today's states would meet the strict requirements of sovereign statehood, describing many countries as 'quasi-states' instead.[41]

Accordingly, the sovereignty recognised by the United Nations is far from being absolute and instead has generally been considered to be contingent. The more significant change of recent times is that it has been reconceived as being instrumental. Its validation rests not in a mystical reification of the state, but in its utility as a tool for the state serving the interests of the citizens – moving tentatively towards the Enlightenment Feurbachian inversion. Internal forms and precepts of governance must conform to international norms and standards of state conduct; that is, sovereignty must be exercised with due responsibility. This crucial normative shift was articulated by Francis M. Deng, the special representative of the secretary-general for internally displaced persons.[42] States are responsible for providing life-protecting and life-sustaining services to the people. When unable to do so, as responsible members of the international community, they must seek and accept international help. If they fail to seek – or obstruct – international assistance and put large numbers of people at risk of grave harm, the world has an international responsibility to respond. In extreme circumstances, the response may include the use of military force.

It is easy to forget that the United Nations was never meant to be a pacifist organisation. Its origins lie in the anti-Nazi wartime military alliance between Britain, the United States and the Soviet Union. Its primary purpose is the maintenance of international peace and security. The UN Security Council (UNSC) is the world's one and only duly sworn in sheriff for enforcing international law and order. But the UN Charter contains an inherent tension between the intervention-proscribing principle of state sovereignty and the intervention-prescribing principle of human rights. The calls for and controversy over

---

[41] Robert H. Jackson, *Quasi-States: Sovereignty, International Relations, and the Third World* (Cambridge: Cambridge University Press, 1990). See also Stephen D. Krasner, *Sovereignty: Organized Hypocrisy* (Princeton: Princeton University Press, 1999).

[42] Francis M. Deng, Sadikiel Kimono, Terrance Lyons, Donald Rothchild and I. William Zartman, *Sovereignty as Responsibility: Conflict Management in Africa* (Washington DC: Brookings, 1996); Francis M. Deng, 'Frontiers of Sovereignty', *Leiden Journal of International Law* 8:2 (June 1995), pp. 249–286.

humanitarian intervention arose from this tension. On the one hand, as noted, individuals became bearers of duties and holders of rights under a growing corpus of human rights and international humanitarian law treaties and conventions such as the UN Charter, the Universal Declaration of Human Rights, as well as the two covenants on civil-political and social, economic and cultural rights, the four Geneva Conventions, plus the two prohibiting torture and genocide, and so on. On the other hand, the cluster of norms inhibiting, if not prohibiting, humanitarian intervention includes, alongside the norm of non-intervention, state sovereignty, domestic jurisdiction, pacific settlement of disputes, non-use of force and, in the case of UN-authorised force, impartiality.

In the first four decades, state sovereignty was privileged over human rights, with the one significant exception of apartheid. The balance tilted in the 1990s and was more delicately poised between the two competing principles at the start of the new millennium. After the end of the Cold War, the United Nations Security Council experienced a surge of enforcement activity within civil war contexts to provide international relief and assistance to victims of large-scale atrocities from perpetrator or failing states.[43] In a number of cases in the 1990s, the Council endorsed the use of force with the primary goal of humanitarian protection and assistance: in the (ineffectual) proclamation of UN safe areas in Bosnia, the delivery of humanitarian relief in Somalia, the restoration of the democratically elected government of Haiti and the deployment of the multinational Kosovo Force.[44] A more activist Security Council engaged in de facto intervention in Iraq to protect the Kurds from the defeated Saddam Hussein's regime, and Britain and the United States enforced a no-fly zone to protect the Kurdish minority in Northern Iraq throughout the 1990s, albeit under a questionable legal basis.[45]

From Liberia and the Balkans to Somalia, Kosovo and East Timor, the conscience-shocking humanitarian catastrophes were explicitly recognised as threats to international peace and security requiring and justifying a forcible response by the international community. When the Security Council was unable to act owing to a lack of enforcement

---

[43] International Commission on Intervention and State Sovereignty (ICISS), *The Responsibility to Protect: Research, Bibliography, Background* (Ottawa: International Development Research Centre, 2001), pp. 79–126.

[44] See Brian D. Lepard, *Rethinking Humanitarian Intervention* (University Park: Pennsylvania State University Press, 2002), pp. 7–23.

[45] Washington and London grounded their declaration and enforcement of the no-fly zone in United Nations Security Council Resolution 688 (5 April 1991). But the resolution contains no obvious basis for such a claim and it never was accepted by any relevant UN authority.

capacity, it subcontracted the military operation to UN-authorised coalitions. And if it proved unwilling to act, sometimes groups of countries forged 'coalitions of the willing' to act anyway, even without UN authorisation. The debate on intervention was ignited in particular by humanitarian crises in Somalia, Rwanda, Srebrenica, Kosovo and East Timor, which revealed a dangerous gap in civilian protection mandates and capacities and a sharp polarisation of international opinion.

There was a second change. From 1945 to the end of the Cold War in 1989–1990, the preservation of peace was privileged over the protection of human rights. The Charter talks of both but provides concrete instruments for the maintenance of the former. The end of the Cold War lessened the fear that international action in defence of human rights would threaten world peace by cutting across the vital interests of Moscow or Washington vis-à-vis their allies. At the same time, the proliferation of complex humanitarian emergencies, and the inappropriateness of the classical tenets of UN peacekeeping for dealing with them, highlighted the inherent tension between the neutrality of traditional peacekeeping and the partial consequences of peace enforcement. The dilemma was confronted squarely in the Brahimi Report, which concluded that political neutrality has often degenerated into military timidity and the abdication of the duty to protect civilians. Impartiality should not translate into complicity with evil. While striving to remain impartial, the United Nations should soften its principle of neutrality between belligerents in favour of 'adherence to the principles of the Charter and to the objectives of [the] mandate'.[46] In retrospect, the Brahimi Report was an important milestone in the normative journey from humanitarian intervention to the Responsibility to Protect.

The ineluctable logic of Feurbachian inversion: sovereign rights are human rights

The final approach is to take the logic of the Enlightenment's Feuerbachian inversion to the next step. Much of the debate leading up to and stemming from the enunciation and endorsement of R2P is based on the potential conflict between human rights and sovereign rights. However, this is a false dichotomy.[47]

The Feuerbachian inversion places citizens above states rather than sovereigns over subjects and locates sovereignty in the citizens, with

[46] *Report of the Panel on United Nations Peace Operations*, Document A/55/305-S/2000/809, (United Nations: New York, 21 August 2000), paragraph 50.
[47] Sampford, 'Sovereignty and Intervention'.

governments only exercising power as delegated to them via the proce-dures adopted by the citizens. Sovereignty can become a collective human right of the citizens (and arguably a broader right to citizenship in an effective state).[48] This reconception of the basis of international constitutional legitimacy largely eliminates most of the conflict between sovereignty and the protection of human rights.[49] Conflict of this kind is always possible when the international community recognises, as the sovereign power, any group which has gained effective political control through the prior successful use of force. This formula does not deny the possibility that such force will be exercised to deny the human rights of the excluded groups. If anything, it actively encourages human rights abuses by rewarding the successful exercise of force to secure dominion over a particular territory. It rewards those who mount anti-democratic coups. It rewards those who rig elections. It rewards those who intimidate the population or who rule through and for one ethnic or social group against others.[50]

If sovereignty is seen as extending only over those to whom the sover-eign power is democratically accountable, then this principle provides members of any group over which that sovereign power is claimed a right to democratic participation. It also accords a right to those who have been excluded to democratic participation in that or another state. Sovereignty is no longer the recognition of a power over a people, but the collective right of a people to participate in and benefit from an independent political community, participating as an equal in the com-munity of nations. To put it another way, sovereignty becomes a human right.[51]

This would be a 'great leap forward' in the Maoist sense, if attempted in a single bound. However, we can take it in smaller steps by applying

---

[48] Charles Sampford, 'The Four Dimensions of Rights and the Means for Their Protection', Charles Sampford and Brian Galligan, eds, *Rethinking Human Rights* (Sydney: Federation Press, 1997).

[49] This does not deal with problems of human rights abuses by democratic states.

[50] This overcomes the problem that Steven David highlights. Although some elites in developing countries may represent little more than themselves, use state power for their own ends and interests, and have come to power by illegitimate means (including support from abroad), they have all the benefits of sovereignty, including non-intervention without consent. Steven David, *Third World Coups d'Etat and International Security* (Baltimore: John Hopkins University Press, 1987), pp. 4–6.

[51] See Krasner, *Sovereignty: Organized Hypocrisy*, p. 231. Some would leave this as a collective right of the people. Others might like to conceive it in terms of individual rights – as a right of all persons to take part in a sovereign government, to be a part of the group to whom a government is accountable. See Sampford, 'The Four Dimensions of Rights and the Means for Their Protection'. Either way, the point is that every human being on the planet has the right to participate in such a community and denying that right constitutes an abuse of human rights.

one of Kofi Annan's fervent hopes that sought to encapsulate a strong normative principle in an empirical outcome. 'Wherever democracy has taken root, it will not be reversed.'[52] Once a people have secured their sovereign rights through the establishment of even a half-decent democracy, no one else can trump those sovereign rights. Democracies can, and should, protect each other – and the African Union has provided a lead by incorporating this principle into its constitutive document. Africans have had more than their fair share of tyrants, both home-grown and among European colonisers. They have had enough of tyrants exercising their right to persecute and are sometimes prepared to act in line with the more recent, as opposed to seventeenth-century, 'R2P'.

[52] Kofi Annan, 'UN Secretary General Kofi Annan's Closing Remarks to the Ministerial Conference', First Ministerial Conference of the Community of Democracies, Warsaw, Poland, 26–27 June 2000, www.demcoalition.org/pdf/un_secertary_gen_kofi_annan.pdf.

4   The Responsibility to Protect and a theory of norm circulation

Amitav Acharya

In this chapter, I reflect on how the Responsibility to Protect (R2P) as an idea and norm relates to the ongoing theoretical debates about the origins and diffusion of norms in international relations literature. Among international relations theories, it is constructivism that pays the most attention to the role of ideas and norms. While realism regards ideas and norms as epiphenomena, and neoliberalism focuses on their instrumental and utilitarian value, or ideas as 'hooks', constructivism regards ideas as having a causal and constitutive effect. And constructivism has produced a rich literature not only on whether norms matter, but also how they matter. More recently, scholars have turned their attention to the processes and mechanisms of the spread of norms, focusing on issues of contestation and agency. Hence, new insights into the outcome of norm diffusion have emerged, which hold that new norms are seldom adopted wholesale, but are localised and translated to fit the context and need of the norm-takers. One of the key points of interest is that to understand how norms matter, one has to look into whose norms matter.

R2P poses a special challenge to these theoretical debates about agency in norm diffusion. Because of its close association with human rights and humanitarian intervention debates that long preceded it, R2P is often associated with Western political theory and agency. While some of the proponents of the norm vigorously deny that R2P reflects the traditional North–South fault line,[1] that perception endures in the developing world. The Canadian hand behind the creation of the International Commission on Intervention and State Sovereignty (ICISS) and the explicit linking by its then Foreign Minister Lloyd Axworthy of R2P with other instruments of human security, such as the International Criminal Court and the Ottawa anti-personnel landmines treaty, has led to the identification R2P with a distinctive Western 'freedom from fear' agenda, at the

---

[1] Ramesh Thakur and Thomas G. Weiss, 'R2P: From Idea to Norm – And Action?', *Global Responsibility to Protect* 1:1 (2009), pp. 22–35, at p. 35.

expense of broader elements of human security (including but not limited to 'freedom from want').

The receptivity to a new international norm is likely to be higher if the responsibility for its creation and diffusion is seen to be more broadly shared than being credited to any particular group – whether the North or the South. The real issue about the diffusion of R2P thus has to do with the question: whose ideas matter? In the absence of a broader framework to investigate the origins of norms, there is likely to be controversy, competition over ownership, mistrust and even rejection of what is without doubt one the most important and attractive of new international principles.

Unfortunately, international relations theories are yet to provide us with a framework for understanding norm diffusion that captures the complex and multifaceted nature of that agency. The early literature on norm diffusion was marked by a distinct 'moral cosmopolitanism' flavour.[2] In essence, it showcased how 'good' global norms promoted mainly by Western norm entrepreneurs displace 'bad' local ideas or practices that are mainly found in the non-Western world. The fact that local actors in the non-Western world may be privy to ideas and practices that are of proven efficacy and prior legitimacy was often missed. Sadly, some of the major writings on R2P and the statements of their key proponents conforms to this stereotype.

Yet even a brief but careful re-examination of the origins of R2P norm highlights several features – including ones that have been identified in the earlier literature but not brought together in the manner suggested in this essay – that might pose a challenge to the 'moral cosmopolitanism' narrative and lead the way to a reformulation of our theoretical approaches to understanding why and how norms emerge. In this essay, I offer such a narrative and propose the concept of 'norm circulation' as a more general framework for studying norm creation and diffusion in world politics.

Structure and agency in R2P's emergence

The leading approach to the study of norm diffusion in international relation theory, constructivism holds that the structure of the

---

[2] Amitav Acharya, 'How Ideas Spread: Whose Norms Matter? Norm Localization and Institutional Change in Asian Regionalism', *International Organization* 58:2 (2004), pp. 239–275; Amitav Acharya, *Whose Ideas Matter: Agency and Power in Asian regionalism* (Ithaca: Cornell University Press, 2009); Amitav Acharya, 'Norm Subsidiarity and Regional Orders: Sovereignty, Regionalism and Rule Making in the Third World', *International Studies Quarterly* 55:1 (2011), pp. 95–123.

international system is not just material, but also ideational. In this sense, the end of Cold War, the 'end of history', the victory of the West, the global spread of human rights and democracy, may be seen as elements of the changing normative structure of world politics that had rendered the emergence of R2P likely or even inevitable. In terms of agency, the work of the ICISS is usually billed as the most important. In an interview in 2012, Gareth Evans, the co-chair of ICISS, stated:

> The 'Responsibility to Protect' (R2P) was an idea born in 2001. The intention was to recast the language and substance of the debate: to change prevailing mind sets, so the reaction to these catastrophic human rights violations taking place behind sovereign state walls would be that they are everyone's business.[3]

This statement of course belies the complex origins of R2P norm, as Evans' himself would acknowledge. The ICISS role in developing R2P was not just about 'recasting' and thereby 'softening' the idea of humanitarian intervention from 'right to intervene' to 'responsibility to protect' because it had become too controversial for the developing countries. The commission's most important contribution might have been in pulling together several prior threads of the norm into a coherent whole. Indeed, there is compelling evidence to suggest that R2P as a norm had its origins in a wide variety of sources and contexts. At least four can be identified: the work of ICISS, the prior idea of responsible sovereignty developed in an African context, evolving human rights policy debates and approaches, and the just war tradition in its classical and contemporary formulations.

Of these diverse threads, particular attention should be given to the idea of responsible sovereignty. The origin of this idea is usually credited to Francis Deng,[4] a Sudanese diplomat who worked at the

---

[3] Gareth Evans, 'Gareth Evans on "Responsibility to Protect" after Libya', Interview with Alan Philps, *The World Today* 68:8–9 (2012), pp. 30–32.

[4] This has been increasingly recognised. See Thakur and Weiss, 'R2P: From Idea to Norm – and Action?'; Ramesh Thakur, *The Responsibility to Protect: Norms, Laws and the Use of Force in International Politics* (London: Routledge, 2011); Thomas G. Weiss, *Thinking about Global Governance: Why People and Ideas Matter* (London: Routledge, 2011); Thomas G. Weiss, 'The Responsibility to Protect (R2P) and Modern Diplomacy', in Andrew Cooper, Jorge Heine and Ramesh Thakur, eds, *The Oxford Handbook of Modern Diplomacy* (Oxford: Oxford University Press, 2013), pp. 763–778; Alex J. Bellamy, *Responsibility to Protect: The Global Effort to End Mass Atrocities* (Cambridge: Polity Press, 2009). It is also notable that the ICISS's initiator, Canadian External Affairs Minister Lloyd Axworthy, and the co-chair, Gareth Evans, have also acknowledged the role of Deng and the Brookings project, but perhaps to a degree that one might deem as insufficient: Lloyd Axworthy, *Navigating a New World: Canada's Global Future* (Toronto: Alfred A. Knopf, 2003), p. 414. Gareth Evans has made clear this historical link in Gareth Evans, *The Responsibility to Protect: Ending Mass Atrocity Crimes Once and for All* (Washington DC: Brookings Institution Press, 2008).

Brookings Institution. Before Deng became the founding director of the Africa Project at Brookings Institution, he served as the ambassador of Sudan to Canada, Denmark, Finland, Norway, Sweden and the United States, as well as Sudan's minister of state for foreign affairs (1976–1980). He also served as the representative of the United Nations secretary-general on internally displaced persons from 1994 to 2004. Deng was part of a collaborative project which included, among others, African expert I. William Zartman, which led to the first and still the most substantive work on the idea of responsible sovereignty. In it, Deng and his colleagues proposed that 'those governments that do not fulfill their responsibilities to their people forfeit their sovereignty. In effect, the authors redefine sovereignty as the responsibility to protect the people in a given territory.'[5] The book was subtitled 'Conflict Management in Africa' – as sure a marker as there can be of the regional context and basis for what would become a global norm, rather than the other way around, as is often assumed in the mainstream literature on the origins of norms.[6]

Another source of R2P norm has been identified by Roberta Cohen, who came to Brookings to work with Deng from a rather different background. Cohen was part of the Carter Administration's human rights team and was closely connected with human rights advocacy groups. Although she joined the Brookings after the publication of the *Sovereignty as Responsibility* volume in 1996, her work with Deng on internally displaced persons (IDPs) continued to stress the responsible sovereignty idea. In her writings, Cohen has linked R2P with the human rights promotion efforts of the Carter Administration, which was the first US presidency to make human rights a central element of US foreign policy.[7]

Thus, the idea of responsible sovereignty came more from issues connected with Africa and the internally displaced persons (IDPs),[8] and

---

[5] Amitai Etzioni, 'Sovereignty as Responsibility', *Orbis* 50:1 (2006), pp. 71–85.

[6] Francis M. Deng, Sadikiel Kimaro, Terrence Lyons, Donald Rothchild and I. William Zartman, *Sovereignty as Responsibility: Conflict Management in Africa* (Washington DC: The Brookings Institution, 1996). See also Francis M. Deng and I. William Zartman, eds, *Conflict Resolution in Africa* (Washington DC: The Brookings Institution, 1991); Francis M. Deng and Terrence Lyons, eds, *African Reckoning: A Quest for Good Governance* (Washington DC: The Brookings Institution, 1998); Francis M. Deng, 'Reconciling Sovereignty with Responsibility: A Basis for International Humanitarian Action', in John W. Harbeson and Donald Rothschild, eds, *Africa in World Politics: Post-Cold War Challenges* (Boulder: Westview Press, 1995), pp. 295–310.

[7] Roberta Cohen, 'From Sovereign Responsibility to R2P', in W. Andy Knight and Frazer Egerton, eds, *The Routledge Handbook of the Responsibility to Protect* (London: Routledge, 2012), pp. 7–21.

[8] Roberta Cohen and Francis M. Deng, *Masses in Flight: The Global Crisis of Internal Displacement* (Washington DC: The Brookings Institution, 1998); Roberta Cohen and

less from the more globally politically prominent idea of humanitarian intervention, or the 'right to intervene'. Moreover, the IDP project itself had to do with the changing role of the UN High Commission for Refugees (UNHCR), which under Sadako Ogata was reorienting itself towards a human security approach. While under the existing mandate of the UNHCR the IDPs were not regarded as a legitimate concern for the UNHCR, the grim situation in Africa and other parts of the world made it imperative for Ogata to call for sovereignty as a responsibility of the state to protect its citizens.

It might be said that R2P, as it was articulated by the ICISS, adds the intervention dimension to the idea of responsible sovereignty. As the UN secretary-general's representative on internally displaced persons from 1992 to 2004, Deng was especially careful not to raise the issue of intervention with governments. When he did, he would raise it indirectly: reminding them that if they refrained from abusing their citizens, they might avoid outside intervention. The ICISS and R2P would be more direct about intervention and its conditions and modalities.

In so doing, the ICISS drew explicitly on the just war tradition, which holds that 'sometimes, states can have moral justification for resorting to armed force'.[9] The ICISS Report's six-fold criteria for intervention, namely right authority, just cause, right intention, last resort, proportional means and reasonable prospects, directly mirrors the *jus ad bellum* principles of the just war theory, which includes just cause, right intention, proper authority, last resort, probability of success and proportionality.[10]

The just war tradition has its roots in the Greco-Roman tradition, Christian ethics, and Western philosophy. The leading sources of this doctrine include Aristotle, Cicero, St Augustine, St Aquinas, Grotius, Suarez, Vattel and Vitoria. The principles of just war thinking had found their way into modern international law governing armed conflict, including The Hague and Geneva Conventions.[11] This makes it only natural that R2P would be seen as a Western concept, no matter how strenuously its proponents would try to deny this claim.

It is also important to note that the origins and emergence of R2P had little to do with hegemonic creation, or US leadership under the

---

Francis M. Deng, eds, *The Forsaken People: Case Studies of the Internally Displaced* (Washington DC: The Brookings Institution, 1998).

[9] 'War', *Stanford Encyclopedia of Philosophy*, www.plato.stanford.edu/entries/war/.

[10] Ibid. See also Amitav Acharya, 'Redefining the Dilemmas of Humanitarian Intervention', *Australian Journal of International Affairs* 56:3 (2002), pp. 373–381.

[11] 'War', *Stanford Encyclopedia of Philosophy*, www.plato.stanford.edu/entries/war/. The best articulation of the just war tradition is Michael Walzer, *Just and Unjust Wars* (New York: Basic Books, 1978).

George W. Bush Administration. Some analysts trace the origins of R2P by pointing to the role of the United States, such as Bush Administration officials like Richard Haass who justified the war on Iraq by citing the diminishing importance of state sovereignty in the face of human suffering.[12] But the available evidence shows that this was as self-serving as it was unconvincing.[13] The Bush Administration simply found R2P a convenient pretext to justify its intervention in Iraq, after its earlier justifications, such as WMDs and Iraq's link with terrorism, had failed to convince the international community. As Thakur and Weiss noted:

> as the WMD justification for the war fell apart and claims of close links between Saddam's regime and al-Qaeda also proved spurious, the coalition of the willing – with Washington and London as the main belligerents – began to apply *ex post facto* humanitarian language and even R2P as the main justification for their actions in Iraq. Richard Haass, the former director of policy planning unit in the US State Department and president of the Council on Foreign Relations, spoke of sovereignty as responsibility and argued that when states fail to discharge their responsibility to fight terrorism: 'America will act – ideally with partners, but alone if necessary – to hold them accountable'.[14]

A positive correlation between power and norms has been claimed by a great deal of writings in international relations.[15] Yet this may not always

---

[12] Bellamy, *Responsibility to Protect*.

[13] This is extensively discussed in Amitav Acharya, 'State Sovereignty After 9/11: Disorganised Hypocrisy?', *Political Studies* 55:2 (2007), pp. 274–296.

[14] Thakur and Weiss, 'R2P: From Idea to Norm,' p,36

[15] Acknowledgement of the importance of material power in norm creation cuts across realism, liberalism and constructivism. Based on an analysis of the four historic cases of norm diffusion, the support for religious toleration, the abolition of slave trade, the protection of minorities in Central Europe and the promotion of individual rights, Stephen Krasner, a realist, argues that 'the most important explanation for the variation in outcomes is the relative power and interest of states': Stephen D. Krasner, 'Sovereignty and Intervention', in Gene M. Lyons and Michael Mastanduno, eds, *Beyond Westphalia?: National Sovereignty and International Intervention* (Baltimore: The Johns Hopkins University Press, 1995). In Ikenberry and Kupchan's liberal theory of hegemonic socialisation, norm diffusion is contingent upon relative power. The main function of norms is to legitimise power: the 'rule based on might is enhanced by rule based on right': G. John Ikenberry and Charles A. Kupchan, 'Socialization and Hegemonic Power', *International Organization* 44:3 (1990), pp. 283–315, at p. 286. Wendt, the key scholar in constructivism and champion of the role of ideas, holds that 'where there is an imbalance in relevant material capability social acts will tend to evolve in the direction favored by the more powerful': Alexander Wendt, *Social Theory of International Politics* (Cambridge: Cambridge University Press, 1999), p. 331. Also from a constructivist perspective, Ann Florini points out that norms held by powerful actors 'have many more opportunities to reproduce through the greater number of opportunities afforded to powerful states to persuade others of the rightness of their views': Ann Florini, 'The Evolution of International Norms', *International Studies Quarterly* 40:3 (1996), pp. 363–389, at p. 375.

be the case; powerful states do not make good norm entrepreneurs; the direct involvement of a hegemon or powerful actors is not essential to the creation and diffusion of a global norm. On the contrary, norms peddled by powerful states easily invite suspicion.

Moreover, the US use of R2P in the context of the Iraq War also suggests what might be yet another feature of the origins of R2P: differences that exist *within* the North, rather than *between* the North and the South. The instrumental US linking of the intervention in Iraq and the idea of humanitarian intervention was based on what constructivists call the 'logic of consequences', contrasting sharply with the positions of Canada and others, who based their support of the norm on the 'logic of appropriateness'.

One important reason why powerful states were not particularly important has to do with the fact that in origins, R2P was not the product of traditional intergovernmental diplomacy. Rather, it resulted from 'inputs by a host of actors who would have been kept away from the policy-formulation and policy-making circles of the past – that is, this dynamic process was neither hierarchical nor dominated by the secretive diplomacy of powerful states'.[16] Such processes are more likely to open up space for a wider variety of actors, including individuals and states from middle powers and developing countries, to engage in norm creation. At the same time, although much credit for R2P has gone to individuals and the countries they come from, such as Canada, and while this is to certain extent well-deserved, this should not come at the expense of recognising the role of others, such as Deng, Mohamed Sahnoun (the co-chair of ICISS) and Ramesh Thakur, a member of the ICISS – a naturalised Australian-Canadian citizen who hailed from India and played an especially important role in the writing and dissemination of the report of the Commission. Among the international policymakers, the UN Secretary-General Kofi Annan's views on sovereignty are of importance, as it clearly echoed the 'sovereignty as responsibility' idea.[17] The fact that Deng and Annan were both from Africa should not be regarded as a mere or unimportant coincidence, but a central aspect of the genesis of R2P.

Indeed, while the idea of humanitarian intervention was made more urgent by the horrific conflicts in several parts of the world, including northern Iraq, Somalia, Rwanda-Burundi and the Balkans, the idea of responsible sovereignty in particular has a strong African context

---

[16] Weiss, 'The Responsibility to Protect (R2P) and Modern Diplomacy'.
[17] Kofi Annan, 'Two Concepts of Sovereignty', *The Economist*, 16 September 1999.

and heritage. Well before R2P acquired global prominence, key African leaders had advocated intervention in response to African problems. Nigerian President Olusegun Obasanjo argued in 1991: 'An urgent aspect of security need is a re-definition of the concept of security and sovereignty . . . we must ask why does sovereignty seem to confer absolute immunity on any government who commits genocide and monumental crimes.' In a similar vein, Uganda's Yoweri Museveni noted at the same Kamapala meeting: 'Sovereignty became a sacred cow and many crimes have been committed in its name . . . If the European countries can surrender some of their sovereignty for greater development, African states can similarly surrender some of their sovereignty for greater security, both at the intra and interstate levels.' As the secretary-general of the Organization of African Unity (OAU), the precursor to the African Union (AU), Salim Ahmed Salim, put it: 'We should talk about the need for accountability of governments and of their national and international responsibilities. In the process, we shall be redefining sovereignty.' At the OAU summit in Ouagadougou in 1998, Nelson Mandela told his fellow leaders: 'Africa has a right and a duty to intervene to root out tyranny . . . we must all accept that we cannot abuse the concept of national sovereignty to deny the rest of the continent the right and duty to intervene when behind those sovereign boundaries, people are being slaughtered to protect tyranny.'[18]

The regional–global nexus: constructing R2P from Africa

Hence, the African and non-Western context of and linkages to R2P deserves special recognition. This is further attested to by the fact that the co-chair of the Commission, Sahnoun, was an Algerian diplomat who had served, among other posts, as adviser to the president of Algeria, deputy secretary-general of the OAU, deputy secretary-general of the League of Arab States, special envoy of the UN secretary-general on the Ethiopian–Eritrean conflict, joint representative of the UN and the OAU in the Great Lakes Region and Central Africa and special representative of the UN to Somalia. Although a global-level operator, his African origins and make-up were unmistakable.[19] Sahnoun turned out to be a very influential member of the Commission. Someone intimately

---

[18] All quotes taken from Adekeye Adebajo and Chris Landsberg, 'The Heirs of Nkrumah: Africa's New Interventionists', *Pugwash Occasional Papers* 2 (2001), www.pugwash.org/reports/rc/como_africa.htm.

[19] Speaking of his own background, Sahnoun observes: 'I started my career with the African Union and immediately I found myself involved in conflict resolutions. In the

involved with the working of the Commission says: 'Sahnoun was really the main voice [of Global South], and a very wise one.' While the Commission made every effort to transcend the North–South divide, 'the views of the global South ... were integrated into the Commission'. Here, Sahnoun played the key role. 'When Sahnoun spoke and said "this will not wash," that was the end of the story ... His voice always put on the brakes, but he also is a partisan of rights (having himself been tortured by the French).'[20]

Sahnoun brings out the African context and contribution to the making of R2P clearly in the following words:

For Africans, the vow to which our leaders subscribed in 2005 was not new. Five years earlier they had already adopted the norm of non-indifference to mass atrocities in the African Union's Constitutive Act. The idea itself of 'sovereignty as responsibility' was developed by the Sudanese scholar and diplomat, Francis Deng. And, unlike other regions, our legal systems have long acknowledged that in addition to individuals, groups and leaders having rights, they also have reciprocal duties. So the responsibility to protect is in many ways an African contribution to human rights.[21]

The importance of the African context of R2P is further underscored by the fact that there seems to be no comparable instances of intellectuals and policymakers from the Balkans, the other major theatre of major conflict and genocide, offering similar visions and ideas or getting involved in debates that fed into R2P doctrine. Moreover, the African context is important not only to the origins of R2P, but also to its diffusion. The African Union Constitutive Act puts the interest of people at the centre of its goals. One of its main objectives is to 'achieve greater unity and solidarity between the African Countries and the peoples of Africa'. It also recognises the 'right of the Union to intervene

1960s and 1970s, many African countries became independent states. Quickly they found themselves confronted with border problems. The [frontiers] had been traced by the colonial powers, and these did not take into account socio-cultural factors, ethnicity and so on. It became urgent to find solutions and to convince the different countries to avoid conflict and eventually to respect the borders as they had been established by the colonial powers. Gradually, we arrived at agreements where the African countries accepted the borders such as they were, but also respecting minorities. Then came internal conflicts. Here we had to implement mediation and try to find a solution. It started with Biafra, and then it went on from there. I gained experience that proved itself to be very useful later, and therefore the successive Secretary-Generals [sic] of the United Nations called on me so that I could take care of these problems.' 'A Distinguished Peacemaker in the United Nations – Ambassador Mohamed Sahnoun', Diva International, www.divainternational.ch/spip.php?article24.

[20] Correspondence with a person closely associated with the ICISS, 21 December 2012.
[21] Mohamed Sahnoun, 'Uphold Continent's Contribution to Human Rights', 21 July 2009, Available at http://allafrica.com/stories/200907210549.html?viewall=1, date accessed 3 May 2013.

in a Member State pursuant to a decision of the Assembly in respect of grave circumstances, namely war crimes, genocide and crimes against humanity'. [22]

The AU is not alone in Africa to embrace the letter or spirit of R2P. In West Africa, the Economic Community of West African States (ECOWAS), through its Mechanism for Conflict Prevention, Management, Resolution, Peacekeeping and Security, provides for both an early warning system as well as collective political or military interventions in humanitarian crises. The Organ on Politics, Defence and Security Co-operation in the Southern African Development Community (SADC) can authorise intervention in domestic conflicts in response to ethnic cleansing, genocide and human rights violations. These African mechanisms 'address the need for collective responses to crises that threaten vulnerable populations through prevention as well as reaction – ideas that are affirmed in R2P principles'.[23] They have been used on multiple occasions; while not always with promptness or success, they do stand in sharp contrast to the notable absence of a single such mechanisms or instance of collective military intervention in other regions such as Asia, the Middle East, or Latin America.

The role of Deng, Annan and Sahnoun; the backdrops of Rwanda and Somalia; the changing views on sovereignty by African leaders well before ICISS Commission were even set up; the African context of the idea of 'responsible sovereignty' and the acceptance of African leaders and regional bodies of the idea of R2P; taken together, these factors point to the futility of trying to explain the origin of a global norm (or an emerging global norm) like R2P without stressing its regional context. In the same vein, ignoring the regional context and opinion in the application of the norm can be counter-productive also.

The African context is especially striking when one looks at the attitude of Asia and its regional bodies towards R2P. Unlike Africa, there were few insider proponents of the norm in Asia. Notable exceptions might be Anwar Ibrahim, the former deputy prime minister of Malaysia, who proposed the idea of 'Constructive Intervention', or Surin Pitsuwan, the former Thai foreign minister and secretary-general of the Association of Southeast Asian Nations (ASEAN), who reframed Anwar's idea to 'Flexible Engagement'. But none of these progressive ideas about diluting sovereignty came close to advocating military intervention or even hard peacekeeping of the kind advocated by

---

[22] 'The Constitutive Act of the African Union', Lome, Togo, 11 July 2000. http://www .africa-union.org/root/au/aboutau/constitutive_act_en.htm.

[23] R2PCS, 'Responsibility to Protect Engaging Civil Society', www.responsibilityto protect.org/files/R2Pcs%20Frequently%20Asked%20Question.pdf.

African leaders and policymakers.[24] Some initial Asian responses to
R2P were couched in earlier misgivings about the idea of humanitarian intervention. In the words of Malaysia's foreign minister, Syed
Hamid Albar: 'We have to be wary all the time of new concepts and
new philosophies that will compromise sovereignty in the name of
humanitarian intervention, in the name of globalisation which is
another form of trying to interfere in the domestic affairs of another
country.'[25]

The differences between Africa and Asia over R2P are especially striking and deserve some explanation because the two regions, which jointly
participated at the 1955 Asia–Africa Conference in Bandung, Indonesia,
started with a similar normative predisposition towards state sovereignty.
Like Asia, Africa used to be a bastion of the non-intervention norm.[26]
The concept of norm subsidiarity is relevant in explaining the changing
African attitudes towards sovereignty. Norm subsidiarity occurs when
local actors feel neglected or marginalised by more powerful central
actors. African leaders in the 1990s did feel neglected and betrayed by
the lack of interest from the United States and the United Nations after
the Somalia episode in 1992.[27]

What is also important in explaining these variations is the availability
of 'insider proponents' (such as South Africa's former President Thabo
Mbeki, Obasanjo and Salim in Africa, in addition to global players of
African background such as Deng, Anan and Sahnoun) in different
regions. Domestic politics and regional ideology are also important factors in deciding the level and quality of acceptance and compliance with a
given norm. Looking again at the variation between Asia and Africa,
Africa's stronger pan-national sentiments and shared sense of vulnerability and neglect, notably weaker in Asia, and the democratic credentials of
post-Apartheid South Africa versus the authoritarian regime in Asia's
most powerful state, China, might have contributed to Africa's greater
receptivity to R2P.[28]

---

[24] Acharya, *Whose Ideas Matter*, pp. 126–128.

[25] 'Malaysia Opposes UN Probe of East Timor Atrocities', *Agence France Presse*, 7 October 1999.

[26] Robert H. Jackson and Carl G. Rosberg, 'Why Africa's Weak States Persist: The Empirical and the Juridical in Statehood', *World Politics* 35:1 (1982), pp. 1–24.

[27] Adebajo and Landsberg, 'The Heirs of Nkrumah'. See also Theo Neethling, 'Reflections on Norm Dynamics: South African Foreign Policy and the No-Fly Zone over Libya', *South African Journal of International Affairs* 19:1 (2012), pp. 25–42.

[28] These explanatory factors are consistent with the framework for studying variations in regionalism provided in Amitav Acharya and Iain Alastair Johnston, eds, *Crafting Cooperation: Regional International Institutions in Comparative Perspective* (Cambridge: Cambridge University Press, 2007).

Compared to other parts of the developing world, Asia remains a tightly sovereignty-bound region. In Latin America, a military takeover of a civilian government could trigger its suspension from the Organization of American States (OAS), which is then mandated to seek the restoration of civilian rule. In Asia, no regional organisation espouses such intrusive measures.

Yet, the regional variations that undoubtedly do exist within the developing world should be put in proper perspective. Box 1 offers a snapshot of these differences.

Box 1. Selected Responses to R2P: 2005-2007

- **CHINA:** 'The concept of the "responsibility to protect" should be understood and applied correctly. At present, there are still various understandings and interpretations about this concept by many member states. Therefore the Security Council should refrain from invoking the concept of "the responsibility to protect". Still less should the concept be abused ... The responsibility to protect civilians lies primarily with the Governments of the countries concerned. While the international community and other external parties can provide support and assistance and urge the parties concerned seriously to implement the provisions of humanitarian law and to avoid harming civilians, they should not infringe upon the sovereignty and territorial integrity of the countries concerned, nor should they enforce intervention by circumventing the Governments of such countries.'
- **INDONESIA:** 'We need a consensus on the responsibility to protect people from genocide, ethnic cleansing and crimes against humanity. To this end, force should be used only when all other means have failed.'
- **MALAYSIA:** 'Actions must be in accordance with the respect for the sovereignty and territorial integrity of states as well as observing the principle of non-interference.'
- **BOTSWANA:** 'We embrace the concept of "responsibility to protect".'
- **GHANA:** 'We hold the view that in the event of the failure by both governments and armed groups to abide by their commitments under international humanitarian law, conventions and agreements, it behoves the United Nations to intervene and protect innocent populations against such crimes as genocide, ethnic cleansing and other gross human rights violations.'
- **NIGERIA:** 'The time has come for the international community to reexamine when it is its responsibility to protect, without prejudice to the sovereignty of Member States. Genocide, ethnic cleansing and crimes committed against unarmed civilians

Box 1. (cont.)

in situations of conflict are grim reminders that the time is right for
the international community to determine when to exercise its
responsibility to protect.'

- **ZIMBABWE:** 'The vision that we must present for a future
United Nations should not be one filled with vague concepts that
provide an opportunity for those states that seek to interfere in the
internal affairs of other states. Concepts such as "humanitarian
intervention" and the "responsibility to protect" need careful
scrutiny in order to test the motives of their proponents.'

- **ARGENTINA:** '[T]he responsibility to protect civilians in conflict is a central principle of humanity that must be depoliticised
and transformed into joint action of Security Council members
and international organisations'.

- **MEXICO:** 'We all know that the debate about the responsibility
to protect is interlinked with the fundamental principles of
international law. Despite the consensus reached in 2005, we
cannot deny that mistrust prevails on this matter. While some
States see in this new principle the mere continuance of
interventionist practices aimed at destabilizing political regimes,
others promote its application in a selective manner, limiting its
scope to cases significant for their political interests.'

- **VENEZUELA:** 'Today we claim from the peoples, in this case
the people of Venezuela, a new international economic order,
but it is also eminently a new international political order, let's
not allow a handful of countries [to] try to reinterpret with
impunity the principles of the International Law to give way to
doctrines like "Preemptive War", how do they threaten us with
preemptive war!, and the now so-called Responsibility to
Protect, but we have to ask ourselves who is going to protect us,
how are they going to protect us.'

*Source: New York: International Coalition for the Responsibility
to Protect, Institute for Global Policy: 'Government statements on
the Responsibility to Protect Asia-Pacific Region, 2005-2007'.
Available at: http://responsibilitytoprotect.org/R2P%20Government
%20statements%20Asia%20Pacific%202005-2007.pdf (accessed 19
April 2015); Government statements on the Responsibility to Protect
Africa Region 2005-2008. Available at: http://www.responsibilitytopro
tect.org/files/Govt%20Statements%202005-2007–Africa%20pdf.pdf
(accessed 19 April 2015); 'Government statements on the Responsibility
to Protect Latin-America Region 2005-2007'. Available at http://www
.responsibilitytoprotect.org/files/R2P%20Government%20statements
%20Latin%20America%202005-2007.pdf.*

Even if some of these reservations about and criticisms of R2P (especially from authoritarian governments) may be self-serving, past instances of promotion of human rights and democracy tells us that they are hardly unjustified. At the same time, these divergent views on R2P do not amount to an outright rejection of the norm. They do, however, indicate caution induced by a certain level of suspicion of the West's intentions and double standards. Of greater importance, however, is the fact that such protestations might be quite healthy. They can act as a check against abuse and create a path towards eventual acceptance. They engender pressures (not always realised) towards greater transparency, accountability and stronger justification for the intervention on the part of the intervening nations and bodies. Moreover, they can also produce a feedback effect by prompting new ideas and mechanisms to govern the application of R2P, including checks and balances – both formal and informal – that could have significant implications for legitimating R2P-governed behaviour. Brazil's subsequent proposal for 'Responsibility While Protecting' is one such possible example.

This was especially evident in the aftermath of the Libya intervention and the well-known and well-founded controversies associated with it that came from the widespread view that the two leading interveners, Britain and France, clearly exceeded the mandate of the UN Security Council when they turned the original mandate of civilian protection into an explicit move for regime change. Despite the fact that the immediate international backlash was limited – although it did include African backers of the authorising UN resolution, Nigeria and South Africa, changing their positions within the African Union from support to opposition of the Libyan intervention – it surely made it more difficult to apply R2P in other cases such as that of Syria, where there have been more government atrocities on citizens leading to greater civilian casualties. In this context, it was inevitable that attempts to reform R2P would emerge. One such clear effort is Brazil's proposal for 'Responsibility While Protecting', RWP, introduced in November 2011. The proposal, coming from a BRICS (Brazil, Russia, India, China, South Africa) nation and G-20 member, not only demands that the application of R2P should be consistent with the principles of last resort and proportionality (which were already in the ICISS Report), but also for greater accountability during the operations undertaken in the name of R2P.[29] To this end, it calls for 'a monitoring and review mechanism whereby it can be ensured that states have the

---

[29] Boon, Kristen, 'The Responsibility to Protect', *Opinio Juris*, www.opiniojuris.org/2012/11/13/the-responsibility-to-protect/.

opportunity to debate the implementation of a UN Security Council mandate'.[30] Although the proposal is yet to be realised, it has garnered a level of sympathy and support, including from Gareth Evans, who described the Brazilian proposal as a 'way forward' for R2P in the wake of the Libyan controversy. As Evans puts it:

The two key proposals are for a set of criteria to be fully debated before the Security Council approves any use of military force, and for some kind of enhanced monitoring and review process that would enable such mandates to be seriously debated by all Council members during their implementation ... If such criteria – all setting quite high hurdles – were visible and consistently applied, it should be a lot easier to avoid the 'slippery slope' argument which has contributed to the Security Council paralysis on Syria, making some countries unwilling to even foreshadow non-military measures such as targeted sanctions or International Criminal Court investigation because of their concern that military coercion would be the inevitable next step if lesser measures failed.[31]

From norm internalisation to norm circulation

The backlash against the abuse of R2P in Libya and the attempts to institute safeguards for its future application, along with my foregoing discussion of the multiple sources and agencies in the genesis of R2P, calls for a reformulated framework for understanding norm diffusion in world politics. The ensuing analysis builds upon my previous works on norms, especially 'localisation' (or 'constitutive localisation') and 'subsidiarity'. I call this new understanding *norm circulation*. As opposed to the 'moral cosmopolitanism' perspective described at the outset, circulation pays attention to norm creation and diffusion as a two-way process. Here, global norms offered by transnational moral actors are contested and localised to fit the cognitive priors of local actors (localisation), while this local feedback is repatriated back to the wider global context along with other locally constructed norms, and help to modify, and possibly defend and strengthen, the global norm in question (subsidiarity). Norm circulation occurs when the less powerful actors feel marginalised in the norm creation process or feel betrayed by the abuse of the norm by the more powerful actors during the implementation stage. Norm circulation is thus a combination of my prior concepts of localisation and subsidiarity. Moreover, the idea of norm circulation requires attention to four dimensions:

---

[30] Crossley, Noele, 'The Responsibility to Protect in 2012: R2P Fails in Syria, Brazil's "RWP" Emerges', *Global Policy*, 28 December 2012.
[31] Evans, 'Gareth Evans on "Responsibility to Protect" after Libya'.

1. Sources: Norms come from a variety of sources, involving multiple actors, issues and contexts. The linkages among them may not be entirely obvious and media reports and promotional action by the norm entrepreneurs may create (mis)perceptions about the exact origins and ownership of the norm.
2. Contexts: What matters in norm circulation is not just the norm entrepreneur, whether it be an individual or a group (like an NGO), but also the context from which he/she draws the norms. Some supposedly global norms can have a regional context in terms of their origins or influences. One should not assume – as most norm scholars do – that regions mere adopt or adapt global norms; it can be the other way around.
3. Agents: Attention must be given not only to how norms originate, but also to how they diffuse. The first mention of a new term or concept of a norm is important, but agency can also lie in who is promoting the norm in question and how it is being promoted. It is also important to note that norm creation is not the prerogative of powerful states. Weak states can also create regional and global norms.
4. Contestations and Feedback: Resistance that leads to the redefinition, contextualisation and localisation of a norm is a form of agency. Norms are seldom likely to be adopted wholesale, even though the very idea of a 'universal' norm in the sense of 'applying to all' masks important variations in the implementation of the norm and the instruments, institutions and processes used for their propagation.

Based on the above, the idea of norm circulation can be presented with the help of the following figures:

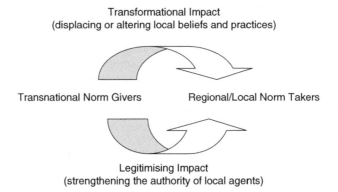

Transformational Impact
(displacing or altering local beliefs and practices)

Transnational Norm Givers   Regional/Local Norm Takers

Legitimising Impact
(strengthening the authority of local agents)

Figure 4.1: Norm internalisation: moral cosmopolitanism

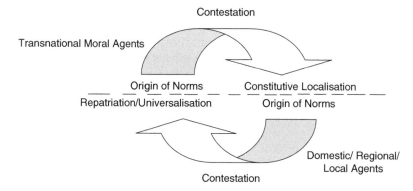

Figure 4.2: Norm circulation

In the existing literature on norm diffusion, there is a heavy emphasis on transnational norms (promoted mainly by Western actors and agents) that alter/displace the beliefs and practices of the local/regional actors (mainly in the non-Western world). While this might provoke some initial resistance, from a moral cosmopolitanism perspective resistance is often seen as futile or illegitimate. Occasionally, however, local actors can borrow transnational norms with a view to strengthening their legitimacy and authority, although this is found more in the Western world or (in the case of the non-Western world) in the case of economic norms (neoliberal economic openness) than political norms such as human rights.

The idea of norm circulation suggests a different pathway to norm diffusion. The scope of normative agency is much broader; they can comprise state and social movements, whether Western or non-Western operating at global, regional or domestic levels. Norm initiation may happen in the transnational space where Western actors dominate or at a local level where the primary voice may be non-Western actors (as articulated through the idea of 'norm subsidiarity'). Whatever the point of initiation, the influences on norm creation are multiple and complex; the prior ideas and agency of actors other than the visible initiators of norms may be present at the point where the norm actually originated. Moreover, the initial norm goes through a period of contestation, leading to its localisation or translation. This might create a feedback/repatriation effect which might travel back to the point of origin of the norm in the transnational space and lead to its modification or qualification. At the same time, locally constructed norms in similar issue areas (including those in the West or non-West) might be exported to the transnational space and acquire a global resonance, thereby modifying the definition or promotion of the more globally prominent norm(s) in similar issue areas. This multiple-agency, two-way, multi-step process of norm diffusion, based on resistance, feedback and repatriation, is the essence of my idea of norm circulation. Such circulation does not imply the weakening of the norm. Instead, it can lead to the strengthening of norms and enhance the prospects of application and compliance.

Conclusion

Viewed in the context of R2P, the idea of norm circulation can be conceptualised as follows. The norm has multiple sources: the work of the ICISS, the idea of humanitarian intervention (the 'right to intervene'), human rights promotion, the just war tradition and the idea of responsible sovereignty developed in the context of Africa and IDPs. The norm had multiple contexts: the Middle East, the Balkans and, above all, Africa. It also had multiple agents or norm entrepreneurs: Canadians, Australians, Africans and others, although a key fact here is that the United States under the George W. Bush Administration was not really among them.

The African context, and the African self-perception of a continent betrayed or abandoned by the West after Somalia, was especially important. African leaders embracing intervention were not simply applying the humanitarian intervention principle that originated in the West; they were also invoking a sense of African ownership and responsibility for finding regional solutions to Africa's problems (an indigenous and pre-existing norm). Hence, the African construction of R2P cannot be easily dismissed as a case of Africa merely following the Western idea of right to intervene. It was qualitatively different in origin and inspiration and would influence the creation and implementation of the R2P norm, not only in Africa but also in other parts of the world.

After the norm was presented, it was contested. There were important regional variations, especially between Asia and Africa but also between the US understanding in the context of the war on terror and those of the other Western countries. After Libya, which is both Arab and African, the norm has faced attempts at redefinition, with safeguards such as those proposed by Brazil. This need not weaken the norm, but may make it more legitimate and applicable if initiatives such as the Brazilian proposal are implemented, thereby completing the process of norm circulation.

In the final analysis, therefore, the creation of international norms is never a *one-source*, *one-way*, or a *one-step* process. Nor is it carried out by a single agent. This is the main lesson of the emergence of R2P for norm scholars and global policymakers concerned with creating and implementing new principles of collective action. R2P offers valuable insights into how norm creation is the result of a diversity of sources, multiplicity of agents and a plurality of contexts. The concept of norm circulation also holds that some norms will remain essentially contested, and subjected to continuous feedback following their last application. If the fundamental and 'established' norms of international relations such as sovereignty, non-intervention and equality of states have been continually contested over their meaning, interpretation and application over time and space, why shouldn't R2P be similarly challenged? This does not devalue the importance of R2P, however. Even if it will never attain the status of a settled norm, it will remain a crucial benchmark for assessing the international community's response to conflicts involving serious loss of civilian life. But it is only by developing a broader framework of agency, feedback and accountability that one can appreciate the complexity of norm creation in world politics. And it is only by employing such a broader framework of understanding that advocates of R2P can make a stronger case for the acceptance of the norm worldwide.

Part II

The Responsibility to Protect, normative
theory and global governance

5   The Responsibility to Protect and world order

Tim Dunne

Intervention for human protection is a key component of liberal thinking on world order. It is as old as the states system itself. A defence of intervention on humanitarian grounds can be found in Grotius' *Laws of War and Peace*, and it featured in the doctrine and practice of European great powers during the period when European hegemony was consolidated.[1] The British effort to abolish the trade in slaves in the early-to-mid-nineteenth century is a case in point, a practice that was recently described as 'the most costly international moral action recorded in modern history'.[2]

Despite the *longue durée* of the practice, protective intervention remains both institutionally complex and normatively contested in world order today.[3] The fissures in the international community were evident both during and after the intervention in Libya in 2011 led by the North Atlantic Treaty Organization (NATO). Supporters of the intervention were quick to argue it was a 'textbook case'.[4] After all, it was multilateral, it was decisive, it had UN Security Council approval and the mission to

---

[1] Hugo Grotius, *The Rights of War and Peace*, translated by Richard Tuck (Indianapolis: Liberty Fund, 2005 [1625]). For a comprehensive historical account of intervention, see Luke Glanville, *Sovereignty and the Responsibility to Protect: A New History* (Chicago: Chicago University Press, 2014).

[2] MacMillan goes on to say: 'it lasted for forty years, incurred the loss of around 5,000 British sea-men (mostly from disease) and cost an average of 2% of British national income annually'. John MacMillan, 'Myths and Lessons of Liberal Intervention: the British Campaign for the Abolition of the Atlantic Slave Trade to Brazil', *Global Responsibility to Protect* 4:1 (2012), p. 98.

[3] 'Protective intervention' is a term that is appropriate in this chapter as it signals a normative-historical practice that includes both the older conception of humanitarian intervention and its most recent variant 'the responsibility to protect'. I borrow the term from Ramesh Thakur, 'Humanitarian Intervention', in Thomas G. Weiss and Sam Daws, eds, *The Oxford Handbook on the United Nations* (Oxford: Oxford University Press, 2007), p. 398; Nicholas J. Wheeler and Tim Dunne, 'Operationalising Protective Intervention: Alternative Models of Authorisation', in W. Andy Knight and Frazer Egerton, eds, *The Routledge Handbook of the Responsibility to Protect* (London: Routledge, 2012), pp. 87–102.

[4] Thomas G. Weiss, 'RtoP Alive and Well after Libya', *Ethics & International Affairs* 25:3 (2011), pp. 287–292; Jon Western and Joshua S. Goldstein, 'Humanitarian Intervention Comes of Age: Lessons from Somalia to Libya', *Foreign Affairs* 90:6 (2011), pp. 48–59.

protect civilians was accomplished with very low casualty figures. For detractors, the acronym NATO once again stood for 'not altogether thought out' (as Ken Booth once put it, only this time during the Kosovo crisis in 1999). The liberal-left intellectual David Rieff argued that 'the campaign in Libya has done grave, possibly even irreparable, damage to R2P's prospects of becoming a global norm'.[5]

Whether Russia and China are right to feel betrayed by the alleged shift in the Libya mandate from the protection of civilians to regime change, what is not in doubt is that the subsequent paralysis inside the Security Council has enabled the Assad regime to commit mass atrocities with virtual impunity. As Lakhdar Brahimi put it in a recent Security Council briefing, 'the solution of that war is in your hands, members of the Security Council'.[6]

Perhaps, when it comes to using force to defend human rights, there will always be normative tension, not least because of the disjuncture between means and ends (as one critic put it, 'how can a bomb ever be humanitarian?'). But was the intensity of the backlash evident since 2011 merited or anticipated? Can we really argue, as R2P supporters imply, that there is a consensus on 'sovereignty as responsibility' in the UN system when two of the Council's permanent members proclaim that non-intervention must be strictly adhered to even when evidence that atrocities were being committed – in Syria – is virtually uncontested?

This chapter aims to shed light on why 'intervention talk' is triggering such disunity and discontent in academic and diplomatic forums. As ever, beneath the diplomatic dissonance lie contested conceptual and moral arguments. One manifestation of these is the current debate about the character of the 'liberal world order' – evident, for example, in Georg Sørensen's contrast between a strategy of 'restraint' versus a strategy of 'coercion'.[7] Yet this is a somewhat limited account of what is at stake in disputes about intervention: as we saw in the case of Libya, an otherwise cautious and pragmatic Obama foreign policy ended up taking a bold stance (in that sense, the strategy of 'leading from behind' was a way of turning consent into coercion). The next section of this chapter considers in more detail the rival accounts of world order and their relevance to questions about intervention.

[5] David Rieff, 'R2P, R.I.P.', *New York Times*, 7 November 2011.
[6] Lakhdar Brahimi in a closed meeting: 'l apologize to the Syrian people'. 'Briefing to the Security Council by the Joint Special Representative of the United Nations and League of Arab States for Syria, 19 April 2013', *UN Report*, 23 April 2013, www.un-report.blogspot .com.au/2013/04/brahimi-in-closed-meeting-l-apologize.html.
[7] Georg Sørensen, *A Liberal World Order in Crisis: Choosing between Imposition and Restraint* (Ithaca, NY: Cornell University Press, 2011).

In the final section I advocate a reconceptualisation of an older distinction in thinking about world order – that of pluralism versus solidarism. Both are normative theories which can be understood in abstract ways, with countervailing commitments; yet both are 'action guiding' theories that give more insight into the tensions within and possibilities for protective intervention in international society today. By thinking about intervention in the context of world order, it is evident that the meta-value of liberal democracy may be in trouble but the narrower agenda of R2P could conceivably be more resilient. Pluralism, far from being the enemy of R2P, might turn out to be its saviour.[8]

Before the chapter gets properly underway, however, it is important to note the caveat that the focal point for R2P is going to be the 'third pillar' (to use Secretary-General Ban Ki-moon's analytical distinctions). It is this third pillar that accords the UN Security Council a unique role in being the protector of the last resort. According to the UN Secretary-General, the international community has a duty to take 'timely and decisive' action when states are 'manifestly failing' to protect their populations. Actions that are permissible include non-coercive means such as diplomacy and humanitarian assistance, and coercive measures such as sanctions or, as a last resort, the use of force (which requires Security Council authorisation).[9]

Conceptions of world order in international relations

World order is regularly invoked by international relations (IR) scholars but is seldom defined. On the rare occasions when it is, we find a diverse set of meanings and understandings. The purpose of this discussion is to consider a few of the dominant framings of world order before providing a justification of an English School account which will be privileged in this chapter because it provides the most persuasive understanding of the modalities of world order building.

Often, world order is used interchangeably with international order.[10] The function of the term 'order' is to signal something purposive while the function of 'world' (or 'international') is to fix a level of analysis that is either state-centric or world systemic. These building blocks of an

---

[8] This possibility is also suggested in Jennifer M. Welsh, 'Norm Contestation and the Responsibility to Protect', *Global Responsibility to Protect* 5.4 (2013) 'Special Issue: R2P and International Theory', pp. 365–396; in the same issue, Tim Dunne 'Distributing Duties and Counting Costs', pp. 443–465.

[9] Ban Ki-moon, *Implementing the Responsibility to Protect*. Report of the Secretary-General, Document A/63/677 (New York: United Nations, 12 January 2009).

[10] Chong Guan Kwa and See Seng Tan, 'The Keystone of World Order', *The Washington Quarterly* 24:3 (2001), pp. 95–103.

ontology familiar to IR enable certain macro-level ascriptions to be applied to the character of world order at a particular moment in history – 'colonial', 'sovereigntist', 'mutlilateralist', 'hegemonic' or, to use Ruggie's term for the post-1945 period, an embedded liberal world order.[11] International or world order is also invoked in relation to the activities of the dominant institutions – be they sovereign states, great powers, regions or international governmental or non-governmental organisations (NGOs). World order is, therefore, both place and purpose: a place where there are flows of ideas and materiality on a global scale and an institutional design that embodies shared values and purposes (however limited these might be). World orders must be built and, once constructed, they become a site of contestation between actors who are oriented towards the status quo versus revisionist actors who believe the artifice to be pathological and unjust.

Beyond this general account of world order, it is useful to consider three specific articulations of it. First, world order is articulated in relation to patterns of governance. Georg Sørensen is an exemplar: he defines world order as 'a governing arrangement' among states designed to meet 'the current demand for order in major areas of concern'.[12] Viewing world order as an aggregate of regimes and international organisations providing 'governance without government'[13] is compatible with recent neoliberal institutionalist thought, with its emphasis on questions of institutional design, regulatory efficiency and state compliance. The main limitation with such an interpretation of world order is that it is both too demanding and too 'thin'. When looking at world order through the optic of R2P, it is apparent that the operative paragraph in the World Summit Outcome Document about the 'international community's responsibilities' is too underdeveloped and contested to be regarded as 'a governing arrangement' in relation to atrocity prevention and response. It is also too thin insofar as the definition lacks attention to the moral purposes underlying world order – which are put to the test when voices are clamouring for UN member states to 'do something' to either halt or contain genocide.

While the relative absence of normative content is a legitimate criticism of some contemporary conceptions of world order, the same cannot be

[11] John Gerard Ruggie, *Constructing the World Polity: Essays on International Institutionalization* (New York: Routledge, 1998), chapter 2, 'Embedded Liberalism and the Postwar Economic Regimes', pp. 62–84.

[12] Georg Sørensen, 'What Kind of World Order? A Response to Critics', *Cooperation and Conflict* 41:4 (2006), p. 393.

[13] See Thomas G. Weiss and Ramesh Thakur, *Global Governance and the UN: An Unfinished Journey* (Bloomington: Indiana University Press, 2010) pp. 32–33.

said for the older 'world order models' thinking characteristic of writers such as Richard Falk, Johan Galtung and Saul Mendlovitz. Their movement was characterised as a project, driven by transformational arguments about the injustices of the current configuration of world order. They were against an order built on sovereign states because of the pathologies and inequities of that order.[14] In place of an interstate order they privileged the idea of global citizenship based on universal rights and protections. Integral to this world order models movement was a distinctive and radical role for academic theorists: the project had to be cross-national, inter-disciplinary and led by scholar-activists. For Richard Falk, perhaps the leading scholar-activist in the project, world order refers to a more complex post-Westphalia world – or a world beyond sovereign authority – in which transnational problems were tackled by the politics and policies of human governance. The principal limitation with this account is the absence of detailed accounts of how means and ends are to be aligned. We might all agree that 'humane governance' is good, or that environmental stewardship is preferable to wanton degradation, but what action is necessary or appropriate to bring these ends about? This question is even harder to answer given the multi-actor ontology of the world order models researchers: aligning spheres of private interests to a notion of the common good, in the absence of a powerful regulator or sovereign, is an age-old dilemma that has yet to be adequately resolved.

The writings of Robert Cox supply a concept of world order with greater theoretical depth. For Cox, world order is a historical structure that is shaped by the interplay of states (in the modern period), transnational material and ideational forces, and the institutionalisation of forms of power and authority. Following Gramsci, Cox saw hegemony as the dominant ordering device in the twentieth century.[15] In a footnote to his famous article on 'Social Forces, States and World Orders', Cox explains his preference for the term world order over 'inter-state system'. The latter was merely one historical configuration of world order; and also, the term 'order' was preferable to 'system' as it implied 'enduring patterns of power relationships' while at the same time avoiding the connotation of 'equilibrium', which is often implicitly associated with systemic theories.[16]

Bull would agree with Cox that the international (or more accurately interstate) system is one historical form of world order; where they disagree is in the priority that is to be accorded to the economic domain.

---

[14] Richard Falk, 'World Orders, Old and New', *Current History* 98:624 (1999), pp. 29–34.

[15] Robert W. Cox, 'Social Forces, States and World Orders: Beyond International Relations Theory', *Millennium* 10:2 (1981), p. 151.

[16] Ibid, p. 249.

While it must be conceded that Bull and the English School artificially bracketed capitalism from their analysis, such a position could be defensible on two grounds. First, a straightforward division of labour is necessary – adopting a systemic level of analysis requires a restrictive focus on certain explanatory variables, and in the case of Bull's *The Anarchical Society*, [17] these were the primary political institutions of international ordering. Second, even if it were possible to produce macro-level analyses of economic, political and military structures, Cox and Bull would no doubt have differed as to the relative priority to be attached to each domain. Despite these differences, Cox and Bull are closer than many contemporary IR scholars would admit. Putting it crudely, Cox saw world order as the meeting point of social forces, interstate relations and the hegemony of global capitalism; Bull saw world order in terms of a hierarchy in which institutions and regimes were in part constituted by world order values – the degree of convergence between the levels required detailed empirical and institutional research. What is not in doubt is that both Cox and Bull believed that world order could *not* be bracketed from normative evaluation – the claim that it is a neutral concept would be an anathema to both theorists. This is well understood as a feature of Cox's work in light of his association with critical theory;[18] yet it is an under-appreciated dimension of Bull's work.[19]

Hedley Bull's theory of order is neatly set out in *The Anarchical Society*. What is seldom acknowledged is that Bull's theory of order was highly derivative, in outline at least, from the thinking of Raymond Aron, Stanley Hoffmann and other leading IR figures in the 1960s. A conference on World Order was held in Bellagio in 1965 in which there was broad agreement that order can productively be understood in terms of the provision of certain minimal conditions for social life. Those conditions – or primary rules – were security from violence, trust and the protection of property.[20] Within international society, it was the responsibility of states to obey these primary rules such that a stable

---

[17] Hedley Bull, *The Anarchical Society: A Study of Order in World Politics* (London: Macmillan, 1977).

[18] Richard Devetak, 'Critical Theory', in Scott Burchill and Andrew Linklater eds, *Theories of International Relations* (London: Macmillan, 2013, 5th edition). This argument is developed considerably in Richard Devetak, 'A Rival Enlightenment? Critical International Theory in Historical Mode', *International Theory* 6:3 (2014), pp.417–453.

[19] For an example of a misrepresentation of Bull's concept of world order as being a morally and political neutral concept, see Sanjay Chaturvedi and Joe Painter, 'Whose World, Whose Order?: Spatiality, Geopolitics and the Limits of the World Order Concept', *Cooperation and Conflict* 42:4 (2007), pp. 375–395.

[20] R. J. Vincent, *Nonintervention and International Order* (Princeton: Princeton University Press, 1974).

order endured. Precisely how these primary rules related to other elements of world politics was under-determined in these earlier debates – a gap that English School theory sought to close in later years.[21]

What significance, if any, should be attached to the fact that Bull primarily wrote about order as though it was an 'arrangement between states'? To begin with, Bull can be criticised for committing the error that Cox warns us about, namely, not recognising that state sovereignty is merely one historical institution of political ordering. This issue is compounded by the fact that 'the role that global social processes have played in the constitution of international orders is occluded'.[22] These points are well taken; nevertheless, it does not require a giant conceptual leap to treat Bull's work as offering contending theories of world order – a theme which drives the discussion that immediately follows.

Pluralism and solidarism as world order models

Pluralism and solidarism are generally represented as contending normative theorisations of international society.[23] In his classic statement of the pluralist and solidarist conceptions of international society, Nicholas J. Wheeler argued that both constituted normative accounts of how the world hangs together.[24] Pluralists attach primary significance to the rules of coexistence that sovereign states have accepted as a means of maintaining order; they do so in the knowledge that there are widely diverse 'comprehensive doctrines' in world politics. What might be considered just in one community could be considered depraved by another. For this reason, the starting point for a cooperative order is reciprocal recognition of sovereignty, an institutional arrangement where all peoples can build a community they call their own – 'we' do not possess the knowledge and understanding of 'others' such that we can judge the rightness of their institutions and values. To do so would be paternalistic, which Kant appropriately regarded as being 'the greatest conceivable despotism'.[25]

---

[21] Barry Buzan, *From International to World Society? English School Theory and the Social Structure of Globalisation* (Cambridge: Cambridge University Press, 2004).

[35] Christian Reus-Smit, 'The Liberal International Order Reconsidered', in Rebekka Friedman et al eds., *After Liberalism? The Future of Liberalism in International Relations* (Houndmills: Macmillan, 2013) p. 168.

[23] Nicholas J. Wheeler, 'Pluralist or Solidarist Conceptions of International Society: Bull and Vincent on Humanitarian Intervention', *Millennium – Journal of International Studies* 21:3 (1992), pp. 463–487; Robert H. Jackson, *The Global Covenant: Human Conduct in a World of States* (Oxford: Oxford University Press, 2000).

[24] Wheeler, 'Pluralist or Solidarist Conceptions of International Society'.

[25] Hans Reiss, ed., *Kant: Political Writings*, 2nd ed., trans H.B. Nisbet (Cambridge: Cambridge University Press, 1970).

Critics of pluralism charge that it is failing to deliver on its promise. The persistence of interstate wars throughout the twentieth century suggests that sovereignty norms were not sufficient to deter predatory states. Moreover, the rule of non-intervention that was central to pluralism was enabling statist elites to violently abuse their own citizens with impunity.[26] For these reasons, both Bull and Vincent were drawn to a different account of international society in which universal values such as human rights set limits on the exercise of state sovereignty. The guiding thought here, and one that is captured by the term solidarism, is that the ties that bind individuals to the great society of humankind are deeper than the pluralist rules and institutions that separate them.

When viewed as world order models, as opposed to political preferences, pluralism and solidarism integrate state strategies to social and historical configurations that are aligned to distinct moral purposes, have different conceptions of agency and prioritise different institutions and mechanisms for ordering. Grasping the model of world order requires adopting a configurative theoretical framework that has been advanced by Reus-Smit and others.[27] These innovative insights from constructivists provide us with new lenses for theorising the multidimensionality of R2P, in particular the relationship between actors, institutions and moral purposes. As will become clear below, pluralism and solidarism are not merely different in their ethical commitments; they are differently configured frameworks of world order. It is only through making this analytical move that it becomes possible to see the way earlier English School theorisations incorrectly placed them on side of an intervention/ non-intervention boundary.

How, then, according to constructivists like Reus-Smit, should we understand the configuration of world order? Figure 5.1 is adapted from Reus-Smit's work.[28] It is based on an analytical characterisation of world order that is composed of the following dimensions. World order is an ideal-typical representation of a historical formation that is

---

[26] Ken Booth, 'Human Wrongs and International Relations', *International Affairs* 71:1 (1995), pp. 103–126.

[27] Christian Reus-Smit, 'The Constitutional Structure of International Society and the Nature of Fundamental Institutions', *International Organization* 51:4 (1997), pp. 555–589; Christian Reus-Smit, *Individual Rights and the Making of the International System* (Cambridge: Cambridge University Press, 2013); Andrew Phillips, *War, Religion and Empire: The Transformation of International Orders* (Cambridge: Cambridge University Press, 2011).

[28] Reus-Smit, 'The Constitutional Structure of International Society and the Nature of Fundamental Institutions', p. 559.

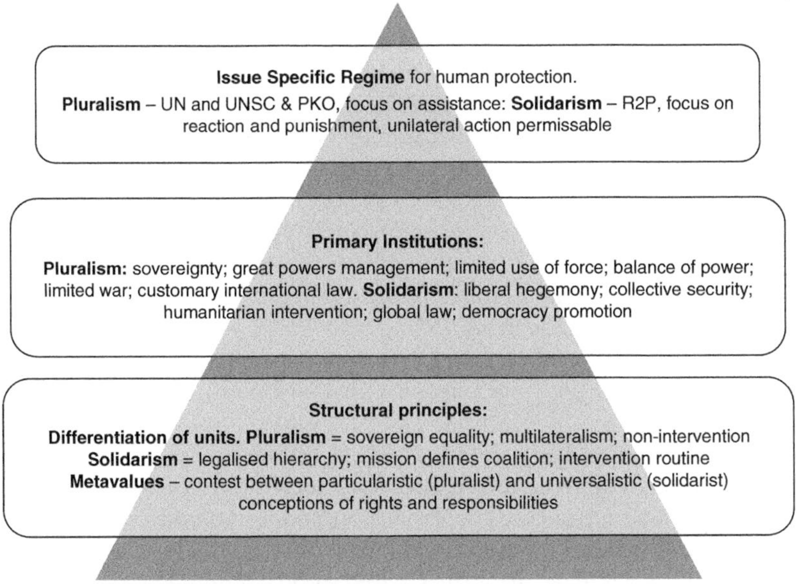

Figure 5.1: Configuring world order models

multi-layered. At the base are the 'structural principles' that operate at any given time – these are usually distinguished by ordering principles of anarchy/hierarchy, or other systemic arrangements such as empire, heteronomy, sovereignty, suzerainty and hegemony. Structural principles are normative as well as historical. This comes through nicely in Reus-Smit's conception of them as principles that 'license a particular systemic configuration of political authority (by privileging a particular organising principle), define what constitutes legitimate political agency (with reference to hegemonic ideas of the moral purposes of the "state", broadly understood), and sanction particular kinds of fundamental institutional practices (in line with an ascendant norm of procedural justice)'.[29] Above the base are the primary institutions[30] which are durable practices or conventions, embodying a mix of norms and rules, which are recognised as being acceptable ways of 'how to go on' (to use a Wittgensteinian

[29] Reus-Smit, 'The Liberal International Order Reconsidered' p. 170.
[30] Reus-Smit refers to them as fundamental institutions but here I invoke Buzan's characterisation of 'primary institutions'. Barry Buzan, 'An English School Perspective on "What Kind of World Order?"', *Cooperation and Conflict* 41:4 (2006), pp. 364–369.

metaphor) in the world. Issue-specific regimes and international organisations are the final layer of world ordering; these institutions are 'secondary' in the sense that their membership and reason for existing is derivative of deeper structural principles, while at the same time being conditioned by the primary institutions. Before outlining each layer of world order and showing how it shapes the possibilities for logics of human protection, it is important to point out the interlinked character of the levels. To illustrate this point, think for a moment about how sovereignty, as the defining quality of the modern state, 'cannot be disentangled from anarchy as the defining quality of system' structure (and therefore the rules of the game)'.[31]

The pluralist world order

Clearly in the post-1945 period the 'end of empire' signalled the triumph of the sovereign state as the rightful 'member' of international society. The meta-value advancing the expansion and completion of the states system was the norm of procedural justice that enabled the coexistence of multiple sovereigns in a rules-based order. Pluralism asserts that states are entitled to equal rights regardless of their capabilities or internal arrangements.

The UN Charter shows how the structural principles of a pluralist order became constitutionally embedded and solidified. The Charter's centre of gravity was very much on the side of states and their right of self-determination: this suited the realist 'turn' in international relations as one by one the great figures of early post-1945 IR turned against the institution of international law and the place of human rights within it. In an era of heightened great power rivalry, putting moral principles at the heart of foreign policy risked the charge of hypocrisy and a repeat of the mistakes of the inter-war period when the 'legalistic-moralistic approach' was in full swing.[32] The indifference shown to the Universal Declaration of Human Rights by lawyers and practitioners was reaffirmed by the politics of decolonisation in which freedom from colonial rule was regarded as a precondition for the enjoyment of all individual rights.

Over and above recognition, pluralists believe that the rules and institutions of international society are generated by custom and practice. The legitimacy of those rules depends critically on whether they

---

[31] Buzan, *From International to World Society*, p. 178.
[32] George F. Kennan, *American Diplomacy* (Chicago: University of Chicago Press, 1984), p. 95.

have been arrived at through a just procedural basis. For pluralists, the two most important rules in international society are to maintain order and tranquillity, related to the prohibition on intervention in the 'domestic jurisdiction' of a state, and restraint with respect to the threat or use of force (Articles 2.7 and 2.4 of the UN Charter respectively). Legalising a right of humanitarian intervention would challenge the primary institution of sovereign equality, which in turn poses challenges to the UN regime and its presumption against the use of force with the sole exception of a credible case of individual or collective self-defence.

Intervention violates a state's rights because it undermines a people's right to live without interference from outsiders. This view is frequently advanced by English School writers. Pluralists, Wheeler argues, 'do not believe that there is, or should be, such a right of humanitarian intervention for individual states'.[33] Alex Bellamy puts the pluralist view of intervention even more strongly, suggesting that pluralists do not accept the implied change in the meta-value of international society. In his words, 'human rights are constructed within a specific cultural context and are not universal'.[34]

For pluralists, the problem here is the unfounded moral universalism that is attributed to the human rights regime that limits, or even prevents, reaching agreement in other international settings – particularly those pertaining to issue-specific regimes such as the control and regulation of weapons of mass destruction, the regime for environmental sustainability or the institutions for the protection of human rights.

The solidarist world order

Bull originally defined solidarism as the collective enforcement of international rules and the guardianship of human rights.[35] Solidarism differs from cosmopolitanism in that the latter is agnostic as to the institutional arrangement for delivering universal values. While some cosmopolitans believe a world government is preferable, others think this would be despotic and would rather abandon formal institutional hierarchies altogether. Solidarism, by contrast, is a moral and political vision of world order that is largely driven by states for the purposes and interests of peoples.

---

[33] Wheeler, 'Pluralist or Solidarist Conceptions of International Society', p. 468.

[34] Alex Bellamy, 'Pragmatic Solidarism and the Dilemmas of Humanitarian Intervention', *Millennium – Journal of International Studies* 31:3 (2002), p. 476.

[35] Hedley Bull, 'The Grotian Conception of International Society', in Herbert Butterfield and Martin Wight, eds, *Diplomatic Investigations: Essays in the Theory of International Politics* (London: Allen & Unwin, 1966).

In a solidarist order individuals are entitled to basic rights. This in turn demands that sovereignty norms are modified such that there is a duty on the members of international society to intervene forcibly to protect those rights. At this point, Bull was hesitant about what was implied by solidarism. He believed that there was a danger that the enforcement of human rights principles risked undermining international order. Until there was a greater consensus on the meaning and priority to be accorded to rights claims, attempts to enforce them – what he described as 'premature global solidarism' – would do more harm than good.[36]

Critical to the solidarist view of international society is the belief that universality of human rights had to be grafted into the primary institutions of international society. Failure to do this undermines the moral purpose of the state. This point is neatly captured by the philosopher Henry Shue:

To claim, on the one hand, that one believes that Hutu and Tutsi alike, like all persons, have a basic right not to be killed arbitrarily (genocide or otherwise), but to claim, on the other hand, that it is the job of 'their' state to protect them ... is not to be serious about implementing rights in the real world. If we do not believe that anyone beyond their own state can reasonably be asked to bear the responsibility of protecting these people against the single most serious threat to their lives – their own state – we do not believe in any practically meaningful way that they have a basic right not to be killed. We simply have not yet admitted to ourselves that these people, at least, we have written off. They must face their own particular terrors without any protection from the rest of us. Even the most basic 'human' rights are not quite universal. Humans divide into two groups, those able to protect themselves, who do not have genocidal states, and the unprotected, who do have genocidal states.[37]

Solidarists recognise that human rights have to be advanced in a world in which sovereign states – and their attendant primary institutions – retain institutional power and authority. For this reason, solidarism is not anti-statist; it is fundamentally a modification of world order rather than a marker of its transcendence. Yet at the same time solidarism brings into question the fitness of the primary institutions of international society. Can great powers be responsible sovereigns? Can international legal duties be binding rather than merely aspirations? Are the issue-specific regimes sufficiently robust such that they meet the reasonable demands of the world's peoples for protection from violence, enslavement and arbitrary death?[38]

[36] Nicholas J. Wheeler and Tim Dunne, 'Hedley Bull's Pluralism of the Intellect and Solidarism of the Will', *International Affairs* 72 :1 (1996), pp. 91–107.
[37] Henry Shue, 'Limiting Sovereignty', in Jennifer M. Welsh, ed, *Humanitarian Intervention and International Relations* (Oxford: Oxford University Press, 2004), p. 21.
[38] Nicholas J. Wheeler, *Saving Strangers: Humanitarian Intervention in International Society* (Oxford: Oxford University Press, 2000).

How did human rights become a moral purpose which liberal states, countless NGOs, dissidents, novelists, workers, artists and ordinary publics embraced? Recent human rights historiography points to a tectonic shift in the meaning and priority accorded to individual rights in the UN system that occurred in the decade or so before the end of the Cold War. There were three drivers of this transformation. First, there was a realisation that while national self-determination might have liberated the new elites in southern capitals, it was often inimical to the promotion and protection of human rights. Second, the Helsinki process of East–West détente crystallised the idea that human rights were an international policy commitment – something that the now burgeoning international NGO sector pursued unrelentingly. The third driver was US domestic politics. President Jimmy Carter's inaugural address, in 1977, mentioned human rights twenty times – 'our commitment to human rights must be absolute', to use his fateful words.[39] Suddenly, a term that had previously had little or no resonance in the US public sphere had been posited as a major policy goal of the government. And in a post-Vietnam era, Americans were desperately looking to press the 'reset' button in order to rehabilitate their reputation as a liberal hegemon. At almost the identical time, the UK Labour government's young foreign secretary – David Owen – was also giving attention to the concept and how it could be applied in government.[40] While the theory and practice of human rights was to be buffeted from many different angles during the 1980s, the genie was out of the bottle. There had been a historic shift in Anglo–American thinking towards a rights-based internationalism, necessitating a corresponding recalibration of the meaning of sovereignty.

What impact did this emergent moral purpose have on the primary and secondary institutions of international society? Mark Mazower neatly captures this in his recent book, *Governing the World*:

New and much more conditional attitudes toward sovereignty, already evident through the human rights revolution of the 1970s, were now taken up within the United Nations itself, and it became the instrument of a new civilizing mission that, much like the old one from which it sprang, relied heavily on the language of international law and the appeal to universal moral values for its legitimation.[41]

---

[39] Samuel Moyn, *The Last Utopia: Human Rights in History* (Cambridge, MA: Harvard University Press, 2010), p. 155.

[40] R. J. Vincent, *Human Rights and International Relations* (Cambridge: Cambridge University Press, 1986).

[41] Mark Mazower, *Governing the World: The History of an Idea, 1815 to the Present* (New York: Penguin Books, 2013), p. 379.

A successful appeal to universal moral values promised a morality that could transcend politics. It was not to last very long in American political history, as Ronald Reagan and then George W. Bush overtly embedded universal rights and liberties in their democracy promotion agendas. At the same time as human rights were being incorporated into the identities of leading liberal states – with very mixed results – their transcendent appeal continued to inform the thinking of human rights practitioners and advocates.[42]

New histories of human rights offer important insights into the emergence of 'atrocity prevention'. Samuel Moyn persuasively argues that the anti-genocide consciousness followed a separate track to the rights-based activism symbolised by Amnesty International and other US-based social movements. The two were belatedly integrated. Moyn dates this convergence in very vague terms – somewhere between the time of the Cambodian genocide and the return of ethnic cleansing on the continent of Europe in the 1990s.[43] The implications of this claim are significant. If genocide prevention and human rights were only coupled together fairly recently, then it is surely worth asking the question whether they should be separated today. As Moyn argues, the two goals 'are absolutely different', with atrocity prevention achieved through 'minimalist' ethical norms, while the individual rights-based view of the global community is 'maximalist'. In a tantalisingly brief conclusion to the book, Moyn hints that advocates of catastrophe prevention and response are better able to 'make room for the contest of genuinely political visions for the future ... Yet then human rights cannot be a general slogan or worldview or ideal'.[44] Such a claim opens up the possibility that pluralism could be hived off from the legalism and universalism of solidarism (discussed further below).

Pluralism, solidarism and world order in the twenty-first century

The solidarist case for humanitarian intervention gathered momentum through the 1990s, spurred on by the collective failure to prevent genocide in Rwanda in 1994 and ethnic cleansing in Srebrenica in 1995. In both cases, the Security Council dithered, individual great powers looked

---

[42] Stephen Hopgood, *Keepers of the Flame: Understanding Amnesty International* (Ithaca: Cornell University Press, 2006).

[43] One flaw in Moyn's account is the American-centric nature of the narrative. He overlooks, for example, the critical contribution made by French thinking in the late 1980s, in which Bernard Kouchner (and others) built an epistemic community around the idea of 'le droit d'ingérence', or 'the right of intervention'. Philippe Guillot, 'France, Peacekeeping and Humanitarian Intervention', *Peacekeeping* 1:1 (1994), pp. 30–43.

[44] Moyn, *The Last Utopia: Human Rights in History*, pp. 226–227.

the other way and transnational civil society was mute when it ought to have been mobilising and shaming. For many inside the UN order, the problem for humanitarian intervention was not so much the danger of 'abuse' but instead the problem of 'will'. As Simon Chesterman put it, 'unhumanitarian non-intervention' was a more apparent pattern than great power 'sheriffs' and their middle power 'deputies' looking for opportunities to enforce the law.[45] In truth, the pluralist rules of the post-1945 order had become far too enabling for governments to commit – or tolerate – egregious and systematic violations of the basic rights of their citizens. This was all too clear to UN Secretary General Kofi Annan – 'No government', he insisted, 'has the right to hide behind national sovereignty in order to violate the human rights or fundamental freedoms of its peoples'.[46]

Solidarist assumptions and commitments informed much of the thinking that took place on the intervention question inside the International Committee on Intervention and State Sovereignty (ICISS), the body funded by the Canadian government to review the conditions under which it is acceptable for coercive intervention to take place without host state consent.[47] Much ink has been spilt on the Commission's findings, and how this epistemic community of global diplomats and scholars settled on the articulation of 'sovereignty as responsibility'; a meta-value that was diffused through international society during the early part of the twenty-first century.

The change in the meta-value of sovereignty from being something that was unconditional to being an entitlement that could be withdrawn if the state failed to meet certain civilised standards of behaviour signalled a critically important world order reform. Modifying the meta-value triggered changes to the primary institutions – for example, the UN Security Council adapted its understanding of 'security' to include domestic crimes against humanity. Alongside the reform to the primary institutions we saw the evolution of an issue-specific regime called 'responsibility to protect'. R2P starts with a presumption that prevention

---

[45] Simon Chesterman, 'Humanitarian Intervention and Afghanistan', in Welsh, ed, *Humanitarian Intervention and International Relations* pp. 163–175; Simon Chesterman, '"Leading from Behind": The Responsibility to Protect, the Obama Doctrine, and Humanitarian Intervention after Libya', *Ethics & International Affairs* 25:3 (2011), pp. 279–285.

[46] Kofi Annan, Statement by the Secretary-General of the United Nations – 55th session of the Commission on Human Rights, Geneva, 7 April 1999; text reprinted in Kofi Annan, 'No government has the right to hide behind national sovereignty in order to violate human rights', *Guardian*, 8 April 1999, www.guardian.co.uk/world/1999/apr/07 /balkans.unitednations.

[47] International Commission on Intervention and State Sovereignty (ICISS), *The Responsibility to Protect* (Ottawa: International Development Research Centre, 2001).

is better than cure; accordingly, all governments have to accept an obligation to protect peoples from genocide, war crimes, ethnic cleansing and
crimes against humanity. Yet R2P recognises that we live in an imperfect
world where states frequently fail to uphold the moral and legal standards
they have agreed to. In cases where a state is 'manifestly failing' to meet its
responsibilities, the wider society of states is obliged to take a range of
decisive measures, with force being the last resort. In channelling all
coercive decisions through the Security Council, advocates of R2P underlined an ongoing preference for multilateralism and for working within
the essentially pluralist constitution of the UN Charter.

The UN General Assembly resisted the view that intervention could
take place without the consent of the Security Council if that body was
unable to agree a resolution when there was clear evidence of a humanitarian catastrophe happening – or about to happen. Yet the earlier
ICISS report was not so restrictive about the question of 'right authority'.
Much was made, at the time, of this 'retreat' from the ICISS proposal;
yet with hindsight, the broad consensus reflected in the 2005 World
Summit document remains compatible with a pluralist configuration of
the primary institutions of world order. At the same time it is true that, in
implying that the international community had general and special
responsibilities to act, R2P went well beyond the International Law
Commission's findings on state responsibilities, which reduced international responsibility to nothing more than a commitment to cooperate
with other states.[48]

Despite the frequency of diplomatic statements supporting R2P, many
fissures and fragments remain – some of which can be traced back to the
co-mingling of universal meta-values of humanitarian protection with
enforcement machinery that is heavily dependent on consensus. This
co-mingling is evident when R2P is said to be a 'norm', a claim that is
made frequently in both academic texts and practitioner speech-acts by
global diplomats, including the UN Secretary-General. While it can be
empirically shown that the phrase 'responsibility to protect' has increasingly found its way into UN Security Council resolutions and countless
diplomatic statements, we also know that its invocation can lead to
radically divergent policy outcomes – timely and decisive action (as in
the case of Libya) and relative indifference (as in the case of the 'forgotten
war' in the Democratic Republic of Congo). Such inconsistencies are
easily reconciled with a pluralist view of the world: action in response to
mass atrocities in one part of the world may have little or no bearing on

---

[48] James Crawford, *The International Law Commission's Articles on State Responsibility:
Introduction, Text and Commentaries* (Cambridge: Cambridge University Press, 2002).

violations elsewhere. In this respect, the meta-value of universal protection is often held in check by pluralist institutional practices, as well as prudential considerations that include the costs of such an action on the part of states undertaking the intervention.[49]

If prudential considerations are permitted to intrude to such an extent, what does it mean to talk about R2P being a 'norm'? It is not a 'legal norm' in the conventional sense as there is no international treaty with specific obligations that take effect when the treaty is ratified by governments. Is it a 'social norm'? While degrees of indeterminacy are compatible with social norms, *this* degree of contingency and inconsistency is open to question. The problem with radical indeterminacy is that it can erode the moral standing of the norm. We do not follow norms or rules 'blindly', as Wittgenstein once famously claimed; we follow them because we think they are right. The norm that retains its moral quality is not R2P per se, but rather, the prohibition against genocide and related crimes against humanity. If this moral principle is appropriately regarded as the foundation of the atrocity prevention regime, then it becomes more logical to regard R2P as a particular issue-specific framework within which responses to these catastrophes – imminent or actual – are deliberated and acted upon. It is here that contemporary pluralists need to begin their account of establishing a prudential moral argument for last-resort interventions in cases of humanitarian catastrophes.

In reconsidering R2P in the context of world order, it is important to decouple R2P from the moral project of creating liberal institutions beyond borders. Such a goal is the pursuit of a subtly different meta-value. Some solidarists see democracy promotion and mass human atrocity prevention as being two sides of the same coin. The renowned Argentinian lawyer and former diplomat Fernando Tesón operates with an understanding of intervention precisely along these lines: intervention is the threat or use of force 'undertaken in principle by a liberal government or alliance, aimed at ending tyranny or anarchy, welcomed by the victims, and consistent with the doctrine of double effect'.[50] Such an understanding of 'humanitarian protective intervention' is what many in the 'global South' fear about the remaking of world order – war as an instrument used to 'emancipate' societies by toppling their governments and replacing them with constitutional liberal orders.

---

[49] Benjamin A. Valentino, 'The True Costs of Humanitarian Intervention', *Foreign Affairs* 90:6 (2011), pp. 60–73.

[50] Fernando Tesón, 'The Liberal Case for Humanitarian Intervention', in J. L. Holzgrefe and Robert O. Keohane, eds, *Humanitarian Intervention: Ethical, Legal and Political Dilemmas* (Cambridge: Cambridge University Press, 2003), p. 94.

Tesón was not alone in linking the practice of intervention to the pursuit of a liberal world-order-building project. Think tanks and policy networks associated with the Democratic Party in the United States were also, around this time, articulating strong doctrines of intervention for liberal ends. Anne-Marie Slaughter was lobbying the second-term Bush Administration to adopt R2P as well as pushing for institutional reforms to NATO, the G20 and the US government in order to more effectively respond to genocide prevention and response.[51] And if existing institutions such as the United Nations were incapable of taking timely and decisive action because of recalcitrant action by other states pursuing their narrow national interest, internationalists such as John Ikenberry and Anne-Marie Slaughter believed that a new league or concert of democracies should be created to provide an alternative site of legitimation.[52] Such expanding normative ambition is a feature of post-Cold War international society – and it is likely to be much harder to contain than sceptics are prone to believe.

The aftermath of the R2P intervention in Libya in 2011 is a good illustration of the political danger that is associated with a perception that the intervening powers allowed R2P to mutate into a war of regime change. The view that those that established the no-fly zone over-reached themselves in relation to the mandate is one that is widely shared by many diplomatic missions. Yet this view elides the fact that, during the weeks leading up to the commencement of military action, US President Barack Obama kept coming back to the point that one imperative with regard to action against Libya was to avoid the mistakes of the 2003 Iraq War, a war in which regime change was a stated goal of the invading and occupying powers. Furthermore, he made it clear that 'broadening our military mission to include regime change would be a mistake'.[53] In reality, when coercive power is unleashed against a regime that is committing atrocities, it is impossible to discretely isolate means and ends; protecting civilians from the air is bound to alter the balance of forces on the ground. Yet it remains important to distinguish between the intentions of the civilian leaders implementing Security Council Resolution 1973 from the unintended consequences of the military action they instigated.

---

[51] Anne-Marie Slaughter, 'Help Develop Institutions and Instruments for Military Intervention on Humanitarian Grounds', in *Restoring American Leadership: 13 Cooperative Steps to Advance Global Progress* (Washington DC: Open Society Institute, and New York: Security and Peace Institute, 2005), pp. 37–43.

[52] G. John Ikenberry and Anne-Marie Slaughter co-directors, '*Forging a World of Liberty Under Law: U.S. National Security in the 21st Century*', final report of the Princeton Project on National Security, 2006. See also Allen Buchanan and Robert O. Keohane, 'The Legitimacy of Global Governance Institutions', *Ethics & International Affairs* 20:4 (2006), pp. 405–437.

[53] Barack Obama, 'Remarks by the President in Address to the Nation on Libya', National Defense University, Washington DC, 2011.

Moreover, it ought to be possible – in a policy sense – to maintain daylight between a policy that seeks a change in the behaviour of a regime from a policy that seeks to overthrow a tyrannical government.

The question of whether Libya was or was not a war of regime change is one that needs future research. Either way, from a policy perspective, the damage has been done. What matters for the R2P epistemic community – scholars and practitioners – is to set out, very clearly, the differences between R2P as an atrocity prevention framework and the more comprehensive liberal project of democracy promotion.

This challenge to articulate a conception of intervention that is more minimalist, and consistent with pluralism, has been taken up recently by Robert Pape.[54] He argues, somewhat erroneously, that R2P is far too broad as a doctrine, creating 'unbounded obligations to help foreigners'.[55] A better target for his critique would have been those academics in pursuit of utopian models of cosmopolitan democracy rather than the practitioner community responsible for documents such as the one adopted at the World Summit in 2005.[56] That aside, his 'new standard' of 'pragmatic humanitarian intervention' is an attempt to ensure the 'issue specific regime' is aligned with a traditional pluralist conception of primary institutions – including the relative freedom of manoeuvre on the part of great powers who retain a strong sense of their sovereign right to independence.

Conclusion

The irreducible core to world order is the complex of meta-values and conventions that 'define what constitutes a legitimate actor' and set the parameters for acceptable forms of interaction. In other words, the ordering principle – and the concomitant modes of differentiation – are enabled and produced by the dominant conception of morality as these are understood and internalised by the leading polities in that order.

The conventional English School reading of pluralism and solidarism continues to capture, better than other heuristic devices, the dynamics of world order building. Pluralists hold on to the presumption that sovereignty is a prerequisite for peoples to live 'the good life' according to their history, culture and traditions. Sovereignty's status as the fundamental

---

[54] Robert A. Pape, 'When Duty Calls: A Pragmatic Standard of Humanitarian Intervention', *International Security* 37:1 (2012), pp. 41–80. For a response by the two authors of the original R2P report, see Gareth Evans, Ramesh Thakur and Robert Pape, 'Correspondence: Humanitarian Intervention and the Responsibility to Protect', *International Security* 37:4 (Spring 2013), pp. 199–214.
[55] Pape, 'When Duty Calls', pp. 43, 51.
[56] Daniele Archibugi, 'Cosmopolitan Guidelines for Humanitarian Intervention', *Alternatives* 29:1 (2004), pp. 1–21.

meta-value has been modified into a prerogative that is dependent on the state protecting its people rather than generating fear or committing grotesque crimes such as those that the Assad government has been undertaking during the Syrian crisis.

The modification of the meta-value of sovereignty owes a great deal to the triumphant march of the human rights story since the early 1970s. At the same time, the character of the primary institutions has not been greatly modified – a world of responsible states is still an interstate order. In the construction of the secondary institution of R2P, we see how the tension between solidarist values and pluralist institutions is being played out. This is why, for most R2P advocates, the doctrine has never been imbued with many of the attributes that its critics appear to want to grant it – then take away. Inconsistency, so often talked about by critics, is for supporters entirely to be expected given the history and composition of the UN Security Council. A slippage from mandate to operations is again all too predictable given how little operational control the fifteen-member Security Council (and Secretariat) is able to exercise upon those countries doing the implementation. In Thakur's words, 'The R2P consensus underpinning Resolution 1973 on Libya was damaged by gaps in expectation, communication, and accountability between those who mandated the operation and those who executed it.'[57]

The chapter has shown the value of thinking about R2P as a specific regime within a world order in which manifest tensions exist within and between primary and secondary institutions. Such a framework problematises the traditional English School claim that only solidarism represents pro-humanitarian intervention. Rather, by looking at world order, we see how pluralism and solidarism coexist. A practical and normative task for theory is to disentangle the configuration. It can do this by giving greater clarity to the meta-value (protection not democracy promotion) and by reassuring sovereign states that R2P is about strengthening their legitimacy rather than weakening their status as the constitutive members of international society.[58] Such arguments remind us that pluralism is not doctrinally opposed to humanitarian intervention, and, looking to the future, pluralism might actually lend the regime important support in R2P's unfinished quest to modify world order today.

---

[57] Ramesh Thakur, 'R2P after Libya and Syria: Engaging Emerging Powers', *The Washington Quarterly* 36:2 (2013), p. 72.

[58] See Simon Chesterman, Michael Ignatieff and Ramesh Thakur, eds, *Making States Work: State Failure and the Crisis of Governance* (Tokyo: United Nations University Press, 2005).

6 International law and the Responsibility to Protect

Michael Byers

'We surely have a responsibility to act when a nation's people are subjected to a regime such as Saddam's'.[1] During its short life, the Responsibility to Protect (R2P) has experienced gains and setbacks, with the greatest setback coming in March 2004 when Tony Blair invoked the concept in an attempt to justify the previous year's invasion of Iraq.

R2P is of interest to international lawyers and international relations scholars alike. It is a result of 'norm entrepreneurship'.[2] It achieved prominence quickly, with only four years separating its birth in 2001 from its inclusion in the United Nations World Summit Outcome Document in 2005. But with success came controversy and compromise. On the key issue of the use of military force, R2P has – by widespread agreement – been confined to the context of UN Security Council decision-making, where it remains permissive but non-binding.

This chapter examines the interaction between R2P, the prohibition on the use of force set out in the UN Charter and the discretionary power of the Security Council to determine the existence of a 'threat to the peace' and authorise military action.[3] It asks: to what degree, if any, has R2P become part of contemporary international law concerning the use of force? And what does the history of R2P tell us, more generally, about 'norm entrepreneurship' and processes of legal change?

---

[1] Tony Blair, 'Blair Terror Speech in Full', *BBC News*, 5 March 2004, www.news.bbc.co.uk /2/hi/3536131.stm.

[2] On norm entrepreneurs, see Martha Finnemore and Kathryn Sikkink, 'International Norm Dynamics and Political Change', International Organization 52 (1998) 887–917; Margaret Keck and Kathryn Sikkink, *Activists Beyond Borders: Advocacy Networks in International Politics* (Ithaca: Cornell University Press, 1998); Ian Johnstone, 'The Secretary-General as Norm Entrepreneur', in Simon Chesterman, ed, *Secretary or General?: The UN Secretary-General in World Politics* (Cambridge: Cambridge University Press, 2007), pp. 123–138.

[3] The broader aspects of R2P are well documented elsewhere. See, for example, Gareth Evans, *The Responsibility to Protect: Ending Mass Atrocity Crimes Once and for All* (Washington DC: Brookings Institution, 2008); Ramesh Thakur, *The Responsibility to Protect: Norms, Laws, and the Use of Force in International Politics* (London: Routledge, 2011).

The chapter concludes that R2P has neither acquired legal status as a new exception to the prohibition on the use of force, nor exerted much influence on the rest of the international legal system. At the same time, the concept may – on an ad hoc basis – be influencing how states respond when another state violates the law while seeking to prevent atrocities. If so, the principal legal effect of R2P might concern mitigation of the consequences of rule breaking, rather than any changes to the rules themselves.

The development of R2P

The central obligation of the 1945 UN Charter is set out in Article 2(4): 'All Members shall refrain in their international relations from the threat or use of force against the territorial integrity or political independence of any state, or in any other manner inconsistent with the Purposes of the United Nations.'[4] According to the international rules on treaty interpretation, a treaty 'shall be interpreted in good faith in accordance with the ordinary meaning to be given to the terms of the treaty in their context and in the light of its object and purpose'.[5] The ordinary meaning of Article 2(4) is clear: the use of force across borders is prohibited. This meaning is supported by the context of the terms and the object and purpose of the treaty, with the Charter's preamble affirming the determination of its members 'to ensure by the acceptance of principles and the institution of methods, that armed force shall not be used, save in the common interest'. The Charter allows only two exceptions to the prohibition: Security Council authorisation and the right of self-defence. Only the first of these exceptions is of much relevance to R2P.

Under Chapter VII, the Security Council has wide powers to 'determine the existence of any threat to the peace, breach of the peace, or act of aggression' and authorise military action. These powers went unexercised during the Cold War, apart from a possible authorisation in Korea in 1950 and a clear but tightly constrained authorisation concerning Rhodesia in 1966. In the latter situation, the Security Council took a significant step in determining that human rights violations – in this case the racist policies of a white minority government – constituted a threat to the peace. It imposed a wide-reaching embargo and, in Resolution 221, called upon the United Kingdom 'to prevent, by the use of force if

[4] United Nations Charter, www.un.org/en/documents/charter/.
[5] 1969 Vienna Convention on the Law of Treaties, Art. 31, www.untreaty.un.org/ilc/texts /instruments/english/conventions/1_1_1969.pdf. The Vienna Convention codified the customary international law of treaty interpretation, as to which see Lord McNair, *The Law of Treaties* (Oxford: Oxford University Press, 1961) pp. 366–382.

necessary, the arrival of vessels reasonably believed to be carrying oil destined for Southern Rhodesia'.[6]

Somalia (1992–1993)

Since the end of the Cold War, the Security Council has used Chapter VII in a number of human rights and humanitarian crises. In January 1992, the Council determined that civil strife and famine in Somalia constituted a threat to the peace and imposed an arms embargo.[7] Later that year, the Council authorised a UN-led peacekeeping force[8] as well as a second, US-led force with a broad mandate to 'use all necessary means to establish as soon as possible a secure environment for humanitarian relief operations'.[9] One year later, the killing of 18 US Army Rangers prompted a public outcry in the United States that led to the collapse of both the US- and UN-led operations. However, Somalia nevertheless represented an important step for the Security Council, which for the first time in the post-Cold War era had authorised the use of force for humanitarian ends.

Bosnia (1992–1995)

The post-Cold War break-up of Yugoslavia resulted in bloody cleavages between ethnic groups. In 1992, the Security Council used Chapter VII to establish a United Nations Protection Force in the former Yugoslavia (UNPROFOR) to provide basic peacekeeping.[10] The next year, it extended UNPROFOR's mandate to include the creation and protection of so-called safe havens for Bosnian civilians,[11] and in Resolution 836 it authorised North Atlantic Treaty Organization (NATO) aircraft to bomb Serbian weapons and supply lines, but only after specific targeting decisions were coordinated and approved by both NATO and the UN secretary-general.[12] As with the Somalia resolutions, Resolution 836 was significant in authorising force for humanitarian ends, but the complex mandate proved ineffective and, in 1995, more than 7,000 men and boys were slaughtered in Srebrenica as UN peacekeepers stood by, their pleas for NATO air support unanswered.

---

[6] SC Res. 221 (9 April 1966), www.un.org/documents/sc/res/1966/scres66.htm.
[7] SC Res. 733 (23 January 1992), www.un.org/documents/sc/res/1992/scres92.htm.
[8] SC Res. 755 (28 August 1992), www.un.org/documents/sc/res/1992/scres92.htm.
[9] SC Res. 794 (3 December 1992), www.un.org/documents/sc/res/1992/scres92.htm.
[10] SC Res. 743 (21 February 1992), www.un.org/documents/sc/res/1992/scres92.htm.
[11] SC Res. 819 (16 April 1993), www.un.org/docs/scres/1993/scres93.htm.
[12] SC Res. 836 (4 June 1993), www.un.org/docs/scres/1993/scres93.htm.

Rwanda (1994)

As the Rwandan genocide began in April 1994, the commander of a small UN peacekeeping operation desperately requested more troops. The Security Council responded by reducing his force from 2,500 to 270 peacekeepers. The withdrawal cannot be attributed to any lack of knowledge on the part of Security Council members. On 23 April, a classified document prepared for senior US officials spoke matter-of-factly about 'the genocide, which relief workers say is spreading south'.[13] Six days later, during a Security Council meeting, the British ambassador reportedly cautioned against designating the massacre as 'genocide' because doing so might compel a response.[14] As in Bosnia, where inadequate and complex mandates hindered action, the problem was a lack of political will. And yet the failure to act in Rwanda might subsequently have shamed some countries into action in Kosovo.

Kosovo (1999)

In 1999, NATO countries launched an air campaign to protect the population of Kosovo from Serbian paramilitaries. The intervention took place without Security Council authorisation and despite the strong objections of Russia, China and numerous developing countries. Although the United Kingdom claimed a right of 'unilateral' (i.e., not Security Council authorised) humanitarian intervention,[15] the United States was more circumspect, referring repeatedly to 'humanitarian concerns' but never explicitly claiming a third exception to the prohibition on the use of force.[16]

---

[13] Central Intelligence Agency, 'National Intelligence Daily', 23 April 2004, www.gwu.edu /~nsarchiv/NSAEBB/NSAEBB117/Rw34.pdf.

[14] Linda Melvern, *A People Betrayed: The Role of the West in Rwanda's Genocide* (London: Zed Books, 2000), p. 180.

[15] See Sir Jeremy Greenstock, UK Permanent Representative to the UN, Statement to the Security Council on 24 March 1999, UN Doc. S/PV. 3988, pp. 11–12, reproduced in *British Yearbook of International Law* 70 (1999), pp. 580–581. See also: *4th Report of the House of Commons Foreign Affairs Committee*, HC-28-I (2000), which points out that the UK government justified humanitarian intervention only 'as an exceptional measure in support of purposes laid down by the UN Security Council ... where that is the only means to overt an immediate and overwhelming humanitarian catastrophe'.

[16] See, for example, 'In the President's Words: "We Act to Prevent a Wider War"', *New York Times*, 25 March 1999. After the war, Secretary of State Madeleine Albright stressed that Kosovo was 'a unique situation *sui generis* in the region of the Balkans' and that it was important 'not to overdraw the various lessons that come out of it'. Press conference with Russian Foreign Minister Igor Ivanov, Singapore, 26 July 1999, cited in International Commission on Intervention and State Sovereignty (ICISS), *The Responsibility to Protect: Research, Bibliography, Background* (Ottawa: International Development Research Centre, 2001), p. 128.

Germany supported the NATO action but insisted it 'must not be allowed to become a precedent'.[17]

The Kosovo War put proponents of human rights and humanitarian assistance in a difficult position. UN Secretary General Kofi Annan's initial reaction was to say: 'Emerging slowly, but I believe surely, is an international norm against the violent repression of minorities that will and must take precedence over concerns of sovereignty.'[18] Following the war, the United Kingdom proposed a framework for a limited right of unilateral humanitarian intervention. According to the British criteria, armed force should only be used as a last resort, in the face of 'an overwhelming humanitarian catastrophe, which the government has shown it is unwilling or unable to prevent or is actively promoting'. The force 'should be proportionate to achieving the humanitarian purpose', carried out 'in accordance with international law', and 'collective'.[19] But the Kosovo War did nothing to alleviate concerns about powerful states abusing any new right to intervene. In 1999 and 2000, the 133 developing states of the Group of 77 twice adopted declarations that unequivocally affirmed the illegality of humanitarian interventions not specifically authorised by the Security Council.[20]

This negative reaction is probably what caused Annan, later in 1999, to acknowledge that no norm of unilateral humanitarian intervention had yet achieved legal status, and that any such norm could have undesirable consequences for the international order: 'What is clear is that enforcement action without Security Council authorisation threatens the very core of the international security system founded on the Charter of the UN. Only the Charter provides a universally accepted legal basis for the use of force.'[21]

---

[17] Foreign Minister Klaus Kinkel said: 'With their decision, NATO states did not intend to create any new legal instrument that could ground a general power of authority of NATO for intervention. The NATO decision must not be allowed to become a precedent. We must not enter onto a slippery slope with respect to the Security Council's monopoly on the use of force'. Deutscher Bundestag, Plenarprotokoll 13/248, 16 October 1998, p. 23129 (my translation), German original available at: www.dip21.bundestag.de/dip21 /btp/13/13248.asc.

[18] Kofi Annan, Statement by Secretary-General of the United Nations – 55th session of the Commission on Human Rights, Geneva, 7 April 1999; text reprinted in Kofi Annan, 'No government has the right to hide behind national sovereignty in order to violate human rights', *Guardian*, 7 April 1999, www.guardian.co.uk/world /1999/apr/07/balkans.unitednations.

[19] Foreign Secretary Robin Cook, 'Speech to the American Bar Association, 19 July 2000', *British Yearbook of International Law* 71 (2000), p. 646.

[20] See Ministerial Declaration, 23rd Annual Meeting of the Ministers for Foreign Affairs of the Group of 77, 24 September 1999, paragraph 69, www.g77.org/doc/Decl1999.html; Declaration of the Group of 77 South Summit, Havana, Cuba, 10–14 April 2000, paragraph 54, www.g77.org/doc/docs/summitfinaldocs_english.pdf.

[21] Kofi Annan, *Preventing War and Disaster*, Annual Report on the Work of the Organization (United Nations, 1999) p. 8, paragraph 66, www.daccess-dds-ny.un.org/doc/UNDOC /GEN/N99/246/59/PDF/N9924659.pdf.

The International Commission on Intervention and State Sovereignty (2001)

After the Kosovo War, the Canadian government established the International Commission on Intervention and State Sovereignty (ICISS) and charged it with finding 'some new common ground'.[22] However, a careful reading of ICISS report, released in December 2001 and entitled *The Responsibility to Protect*, shows the commissioners failing to agree on the central issue of the use of force. Some passages seem to favour a right of humanitarian intervention in the absence of Security Council authorisation:

> Based on our reading of state practice, Security Council precedent, established norms, emerging guiding principles, and evolving customary international law, the Commission believes that the Charter's strong bias against military intervention is not to be regarded as absolute when decisive action is required on human protection grounds.[23]

Other passages lean the other way, albeit with a nod to the 'Uniting for Peace' resolution adopted by the General Assembly in 1950:

> As a matter of political reality, it would be impossible to find consensus . . . around any set of proposals for military intervention which acknowledge the validity of any intervention not authorized by the Security Council or General Assembly.[24]

In addition to coining the term 'responsibility to protect', the ICISS usefully expanded the focus of attention to include preventive and post-crisis measures. But it did little to resolve the controversy over unilateral humanitarian intervention, leaving that for states to decide.

The Constitutive Act of the African Union (2002)

In 2002, the Organization of African Unity renamed and reconstituted itself through the Constitutive Act of the African Union.[25] Part of the reconstitution was a provision described by Dan Kuwali as 'by and large,

---

[22] *The Responsibility to Protect* (Ottawa: International Development Research Centre, 2001), p. vii.

[23] Ibid., p. 16, paragraph 2.27.

[24] Ibid., pp. 54–55, paragraph 6.36. On 'Uniting for Peace' see UNGA Res. A-RES-377(V) (3 November 1950), www.un.org/depts/dhl/resguide/r5.htm; and Dominik Zaum, 'The Security Council, the General Assembly and War: The Uniting for Peace Resolution', in Vaughan Lowe, Adam Roberts, Jennifer Welsh and Dominik Zaum, eds, *The United Nations Security Council and War: The Evolution of Thought and Practice since 1945* (Oxford: Oxford University Press, 2008), p. 154.

[25] Constitutive Act of the African Union, 11 July 2002, OAU Doc. CAB/LEG/23.15, www.africa-union.org/root/au/aboutau/constitutive_act_en.htm.

on all fours with the notion of R2P'.[26] Article 4(h) asserts the 'right of the Union to intervene in a Member State pursuant to a decision of the Assembly [of Heads of State and Government] in respect of grave circumstances, namely: war crimes, genocide and crimes against humanity'.[27] Article 4(h) also implies that African Union member states do not consider themselves bound to obtain UN Security Council authorisation when using force collectively in response to such atrocities.[28]

Despite having faced some major human rights and humanitarian crises, the African Union has yet to invoke Article 4(h). Paul Williams has identified three possible reasons for this: 'first, the strength of the host state; second, the residual power of the principles of noninterference and anti-imperialism within the African society of states; and third, the AU's lack of practical military capacity for humanitarian intervention'.[29] A fourth and equally important reason may be that, whenever the African Union has wished to intervene in a human rights or humanitarian crisis, the UN Security Council has provided a Chapter VII resolution.

There may well be a causal connection between the 2001 ICISS report and the Constitutive Act of the African Union, since the former preceded the latter by just six months. At the same time, the right asserted in Article 4(h) is entirely consistent with established international law because the member states of the African Union, when ratifying the Constitutive Act, consented to the new power.[30] Article 4(h) is analogous to Chapter VII, where the powers of the Security Council are derived from the consent expressed by member states when ratifying the UN Charter. For this reason, Article 4(h) is not a precedent for unilateral humanitarian intervention, even if it does create a new, strictly regional, treaty-based exception to the prohibition on the use of force.

---

[26] Dan Kuwali, 'The End of Humanitarian Intervention: Evaluation of the African Union's Right of Intervention', *African Journal on Conflict Resolution* 9:1 (2009), p. 48.

[27] In 2003, the adoption of a 'Protocol relating to the establishment of the Peace and Security Council of the African Union' provided an implementing mechanism for decisions to intervene taken by the Assembly; www.africa-union.org/root/au/organs/psc /Protocol_peace%20and%20security.pdf.

[28] Art. 17 (1)of the Protocol (ibid.) reads: 'In the fulfillment of its mandate in the promotion and maintenance of peace, security and stability in Africa, the Peace and Security Council shall cooperate and work closely with the United Nations Security Council, which has the primary responsibility for the maintenance of international peace and security'. Nothing in the words 'cooperate and work closely with' or 'primary responsibility' implies a relationship of legal dependence.

[29] Paul D. Williams, *The African Union's Conflict Management Capabilities*, Council on Foreign Relations, October 2011, p. 5, www.cfr.org/content/publications/attach ments/IIGG_WorkingPaper7.pdf.

[30] See, similarly, Kuwali, 'The end of Humanitarian Intervention', pp. 45–46.

The Iraq War (2003)

Again, Tony Blair has provided a worrisome example of how R2P could be abused. One year after the Iraq War, the British prime minister implied that a right of unilateral humanitarian intervention already existed in situations of 'humanitarian catastrophe':

It may well be that under international law as presently constituted, a regime can systematically brutalise and oppress its people and there is nothing anyone can do, when dialogue, diplomacy and even sanctions fail, *unless* it comes within the definition of a humanitarian catastrophe.[31]

He then invoked R2P in support of a right to intervene in less severe circumstances:

The essence of a community is common rights and responsibilities. We have obligations in relation to each other ... We do not accept in a community that others have a right to oppress and brutalise their people. We value the freedom and dignity of the human race and each individual in it. Emphatically I am not saying that every situation leads to military action. But ... we surely have a responsibility to act when a nation's people are subjected to a regime such as Saddam's.[32]

Thus, a war that Blair had previously sought to justify with contested readings of Security Council resolutions was suddenly being rationalised with a concept that, as a possible legal basis for force, had already been widely rejected by most governments.[33] This development was of pivotal importance for the future direction of R2P.

The High-Level Panel on Threats, Challenges and Change (2004)

After Blair's invocation of R2P, many proponents of the concept refocused their efforts on addressing the problem of political will within the context of existing legal constraints. This adjustment was visible in a speech given to the UN General Assembly by Canadian Prime Minister Paul Martin in

---

[31] Blair, 'Blair terror speech in full', emphasis added.
[32] Ibid. However, ICISS co-chair Evans and Commissioner Thakur were quick to reject the relevance of R2P to the Iraq war: Gareth Evans, 'Humanity Did Not Justify This War', *Financial Times*, 15 May 2003; Ramesh Thakur, 'Chrétien Was Right: It's Time to Redefine a "just war"', *Globe and Mail* (Toronto), 22 July 2003.
[33] Russian Foreign Minister Sergey Lavrov likewise invoked the term 'responsibility to protect' to justify the invasion of Georgia in 2008, but it is clear that he was referring to a principle in Russian *domestic* law concerning the duty of the Russian government to protect its citizens. See 'Interview by Minister of Foreign Affairs of the Russian Federation Sergey Lavrov to BBC', Moscow, 9 August 2008, www.un.int/russia/new/MainRoot/docs/off_news/090808 /newen2.htm.

September 2004.[34] Martin stressed that the 'responsibility to protect is not a licence for intervention; it is an international guarantor of political accountability'. Although 'customary international law is evolving to provide a solid basis in the building of a normative framework for collective humanitarian intervention', this basis was not yet complete. Martin called for the Security Council to 'establish new thresholds for when the international community judges that civilian populations face extreme threats'.

In December 2004, the UN secretary-general's High-Level Panel on Threats, Challenges and Change reported that 'the Council and the wider international community have come to accept that, under Chapter VII ... it can always authorize military action to redress catastrophic internal wrongs if it is prepared to declare that the situation is a "threat to international peace and security", [which is] not especially difficult when breaches of international law are involved'.[35] With respect to R2P specifically, the Panel wrote:

There is a growing recognition that the issue is not the 'right to intervene' of any State, but the 'responsibility to protect' of *every* State when it comes to people suffering from avoidable catastrophe – mass murder and rape, ethnic cleansing by forcible expulsion and terror, and deliberate starvation and exposure to disease.[36]

The Panel stressed that this 'emerging norm' was – in terms of military intervention – only 'exercisable by the Security Council'.[37] Echoing the ICISS report, the Panel proposed 'criteria of legitimacy' for when force should be used: seriousness of intent, proper purpose, last resort, proportional means, and balance of consequences.[38] It recommended that these criteria be embodied in declaratory resolutions of the Security Council and General Assembly.[39]

The secretary-general's report and World Summit Outcome Document (2005)

In March 2005, Kofi Annan issued a report entitled 'In Larger Freedom' in which he endorsed R2P while affirming the Security Council's monopoly on the use of force:

[34] 'Address by Prime Minister Paul Martin at the United Nations', 21 September 2004, www.news.gc.ca/web/article-eng.do?crtr.sj1D=&mthd=advSrch&crtr.mnthndVl=&nid=98589&crtr.dpt1D=&crtr.tp1D=&crtr.lc1D=&crtr.yrStrtVl=&crtr.kw=Haiti&crtr.dyStrtVl=&crtr.aud1D=&crtr.mnthStrtVl=&crtr.yrndVl=&crtr.dyndVl.

[35] *A More Secure World: Our Shared Responsibility*. Report of the High-Level Panel on Threats, Challenges and Change, Document A/59/565 (New York: United Nations, 2004), p. 57, paragraph 202, www.un.org/secureworld/report.pdf.

[36] Ibid., pp. 56–57, paragraph 201, emphasis in original.

[37] Ibid., p. 57, paragraph 203.   [38] Ibid., pp. 57–58, paragraph 207.

[39] Ibid., p. 58, paragraph 208.

If national authorities are unable or unwilling to protect their citizens, then the responsibility shifts to the international community to use diplomatic, humanitarian and other methods to help protect the human rights and well-being of civilian populations. When such methods appear insufficient, the Security Council may out of necessity decide to take action under the Charter of the United Nations, including enforcement action, if so required.[40]

Six months later, at the conclusion of the UN World Summit, the member states not only endorsed R2P; they declared themselves 'prepared to take collective action ... in a timely and decisive manner'.[41] However, they also specified that any such action would take place 'through the Security Council, in accordance with the Charter, including Chapter VII', that it would only be 'on a case-by-case basis', and only 'should peaceful means be inadequate and national authorities are manifestly failing to protect their populations from genocide, war crimes, ethnic cleansing and crimes against humanity'.

The inclusion of R2P in the 'World Summit Outcome Document' was a significant development. At the same time, the role of the concept was deliberately limited by: (1) the reaffirmation of the exclusivity of Security Council decision-making;[42] (2) the use of non-committal language such as 'prepared' and 'on a case-by-case basis'; and (3) the raising of the ICISS threshold of 'population suffering serious harm' to 'genocide, war crimes, ethnic cleansing, and crimes against humanity'. Moreover, the World Summit Outcome Document did not create any new rights, obligations or limitations for the Security Council, since the Council already had the discretionary power to authorise force for the full range of human rights and humanitarian concerns. At the most, the World Summit Outcome Document created a new point of *political* leverage, since proponents of action can now point to this collective statement of intent.

---

[40] Kofi A. Annan, *In Larger Freedom: Towards Development, Security and Human Rights for All*. Report of the Secretary-General, Document A/59/2005 (New York: United Nations, 21 March 2005), paragraphs 132 and 135, www.un.org/largerfreedom/con tents.htm.

[41] *World Summit Outcome*, Document A/RES/60/1 (New York: United Nations, 24 October 2005), paragraphs 138–139, www.un.org/summit2005/documents.html.

[42] That said, Carsten Stahn has argued that 'states did not categorically reject the option of (individual or collective) unilateral action in the Outcome Document. This discrepancy leaves some leeway to argue that the concept of responsibility to protect is not meant to rule out such action in the future'. Carsten Stahn, 'Responsibility to Protect: Political Rhetoric or Emerging Legal Norm?' *American Journal of International Law* 101 (2007), p. 120. However, as a general principle of interpretation, a text's silence on any particular issue does not imply a gap.

Security Council Resolution 1674 (2006)

In April 2006, the Security Council followed the recommendation of the High-Level Panel by adopting a declaratory resolution. Resolution 1674 addresses numerous aspects of the 'protection of civilians in armed conflict', including R2P. Paragraph 4 *'Reaffirms* the provisions of paragraphs 138 and 139 of the World Summit Outcome Document regarding the responsibility to protect populations from genocide, war crimes, ethnic cleansing and crimes against humanity'.[43] It thus confirms the Council's post-Cold War practice of including human rights and humanitarian crises within the scope of possible determinations of 'threats to the peace'. However, it does not signal or contribute to any change in international law, because the scope of the Council's discretionary power is so very wide that, from a legal perspective, it might only be limited by *jus cogens* rules.[44]

The adoption of Resolution 1674 might increase the likelihood of the Security Council acting in situations of 'genocide, war crimes, ethnic cleansing and crimes against humanity', but only because its references to R2P and the World Summit Outcome Document gives proponents of action an additional point of political leverage. It is important to note that the resolution does not include any criteria such as those recommended by the High-Level Panel. Nor did the Council follow the lead of the General Assembly and declare it was 'prepared to take collective action . . . in a timely and decisive manner'.

The greatest challenge with respect to humanitarian and human rights crises remains generating the political will to act, which in the context of the Security Council means both adopting *and* implementing a resolution. That political will is required over both stages was demonstrated with respect to Darfur. In August 2006, after more than two years of atrocities, the Security Council finally used its Chapter VII powers to authorise the deployment of a UN peacekeeping force with a robust mandate to protect civilians.[45] Resolution 1706 made an indirect reference to R2P by noting that Resolution 1674 'reaffirms inter alia the

---

[43] United Nations, Security Resolution 1674 (28 April 2006), www.un.org/en/sc/docu ments/resolutions/2006.shtml, emphasis in original.

[44] See Separate Opinion of Judge ad hoc E. Lauterpacht, *Application of the Convention on the Prevention and Punishment of the Crime of Genocide* (Bosnia and Herzegovina v. Serbia and Montenegro), Order of 13 September 1993, p. 440, paragraph 100, www.icj-cij.org /docket/files/91/7323.pdf.

[45] In paragraph 12 of Resolution 1706, adopted on 31 August 2006, the Security Council, 'Acting under Chapter VII of the Charter of the United Nations: (a) *Decides* that UNMIS is authorized to use all necessary means, in the areas of deployment of its forces and as it deems within its capabilities . . . to protect civilians under threat of physical violence'; www.un.org/en/sc/documents/resolutions/2006.shtml.

provisions of paragraphs 138 and 139 of the 2005 United Nations World Summit outcome document'.[46] However, most governments, instead of rushing to participate in this new and legally robust mission, either ignored the authorisation or cited commitments elsewhere.[47]

Resolution 1973 (Libya, 2011)

In March 2011, Libyan dictator Muammar Gaddafi used deadly force against peaceful protesters and threatened to show no mercy to the residents of rebel-held cities.[48] The Security Council responded by adopting Resolution 1973, which provided two parallel authorisations to use force, the first of which was much broader than the second.[49]

In paragraph four, the Council: '*Authorizes* Member States ... to take all necessary measures ... to protect civilians and civilian populated areas under threat of attack in the Libyan Arab Jamahiriya, including Benghazi, while excluding a foreign occupation force of any form on any part of Libyan territory.' This first authorisation would cover a great deal of military activity, because 'all necessary measures' is the language normally used by the Council to grant full powers to intervening countries.[50] Even the exclusion of a 'foreign occupation force' does not preclude the use of some ground forces, since 'occupation' is a technical term of international humanitarian law defined in the 1907 Hague Regulations: 'Territory is considered occupied when it is actually placed under the authority of the hostile army. The occupation extends only to the territory where such authority has been established and can be exercised.'[51]

The second authorisation that deals with airspace is arguably redundant. It appears in paragraph six, where the Council '*Decides* to establish a ban on all flights in the airspace of the Libyan Arab Jamahiriya in order to help protect civilians', and in paragraph eight, where the Council

---

[46] Ibid.

[47] See, for example, 'UN force for Darfur takes shape', *New York Times*, 1 August 2007, www.nytimes.com/2007/08/01/world/africa/01iht-darfur.4.6942617.html?_r=0.

[48] In one TV broadcast, Gaddafi told the residents of Benghazi to lay down their arms; otherwise, he warned, his troops would come that night and 'find you in your closets; we will have no mercy and no pity'. Dan Bilefsky and Mark Landler, 'As U.N. Backs Military Action in Libya, U.S. Role Is Unclear', *New York Times*, 17 March 2011, www.nytimes.com/2011/03/18/world/africa/18nations.html.

[49] SC Res. 1973 (17 March 2011), www.un.org/en/sc/documents/resolutions/2011.shtml, all emphases below in original.

[50] Of course, all military actions remain subject to the rules of international humanitarian law, including those set out in the 1949 Geneva Conventions.

[51] Art. 42, Hague Regulations concerning the Laws and Customs of War on Land, as annexed to the 1907 Convention (IV) respecting the Laws and Customs of War on Land, www.icrc.org/ihl.nsf/FULL/195?OpenDocument.

'*Authorizes* Member States ... to take all necessary measures to enforce compliance with the ban on flights imposed by paragraph 6 above, as necessary'.

Resolution 1973 does not endorse an expansive conception of R2P, with just one paragraph in the preamble making reference to it: '*Reiterating* the responsibility of the Libyan authorities to protect the Libyan population and *reaffirming* that parties to armed conflicts bear the primary responsibility to take all feasible steps to ensure the protection of civilians.'[52] Apart from the word 'primary', there is nothing in the paragraph that suggests a responsibility to protect on the part of outside countries.

Resolution 1973 also fails to declare that any of the crimes identified by the World Summit Outcome Document as falling within the ambit of R2P were actually taking place. Although the resolution condemns 'the gross and systematic violation of human rights, including arbitrary detentions, enforced disappearances, torture and summary executions', it adopts a decidedly cautious stance as to these actually being crimes against humanity: '*Considering* that the widespread and systematic attacks currently taking place in the Libyan Arab Jamahiriya against the civilian population may amount to crimes against humanity.'

Resolution 1973 is consistent with R2P insofar as it authorises the use of force for human rights purposes.[53] But in terms of the development of R2P, Resolution 1973 proves only that the concept has become part of the context of Security Council deliberations. Of course, in some situations that role as context may still be significant.

Post-Libya consequences for R2P

There are those who believe that R2P was set back by the controversy over NATO's campaign in Libya, and that this reversal is evident in the lack of a meaningful response to the Syrian civil war.[54] As Vitaly Churkin, Russia's ambassador to the United Nations, said:

[52] Similar references appear in the preambles of SC Res. 1975 (30 March 2011, Côte d'Ivoire), SC Res. 1996 (8 July 2011, South Sudan) and SC Res. 2014 (21 October 2011, Yemen).

[53] That human rights were the principal motivating factor behind Resolution 1973 is supported by the fact that, at the time of the intervention, the Libyan regime posed no threat to other countries. Gaddafi forswore his nuclear and chemical weapons programmes in 2003 and was removed from the US list of state sponsors of terror in 2006.

[54] See, for example, Gareth Evans and Ramesh Thakur: 'The R2P consensus underpinning Resolution 1973 fell apart over the course of 2011, damaged by gaps in expectation, communication, and accountability between those who mandated the operation and those who executed it', 'Correspondence: Humanitarian Intervention and the Responsibility to Protect', *International Security* 37:4 (2013), p. 206; Spencer Zifcak,

The situation in Syria cannot be considered in the Council separately from the Libyan experience. The international community is alarmed by statements that compliance with Security Council resolutions on Libya in the NATO interpretation is a model for the future actions of NATO in implementing the Responsibility to Protect.[55]

However, the authorisations in Resolution 1973 gave space for different public positions concerning the permissible extent of force.[56] This would not be the first time the Security Council has crafted a resolution with a view to providing room for divergent interpretations.[57] The result is an intermediate zone on the legal–illegal spectrum of military action: between the legal and the illegal, there is now the deliberately arguable. One benefit of this grey zone is that it provides space for states to disagree in public while 'agreeing to disagree' in private. Another benefit may be that it creates a form of temporary, conditional permission that can harden into legality or illegality – depending on how contested facts are subsequently clarified, for instance, by the presence or absence of weapons of mass destruction, or the actual existence and scale of atrocities.

It is also significant that Resolution 1973 had the support of the Arab League. Indeed, the resolution refers explicitly to 'the decision of the Council of the League of Arab States of 12 March 2011 to call for the imposition of a no-fly zone on Libyan military aviation, and to establish safe areas in places exposed to shelling as a precautionary measure that allows the protection of the Libyan people and foreign nationals residing in the Libyan Arab Jamahiriya'. The involvement of the Arab League made it politically difficult for China and Russia to cast their vetoes, and thus increased the incentive to agree on language that enabled the resolution to be interpreted in different ways.

The Arab League has also been active with respect to the Syrian crisis: suspending Syria's membership in the League, imposing economic sanctions, pushing for a Security Council resolution that would have called on President Bashar al-Assad to step aside, and proposing a UN-authorised

'The Responsibility to Protect after Libya and Syria', *Melbourne Journal of International Law* 13:1 (2012), pp. 59–93; Noele Crossley, 'The Responsibility to Protect in 2012: R2P fails in Syria, Brazil's "RWP" Emerges', *Global Policy Journal Blog*, 28 December 2012, www.globalpolicyjournal.com/blog/28/12/2012/responsibility-protect -2012-r2p-fails-syria-brazil's-'rwp'-emer.

[55] UN SCOR, 66th session, 6627th meeting, UN Doc S/PV.6627 (4 October 2011), p. 4.
[56] As Hugh Roberts writes, 'Those who subsequently said that they did not know that regime change had been authorised either did not understand the logic of events or were pretending to misunderstand in order to excuse their failure to oppose it'. Roberts, 'Who said Gaddafi had to go?', *London Review of Books* 33:22 (17 November 2011), www.lrb.co.uk/v33/n22/hugh-roberts/who-said-gaddafi-had-to-go.
[57] Michael Byers, 'Agreeing to Disagree: Security Council Resolution 1441 and Intentional Ambiguity', *Global Governance* 10:2 (2004), pp. 165–186.

peacekeeping mission.[58] However, there are many factors associated with Security Council decision-making. In the case of Syria, complicating factors include its geographic location, the presence of Russian electronic intelligence-gathering and naval facilities, and advanced air defences which would likely cause the loss of aircraft and pilots if any attempt was made to impose a no-fly zone.[59]

The controversy concerning the implementation of Resolution 1973 in Libya will eventually subside, for there is more pragmatism in international relations than the public statements of governments might indicate. The concept of R2P will survive, and have influence politically, even if it never changes the core prohibition on the use of force.

The legal status of R2P

Prior to Blair's 2004 speech, much of the literature on R2P either continued the debate that had previously been framed as 'unilateral humanitarian intervention', or discussed the concept in the post-9/11 context of self-defence and preventive military action.[60] However, even before Blair's demonstration of the potential for the abuse of R2P by powerful states, it was already apparent that the threshold for changing the prohibition on the use of force was unachievable. Both the widespread opposition of developing states and the *jus cogens* character of the prohibition rendered the idea of an R2P exception a non-starter in a legal system where rules are changed through the actions and opinions of nearly 200 states, and where a small number of rules are more deeply entrenched than the others.[61] Gareth Evans, one of the 'norm entrepreneurs'; behind R2P, has summarised the new consensus: 'The 2005 General Assembly position was very clear that, when any country seeks to apply forceful means to address an R2P situation, it must do so through the Security Council ... Vigilante justice is always dangerous.'[62]

---

[58] 'The League and Syria', in 'Times Topics: Arab League', *New York Times* website, at www .topics.nytimes.com/topics/reference/timestopics/organizations/a/arab_league/index.html.

[59] Julian Borger, 'Russian military presence in Syria poses challenge to US-led intervention', *Guardian*, 23 December 2012, www.guardian.co.uk/world/2012/dec/23/syria -crisis-russian-military-presence.

[60] See, perhaps most problematically, Lee Feinstein and Anne-Marie Slaughter, 'A Duty to Prevent', *Foreign Affairs* 83:1 (2004), pp. 136–150.

[61] See Michael Byers and Simon Chesterman, 'Changing the Rules about Rules? Unilateral Humanitarian Intervention and the Future of International Law', in J.L. Holzgrefe and Robert O. Keohane, eds, *Humanitarian Intervention: Ethical, Legal and Political Dilemmas* (Cambridge: Cambridge University Press, 2003), pp. 183–184.

[62] Gareth Evans, 'Russia and the "responsibility to protect"', *Los Angeles Times*, 31 August 2008, www.latimes.com/news/opinion/commentary/la-oe-evans31-2008aug31,0,363 2207.story.

This chapter could end here: with the conclusion that R2P, insofar as it concerns the use of force, is now limited to being part of the context of Security Council decision-making. However, it may prove useful to extend the analysis one step further by examining whether R2P is having any influence on the margins of the prohibition on the use of force, and specifically on the rules proscribing the provision of aid, assistance, training, equipment and arms to rebels.[63]

Support for rebels

The prohibition on the use of force has long been understood to encompass the provision of aid, assistance, training, equipment, and arms to rebels.[64] In 1970, the UN General Assembly adopted a 'Friendly Relations Resolution' that encapsulated the rule in two paragraphs:

> Every State has the duty to refrain from organizing, instigating, assisting or participating in acts of civil strife or terrorist acts in another State or acquiescing in organized activities within its territory directed towards the commission of such acts, when the acts referred to in the present paragraph involve a threat or use of force . . .
>   Also, no State shall organize, assist, foment, finance, incite or tolerate subversive, terrorist or armed activities directed towards the violent overthrow of the régime of another State, or interfere in civil strife in another State.[65]

Although the rule was often violated during the Cold War, as the two superpowers engaged in 'proxy wars', it was not altered by that contrary practice. One explanation for the lack of change is that support for rebels was usually provided covertly, and only overt actions can contribute to changing international law.[66]

---

[63] As the International Court of Justice explained in the *Nicaragua Case*, it is sometimes necessary 'to distinguish the most grave forms of the use of force (those constituting an armed attack) from other less grave forms'. *Military and Paramilitary Activities in and against Nicaragua* (Nicaragua v. US), (1986) ICJ Reports 14, p. 101, paragraph 191, www.icj-cij.org/docket/files/70/6503.pdf.

[64] See Ian Brownlie, *International Law and the Use of Force by States* (Oxford: Oxford University Press, 1963), pp. 370–371. The only possible and controversial exception to this ban has concerned the provision of support to groups engaged in wars of 'national liberation'. For example, in 1981 the UN General Assembly appealed 'to all States to provide all necessary humanitarian, educational, financial and other necessary assistance to the oppressed people of South Africa and their national liberation movement in their legitimate struggle'. GA Res. 36/172 (1981), paragraph 16, www.daccess-dds-ny.un.org /doc/RESOLUTION/GEN/NR0/407/98/IMG/NR040798.pdf.

[65] Declaration on Principles of International Law Concerning Friendly Relations and Cooperation Among States in Accordance with the Charter of the United Nations, GA Res. 2625 (1970), www.un.org/ga/search/view_doc.asp?symbol=A/RES/2625(XXV).

[66] See Anthony D'Amato, *The Concept of Custom in International Law* (Ithaca: Cornell University Press, 1971), p. 469, where the author writes, with respect to the widespread

The rule was affirmed in the 1986 *Nicaragua Case* where the International Court of Justice found that the United States had illegally trained and equipped rebels. The Court addressed the possibility that the law might be different when rebels have a 'particularly worthy' cause:

[The Court] has to consider whether there might be indications of a practice illustrative of belief in a kind of general right for States to intervene, directly or indirectly, with or without armed force, in support of an internal opposition in another State, whose cause appeared particularly worthy by reason of the political and moral values with which it was identified. For such a general right to come into existence would involve a fundamental modification of the customary law principle of non-intervention.[67]

The Court went on to emphasise that, 'for a new customary rule to be formed, not only must the acts concerned "amount to a settled practice," but they must be accompanied by the *opinio juris sive necessitates*'. In short, 'Reliance by a State on a novel right or an unprecedented exception to the principle might, if shared in principle by other States, tend towards a modification of customary international law', but only if states 'justified their conduct by reference to a new right of intervention or a new exception to the principle of its prohibition'.[68] The Court in the *Nicaragua Case* found neither a settled practice nor evidence of *opinio juris*.

The end of the Cold War brought three developments that might have affected the rule. First, there was an increase in the practice of selling weapons to rebel groups, as arms producers, squeezed by a reduction in military spending by NATO and former Warsaw Pact countries, became less scrupulous about their buyers.[69] Second, and as explained above, the Security Council expanded its conception of 'threat to the peace' to include human rights and humanitarian crises. Third, a difficult debate about unilateral humanitarian intervention took place, which ultimately led to the ICISS reframing the issue as 'responsibility to protect'.

The debate about unilateral humanitarian intervention has also spilled over into an academic debate over the permissibility of supplying weapons to rebels who are fighting to prevent atrocities.[70] There are authors who support arms transfers based on an inherent right to self-defence against

---

use of torture by states, that the 'objective evidence shows hiding, cover-up, minimization, and non-justification – all the things that betoken a violation of the law'.

[67] *Nicaragua Case*, p. 108, paragraph 206.   [68] Ibid., pp. 108–109, paragraph 206.

[69] See Joanna Spear, 'Arms Limitations, Confidence-Building Measures, and Internal Conflict', in Michael Edward Brown, ed, *The International Dimensions of Internal Conflict* (Cambridge, MA: Center for Science and International Affairs, 1996), pp. 377–410.

[70] See Frédéric Mégret, 'Beyond the "Salvation" Paradigm: Responsibility To Protect (Others) vs the Power of Protecting Oneself', *Security Dialogue* 40:6 (2009), pp. 575–595.

genocide,[71] and those who accept the 'normative legitimacy' of such transfers but insist on the continued requirement of 'some form of approval within the UN system'.[72] However, there has been little movement with respect to state practice and *opinio juris*, as an examination of some recent developments demonstrates.

Bosnia-Herzegovina

Bosnia-Herzegovina was recognised as an independent state before Iran began shipping weapons in 1994 in an effort to help the Bosnian government counter well-armed Serbian paramilitaries who were committing atrocities against civilians. As a result, the legal controversy that ensued was not over any possible infraction of the rule prohibiting arms shipments to rebels, but rather of the apparent violation of a UN arms embargo that had been imposed on both sides.

Nevertheless, the situation cast some light on whether – and how – the justness of a cause might matter to the legality of weapons shipments. When the *Los Angeles Times* reported that the United States had known about the Iranian shipments and failed to discourage them,[73] the White House responded that it had 'upheld the letter of the law and the requirements of the U.N. Security Council resolution' imposing the embargo.[74] But another newspaper reported an anonymous US official as saying: 'Were we in a position to stop them? Not really. And was there sympathy for Bosnia here? The answer is, yes.'[75]

Libya

In February 2011, the Security Council imposed an arms embargo on Libya by way of paragraph 9 of Resolution 1970.[76] One month later it adopted Resolution 1973, which authorised 'all necessary measures,

---

[71] Daniel D. Polsby and Don B. Kates, 'Of Holocausts and Gun Control', *Washington University Law Quarterly* 75:3 (1997), pp. 1237–1275.

[72] Kenneth D. Heath, 'Could We Have Armed the Kosovo Liberation Army – The New Norms Governing Intervention in Civil War', *UCLA Journal of International Law and Foreign Affairs* 4 (1999–2000), p. 259.

[73] James Risen and Doyle McManus, 'U.S. OKd Iranian Arms for Bosnia, Officials Say', *Los Angeles Times*, April 1996, www.articles.latimes.com/1996-04-05/news/mn-55275_1_iranian-arms-shipments.

[74] James Risen, 'Administration Defends Its OK of Bosnia Arms', *Los Angeles Times*, 6 April 1996, www.articles.latimes.com/1996-04-06/news/mn-55492_1_arms-embargo.

[75] Rupert Cornwell, 'US "secretly agreed Iran arms for Bosnia"', *Independent*, 6 April 1996, www.independent.co.uk/news/world/us-secretly-agreed-iran-arms-for-bosnia-1303474.html.

[76] SC Res. 1970 (26 February 2011), www.un.org/en/sc/documents/resolutions/2011.shtml.

notwithstanding paragraph 9 of resolution 1970 (2011), to protect civilians
and civilian populated areas'.[77] This language can easily be interpreted as
authorising the supply of weapons to the rebels, and arguably reflects
something of a change in the international community's attitude to providing such support. However, the 'notwithstanding paragraph 9' language in no way contributed to a change in the general rule because the
authorisation was provided by the Security Council. The question, as to
whether there has been any change in the rule *outside* of Chapter VII,
remained unanswered.

Syria

In 2011–2013, Syria was not subject to a UN arms embargo because
Russia and China were opposed to such a measure. Syria thus provides an
opportunity to examine whether the prohibition on providing aid, assistance, training, equipment and arms to rebels has been relaxed in parallel
with (and perhaps as a consequence of) the development of international
human rights and R2P. As we will see, a number of governments have
been willing to openly provide aid, assistance and 'non-lethal' equipment
to the Syrian rebels. But some of those governments have stopped short of
providing arms, while others have only done so covertly.

In July 2012, Switzerland suspended arms exports to the United Arab
Emirates after a Swiss-made hand grenade originally shipped to that country was found in Syria.[78] The next month, Reuters reported that US
President Barack Obama had 'signed a secret order authorizing U.S. support for rebels seeking to depose Syrian President Bashar al-Assad and his
government', but that the United States was 'stopping short of giving the
rebels lethal weapons'.[79] France also indicated that it would provide
'non-lethal elements' to the rebels, including 'means of communication
and protection'.[80] And when British Foreign Secretary William Hague
announced that his government would provide £5 million in non-lethal
equipment to the Syrian opposition, he emphasised that the funding
would go to 'unarmed opposition groups, human rights activists and

[77] SC Res. 1973, paragraph 4.
[78] 'Switzerland Halts Arms Exports to U.A.E., as Report Says Swiss Arms Used by Syria
Rebels', Haaretz and Reuters, 5 July 2012, www.haaretz.com/news/middle-east/switzerland
-halts-arms-exports-to-u-a-e-as-report-says-swiss-arms-used-by-syria-rebels-1.449022.
[79] Mark Hosenball, 'Exclusive: Obama Authorizes Secret U.S. Support for Syrian Rebels',
Reuters, 1 August 2012, www.reuters.com/article/2012/08/01/us-usa-syria-obama
-order-idUSBRE8701OK20120801.
[80] 'France Gives Non-Lethal Military Aid to Syrian Opposition: PM', *Al Arabiya News*, 22
August 2012, www.english.alarabiya.net/articles/2012/08/22/233570.html.

civilians'.[81] In January 2013, when Hague announced that the United Kingdom was seeking modifications to EU sanctions on Syria 'so that the possibility of additional assistance [to the rebels] is not closed off',[82] he indicated any military equipment provided would still be of a non-lethal character, such as body armour.[83]

This differentiation between the provision of aid, assistance, training and non-lethal equipment on the one hand, and weapons on the other, is consistent with another recent development in international politics. It has become widely accepted that curtailing arms transfers to non-state groups is one of the most effective means of reducing long-term risks to civilians. This new acceptance has led to the drafting of an Arms Trade Treaty that was adopted by the United Nations on 2 April 2013.[84] The draft treaty makes no exception for the provision of arms to rebels, not even those fighting to prevent atrocities, and ratifications of the treaty will soon be contributing important state practice to the prohibition against such transfers.[85]

Of course, weapons will still find their way into rebel hands. In June 2012, the *New York Times* reported that CIA operatives in southern Turkey were helping to direct arms – paid for by Turkey, Saudi Arabia and Qatar – to Syrian opposition fighters.[86] In January 2013, *The Guardian* reported that: 'Along with Qatar, Turkey and the UAE, the Saudis are believed to be the rebels' principal suppliers and financiers.'[87] However, the latter report also observed that 'public discussion of the issue is extremely rare and the demarcation between government and private initiatives is blurred'. In other words, although there is state practice in support of providing weapons to rebels, it is not accompanied by the *opinio juris* necessary to change a rule of customary international law, and certainly not one of *jus cogens* status that is set out in a foundational treaty such as the UN Charter.

[81] 'Syria conflict: UK to give extra £5m to opposition groups', *BBC News*, 10 August 2012, www.bbc.co.uk/news/uk-19205204.
[82] 'Hague: "Options open" on Military Support for Syrian Rebels', *BBC News*, 10 January 2013, www.bbc.co.uk/news/uk-politics-20969386.
[83] Ibid.
[84] Draft of the Arms Trade Treaty, 1 August 2012, www.daccess-dds-ny.un.org/doc/UNDOC/GEN/N12/448/96/PDF/N1244896.pdf.
[85] On the role of treaties as state practice, see Richard Baxter, 'Treaties and Custom', *Recueil des Cours* 129 (1970–1971), pp. 25–105; D'Amato, *The Concept of Custom*, pp. 89–90 and 160; Mark Villiger, *Customary International Law and Treaties* (Dordrecht: Martinus Nijhoff, 1985).
[86] Eric Schmitt, 'C.I.A. Said to Aid in Steering Arms to Syrian Opposition', *New York Times*, 21 June 2012, www.nytimes.com/2012/06/21/world/middleeast/cia-said-to-aid-in-steering-arms-to-syrian-rebels.html.
[87] Ian Black, 'Arm Syrian Rebels to Contain Jihadis, Says Saudi Royal', *Guardian*, 25 January 2013, www.guardian.co.uk/world/2013/jan/25/arm-syrian-rebels-jihadis-saudi.

As former US State Department Legal Adviser John B. Bellinger III explained in January 2013:

> The U.N. Charter prohibits member states from using force against or intervening in the internal affairs of other states unless authorized by the U.N. Security Council or justified by self-defense. These rules make it unlawful for any country to use direct military force against the Assad regime, including establishing 'no-fly zones' or providing arms to the Syrian opposition without Security Council approval.[88]

However, states are increasingly behaving as if the same general prohibition on the use of force no longer precludes the provision of aid, assistance, training and 'non-lethal' equipment to rebels – at least in cases where the rebels are fighting to prevent atrocities. Moreover, this change has occurred in parallel with, and perhaps partly as a result of, developments concerning international human rights that include the Security Council taking a broader approach to 'threat to the peace', as well as the emergence of R2P.

The role of R2P in contributing to mitigation

When a state feels compelled by humanitarian concerns to violate the prohibition on the use of force, the circumstances might be taken into account in mitigation. Mitigation is a concept familiar to international law. In the 1949 *Corfu Channel Case*, when Albania took the United Kingdom to the International Court of Justice in circumstances where both countries had acted illegally, the Court held that a declaration of illegality was a sufficient remedy for the British violation.[89] In 1960, after Israel abducted Adolf Eichmann from Argentina to face criminal charges, Argentina lodged a complaint with the Security Council, which passed a resolution stating that the sovereignty of Argentina had been infringed and requesting Israel to make 'appropriate reparation'.[90] However the Council, 'mindful' of 'the concern of people in all countries that Eichmann be brought to justice', made no indication that Eichmann should be returned to Argentina.[91]

Shortly after the Kosovo War, Simon Chesterman and I wrote:

> In accordance with such an approach, the human rights violations that prompted a unilateral humanitarian intervention would have to be considered, and to some

---

[88] John B. Bellinger III, 'U.N. rules and Syrian intervention', *Washington Post*, 17 January 2013, www.articles.washingtonpost.com/2013-01-17/opinions/36410395_1_syrian -opposition-assad-regime-intervention.

[89] (1949) ICJ Reports 4 at 36, www.icj-cij.org/docket/files/1/1645.pdf.

[90] SC Res. 138 (23 June 1960), www.un.org/documents/sc/res/1960/scres60.htm.

[91] Ibid.

degree weighed against the actions of the intervening state, in any determination as to whether compensation for violating the rules concerning the use of force is required. Given the fundamental character of the rights violated when mass atrocities occur ... the intervening state might fare quite well in any such after-the-fact balancing of relative violations.[92]

Since then, the development of R2P has introduced criteria that might guide the Security Council and individual states on the appropriateness and degree of mitigation. Resolution 1674 identified that 'genocide, war crimes, ethnic cleansing and crimes against humanity' are of particular concern to the Council, and therefore most likely to trigger an authorised intervention. The paragraphs on R2P in the World Summit Outcome Document, which were 'reaffirmed' in Resolution 1674, specified that an intervention may only be contemplated 'should peaceful means be inadequate and national authorities are manifestly failing to protect their populations'. And while the report of the High-Level Panel on Threats, Challenges and Change was not explicitly endorsed by the Security Council or General Assembly, its 'criteria of legitimacy' – seriousness of intent, proper purpose, last resort, proportional means and balance of consequences – might be considered by the Council and individual states as they decide how to respond to another state's violation of the prohibition on force.

Mitigation itself could come in the form of *ex post facto* authorisation from the Security Council, and it is instructive that such authorisation was granted with respect to the ECOWAS (Economic Community of West African States) interventions in Liberia and Sierra Leone, but not the US-led interventions in Kosovo or Iraq.[93] It could also come in the form of a waiver or reduction of reparations owed, a possibility foreseen in Article 39 of the International Law Commission's Articles on State Responsibility: 'In the determination of reparation, account shall be taken of the contribution to the injury by wilful or negligent action or omission of the injured State or any person or entity in relation to whom reparation is sought.'[94]

Mitigation may already be happening with respect to transfers of weapons to rebels. As was explained above, such transfers are generally covert, and covert actions cannot make or change international law. However, to the degree such transfers are known to be happening, as in Syria, they now attract little reprobation from other states – if and when they are directed

[92] Byers and Chesterman, 'Changing the Rules about Rules?', pp. 200–201.
[93] See SC Res. 788 and 866 (19 November 1992 and 22 September 1993, Liberia) and 1181 (13 July 1998, Sierra Leone), www.un.org/en/sc/documents/resolutions/index.shtml.
[94] James Crawford, *The International Law Commission's Articles on State Responsibility. Introduction, Text and Commentaries* (Cambridge: Cambridge University Press, 2002).

at rebels who are fighting to prevent atrocities. One can therefore spec-
ulate that, instead of changing the rule to accommodate the exception, the
international community is simply choosing to ignore or at least downplay
particular violations.

Implications for the international legal system

The ongoing development of R2P offers a number of insights into the
international legal system. First, 'norm entrepreneurs' who act strategically and persistently can have a significant influence on the framing of
debates concerning specific issues of international law. Second, such
efforts can be interrupted by unanticipated events, including attempts
to distort or hijack the norm by other actors. Third, unanticipated events
can necessitate compromise and redirection, which in the case of R2P
involved the limitation of the concept, insofar as it concerns the use of
force, to being part of the context of Security Council decision-making.

Fourth, compromise and redirection may also result when 'norm
entrepreneurs' realise that some aspects of the international legal system,
such as the prohibition on the use of force, are deeply imbedded and
therefore highly resistant to change. This is not to say that ICISS members were naïve about the existence of *jus cogens* rules or the necessity for
widespread support from the developing world for any change.
Strategically, it is sometimes useful to set one's public goals higher than
the results one realistically hopes to achieve. For this reason, acceptance
of R2P as relevant context for Security Council decision-making has to be
considered a victory, even if some proponents of the concept remain
dissatisfied.[95]

Fifth, the failure of 'norm entrepreneurs' to change a rule does not
necessarily mean that they have failed to influence associated or derivative
aspects of the legal system. In the case of R2P and the prohibition on the
use of force, the failure to change the rule concerning military interventions has not precluded a possible change to the same rule as it applies to
the provision of aid, assistance, training and non-legal equipment to
rebels fighting to prevent atrocities. Practitioners and scholars of

---

[95] See, for example, the International Coalition for the Responsibility to Protect, a coalition
of 49 NGOs which includes the following 'essential element' in its 'common understanding' of R2P: when a state 'manifestly fails' in its protection responsibilities, and
peaceful means are inadequate, the international community *must* take stronger measures
including Chapter VII measures under the UN Charter, including but *not limited to the
collective use of force authorized by the Security Council*. Available at: www.responsibilityto
protect.org/index.php/about-coalition/our-understanding-of-rtop (emphasis added).

international law would be wise to pay attention, not just to the central aspect of any rule, but also its often more mutable margins.

Finally, the effects of 'norm entrepreneurship' can include changes that are additional or alternative to changes to rules. In the case of R2P, both as it concerns unilateral humanitarian intervention and the provision of arms to rebels, it is important to consider whether the development of the concept will lead to increased mitigation of the consequences – for states whose moral compulsion to violate international law is both genuinely felt and well-founded.

In the future, R2P may lead to more changes in the international legal system. But instead of beginning at the core of the prohibition on the use of force, the changes will most likely commence at the margins. International law is often like that, moving forward sideways.

7   The Responsibility to Protect, multilateralism and international legitimacy

Edward Newman

The principle of the Responsibility to Protect (R2P) has won broad support around a clear definition that is relevant to a narrow and specific range of atrocities: genocide, war crimes, ethnic cleansing and crimes against humanity. Controversies remain, especially in how R2P is operationalised and implemented, and in terms of international action when governments are unwilling or unable to prevent or stop atrocities. Where there is less controversy is in the legal and political distinction between coercive international action for human protection purposes which is authorised through multilateral organisations such as the UN, and that which is undertaken unilaterally or by groups of states acting without UN authorisation. Multilateral action on R2P – whether to promote a general doctrine in support of human protection norms or to respond to specific humanitarian crises – is inherently legitimate *because* it is conducted through established multilateral channels, the most important of which is the UN. R2P is therefore anchored to a Westphalian, pluralist conception of international society and existing norms of world order.

In line with this, the most important progress in the protection agenda is that which has occurred in or through multilateral settings, such as the 2005 World Summit Outcome's endorsement of R2P, United Nations Security Council resolutions on the protection of civilians in armed conflict, the appointment of UN advisers on genocide and on R2P and thematic General Assembly debates on R2P, among other examples. The procedural legitimacy of multilateral decisions and processes is generally assumed, and from the liberal perspective this is an expression of popular will. Even when scholars challenge the ethical distinction between coercive humanitarian action undertaken through multilateral organisations such as the UN and action undertaken without UN approval, they generally do not challenge the legitimacy of the UN when that organisation does take action. Moreover, despite the limitations and problems associated with the multilateral implementation of R2P – especially in responding to atrocities – most UN member states would be steadfastly against any coercive action for humanitarian purposes outside the UN framework, irrespective of arguments about effectiveness. Safeguards against the misuse of force for 'humanitarian' purposes – and concerns over the proportionality of and accountability for international action – therefore appear to transcend human solidarism, at least in policy circles.

From the perspective of analysts who advocate R2P, the success or legitimacy of multilateral organisations in relation to war crimes, genocide, crimes against humanity and ethnic cleansing should be judged according to the extent to which the R2P agenda is implemented. Multilateral output legitimacy, therefore, is a function of how multilateral organisations such as the UN effectively promote R2P as an emerging norm, and how effectively they invoke it to prevent or respond to atrocities.

This chapter will explore and critique the sources and the robustness of this assumed multilateral legitimacy. It will describe the evolution of R2P as an essentially multilateral principle and consider the extent to which multilateral progress on this emerging norm reflects acceptable standards of input and output legitimacy, focusing upon its democratic credentials and the constitutive values of the multilateral organisations – in particular, the UN – through which it is promoted. The chapter approaches these topics in the context of a changing international order.

The chapter argues that the progress of R2P multilaterally, both as a doctrine and in response to specific humanitarian crises, masks fundamental problems with the principle. Despite the apparent emerging multilateral consensus there are fundamental controversies about the definition, scope and implementation of R2P, and about the actors who are driving the R2P agenda. In turn, this points to conflicts about the diffusion of norms and the structure of multilateral values and institutions. Some of these multilateral tensions relate to broader fissures in international order at a time of transition as rising or resurgent powers – such as India, China, Brazil and Russia – increasingly seek to make an impact upon international affairs. Multilateral friction related to R2P also reflects a tension in international relations between solidarist and pluralist worldviews in terms of the relationship between individual justice and international order. In addition, in a multilateral context, R2P suffers from the inherent difficulties of international collective action; in particular, the logic of reciprocity and the incentives of saving transaction costs, among other multilateral principles, do not operate effectively in this area of international politics.

In conclusion, multilateral progress on R2P depends not only upon resolving some of the operational controversies which continue to be associated with the principle, but also in addressing some of the systemic tensions which are manifested in the values and institutions of multi-lateralism. Ultimately, however, given the difficulties of achieving a multilateral system in such a sensitive policy area, the implementation of R2P is likely to remain inconsistent, controversial and contested.

The evolving multilateral protection agenda

The international protection agenda has evolved since the 1990s as an essentially multilateral phenomenon, through established multilateral arrangements and with the assumption of multilateral legitimacy. In parallel, the idea of unilateral 'humanitarian intervention' outside the framework of the UN has become increasingly distanced from the debate. The performance of existing multilateral organisations in the area of human protection may well be unsatisfactory, and some scholars have argued that this raises questions regarding their legitimacy.[1] Nevertheless, multilateral approaches are endowed with an inherent legitimacy and R2P cannot be readily examined in isolation from the politics of multi-lateralism. Multilateral action – especially through the UN – is generally considered to reflect some form of international consensus and due process; unilateral intervention, even if ostensibly to prevent or stop human rights abuse, is considered to be prone to self-serving abuses of power.

In recent decades, in response to human tragedies in the midst of conflict in places such as Iraq, Somalia, Rwanda, Bosnia, Kosovo, East Timor, Sudan, Libya and Syria, consensus has gradually – and unsteadily – emerged on the principle that atrocities should be collectively addressed. Since the 1990s two broad lines of argument have emerged, both tied closely to multilateral politics. First, there is a solidarist or cosmopolitan claim that widespread and egregious human rights abuse must be addressed by the international community, even without the consent of the target territory and irrespective of broader issues of international peace and security. Second, there is the argument that severe human rights abuses have destabilising consequences that are not confined to the state in which they occur, and therefore such abuse constitutes a threat to international peace and security. According to this argument, international action may be justified and necessary, including coercive responses under Chapter VII of the UN Charter.

There arguably has been – in theory and practice – a broadening interpretation of 'threats to international peace and security' in this way,

---

[1] Allen Buchanan and Robert O. Keohane, 'Precommitment Regimes for Intervention: Supplementing the Security Council', *Ethics and International Affairs*, 25:1 (2011), pp. 41–63.

in line with the evolving security agenda. But this does not – in principle, at least – challenge Westphalian norms of international order based upon sovereignty and non-interference. The Security Council issued resolutions in relation to Iraq, Somalia, Haiti, Rwanda, the Democratic Republic of Congo (DRC) and East Timor that made a link between human rights and international peace and security. However, the solidarist claim – that human rights abuses, even without a clear threat to international peace and security, demand Security Council action – is far less accepted and more contingent. Coercive international action for human protection purposes outside the UN framework is more controversial still. Indeed, the 1999 Kosovo conflict was the event that best defined the dilemmas inherent in humanitarian intervention, where the failure to achieve a Security Council endorsement – thus failing the test of multilateral legitimacy – created a lasting legacy, irrespective of the pressing humanitarian issues related to that case.

In the broader context this debate meant that a fundamental dichotomy between order/legality and justice had to be tackled. The report of the International Commission on Intervention and State Sovereignty (ICISS), *The Responsibility to Protect*, sought to do that, and it accomplished a rare feat in winning both policy and intellectual acclaim. The core argument was that the primary responsibility for the protection of its people lies with the state itself, but where a population is suffering serious harm and the state in question is unwilling or unable to halt or avert it, the principle of non-intervention yields to the international responsibility to protect.[2]

It is worth reiterating the importance of multilateralism in the ICISS report as a source of authority and legitimacy for R2P. The foundations of R2P lie in the obligations inherent in the concept of sovereignty, the responsibility of the UN and specific human rights obligations reflected in international legal instruments. The report firmly established the authority of R2P within the UN Security Council, especially when a government is unwilling or unable to protect populations from egregious abuses of human rights. Anticipating the political difficulties of working through the Security Council, the ICISS report urged the permanent Security Council members to agree not to apply their veto to the passage of resolutions relating to human protection if there is otherwise majority support, especially if they have no direct national interest. If the Security Council fails to act, the consequences in the ICISS report are also premised upon the principle of multilateral legitimacy: the matter could be considered by

---

[2] International Commission on Intervention and State Sovereignty (ICISS), *The Responsibility to Protect* (Ottawa: International Development Research Centre, 2001).

the General Assembly under the 'Uniting for Peace' procedure, and action by regional organisations under Chapter VII of the Charter could be undertaken, subject to their seeking subsequent authorisation from the Security Council. The report did not rule out international action outside the UN – if the Security Council 'fails to discharge its responsibility to protect in conscience-shocking situations crying out for action'[3] – but it is clear that the original R2P principle should be seen as a multilateral agenda. The operational principles of the ICISS report similarly reflect this assumption of multilateral legitimacy.

The decade following the launch of the ICISS report saw significant progress on the protection agenda and – although this is controversial – there has arguably been growing agreement on a solidarist vision of an international responsibility to protect as an emerging multilateral norm.[4] This can be illustrated with reference to a number of landmark multilateral developments. The Security Council gave an unequivocal human protection mandate to UN peace operations deployed in Sierra Leone, Haiti, Burundi, Liberia, Sudan, DRC, East Timor and Côte d'Ivoire on occasions under the Chapter VII enforcement authority of the Charter. The plight of civilians in armed conflict has become a major political theme in UN – including Security Council – deliberations. Most significantly, in 2005 the UN Summit Outcome document explicitly endorsed a revised, more conservative, version of R2P.

The Summit Outcome and beyond: from definition to implementation

For most people involved in R2P discussions within academic and policy circles – including the ICISS report authors Gareth Evans and Ramesh Thakur[5] – the principle is now defined with reference to the 2005 UN Summit Outcome (and *not* the ICISS report of 2001, which envisaged a broader application of R2P in the event that the Security Council cannot respond to mass atrocities). This further reinforces the idea of R2P as a multilateral principle. The summit agreed that individual states have the responsibility to protect their populations from genocide, war crimes, ethnic cleansing and crimes against humanity, and also to prevent such crimes, including their incitement. It stipulated that the international community should encourage and help states to exercise this responsibility and develop an early warning capability. The agreement also

---

[3] ICISS, *Responsibility to Protect*, p. 55.
[4] Ruti G. Teitel, *Humanity's Law* (Oxford: Oxford University Press, 2011).
[5] Gareth Evans and Ramesh Thakur, 'Correspondence: Humanitarian Intervention and the Responsibility to Protect (R2P)', *International Security*, 37:4 (2013), pp. 199–207.

indicated that the international community, through the UN, has the responsibility to help to protect populations from these atrocities where national authorities are manifestly failing to protect their populations.[6]

The UN secretary-general's 2009 report, *Implementing the Responsibility to Protect*, has formed the reference point for how this international consensus should be operationalised, and this is based upon three pillars, of which two are multilateral: (1) The protection responsibilities of the state to uphold its obligations to international human rights standards; (2) international assistance and capacity-building to help enable, where necessary, states to meet these obligations; and (3) the responsibility of UN members to respond collectively in a timely and decisive manner, using a range of peaceful tools and in exceptional circumstances coercive measures under Chapter VII of the UN Charter.[7] The vision of R2P that has gained traction since 2005 emphasises the importance of preventing the emergence of circumstances in which atrocities are more likely to occur, promoting existing norms and assisting states to build their capacity to uphold relevant human rights.[8] Far less emphasis is placed upon the use of coercion, and in particular the use of armed force, for human protection purposes; moreover, greater emphasis is placed upon non-military forms of coercion, such as sanctions and referral to the International Criminal Court.

The language of R2P has become internalised in diplomatic discourse in terms of how mass atrocities are discussed and addressed, even when it has been difficult to agree upon action. R2P advocates and champions have quite successfully argued that the debate is no longer about 'humanitarian intervention'; the principle of R2P has consensus, and the challenge ahead is implementation.[9] The support that R2P has received is, especially in policy circles, based on the assumption that R2P is (no longer) at odds with conventional Westphalian norms of international order given that it is anchored to the UN Charter and international law. Again, the assumption of multilateral legitimacy is an essential component of this.

---

[6] *World Summit Outcome*, Document A/RES/60/1 (New York: United Nations, 24 October 2005), paragraphs 138–139.

[7] *Implementing the Responsibility to Protect.* Report of the Secretary-General, Document A/63/677, (New York: United Nations, 12 January 2009).

[8] Edward C. Luck, 'The Responsibility to Protect: Growing Pains or Early Promise?', *Ethics and International Affairs*, 24:2 (2010), p. 352.

[9] Gareth Evans, *The Responsibility to Protect: Ending Mass Atrocity Crimes Once and for All* (Washington DC: Brookings Institution Press, 2008); Louise Arbour, 'The Responsibility to Protect as a Duty of Care in International Law and Practice', *Review of International Studies*, 34:3 (2008), pp. 445–458.

The problems of R2P as a multilateral principle

International order in transition

A number of problems suggest that the assumption of multilateral legitimacy in the evolution of R2P – in terms of how it is defined, operationalised and implemented – can be questioned. Firstly, it is possible to challenge the idea that multilateral R2P landmarks truly reflect international consensus. The 2005 Summit appeared to represent a global endorsement of R2P, yet in the years that followed reservations have been expressed by many states. Influential non-Western states – such as China, Brazil, India, Russia and South Africa, among others – have also expressed concerns about the manner in which the R2P agenda has been dominated by liberal, Western centres of power.

Some of the reservations regarding R2P reflect tensions relating to international order and the relationship between sovereignty and individual justice.[10] States which have been championing R2P – such as the United Kingdom, France and sometimes the United States – are associated with a broader, assertive liberal internationalism geared towards the promotion of democracy and market economics, as well as the containment of 'rogue' states. This is a part of a liberal agenda – of course, contingent upon geopolitical interests – that serves to internationalise human rights abuse and to make the legitimacy of sovereignty conditional upon upholding certain standards of human rights. Despite attempts to define R2P narrowly, controversy surrounding the principle can be explained in part by its association with this broader agenda. A number of powerful and rising powers, reflecting a more pluralist worldview, have expressed strong reservations towards this liberal internationalism and the multilateral tensions seen in R2P debates and with respect to decisions should be seen in this light. The idea of a fundamental change in the nature of sovereignty – which was featured in the ICISS report, discarded by the 2005 agreement, but which is nevertheless still associated with R2P – is pointedly not accepted by many states. The 2005 R2P vision masked over this tension between cosmopolitan and pluralist thinking, but it remains relevant to understanding some of the political problems that exist. This tension is all the more significant because it exposes an apparent fault line between liberal states which promote a more robust R2P agenda and a number of rising powers which reflect a more conservative worldview.

---

[10] Edward Newman, 'R2P: Implications for World Order', *Global Responsibility to Protect*, 5:3, 2013.

General Assembly debates on R2P illustrate many of these sensitivities.[11] In a landmark debate in 2009, state representatives, especially among non-Western countries, reiterated the sanctity of state sovereignty, international law and the UN Charter, and the need to strictly limit the application of R2P. This theme was reiterated so often that it was more prominent than the desire to endorse the R2P concept as a guide to policy. A number of other themes in the debate similarly pointed towards fundamental disagreements. States stressed the need to consider broader issues of poverty, structural inequality and under-development, implying that the social and economic conditions that form the background to humanitarian crises and broader issues of international justice have been neglected.

From this perspective any global debate on human rights abuse must take deprivation into consideration, especially when it has such a terrible impact – even more than R2P crimes – in the developing world. Many contributions to the General Assembly debate also raised concerns about double standards and selectivity in the international community's attention to human rights abuses, with a number of references to the Palestinian issue, and the danger of the principle of R2P being abused by powerful states. A number of state representatives problematised the special role of the Security Council and thus the unrepresentative nature of the organ which stands at the top of the operationalisation of R2P. Connected to this, there was some concern about the countries which are championing R2P in terms of the interests they represent – and their own human rights records – bringing their moral legitimacy into doubt. The debate also suggested that there is a lack of clarity about the circumstances in which coercive action should be considered and who would decide whether it should be taken.

It is tempting to suggest that the opposition to R2P is at the margins and comes from the 'usual' spoilers – but this would be to misrepresent the tone of the UN debates on R2P, which reflects far broader concern. Behind a declaratory commitment to an abstract principle of R2P stands a more pronounced reaffirmation, especially among some non-Western states and notably rising powers, of the Westphalian norms of sovereignty, non-interference and territorial integrity. This was, therefore, a reaffirmation of a pluralist worldview in terms of the balance between individual justice and international order. Subsequent UN debates reflected these same divergent views. The September 2012 General Assembly thematic debate, which focused specifically on Pillar Three

---

[11] The International Coalition for the Responsibility to Protect website contains the country statements: www.responsibilitytoprotect.org/.

and the secretary-general's report on timely and decisive response, rehearsed a number of these concerns.

These issues have also been illustrated in the multilateral application of R2P. A number of key Security Council resolutions have seen abstentions from important states and there has been a pattern of behaviour demonstrating fundamental reservations towards R2P among some states. The decision to authorise the use of military force against Libya has been regarded as a step forward for R2P, as an example of the Security Council authorising the use of force against the wishes of a functioning state for human protection purposes (under Resolution 1973). The resolution reaffirmed the sovereignty, independence, territorial integrity and national unity of Libya; determined that the situation in Libya constituted a threat to international peace and security (and thus, not purely a 'domestic matter'); and it also excluded foreign occupation. Nevertheless, Brazil, India, China, Russia and Germany abstained, the two permanent Security Council members among this group apparently unwilling to veto the resolution and be responsible for 'allowing' a massacre, but clearly uncomfortable with the open-ended mandate and the authorisation of all necessary measures.

The multilateral aftermath of the Libya resolution exposed even more the fundamental difficulties of implementing R2P. While this case is hardly representative of international R2P action broadly speaking – because R2P emphasises assistance to national authorities to prevent atrocities from occurring – the fact that R2P advocates have suggested that the principle 'came of age' with Resolution 1973 suggests that this case, and the reactions to it, are illustrative of the broader debate.[12] There has been wide agreement within non-Western states, and in particular the BRICS (Brazil, Russia, India, China and South Africa), that Resolution 1973 was abused by NATO states as a pretext for pursuing regime change and that it was stretched to cover activities not authorised in the resolution, such as attacks against government and media facilities. Indeed, a joint statement by US President Barack Obama, UK Prime Minister David Cameron and President Nicolas Sarkozy of France published in a number of international newspapers in April 2011 openly suggested that the objective of the operation in Libya was regime change.[13] The apparent unwillingness of states involved in the military operation to put more effort into negotiating with the government of Libya for a settlement, their assistance to the rebels – including the transfer of weapons – and the speed

---

[12] Jon Western and Joshua S. Goldstein, 'Humanitarian Intervention Comes of Age: Lessons from Somalia to Libya', *Foreign Affairs*, 90:6 (2011), pp. 48–59.

[13] Barack Obama, David Cameron and Nicolas Sarkozy, 'Libya's Pathway to Peace', *International Herald Tribune*, 14 April 2011.

with which key members of the alliance recognised the Libyan National Transitional Council, all reinforced the impression that the implementation of this resolution went beyond the protection of human rights. All of the signals coming from Russia, China, India and other states – and this is illustrated in the international community's dealing with Syria – suggest that it would be extremely difficult to gain Security Council support for a similar action in the future.

The Brazilian government's 2011 'responsibility while protecting' proposal promoted a more cautious vision of R2P. It also illustrated a widely supported sentiment – especially in light of the blank cheque of Resolution 1973 – that existing multilateral arrangements do not contain the necessary safeguards against the abuse of power in the context of R2P. The proposal suggested that the three R2P pillars should be sequential and step-by-step, presumably to underscore the importance of safeguards against unwarranted coercion. It also argued for better monitoring of the manner in which resolutions are implemented, and stronger accountability of those who are granted the authority to use force while protecting.[14] China's notion of 'responsible protection' reflected a more conservative worldview still, emphasising the importance of state sovereignty, non-intervention and respect for national authorities.[15]

The response of the international community to the uprising and violence in Syria in 2011–2014 reflected the legacy of Libya. It also reflected the limitations of R2P as a multilateral principle given the inherent constraints of existing (pluralist) multilateral values and institutions. Again, while these cases are not representative of the broader R2P debate, they are tests for the application of R2P in the most difficult cases. Russia and China vetoed Security Council Resolutions in October 2011, February 2012 and July 2012. Following the 2011 veto, Russia and China gave statements which clearly displayed their pluralist view of international order. An alternative Russian–Chinese draft resolution – which, according to Russia, had the support of the BRICS – was characterised by 'respect for the national sovereignty and territorial integrity of Syria and non-interference, including military, in its affairs, the logic of the unity of the Syrian people, the rejection of confrontation and an invitation to all for an equal and substantive dialogue'.[16] According to this, the vetoed

---

[14] See Kai Michael Kenkel, 'Brazil and R2P: Does Taking Responsibility Mean Using Force?', *Global Responsibility to Protect*, 4:1 (2012), pp. 5–32.

[15] Ruan Zongze, 'Responsible Protection: Building a Safer World', *China International Studies*, 34, (2012), available at www.ciis.org.cn/english/2012-06/15/content_5090912.htm.

[16] Statement in Explanation of Vote by Vitaly Churkin, Permanent Representative of the Russian Federation to the UN, on the Draft Resolution on the Situation in Syria, 1493-05-10-2011 (New York, 4 October 2011).

resolution reflected an 'entirely different philosophy, the philosophy of confrontation', and undermining Assad's legitimacy would promote full-scale conflict in Syria and destabilise the whole region.

Clearly, Russia has important strategic and economic interests in Syria, tied to the Assad regime, and this in part explains its obstruction of Security Council action. It is also notable that Russia explicitly linked its veto of the Syria resolution to its belief – shared by many – that the implementation of resolution 1973 on Libya had been an abuse of UN authority. However, Russia's position – alongside China and others – is characteristic of a more fundamental difference in dealing with 'domestic' human rights abuses. Moreover, even if Russia's position was entirely a consequence of its pragmatic self-interest, the manner in which it presented its position – and its broader resistance against R2P – in pluralist terms is highly significant. For example, irrespective of human rights abuses, Russia indicated that the sovereign government deserves the assumption of legitimacy; or at least if that legitimacy is to be challenged, that must come from domestic – not external – actors.[17] China – with far fewer direct interests in Syria – similarly explained its position in relation to Syria's sovereignty, independence and territorial integrity. The third veto by China and Russia of a draft resolution on Syria in July 2012 was accompanied by similar non-interventionist statements, as were the negative votes in a General Assembly vote in February 2012.[18] The pluralist worldview is certainly shared by a much larger number of states in broader perspective and it represents a challenge to the multilateral legitimacy of R2P as an emerging norm because it suggests that egregious human rights abuses in politically charged cases will all too often not be addressed.

The position of Russia and China on Syria is an extreme example of this broader tension in international relations related to international order and human rights, especially in 'domestic' situations. In turn, there is a tension between established, often liberal, powers – such as the United States and West European states, and their allies in various parts of the world – and the rising and increasingly assertive BRICS powers and others,[19] including non-Western groupings such as the Non-Aligned Movement and the Shanghai Cooperation Organisation. Some of the reservations regarding R2P therefore derive from fundamental tensions regarding international order and justice. Again, this represents a challenge to the legitimacy of established multilateral arrangements as the principal vehicle for building consensus on R2P.

---

[17] Ibid.

[18] Zhao Shengnan, 'Beijing defends UN vote on Syria', *China Daily*, 18 February 2012.

[19] See Ramesh Thakur, 'R2P after Libya and Syria: Engaging Emerging Powers', *The Washington Quarterly*, 36:2 (2013), pp. 61–76.

The problem of output legitimacy

A further, obvious problem relating to the multilateral application of R2P is that the rules of procedure of multilateral organisations – such as the Security Council of the UN – do not assure that terrible human rights abuses are addressed, even when there is apparently a compelling case for international action. International attention to critical human rights abuses is selective and discretionary, and most obviously it neglects cases where powerful states have an interest in keeping things off the multilateral agenda. Insofar as R2P is essentially a multilateral concept, this problematises the legitimacy both of R2P itself and multilateral values and institutions. Multilateral action did not end egregious human rights abuses in Syria in 2011–2014 and this inaction was – perversely – 'legitimate' according to the rules of procedure of the UN Security Council. Lesser, but still lamentable, human rights abuses elsewhere – in Zimbabwe, Palestine, Sri Lanka, Russia, China – and those allegedly perpetrated by the United States in its 'war on terror' evade significant international attention and censure.

In addition, for many state and non-state observers the Western neglect of certain forms of human rights deprivation – such as the Palestinian case – despite various UN declarations and resolutions makes any moral R2P stance rather hollow because it is not applied consistently. Inadequate international action in the face of preventable disease, mal-nutrition and other forms of terrible deprivation – which claim countless lives in the developing world each year – is a further illustration of this inconsistency. For many R2P sceptics this represents a double standard that threatens to undermine the entire legitimacy of the principle. If the Security Council is able to act in the case of Libya but not in Syria, then the output legitimacy of the organ as the highest authority of R2P is in doubt. R2P advocates might argue that just because the international community cannot help people everywhere, it does not mean that it should not help where it can, but inconsistency and selectivity are deeply problematic in an emerging multilateral norm.

In the policy world R2P must be seen in the context of existing multi-lateral norms. The broader ICISS conception of R2P – which did not endorse, but equally did not absolutely rule out international action to prevent or stop atrocities outside the UN if the Security Council could not or would not act – has been rejected in favour of the more limited version of R2P outlined in the 2005 UN Summit Outcome. There have been some policy recommendations aimed at strengthening the effectiveness of the UN in implementing R2P – for example, a moratorium on veto use in matters related to R2P – and Brazil's 'responsibility while protecting' sought to make the behaviour of powerful states more accountable to multilateral processes. Nevertheless, the assumption remains that established multilateral institutions and norms, however imperfect, are the only legitimate framework for the implementation of R2P.

Some scholars have, however, considered the possibility of alternative approaches when the UN is unable or unwilling to act. According to Buchanan and Keohane, while the Security Council is a legitimate organisation for making decisions related to humanitarian action, it does not possess unconditional exclusive legitimacy and therefore in certain circumstances coercion could be legitimately authorised through other means. They argue that the Security Council has sometimes failed to authorise justifiable intervention to stop or prevent human rights abuses, it lacks procedures for accountability and so there is little prospect for substantial improvement and it obstructs other parties from fulfilling the function of human protection, meaning it is therefore permissible to seek to develop a superior institutional alternative.[20]

Despite the problems with the existing rules of procedure and composition of the UN Security Council, proposals such as these have gained little or no traction – especially in policy circles – because they tend to reinforce the perennial controversies associated with 'humanitarian intervention', even if they might produce a more effective response to atrocities. The multilateral legitimacy deficit is therefore an inherent and seemingly inevitable feature of the multilateral responsibility to protect, but surely not an unexpected one since multilateral institutions are embedded in pluralist, Westphalian norms which reflect both the imperfect politics of consensus and the realities of power. In this context incremental progress can and has occurred, but only very slowly and unevenly, and on a case by case basis. The gap between legality and legitimacy in terms of the use of military force to alleviate terrible human suffering is a challenge to the moral legitimacy of international organisations, but perhaps not as much as the failure of international organisations to perform. In the wake of Libya, the unwillingness of Russia and China to support resolutions on Syria points to the possibility of multilateral deadlock for R2P in the most difficult cases, which would bring the legitimacy both of the principle and the organs charged with its implementation further into doubt.

The problem of input legitimacy

Insofar as R2P is essentially a 'multilateral concept', it is also problematised by broader controversies about rules of procedure and

---

[20] Buchanan and Keohane, 'Precommitment Regimes for Intervention', p. 41.

representation in established multilateral arrangements. These contro-versies, in turn, can be linked to changes in world order – including the rise of countries such as Brazil, India, Russia and China – which make problems related to the control of the multilateral agenda even more conspicuous. The special role of the Security Council and the unrepre-sentative nature of the organ which stands at the top of the operationali-sation of the R2P is clearly a problem for many states on the periphery, but also those states – such as Brazil, India and South Africa – which see the current architecture of global governance as being out of alignment with current global realities. Therefore, the multilateral operationalisa-tion of R2P arguably does not pass the test of 'input legitimacy'.[21] This has been illustrated in a number of General Assembly debates on R2P, in which many countries have insisted that the General Assembly should play a more significant role in implementing the R2P agenda.

No country would refute the basic principle of R2P, but the manner in which it is promoted and applied are characteristic of broader contestation in the international system related to structural inequal-ities and unrepresentative institutions. In this sense, R2P has become hostage to broader frictions related to the transitional international order. Many states, including some which are rising in power and influence, are instinctively guarded towards the principle *because* it is championed by Western states, and because it is promoted through organisations – such as the UN and NATO – that are regarded by some of these states as being unrepresentative or unaccountable. In this sense, therefore, R2P raises tensions in relation to the question of how, and by whom, norms are created and diffused. If R2P is asso-ciated with the perception of unaccountable and unrepresentative international decision-making, then the principle itself is problematic and its legitimacy is weakened.

A multilateral democratic deficit?

Part of the multilateral legitimacy of R2P relates to the assumption that the principle reflects the will of publics around the world. There is some evidence that publics do support the international promotion of human rights and international action – in some circumstances – to prevent or stop atrocities against civilians. Surveys of world opinion – including in China, India and the United States – have suggested that a role for

---

[21] For a discussion on input and output legitimacy with reference to multilateralism see Robert O. Keohane, 'The Contingent Legitimacy of Multilateralism', in Edward Newman, Ramesh Thakur and John Tirman, eds, *Multilateralism under Challenge? Power, International Order, and Structural Change* (Tokyo: UN University Press), 2006.

international society in meeting the responsibility to protect human life is broadly supported.[22] The liberal champions of R2P apparently assume that the publics of democratic societies support international action to promote human rights norms, and this is intuitively reasonable. Some scholars have made a clear link between international action in response to human rights abuse and democratic legitimacy.[23] However, this is also not without its difficulties. Democratic will may form a part of the liberal assumption of R2P's legitimacy, but the idea that the R2P is an expression of popular will – or specifically, the will of those states which champion the principle – is not seriously argued or tested. Survey data is far too scant to claim that the R2P agenda reflects a democratic impulse, and there is certainly evidence that some publics are hostile to the connection between human rights and intervention when it entails risk, long-term involvement or when it appears to be a pretext for ulterior motives.[24] Public reservations were underscored in 2013 when the UK government failed to achieve majority support in a House of Common's vote for possible military action in Syria on humanitarian grounds. In turn, the US government decided not to seek the support of Congress for military action due to public and political unease. The inclination to seek public support – although this was not forthcoming – reflects a move towards the democratisation of humanitarian action, but it also exposes the fact that in most cases there is little or no public input into such decisions. Thus, the 'democratic' part of the R2P agenda is unclear and therefore not a solid foundation upon which to base its multilateral legitimacy. Moreover, when public opinion turns away from international action for human protection purposes it surely problematises this action if the legitimacy of the R2P agenda is premised upon supportive public opinion. Similarly, it is questionable whether states have a duty to promote the R2P if their citizens are collectively isolationist. If R2P is essentially a solidarist, cosmopolitan principle, the disconnect between the principle and the citizen is inherently problematic.

---

[22] 'Publics Around the World Say UN Has Responsibility to Protect Against Genocide', World Public Opinion.org and the Chicago Council on World Affairs, April 2007.

[23] J. L. Holzgrefe and Robert O. Keohane, *Humanitarian Intervention: Ethical, Legal and Political Dilemmas* (Cambridge: Cambridge University Press, 2003).

[24] For example, Timothy Hildebrandt, Courtney Hillebrecht, Peter M. Holm and Jon Pevehouse, 'The Domestic Politics of Humanitarian Intervention: Public Opinion, Partisanship, and Ideology', *Foreign Policy Analysis*, article first published online: 3 July 2012; Ole R. Holsti, *American Public Opinion on the Iraq War* (Ann Arbor: University of Michigan Press, 2011); Linda Feldmann, 'Why Iraq War Support Fell so Fast', *The Christian Science Monitor*, 21 November, 2005; Jon Western, 'Humanitarian Intervention, American Public Opinion, and the Future of R2P', *Global Responsibility to Protect*, 1:3 (2009), pp. 324–345; Ned Dobos, 'Justifying Humanitarian Intervention to the People Who Pay for It', *Praxis*, 1:1 (Spring 2008), pp. 34–51.

Collective action problems

A further difficulty related to the multilateral implementation of R2P concerns the inherent limitations of collective action at the international level. Multilateralism brings stability and regularity to the behaviour of states, it reduces the transaction costs of making, monitoring and enforcing rules, and it facilitates the making of credible commitments.[25] These public goods, according to the institutionalist school of international relations, involve a number of operating principles. There should be sustained commitment by members to the multilateral arrangement across a range of issue areas and the expectation of reciprocity in terms of the costs and benefits associated with participation.[26] This means that members of a multilateral grouping should fulfil the obligations of membership without reservations or conditions based upon the circumstances of a particular issue or their perception of their particular interests.

Even in policy areas far less sensitive than the international protection of human rights, the multilateral management of collective problems can be extremely difficult. The international system is basically anarchical. States vary in power, political outlook and interests. They are formally sovereign and generally driven by self-interests which are frequently in conflict. Leaders and hegemons – invariably the chief sponsors of international regimes – decline or increase in relative power and perceive negative changes in the costs and benefits related to international regimes. Thus, multilateral arrangements are a reflection of the dynamics and processes of international power, as well as the development of norms of cooperation over time. This does not mean that formal or informal multilateral institutions are not effective or important, or cease to be effective in changing circumstances, but it highlights the inherent difficulties of international collective action.[27]

The institutionalist logic of multilateralism – based upon reciprocity, regularity and burden sharing – arguably does not operate with respect to international responses to grave human suffering, so there cannot be a robust system to aid innocent civilians in dire need. Even when state leaders are genuinely moved by egregious human rights abuses, the political, material and human costs of intervention, whether unilateral or through an international organisation, often outweigh the

[25] Robert O. Keohane, *Power and Governance in a Partially Globalized World* (London: Routledge, 2002).

[26] John Gerard Ruggie, ed, *Multilateralism Matters: The Theory and Praxis of an Institutional Form* (New York: Columbia University Press, 1993).

[27] Edward Newman, *A Crisis of Global Institutions? Multilateralism and International Security*, (London: Routledge, 2007).

humanitarian impulse. Moreover, reciprocity arguably does not function in this realm; it is highly unlikely that powerful states would become involved in international action to protect human lives where no other interest exists on the basis that they might require support from other states for a similar intervention which is in their interests in the future. States are reluctant to accept a norm which may embroil them in politically risky and unforeseen international action, preferring to respond on a case by case basis. Experience suggests that their support for such action will always be contingent upon the specific circumstances of each case, and not a commitment to a general rule or doctrine. Indeed, in cases of grave human suffering, consensus on inactivity is far more common (the 2005 UN Summit Outcome document itself committed UN members to respond 'on a case-by-case basis' if national authorities are manifestly failing to protect their populations). By definition, this is not a multilateral system, which requires commitment to action in a particular policy area, even in unforeseen circumstances. Given the sensitivities of being involved in such action it is doubtful whether states will commit themselves to act in a non-discriminatory manner through a binding collective responsibility to protect, especially relating to the Pillar Three agenda.

Conclusion

Over the last twenty years there has been remarkable progress in the human protection agenda, and the R2P principle – in both its ICISS and 2005 guises – has played a central role in this, both as a doctrinal guide and as a fledgling framework for action. This progress must be acknowledged, despite the controversies of recent years. Brazil, China and India have considerably softened their position on R2P from firm resistance around the launch of the ICISS report to guarded support in principle since 2005. Brazil has sought to take a leadership role, not in resisting R2P outright, but by seeking to make it more accountable and sensitive to concerns relating to sovereignty, intervention and the exercise of power internationally. China has given repeated endorsements of R2P since 2005 and supported – or at least not vetoed – a number of UN decisions related to R2P.[28] However, without denying this progress, as the pace of R2P has accelerated and with attempts to operationalise it – especially in difficult circumstances – significant problems have emerged. Some of these fault lines can be linked to the multilateral context within which R2P has evolved and is now embedded.

---

[28] Gregory Chin and Ramesh Thakur, 'Will China Change the Rules of Global Order?', *The Washington Quarterly*, 33:4 (2010), pp. 119–138.

The multilateral framework has been politically essential for the progress of R2P. However, the input legitimacy of multilateral arrangements which promote R2P is – especially in the difficult cases of responding to atrocities when states are unwilling or unable to do so – in tension with output legitimacy, defined as an effective means of preventing or ending egregious human rights abuses. R2P is now embedded into a Westphalian, pluralist international society which enshrines state sovereignty and non-intervention, apart from in the most exceptional circumstances. In too many cases the rules of procedure of international organisations have not facilitated an effective response, or they have been actively obstructive. There are, therefore, internal inconsistencies in the manner in which R2P is embedded in multilateral institutions and norms, in particular in the manner in which pluralist and solidarist worldviews are uncomfortably combined. Somehow, there is a need to ensure that multilateral arrangements have safeguards to protect small countries against the predations of hegemony and the abuse of power, while also facilitating the protection of humans in the broad sense of R2P.[29] For R2P, multilateralism is therefore an unfinished journey.

The role of multilateral arrangements – such as the UN – as the framework for conceptualising and implementing R2P is also problematised by transitional world order. The institutions and values reflected in existing multilateral arrangements are increasingly out of alignment with power political realities, and therefore the diffusion of norms through these multilateral forums often suffers from a lack of traction – or, worse still, these norms are resisted. Whether fairly or unfairly, the perception is that the R2P agenda has been dominated by liberal, Western centres of power, through multilateral organisations in which they have a disproportionate amount of influence. The countries and regional groupings that have shown resistance to parts of the R2P agenda include some – such as Russia, China, India and Brazil – which are on the rise and which challenge the balance of power internationally. To some extent, R2P must therefore better reflect the changing political landscape and so – as the principal framework for R2P – must multilateral organisations.

A few implications follow from this. There is a need to give a voice to a more diverse range of policy actors in the promotion of R2P, which would go some way to lessen the perception of R2P as a 'Western' principle and reduce the polarisation of opinion which exists. Brazil's 'responsibility while protecting' initiative demonstrated the potential for broadening the debate in this way. Greater efforts are also needed to address broader questions about multilateral decision-making and

[29] Thakur, 'R2P after Libya and Syria', p. 62.

accountability and the manner in which international norms are promoted. In addition, there is a need for greater consistency in international attention to human rights abuses, both in general and in relation to R2P atrocities, in order to address the impression that action is only taken when it dovetails with the interests of major Western powers.

There are also problems with the democratic, cosmopolitan credentials of R2P within the legitimising framework of multilateralism, because of the disconnect between international norms and public opinion. There is some evidence of public support for R2P – and international attention to human rights crises more broadly – but this support is not adequately tested and it does not play a role in decisions on the initiation of international R2P activities, or in monitoring these activities when they are undertaken, or in holding actors to account when they perpetrate R2P crimes. There is also no direct public role in holding those states which undertake international action in the name of R2P to account, notably when there are claims that such action is being undertaken disingenuously or disproportionately. All of this suggests that there is a democratic deficit in the implementation of R2P – and, indeed, an internal contradiction to the R2P agenda – which needs to be addressed by strengthening the role of civil society in decision-making and by promoting the principle as a part of democratic debate. R2P cannot legitimately remain the exclusive realm of 'high politics' while also claiming to have cosmopolitan, democratic credentials.

Finally, R2P raises important implications for the study of multilateralism more broadly. The dominant institutionalist framework – providing a rationalist explanation of international cooperation in an anarchical environment – is an inadequate theoretical framework for understanding R2P. Ideas of reciprocity, transaction costs and state-centricity do not explain the traction that R2P has gained in multilateral settings, or the importance of non-state actors in promoting this agenda. Both the theory and practice of multilateralism clearly need to evolve in order that R2P can fulfil its crucial service to humankind.

8   Global governance and the Responsibility to Protect

Abiodun Williams

> Ours is a world in which no individual, and no country, exists in isolation. All of us live simultaneously in our own communities and in the world at large.
>
> Kofi A. Annan.[1]

National worldviews have been historically constricted by geography. Even the supposed global conflicts of the twentieth century featured Western powers playing out their political struggles in buffer or proxy states. This world in which social and economic interactions were driven by geographic restrictions, and warfare was primarily conducted between neighbouring nations, is now long gone, however.

The political realities of the past have crumbled as the traditional vehicle for change – technology – has broken down the barriers restraining international commerce, migration and information exchange even as it has increased the interconnectedness between individuals and states. Positive externalities of this process – which we refer to as globalisation – include a higher global standard of living through lowered trade barriers, and increased opportunities for travel or cultural exchange through reduced costs of transportation and communication. However, along with the perception of a global community comes a new threat, from a cast of emerging actors and maladies such as genocide and organised crime. Nations are increasingly affected by interrelated events occurring in faraway places: 'the environmental policies of China, the health situation in Africa, nuclear safety in Russia, and water management in the Middle East will affect the lives of millions of people who are not citizens of the countries that will make the decisions'.[2] The combination of new

---

[1] Kofi Annan, 'Problems without Passports', *Foreign Policy*, 132 (2002), p. 30

[2] Jean-Marie Guehenno, 'The Impact of Globalization on Strategy', in Chester A. Crocker, Fen Osler Hampson and Pamela Aall, eds, *Turbulent Peace* (Washington DC: US Institute of Peace Press, 2001), pp. 83–96, at p. 86.

perils and opportunities triggers the search for standards for trade, the environment, human rights and arms control in the absence of a true international authority. Even without such authority – or 'global government' – multilateral sanction regimes are installed, people in need receive food aid and the perpetrators of war crimes are brought to justice.

A deluge of scholarly work on global governance has accompanied the advancement of globalisation. Definitions attempting to grasp this evolving concept abound as more and more countries see the benefit of applying global governance tools in addressing their security concerns. This chapter demonstrates the importance and utility of global governance in addressing one of the most important challenges of the modern era: the protection of civilians from mass atrocity crimes. The improving capacity of states and the international community to prevent violent atrocities, as well as their ability to respond to such crimes should they occur, under the Responsibility to Protect (R2P) doctrine generate hope that global governance will prove to be a corrective steering mechanism to address the increasingly complex and transnational challenges of the twenty-first century.

Global governance

The transformation throughout the twentieth century in the spatial organisation of social relations and transactions, typically referred to as globalisation, created new ways in which political authority was exercised. International organisations, non-governmental organisations and business actors would increasingly complement the role of states by initiating or steering decision-making. The concept of global governance only gained solid footing in the aftermath of the Cold War, the end of which resulted in a relocation of authority 'both outwards toward supranational entities, and inwards toward sub-national groups'.[3]

Accompanying this systemic shift from bipolarity to multipolarity, the scholarship on global governance flourished, demonstrated by its centrality in discussions across a broad range of fields, from security studies and international political economy to social policy and environmental studies. Three landmark thresholds shaped the development of global governance from its inception to the modern understanding of the concept.

---

[3] James N. Rosenau, 'Governance, Order, and Change in World Politics', in James N. Rosenau and Ernst-Otto Csempiel, eds, *Governance without Government: Order and Change in World Politics* (New York: Press Syndicate of the University of Cambridge, 1992), pp. 1–29, at pp. 2–3.

James Rosenau's writings on globalisation set the stage in the early 1990s by advancing the idea of governance without government. He questioned the nature of citizenship in a global society and 'the kind of choices and responsibilities that seem increasingly likely to confront citizens . . . as the world shrinks and its parts become both more interdependent and less coherent'.[4] Effective global governance institutions would be necessary to help manage this growing interdependence and regulate transnational practices.

The second threshold was introduced by the Commission on Global Governance, established in 1992 with the support of UN Secretary-General Boutros Boutros-Ghali. The commission defined global governance as 'the sum of the many ways individuals and institutions, public and private, manage their common affairs'. Global governance included both 'formal institutions and regimes empowered to enforce compliance, as well as informal arrangements that people and institutions have either agreed to or perceive to be in their interest'.[5] The commission's seminal report, issued in 1995, created a great stir with its call for broad UN reform and led to a stronger and more centralised body. Inspired by the 1945 San Francisco Conference that gave birth to the United Nations, the commission framed its report as an agenda for change by creating new institutions to address the growing complexity of the international arena. The report suggested broadening the international security concept away from its traditional focus on states, to include 'the security of people and the planet'.[6] The same year the report was published, *Global Governance*, the widely known journal on the subject, was established to fill the need for a common intellectual history on the issue.[7]

The final milestone occurred with the Millennium Summit, the largest gathering to date of world leaders. Framed as a comprehensive effort to examine the status of the United Nations for the coming millennium, the summit supported the findings of the Global Governance Commission in urging institutional reform: 'while the post-war multilateral system made it possible for the new globalisation to emerge and flourish, globalisation, in turn, has progressively rendered its designs antiquated'.[8] In the wake of

---

[4] James N. Rosenau, 'Citizenship in a Changing Global Order', in *Governance without Government*, p. 272.

[5] Commission on Global Governance, *Our Global Neighbourhood* (New York: Oxford University Press, 1995), p. 2.

[6] Ibid., p. 78.

[7] *Global Governance* is the journal of the Academic Council on the United Nations System (ACUNS). The present author is a former chair of the ACUNS Board, and Ramesh Thakur, co-editor of this book, is the present editor-in-chief of *Global Governance*.

[8] 'Globalization and Governance', in *We the peoples: The Role of the United Nations in the 21st Century* (New York: United Nations, Department of Public Information, 2000), p. 11.

the catastrophes in Rwanda and Bosnia, world leaders recognised that interstate conflict no longer constituted the main threat to international peace and security. 'In recent decades, more people have been killed in civil war, ethnic cleansing, and acts of genocide', the report concluded.[9] Summit participants committed to work towards fulfilling the Millennium Development Goals, to improve the coordination between the disparate levels of authority throughout the United Nations and to create structures that reflect the political realities of our times.

The plethora of definitions of global governance reflects the disaggregated nature of the concept, but Thomas Weiss and Ramesh Thakur provide close to an all-encompassing summary of the term:

'[G]lobal governance' is the sum of laws, norms, policies, and institutions that define, constitute, and mediate relations among citizens, society, markets, and the state in the international arena – the wielders and objects of international public power. Even in the absence of an overarching central authority, existing collective arrangements bring more predictability, stability, and order to transboundary problems than we might expect.[10]

This definition reflects four central components of global governance: the conditions for political activity, which are laws, norms, policies and institutions; the scope of relevant actors, moving beyond states; the utility of global governance in providing order; and, finally, the transnational nature of the challenges it aims to address. Global governance is thus a diverse collection of multilevel and multisectoral authorities aimed at structuring the behaviour and interaction of state and non-state actors.

Global governance is generally accepted to include all levels of organised human activity, from grassroots movements to international organisations, including state entities, through which collective interests are articulated. It should not be equated with the manifestation of a centralised global authority, as it presents an 'indistinct patchwork of authority that is as diffuse as it is contingent'.[11] Indeed, global governance is one of the few concepts that equally matches the number of definitions to the instances of application. Steps towards more effective global governance are commonly framed as a push for institutional reform in the face of challenges states are unable to address by themselves. The discussion on the principle of the responsibility to protect within this chapter highlights

---

[9] Ibid., p. 3.

[10] Thomas G. Weiss and Ramesh Thakur, *Global Governance and the UN: An Unfinished Journey* (Bloomington: Indiana University Press, 2010), p. 6.

[11] Thomas G. Weiss, 'The UN's role in Global Governance', *UN Intellectual History Project*, briefing note no. 15 (New York: Ralph Bunche Institute for International Studies, 2009), p. 2.

the importance of effective global governance in ensuring the protection of civilians from atrocities.

Institutional manifestations of global governance

As the scope of threats and opportunities expands under the relentless pressure of globalisation, individuals and states increasingly turn to institutions to structure their cooperation and information exchange in the pursuit of common interests and values. Transnational institutions are tangible manifestations of global governance, featuring interaction between government and non-government entities, including political, economic, commercial and media actors active at the supranational and subnational level. Institutions interact in dynamic ways through a complex web of networks, in which the lead authority depends on the challenge of the day. A distinctive feature of the diverse assortment of global governance institutions is their role in shaping conditions for political activity at the supranational level as they develop or shape norms, laws and policies.

The most prominent set of global actors exists in the category of inter-governmental organisations (IGOs). These are established by treaty, consist of sovereign member states and take collective action in the interest of all represented nations and their people. Paramount among these IGOs, the United Nations (UN) is unique, given its unrivalled international legitimacy and experience. Despite its shortcomings, the UN is the principal mechanism through which state and non-state actors collaborate in the management of affairs that cross countries and continents, as it 'develops norms, promulgates recommendations, and institutionalises ideas'.[12] The UN Security Council and the UN General Assembly were established as forums for international policy debate and sources of coordinated action in the collective interest of UN member states. These principal organs, however, suffer from two mirrored problems. The composition of the Security Council is outdated, leading to frequent inaction or suboptimal decisions that represent the narrow interests of its permanent members. 'Based on the distribution of power and alignments in 1945, the composition of the Council today does not fully represent either the character or the needs of our globalised world.'[13] Conversely, the UN General Assembly is the closest governance has come to a world parliament as its 'one member, one vote' rule embodies a form of global democracy. However, the body suffers from a lack of binding decision-making capacity and frequently

[12] Ibid., p. 5.
[13] Commission on Global Governance, *Our Global Neighbourhood*, p. 13.

features inconclusive debates along North–South dimensions. The perennial calls for reform in both bodies and the inability to adequately address the political divides between member states continue to plague the global institution which otherwise represents the progress made towards true global governance.

An important subcategory of IGOs includes institutions operating at the regional level, like the European Union (EU) and the African Union (AU). These institutions represent the integration of sometimes historically contentious neighbouring states into a regional body, creating economies of scale and addressing shared interests. Smaller organisations with a more limited range of responsibilities and geographic scope, such as the League of Arab States or the Association of Southeast Asian Nations (ASEAN), carry out those tasks their constituent members ascribe to them, providing forums for subregional coordination in the face of challenges none of their members are able to resolve singlehandedly. Most IGOs operate in traditional intergovernmental fashion and maintain little independent authority to ensure compliance with their decisions. A small but expanding group of institutions carries true supranational decision-making capacity, among them the European Commission. European commissioners do not represent their home countries, but instead exercise independent authority in the European general interest by subjecting member states, companies and individuals to binding regulations. 'Most other key global actors', the US National Intelligence Council notes, 'are reluctant to delegate regulatory powers, let alone assign jurisdiction, to an international body, as to share sovereignty under majority decision-making.'[14]

IGOs can be multifunctional like the United Nations, or adopt specific tasks, like the International Atomic Energy Agency (IAEA). IGOs can focus on thematic areas as diverse as arms control, environmental sustainability or international migration. International financial institutions such as the World Trade Organisation (WTO) and the Bretton Woods Institutions characterise the need for states to ensure financial and monetary stability worldwide and facilitate the entry of developing countries in the global economy. Issue-based organisations reflect a trend towards specialisation in addressing the niche-based challenges. The International Organisation for Migration (IOM), the United Nations Children's Fund (UNICEF) and the World Food Programme

---

[14] National Intelligence Council and European Union Institute for Security Studies (NIC-EUISS), 'Global Governance 2025: At a Critical Juncture', (NIC 2010–2008, September 2010), p. 12.

(WFP) have grown especially adept at responding to cross-border humanitarian challenges.

Apart from IGOs, global governance is steered by a plethora of civil society organisations (CSOs), business actors and ad hoc arrangements. CSOs have grown tremendously in size, influence and diversity over recent decades. Humanitarian non-governmental organisations (NGOs) play a growing role in global governance through agenda-setting and implementation as they monitor human rights, provide microcredit loans or assist in administering elections. The mass media affect global governance as journalists investigate the situation in desolate places to shape views on global events. Filling the niche of global justice are judicial bodies like the International Criminal Court (ICC), the International Court of Justice (ICJ), international criminal tribunals and special courts. Multinational corporations proliferate as connections between capital and consumer markets span international borders, and private bond-rating agencies steer the decision-making of powerful economies. Finally, the Doha Development meetings and informal forums such as the Group of Eight (G8) and Group of Twenty (G20) show an increased willingness on the part of world leaders to coordinate their activities and solve transnational problems through ad hoc conferences and summits. 'The proliferation of regular summit-level meetings based outside global or regional institutions is a key feature of recent global governance innovation.'[15] These recent manifestations of global governance play an important agenda-setting role, but their decisions are generally non-binding.

The field of global governance is vast. 'There is no single model of global governance to fit all issues and policy problems, just as there is no single structure of global governance but a multitude of pieces that do not fit together in a complete puzzle. Such is the nature of global governance.'[16] If the global community aims to confront the complex challenges of the twenty-first century, it must first address its internal flaws.

Challenges to global governance

Social, political and economic interactions continue to evolve at a breakneck pace, but the search for effective global governance remains at an early stage. Global governance applies lessons learned following

---

[15] Ibid., p. 19.
[16] Margaret P. Karns and Karen A. Mingst, *International Organizations: The Politics and Processes of Global Governance* (Boulder, CO: Lynne Rienner, 2004), p. 511.

each achievement and failure, a required flexibility allowing the same network of actors to respond to deforestation challenges in the Amazon region and refugee flows in western Africa. Political realities – including intransigence against structural or immediate change and the difficulties in organising and maintaining consistent, willing coalitions – require that institutional structures continue to adjust. The network of global governance actors must overcome three primary challenges to enhance its effectiveness: state dominance, compliance and institutional proliferation.

State Dominance. The dominant role of states within the international system is a significant impediment to globally coordinated action. Early writings on global governance invariably predicted the decline of the nation state and the centralisation of regulatory instruments. 'States are still active and important', Rosenau argued, 'but their participation in the processes of world politics is nevertheless of a different, less dominating kind, thereby leading to the interpretation that fundamental systemic change has occurred'.[17] Several scholars introduced global governance in an effort to break away from post-Second World War systems and to challenge the traditional Realist theorists that dominated the study of international relations in the 1970s and 1980s. Cochrane and his colleagues affirm this notion: 'The global governance project . . . is normatively about dispersing power away from hegemonic centres of power, especially states.'[18] In this view, the United Nations is perceived as an independent organisational entity that complements, and in some instances supersedes, the role of nation states by facilitating cooperation in the international peace and security domain.

Although global decision-making processes have opened up to acknowledge the voices of middle powers, developing nations and non-state entities, powerful states continue to wield significant influence over the institutional system. Even within regional and international organisations, dominant nations shape the institutional and operational direction. From the UN Security Council to the WTO and the G8, institutional reform or robust multilateral action will require consent from key states, some of which have a vested interest in maintaining the status quo. Global governance should not be equated with supranational governance because the former remains dominated by intergovernmental procedures. Instead of operating as an independent entity,

[17] Rosenau, 'Governance, Order, and Change in World Politics', p. 23.
[18] See Jan Selby, 'Introduction', in Feargal Cochrane, Rosaleen Duffy and Jan Selby, eds, *Global Governance, Conflict and Resistance* (New York: Palgrave Macmillan, 2003), pp. 1–18, at p. 6.

global institutions generally remain the sum of their parts, with little ambition or potential to exert supranational authority.

For global governance institutions to be effective and sustainable, stable national environments are therefore indispensable. Particularly in times of domestic instability, states struggle to transcend narrow self-interest and demonstrate flexibility in multilateral diplomacy and other international settings. In dealing with transnational challenges, permanent representatives at the UN act primarily in the interest of their home capital, deliberating within the parameters set out by their national governments. In the face of politically sensitive challenges that require coercive action, the United Nations is merely as effective as its members enable it to be. IGOs and NGOs lack independent resources and autonomy, forcing them to rely on the governments from which they originate. UN member states often prove unwilling to contribute financial or human resources to missions not in their direct political interest. According to Rosenau, 'governance refers to activities backed by shared goals'.[19] Unfortunately, the list of goals universally shared among nation states remains limited, reducing the potential impact of global governance. It seems clear that the presence of global challenges and the creation of global institutions do not automatically result in shared goals, a global community or global values. The prevention of mass atrocities may well be one of the few objectives shared worldwide, explaining the unprecedented normative development of atrocity prevention principles like the responsibility to protect.

Compliance. Like national governments, global institutions require authority to protect the interest of their constituents. Yet most manifestations of global governance uphold limited independent power and legitimacy. 'Shortfalls in moral standing, legal foundations, material delivery, democratic credentials and charismatic leadership have together generated large legitimacy deficits in existing global regimes.'[20] Few global governance actors have the authority, responsibility and capacity to ensure that legal commitments are met. De facto, international law-abiding behaviour comes from peer pressure by allies or the 'golden rule' of 'doing unto others as you would have them do unto you'.[21] International institutions have issued indictments, installed sanctions regimes and even authorised the deployment of coercive force. However, the number of IGOs issuing binding decisions that

---

[19] Rosenau, 'Governance, Order, and Change in World Politics', p. 4.

[20] Jan Aart Scholte, 'Civil Society and the Legitimation of Global Governance', CSGR working paper no. 223/07 (University of Warwick, 2007), p. 1.

[21] Karns and Mingst, *International Organizations*, p. 6.

can be enforced through hard power remains limited. The UN Charter calls for standing UN military forces, but none yet exist.[22] Any form of supranational legislation lacks a robust enforcement mechanism to ensure consistent compliance.

Institutional Proliferation. Globalisation is characterised by a diversification of rule systems and spheres of authority that cross state borders.[23] With such an institutional diversity, inefficiencies, occupational overlap and turf battles become standard practice. 'Intersectoral polarization can produce struggles to control decisions in domains where many actors have important stakes. Governments and intergovernmental organizations may seek to exclude multinational corporations and transnational civil society alliances from input to important international decisionmaking processes.'[24] To overcome this fragmentation, greater coordination is required, both within large bureaucracies and between them. Institutional proliferation strengthens the need for effective networks, coalitions and partnerships, both formal and informal, to coordinate decision-making early on. A more defined hierarchy must be developed to overcome situations in which organisations with overlapping authorities aspire to different or even competing goals. The frequent disagreements between civil society organisations, regional organisations and the United Nations about the utility of intervention in a country at risk of violence or atrocities illustrate the complexity of these relationships.

The ability of the current set of intergovernmental organisations to transcend these challenges will determine the future of global governance. 'The nexus between evolving global order and changes to the concrete manifestations of multilateralism can reveal much about the extent of the relevance and legitimacy of multilateral institution.'[25] The addition of permanent members, the creation of more rotational seats or comprehensive UN Security Council reform may be a promising start to overcoming some of the impediments to global decision-making.

---

[22] Weiss, 'The UN's Role in Global Governance', p. 5.

[23] James N. Rosenau, 'Governance in a New Global Order', in David Held and Anthony McGrew, eds, *The Global Transformations Reader* (Cambridge: Polity Press, 2000), pp. 223–233.

[24] L. David Brown, Sanjeev Khagtam, Mark H. Moore and Peter Frumkin , 'Globalization, NGOs, and Multisectoral Relations', in Joseph S. Nye and John D. Donahue, eds, *Governance in a Globalizing World* (Washington DC: Brookings Institution Press, 2000), pp. 271–296, at p. 289.

[25] W. Andy Knight, 'The Future of the UN Security Council: Questions of Legitimacy and Representation in Multilateral Governance', in Andrew F. Cooper, John English, and Ramesh Thakur, eds, *Enhancing Global Governance: Towards a New Diplomacy?* (New York: United Nations University Press, 2002), pp. 19–37, at p. 19.

The Responsibility to Protect

The use of deadly force against civilians remains a disturbing feature in the twenty-first century. Large-scale killings cost thousands of innocent lives annually in vulnerable societies, mainly throughout Central and South Asia and sub-Saharan Africa.[26] Historically, governments operated with a sense of impunity when exercising their authority within the confines of their territory or reaping the spoils from military victory abroad. From the destruction of Melos during the Peloponnesian War to the assault against Armenians by the Ottoman Empire, individuals have always lethally targeted innocent populations in a spirit of revenge, fear or sheer convenience.[27] National sovereignty and victor's justice provided a powerful shield protecting abusive regimes from international reprimands. Additionally, 'the peace and security provisions of the UN Charter were designed to deal with wars between states, and it was not envisaged that the UN would intervene in the domestic affairs of sovereign states'.[28]

However, in a globalised world featuring a plethora of peacebuilding actors and an immediacy of information, atrocity crimes are no longer regarded as the unfortunate residual consequence of state consolidation and authority. 'The revolution in global communication has created new expectations that humanitarian suffering will be alleviated and fundamental rights vindicated.'[29] The images of bodies strewn about the streets of Kigali, Srebrenica or Goma and displayed on international media create a political atmosphere less tolerant of atrocities. Mass killing has been prioritised as a new transnational or global challenge together with pandemics, terrorism, organised crime and climate change. Although the conduct of one-sided violence is nothing new, its perceived impact on international security and the urge to halt such heinous crimes are unprecedented.

Coupled with the increased inclusiveness of human security is the new ability to hold individuals accountable for atrocious crimes against civilians within their borders. The emerging notion of a responsibility of both national governments and the international community to protect civilians is the latest effort by a globalised world to prevent mass killing, to react to incidences of such crimes and to rebuild in their aftermath. The

---

[26] The Human Security Report Project, *Sexual Violence, Education, and War: Beyond the Mainstream Narrative* (Vancouver: Human Security Press, 2012), pp. 203–204.
[27] Daniel Chirot and Clark McCauley, *Why Not Kill Them All? The Logic and Prevention of Mass Political Murder* (Princeton, NJ: Princeton University Press, 2010), pp. 19–44.
[28] Commission on Global Governance, *Our Global Neighbourhood*, p. 16.
[29] United Nations, 'Globalization and Governance', p. 12.

Responsibility to Protect serves as a corrective mechanism for the collection of authorities that constitute a complex and emerging system of global governance.

R2P's conceptual and operational development is inextricably linked with the public face of global governance, the United Nations. Francis Deng, in his earlier incarnation as representative of the UN secretary-general on internally displaced persons, provided the early foundations by questioning the tension between national sovereignty and international action to halt atrocity crimes within a sovereign state. Together with his colleagues at the Brookings Institution, Deng articulated the idea of 'sovereignty as a responsibility' in 1996 in an effort to overcome the intervention dilemma. His conceptual work, in combination with the political leadership of former UN Secretary-General Kofi Annan, paved the way for the birth of a new concept aimed at countering the increased use of extreme violence against unarmed civilians. Against the backdrop of UN failures to prevent mass killings in Rwanda and Srebrenica, and the 'illegal but legitimate'[30] intervention in Kosovo, Annan declared that 'the United Nations also has a moral responsibility to ensure that genocides such as that perpetrated in Rwanda are prevented from ever happening again'.[31] The International Commission on Intervention and State Sovereignty (ICISS) took up this call by issuing a report in 2001 that first coined the term 'responsibility to protect' in an illustration of global governance in action. At the 2005 UN World Summit, all heads of state/government unanimously embraced the principle and pledged to act in accordance with it. R2P posits that each state has the primary responsibility to protect its population. If the regime is unable or unwilling to fulfil these duties, it proves itself no longer a legitimate sovereign, leading to a transfer of responsibilities to the international community to counter acute risks of brute violence against civilians.

Global governance actors continue to play a vital role in the development of R2P. Humanitarian NGOs advance the principle by monitoring human rights abuses, calling for action and conducting public advocacy campaigns. Regional organisations – the Economic Community of West African States (ECOWAS), the North Atlantic Treaty Organization (NATO) and the EU in particular – implement R2P doctrine in the field, often in partnership with the United Nations. The African Union

---

[30] Independent International Commission on Kosovo, *The Kosovo Report* (New York: Oxford University Press, 2000).
[31] Kofi A. Annan, *Prevention of Armed Conflict*. Report of the Secretary-General, Document A/55/985-S/2001/574 (New York: United Nations, 7 June 2001), Executive Summary.

enshrined key elements of R2P in its Constitutive Act, marking a significant shift from 'non-intervention to non-indifference'.[32] Although the Responsibility to Protect embodies the functioning of global governance, middle and great power states still played a fundamental role in establishing and implementing the principle: former Canadian Foreign Minister Lloyd Axworthy was the driving force behind the establishment of ICISS in 2000; the discussions before the 2005 World Summit shaped the way R2P is still conceived of today; the governments of the Netherlands and Rwanda play an important mobilising role as co-chairs of the informal Group of Friends of R2P; and advocates such as Australia, Costa Rica and Switzerland ensure that atrocity prevention remains high on the international policy agenda.

The development of R2P illustrates the rise and centrality of global governance and its champions. Global governance is vital to the development of R2P, which in turn provides the foundation that allows global governance to sustain itself. The transnational scope of the challenge, the variety of actors responsible and the depth of the cognitive and behavioural change required leads to the conclusion that only more effective global governance can address the risk posed by atrocity crimes to unarmed civilians. A functioning system of global governance will empower both state and non-state actors to uphold their responsibility to protect and deter potential perpetrators. Global governance faces a grave test in addressing this challenge.

The problems it aims to address

The framers of the Responsibility to Protect did not set out to cure all the ills of the world. R2P has a narrowly defined objective and does not aspire to cover all human protection issues, rid the world of the scourge of war or foster equitable economic growth worldwide. However, in its role as a political alarm bell, R2P sets a deliberately high threshold. The challenges R2P seeks to address are limited to the four crimes listed in the 2005 World Summit Outcome Document: genocide, war crimes, ethnic cleansing and crimes against humanity. Despite the overlap between conflict prevention, human rights promotion and R2P tools, stretching the R2P concept could arguably undermine its political utility.

---

[32] Paul D. Williams, 'From Non-Intervention to Non-Indifference: The Origins and Development of the African Union's Security Culture', *African Affairs*, 106:423 (2007), pp. 253–279, at p. 256.

Today, mass atrocities present a transnational challenge that the patch-work of diffuse authorities is aiming to address. The process of globalisation has broadened the interpretation of threats to international peace and security, opening the door for military force authorised by the UN Security Council under Articles 38 and 42 of the UN Charter. Atrocities present a singular challenge in having widespread destabilising effects: refugee streams, radicalisation and the erosion of the international legal framework. 'In an increasingly globalized and interdependent world, few events are ever totally local in their impact ... Clear breaches of interna-tional human rights standards, and indeed crimes against international law, are invariably involved in these cases.'[33] Even when committed in faraway places, national governments increasingly perceive mass atrocities as a threat to their national security. In the recent US presidential directive on mass atrocities, President Barack Obama considered the prevention of mass atrocities and genocide 'a core national security interest and a core moral responsibility of the United States'.[34]

Prioritising multilateral efforts to halt atrocious acts against civilians resonates with the emerging human security paradigm. As globalisation complemented state-based governance with new layers of subnational and supranational authority, so too has the trend towards universality broadened the traditional understanding of national security as prior-itising the defence of state boundaries from external military threats. Within this new global order, populations want protection from a broader range of threats that include disease, pollution and extreme economic deprivation. The human security perspective is people-centred, focusing on freedom from 'fear' and 'want',[35] and account-ability when political elites abuse their power. Correspondingly, the focus of conversations about humanitarian interventions shifted from 'the right of states to intervene' to 'the responsibility to protect civilians'. The Global Governance Commission confirmed the growing accep-tance that the international community was authorised, and in excep-tional cases obligated, to act in cases 'that constituted a violation of the security of people so gross and extreme that it requires an international response on humanitarian grounds'.[36]

---

[33] Gareth Evans, *The Responsibility to Protect: Ending Mass Atrocity Crimes Once and for All* (Washington DC: Brookings Institution Press, 2008), p. 134.

[34] The White House, 'Presidential Study Directive on Mass Atrocities', PSD-10 (Washington DC: Office of the Press Secretary, 4 August 2011.)

[35] National Research Council, 'America's Climate Choices', in *Advancing the Science of Climate Change* (Washington DC: National Academies Press, 2010), p. 389.

[36] Commission on Global Governance, *Our Global Neighbourhood*, p. 90.

The actors it aims to steer

Even in today's globalised world, powerful states maintain a firm hold on formal international security arrangements. It is therefore no surprise that states carry the primary responsibility for implementing the Responsibility to Protect, and that global governance actors or the international community play complementary roles. States carry a three-tier responsibility that corresponds with the three R2P pillars presented by Secretary-General Ban Ki-moon in his 2009 report *Implementing the Responsibility to Protect*.[37] States have a responsibility to protect their populations, request help from the international community if necessary and accept an international presence taking collective action within their territory in case of manifest failure. More particularly, each government is expected to mitigate the risk of atrocities by banning institutionalised discriminatory practices, engaging in regional integration, fighting corruption or controlling the spread of small arms and light weapons. Despite their principal responsibilities, states are often directly or indirectly involved in the killing as the political elite exploits its authority in a polarised society for political gain. In this case, international access may be limited, triggering the consideration of non-consensual enforcement measures as a last resort.

The Responsibility to Protect also serves as a behavioural guideline for intergovernmental and civil society organisations capable of affecting the structural and short-term dynamics leading up to mass violence. In a case of latent or imminent risk, all relevant actors are expected to examine and apply the appropriate tools at their disposal: human rights organisations by monitoring and reporting ongoing abuses, multinational corporations by upholding the principles of corporate social responsibility, and regional organisations by demanding good governance in return for access to their common market. Given its exclusive ability to authorise the use of force, the UN Security Council plays a unique role in this regard. The 1995 Commission on Global Governance recognised the centrality of the Council in sharpening the mass atrocity response system: 'The use of force would be authorised only if these means of peacefully resolving disputes failed and the Security Council determined that under the Charter amendment [legitimising interference], such intervention was justified on the basis of the violation of the security of people.'[38]

---

[37] Ban Ki-moon, *Implementing the Responsibility to Protect*, Document A/63/677 (New York: United Nations General Assembly, 12 January 2009). The three pillars of R2P are the protection responsibilities of the state, international assistance and capacity-building, and timely and decisive collective response.

[38] Commission on Global Governance, *Our Global Neighbourhood*, p. 92.

The conduct it aims to generate

The 2001 report of the International Commission on Intervention and State Sovereignty identified three action components within the Responsibility to Protect: prevention, reaction and rebuilding.

The importance of prevention in governance was first introduced in relation to violent conflict. The 1992 *Agenda for Peace*, by UN Secretary-General Boutros Boutros-Ghali, emphasised the UN's role in seeking to 'identify at the earliest possible stage situations that could produce conflict, and to try through diplomacy to remove the sources of danger before violence results'.[39] Just a few years later, the Global Governance Commission Report stated that 'the primary goals of global security policy should be to prevent conflict ... by anticipating and managing crises before they escalate into armed conflict'.[40] In R2P discussions, the responsibility to prevent is widely recognised as the principle's single most important pillar given that preventive action is deemed preferable to reactive approaches in strategic, moral and financial terms. The four areas of R2P prevention introduced by Alex Bellamy are early warning, preventive diplomacy, ending impunity and preventive deployments.[41] Identifying the underlying causes of atrocities through sound analysis and early warning are a first step towards effective prevention. When the risk is latent, domestic and international prevention efforts focus on coordinated capacity-building and empowering local communities. Before atrocities, non-coercive diplomatic, economic and legal measures take precedence. When atrocities are considered more imminent, crisis management efforts are rapidly set in motion – managing the role of potential spoilers, conditioning aid or issuing threats to intervene.

The responsibility to react is often mistakenly equated with the use of force. The use of coercive military force authorised by the Security Council under Chapter VII of the UN Charter remains a last resort option in case the crimes committed go beyond the pale and grounds are reasonable to believe non-military and non-coercive options would fail. R2P served as a central motivation for the robust interventions in Côte D'Ivoire and Libya, where 'all means necessary' were authorised to protect civilians. Critical governments stress the potentially corrosive effects of R2P on their national sovereignty, as well as the potential for Western abuse of R2P to legitimise self-interested unilateral

---

[39] Boutros Boutros-Ghali, *An Agenda for Peace*, Document A/47/277-S/24111 (New York: United Nations, 1992).

[40] Commission on Global Governance, *Our Global Neighbourhood*, pp. 84–85.

[41] Alex Bellamy, *Responsibility to Protect: The Global Effort to End Mass Atrocities* (Cambridge: Polity Press, 2009), p. 106.

interventions. In a constructive effort to express post-Libya concerns, Brazil introduced the term 'responsibility while protecting', a proposal aimed at complementing the R2P principle in emphasising the need for international accountability. Accountability is vital during any multi-lateral engagement because an external presence may further escalate an already fragile situation.

The reaction repertoire, however, is not limited to the use of force. Non-military measures such as condemnations, the creation of safe havens, the imposition of travel bans and the referral of individuals to the ICC can affect the decision-making calculus of potential perpetrators and protect vulnerable civilians. The distinction arrived at by Weiss and Hubert, between tools aimed at coercing perpetrators and instruments that seek to protect civilians, is productive when assessing non-military reactive measures.[42]

The responsibility to rebuild encapsulates efforts to prevent a stabilis-ing yet fragile post-atrocity environment from relapsing into mass vio-lence against civilians. Rebuilding means 'to provide, particularly after a military intervention, full assistance with recovery, reconstruction and reconciliation, addressing the causes of the harm the intervention was designed to halt or avert'.[43] Addressing deep-rooted grievances, support-ing transitional justice and ensuring reconciliation following atrocities are critical to discouraging future atrocities. This preventive dimension explains the overlap between tools for prevention and rebuilding. However, the memory of past atrocities among both perpetrators and victims provides a distinctive challenge in rebuilding efforts. Rebuilding operations typically feature the disarmament, demobilisation and reinte-gration of armed units, the installation of truth and reconciliation mechanisms and security sector reform.

Several successes and failures typify the mixed legacy of atrocity pre-vention and R2P initiatives. Prevention efforts were successful in subvert-ing a potential crisis in Macedonia following its independence from the former Yugoslavia in the early 1990s, whereas the international mobilisa-tion in Kenya in 2008 illustrates how a rapid reaction can effectively quell an ongoing atrocity. Likewise, rebuilding efforts in Bosnia-Herzegovina following the atrocities committed in the mid-1990s have helped to pre-vent the country from regressing to large-scale violence for nearly twenty years. However, the failures in Srebrenica, Rwanda and Syria show that

[42] International Commission on Intervention and State Sovereignty (ICISS), *The Responsibility to Protect: Research, Bibliography, and Background* (Ottawa: International Development Research Centre, 2001).

[43] International Commission on Intervention and State Sovereignty, *The Responsibility to Protect* (Ottawa: International Development Research Centre, 2001), p. xi.

the imperfect mechanisms in place need further polishing before R2P's ambitious objectives become reality.

Conclusion

Previous R2P failures demonstrate the imperfect nature of global governance. 'If global governance structures and processes do not keep up with the changes in the balance of power in the international system, they run the risk of becoming irrelevant.'[44] At the nexus between global governance and R2P is the need for institutional reform and enhanced coordination, both at the international level among UN entities and at the national level to increase government and non-profit efficacy and accountability. A future assessment study by the National Intelligence Council and the European Union Institute for Security Studies found that 'the multiple and diverse frameworks, however flexible, probably are not going to be sufficient to keep pace with the looming number of transnational and global challenges absent extensive institutional reforms and innovations'.[45] Institutions need to reflect the modern normative and political context and the evolved security prioritisation of our times.

Central to any transformational change will be a reform of the UN Security Council. Sheer expansion of its permanent and non-permanent membership may not suffice, because the interests of its member states will continue to differ in case of imminent or ongoing atrocities. Unless the council reconsiders the use of the veto to block action against atrocity situations and strengthens the UN's early warning capacity, its voice in international politics may continue to stagnate. However, such an overhaul requires an unprecedented gesture on the part of permanent council members. 'Interests and ideas will always clash. But the world can improve on the last century's dismal record. The international community is a work in progress.'[46]

[44] NIC-EUISS, 'Global Governance 2025', p. 17.   [45] Ibid., p. 30.
[46] Annan, 'Problems without Passports'.

9   International law, the Responsibility to Protect and international crises

Jean-Marc Coicaud

As described in the genealogy provided in Chapter 2 of this volume by Gareth Evans, the notion and agenda of the Responsibility to Protect (R2P) emerged against the backdrop of the controversies over humanitarian crises and interventions in the 1990s. This amounted to less than a straightforward international legal obligation, but more than the simple appeal to moral decency that had prevailed previously, for instance in the context of the Convention for the Prevention and Punishment of the Crime of Genocide.[1] Later, on the occasion of the 2005 United Nations (UN) World Summit, the international community, in agreeing to the wording of paragraphs 138–139 of the Outcome Document, went further by officially endorsing R2P as a legitimate norm and tool. As a result, in the following years it became rather normal to use the notion of R2P in the UN context, as illustrated by the various resolutions and statements of the UN Security Council referring to it, or, since 2009, by the annual reports of the UN secretary-general on the operationalization of R2P (reports followed by an informal dialogue in the General Assembly to discuss the secretary-general's findings and recommendations).[2]

This evolution has not, however, settled the debates about R2P. Discussions continue on the circumstances and conditions in which this approach makes sense. This is especially the case concerning the

---

[1] 'Perhaps the greatest unresolved question in the Convention is the meaning of the enigmatic word "Prevent" ... In article I, States Parties undertake to prevent genocide ... [but] the Convention has little specific to say on the question. The obligation to prevent genocide is a blank sheet awaiting the inscriptions of State practice and case law'. William A. Schabas, *Genocide in International Law* (New York: Cambridge University Press, 2000), pp. 545–546.

[2] The first UN secretary-general report on R2P was released in January, 2009, under the title *Implementing the Responsibility to Protect*. Subsequently, the following UN secretary-general reports were published: *Early Warning, Assessment, and the RtoP* (June 2010), *Role of Regional and Sub-Regional Arrangements on Implementing RtoP* (July 2011), *Responsibility to Protect – Timely and Decisive Response* (August 2012), *Responsibility to Protect: State Responsibility and Prevention* (August 2013), *Responsibility to Protect: International Assistance* (August 2014). On this, see *RtoP at the United Nations* (New York, International Coalition for the Responsibility to Protect, September 2014).

use of force, by far the most controversial aspect of R2P and to which we particularly refer in this chapter. This situation is not surprising, especially considering the two types of challenges at the heart of the question of R2P. On the one hand, there is the structural challenge of R2P exacerbating the tensions and the dilemmas that can exist among the fundamental principles and values that national sovereignty, respect for human rights, national interest, solidarity and responsibility beyond borders constitute for the current systems of international relations and international law. On the other hand, there is the contextual and practical challenge of never being sure of what is the best course of action to address a humanitarian crisis, so that in the long run the situation gets better rather than worse.

This chapter analyses R2P, with special attention given to its use of force component, in relation to the structure of international law and some of the latest crises of the period. It is organised in three parts. First, it examines how the normative and power structures of international law are key to understanding the extent and limit of the Responsibility to Protect. Second, it refers to R2P in the context of three of the defining crises of recent years: Syria, Ukraine and Gaza. Third and finally, the chapter draws some lessons and touches upon the future of R2P.

International law and the extent and limits of the Responsibility to Protect

International law is in large measure built around fundamental principles and the nature and dynamics of international rights that come with them. Clarifying this reality is crucial for understanding how the notion of R2P came to emerge and to be viewed as an option in international politics. Indeed, the fundamental principles of international law, including their relations of compatibility, competition and hierarchy, and how these translate in the conception and organisation of international right-holders, hierarchies of right-holders and rightful conduct in international law, are essential to understanding the theory and practice, as well as the extent and, more importantly, the limits of R2P.

Principles of international law and their relations

At the core of international law are a number of fundamental principles. They were officially recognised when the 'Declaration on Principles of International Law Concerning Friendly Relations and Cooperation among States, in Accordance with the Charter of the United Nations' was adopted by the United Nations General Assembly Resolution 2625 on 24 October 1970. More than thirty years later, on the occasion of the World Summit held at the UN in 2005, the heads of state and government rededicated themselves to them as basic guidelines for the life of the whole community.[3] As mentioned in the UN Declaration of 1970 and, again, in the 2005 resolution, these principles are the following: sovereign equality of states, self-determination of peoples, prohibition of the threat or use of force, peaceful settlement of disputes, non-intervention in the internal affairs of other states, respect for human rights, international cooperation and good faith.[4]

The nature and function of these principles are to serve as normative, political and policy guidelines for the thinking, deliberations, decisions and, ultimately, actions of the people in charge of formulating and implementing what is right internationally, especially in the multilateral framework. Both individually and aggregated together, they are central to the legitimacy of the international system underwritten by international law, and they are meant to contribute to the empowerment of actors, nationally and internationally. This ability to help empower actors rests as well on the compatible, competitive and hierarchical relationships that exist between them.

The merit of compatibility among the key principles of international law is to ensure that they complement one another and point in the same direction. We can identify three types of compatibility among the principles. First, there is compatibility among the principles of sovereign equality of states, prohibition of the threat or use of force, peaceful settlements of disputes and non-intervention in the internal affairs of other states. Such compatibility is designed to facilitate the coexistence among international actors. Second, the principles of self-determination of peoples and respect for human rights are in theory compatible as well, as they concern the quality of life within the collective units of the international system, although it should be noted that self-determination does not necessarily serve respect for human rights.[5] Third, the principles of

---

[3] *World Summit Outcome*, Document A/RES/60/1 (New York: United Nations, 24 October 2005), section 1, paragraph 5.

[4] For a study of the fundamental principles, Antonio Cassese, *International Law in a Divided World* (Oxford: Oxford University Press, 1994), pp. 126–165. For another perspective, see Hedley Bull, *The Anarchical Society: A Study of Order in World Politics* (New York: Columbia University Press, 1995), pp. 64–68.

[5] As part of the dynamics of nationalism and the mixture of inclusive solidarity and exclusive particularism that it is, self-determination can play a contradictory role: asking for rights of people to be respected but also, with nationalist forces clashing, being a source of violations of human rights. See Martti Koskenniemi, 'National Self-Determination Today: Problems of Legal Theory and Practice', *International And Comparative Law Quarterly* 43:2 (1994); Nathaniel Berman, *Passions et ambivalences: Le colonialisme, le nationalisme et le droit international* (Paris: Editions Pedone, translated under the direction of

good faith and cooperation are also compatible, for good faith conveys the idea that states must not take undue advantage of their rights or discharge their obligations, so as to thwart the purpose and object of international legal rules. In other words, without good faith, trust and, consequently, cooperation are not conceivable.

Competitive relationships among fundamental principles are problematic but essential. They are problematic because they cause tensions. However, competitive principles cannot be omitted; like compatible principles, the principles in competition are strategic and a central part of international legitimacy. As long as identifying with and mobilising them does not upset the international legal and political framework, they provide and accommodate alternative and pluralistic views. In this perspective, they offer flexibility and maneuvering space in the handling of international demands that help preserve the overall normative and political architecture and credibility of the international system more than a rigid, total convergence of principles would.

Competition among fundamental principles tends to be found between the sovereign equality of states and non-intervention in the internal affairs of other states, on the one hand, and self-determination of peoples and respect for human rights on the other (keeping in mind the restriction mentioned above concerning self-determination). The latter, indicative of the post-Westphalian pattern, is the product of new trends that have emerged after the First World War and particularly after the Second World War, partly deriving from Third World advocacy and partly from the universalisation of Western democratic values.

Against this background, hierarchy among fundamental principles is crucial, for, although all of the principles are essential, they are not on an equal plane. Some prevail over others. As such, the function of hierarchy among the principles of international law is to organise relations among them according to priorities, with some predominating over others without overlooking or even disregarding those that come in second.

Right-holding in international law

These principles and their relations find their complement in the nature and dynamics of right-holding in international law. And, as we are about to see, it is in this double context of principles and right-holding that the emergence and extent and limits of R2P have to be understood.

Nathaniel Berman and Emmanuelle Jouannet by Lucie Delabie, Marie Blocteur, Leila Choukroune, Céline Clerfeuille and Olivia Harrison, 2008), pp. 393–401.

At the most general level, right-holding in international law is about the determination of who is recognised as a member of the international community and is, as such, a right-holder, and vice versa. That said, the determination of who is 'in' and who is 'out' of the international community of legitimacy, so to speak, is not the only distinction at work regarding the issue of right-holding. For among those actors who are right-holders, there is a hierarchy. Some are more important than others, both in normative and practical/policy/political terms. The hierarchy that exists between the state and the individual as international right-holders is a case in point.

When it comes to the state as an international right-holder, the fact that the principles of international law that are firmly rooted in the Westphalian model – in particular sovereign equality of states and non-intervention in the internal affairs of other states – have historically been given primacy has led the state being the primary international right-holder on which other right-holders mainly depend. This has made it the cornerstone of a system of law, both internationally and nationally, geared towards making it the main executor and beneficiary of agency in international law–international relations. From this privileged standing has followed the fact that the possibility, defence and evolution of the international system cannot, to a large extent, be dissociated from the state. Interestingly, this also applies to the rise of the principles belonging to the post-Westphalian paradigm. Without the support of the state, even if at times it had to be pressured to provide such support, principles such as the self-determination of peoples, prohibition of the threat or use of force, peaceful settlement of disputes, respect for human rights and cooperation would not have officially become part of international law and the international system.

By comparison, the individual is a rather secondary international right-holder. To be sure, over time, with the spread of democratic values, the rights of states, which at one point had been more or less absolute at home and abroad, were curtailed. This is how individuals were made right-holders, first internally within those countries embracing the democratic agenda, and then internationally, with international law, particularly after the Second World War and even more so since the end of the Cold War, acknowledging and supporting the relevance of human rights more and more. Nevertheless, individuals, probably more important today than ever as international right-holders, continue to be in a position of relative weakness vis-à-vis the state.

This relationship explains the contrasting picture of international rightful conduct in international law–international relations and, ultimately, that of the notion of R2P. On the one hand, international rightful conduct is no longer limited to the state. If the state remains a key agent and beneficiary of both international law and the system of international relations international law helps to monitor, it is no longer its only beneficiary. With the individual having become a significant international right-holder, it is also in connection with how states behave towards individuals, internally and externally, that their international rightful conduct is defined and measured. On the other hand, it continues to be the case that what is owed to individuals is never as decisive and significant as that which is owed to states. This is shown by the fact that the accountability of political leaders and institutions based on what is owed to individuals remains more an idea, if not an ideal, than an uncontested and automatic and systematic reality. To this day, victims of mass crimes cannot be certain that when states violate their individual and human rights the international community will act to stop them and bring perpetrators to justice.

What this means for the Responsibility to Protect

Having these elements in mind is key to making sense of the emergence of R2P as well as its extent and limitations.

The end of the Cold War and the multiplication of the local/intranational conflicts and the human rights/humanitarian crises that accompanied them made it simultaneously possible and urgent to build upon and push further the importance that international law had previously accorded to the principle of respect for human rights. In the process, this altered what had, to that point, been the order of priorities for principles and right-holding in international law. As human rights treaties had not created a true legal obligation for the international community and its member states to ensure human rights protection, the adoption of R2P served as a middle ground between establishing a real obligation to intervene, for which there was no appetite, and the normative status quo, which amounted to doing nothing. As such, it constituted a significant normative/policy/political step forward. In particular, with R2P, international rightful conduct of states, rather than being primarily evaluated on how states act towards one another, came to include how they extend to individuals a sense of responsibility and solidarity. In this perspective, the three Western democratic permanent members of the United Nations Security Council – the United States, the United Kingdom and France – which had been quite supportive of the idea of international humanitarian interventions and the possibility of using force in the 1990s, pursued their leading role in the 2000s in support of the endorsement of R2P so that it would become part of the portfolio of resources available when addressing humanitarian and human rights crises.

This evolution and the extent it gave to R2P did not imply, however, a full reversal of the hierarchy and priorities that had put national sovereignty, the state as an international right-holder and the national interest at the top of the normative and policy pyramid of international law, and the system of international relations. It only changed it slightly, making it marginally more progressive, while preserving its overall equilibrium and logic. The international relevance of the individual, as expressed in the principle of respect for human rights and the status of international right-holder, had to be acted upon more urgently now than in the past. This was the positive message of R2P. However, R2P, especially when it entails the use of force to protect civilian populations, has been no more than a limited tool of limited use. The state, and its rights and interests, more than international human rights, have remained the building blocks of international law and the international system. In this context, in the UN Security Council, the United States, the United Kingdom and France have been much more willing than Russia and China to call upon R2P and its use of force component, at times pressing for it to be used as a justification for international intervention, like in the case of Libya. But their commitment to R2P has taken place within limits, shaped and constrained by their own continued alignment on the philosophy of national sovereignty and national interest, and the political and geopolitical calculations this philosophy entails. The way in which the humanitarian and human rights crises have been handled recently in Syria, Gaza and Ukraine illustrates this state of affairs.

The crises in Syria, Ukraine and Gaza, and the Responsibility to Protect

In recent years the notion of R2P has been referred to many times by the UN Security Council, mainly in relation to conflicts in Africa and the Middle East. But it has also been more or less ignored on a variety of occasions, despite the fact that very serious humanitarian crises and massive human rights violations have been occurring. This shows how the place and use of R2P and its so-called three pillars[6] are anything but secure and straightforward tools in international policy. In this regard, we touch

---

[6] Pillar One: every state has the responsibility to protect its population from the four mass atrocity crimes of genocide, war crimes, ethnic cleansing and crimes against humanity. Pillar Two: the wider international community has the responsibility to encourage and assist individual states in meeting that responsibility. Pillar Three: if a state is manifestly failing to protect its populations, the international community must be prepared to take appropriate collective action, in a timely and decisive manner and in accordance with the UN Charter.

upon three recent crises below in connection with R2P. We start with Syria. In this case, the extent and the modalities of the humanitarian and human rights crises have made calling upon R2P appropriate. Yet it is as if R2P was never really an option in Syria. This inaction has taken place at the expense of the civilian population and now, with the Islamic State of Iraq and the Levant (ISIL)[7] being a threat, of the stability of an already fragile and traumatised region. Next, we move on to Ukraine, where, despite the fact that the situation on the ground has not fit the R2P conditions, Russia has called upon Responsibility to Protect rhetoric to justify its own agenda. Finally, we end with Gaza, where, in the context of the most recent Israeli–Palestinian confrontation (the summer of 2014), we ask to what extent R2P is relevant.

Syria as a prime candidate for R2P, and yet ...

The Global Centre for R2P indicated in its bimonthly bulletin of 15 September 2014, that after more than three years of conflict in Syria, around 200,000 people had been killed. In addition, there were over 3 million Syrian refugees in neighbouring countries and over 6.5 million internally displaced persons (IDPs) as a result of the war. Moreover, ongoing fighting had been so ferocious and widespread that it had left at least 10.8 million Syrians in need of humanitarian assistance, 4.7 million of whom remained in inaccessible areas.[8] Furthermore, the civilian populations have often been used as a target. The United Nations has reported that all parties to the conflict have, at one time or another, impeded humanitarian access to civilian populations trapped or displaced by fighting. Also, the Syrian regime of Bashar al-Assad has utilised its military resources to retain power at all costs and perpetrate mass atrocities, some of them happening via the use of indiscriminate bombardments in populated areas and, apparently, chemical attacks delivered by rockets. In addition, government-allied militias have repeatedly committed large-scale massacres and perpetrated war crimes and gross violations of international humanitarian law as a matter of state policy.[9]

Nevertheless, none of this has been enough to trigger decisive international action, including the use of force, on the basis of R2P.[10] At the

---

[7] Also called Islamic State of Iraq and Syria (ISIS) or simply the Islamic State (IS).

[8] *R2P Monitor. A Bimonthly Bulletin by the Global Centre for the Responsibility to Protect* (New York, Responsibility to Protect, Issue 17, 15 September 2014), p. 2.

[9] Ibid.

[10] On R2P in the context of Syria, refer for example to Graham Cronogue, 'Responsibility to Protect: Syria, The Law, Politics and Future of Humanitarian Intervention Post-Libya', *Journal of International Humanitarian Legal Studies* 3:1 (2012), Paul

time of writing (September 2014) twice had the UN Security Council referred to R2P in connection with Syria, and not in the strong terms that could have led to an international intervention: once on 2 October 2013, when one of the Security Council presidential statements indicated that 'the Council recalls ... that the Syrian authorities bear the primary responsibility to protect their populations',[11] and another time, in Resolution 2139 (22 February 2014), when the Security Council demanded that 'all parties take all appropriate steps to protect civilians, including members of ethnic, religious and confessional communities, and stresses that, in this regard, the primary responsibility to protect its population lies with the Syrian authorities'. Thus, despite the fact that the war, which started as initially peaceful pro-democracy protests that the government decided to fiercely repress, worsened over time and that the attempts of the international community to find a diplomatic solution to the crisis went nowhere[12], using force in the context of R2P to stop the humanitarian and human rights violations in Syria did not emerge as a serious alternative. The closest the Western powers came to launching air strikes against the Syrian regime was following the large-scale sarin attack on 21 August 2013 that killed an estimated 1,400 people, when Bashar al-Assad's forces were suspected to have been behind the attack.[13]

This is not to say that the Syrian conflict does not entail complexities that have made calling upon R2P particularly challenging, if not highly risky. In this regard, political scientist and international relations specialist (and also one of the co-editors of this volume) Ramesh Thakur, is right to stress, in a very pointed essay titled 'Syria and the Responsibility to Protect',[14] that the failure to protect Syrian civilians, including with the support of force, is due to five sets of factors which would have been wrong to dismiss or overlook:

R. Williams, J. Trevor Ulbrick and Jonathan Worboys, 'Preventing Mass Atrocity Crimes: The Responsibility to Protect and the Syria Crisis', *Case Western Reserve Journal of International Law* 45 (2012), and Carsten Stahn, 'Between Law-Breaking and Law-Making: Syria, Humanitarian Intervention and "What the Law Ought to be"', *Journal of Conflict & and Security Law* 19:1 (2014).

[11] S/PRST/2013/15 (2 October 2013).

[12] See for instance the failure of the various Syria peace talks in Geneva from 2012 to 2014.

[13] For the investigative journalist Seymour M. Hersh the responsibility of the Syrian regime in the use of chemical weapons in August 2013 is doubtful. See Seymour M. Hersh, 'The Red Line and the Rat Line', *London Review of Books* 36:8 (2014). For an analysis of the use of chemical weapons in the Syrian context from an international law perspective, refer to Jillian Blake and Aqsa Mahmud, 'A Legal "Red Line"? Syria and the Use of Chemical Weapons in Civil Conflict', *UCLA Law Review Discourse* 61:244 (2013).

[14] Ramesh Thakur, 'Syria and the Responsibility to Protect' in Robert W. Murray and Alasdair McKay, eds, *Into the Eleventh Hour: R2P, Syria and Humanitarianism in Crisis* (Bristol: e-International Relations Publishing, January 2014).

1. Conceptual conundra in relation to an armed civil war (one of them being: what is the appropriate boundary demarcation between responsibility to protect/protection of civilians, one the one hand, and international humanitarian and human rights laws, on the other, in regulating the conduct of conflict parties in civil war);
2. The difficulty at times of establishing culpability for atrocities with sufficient clarity;
3. Parallel difficulties of satisfying the balance of consequences test with possible unsavoury outcomes both internally (including the risks of more atrocities to be committed against civilians and minority groups if the Bashar al-Assad regime were to collapse entirely) and externally (further inflaming an extremely volatile region, with the possible deepening Sunni–Shia divide all around the Middle East, and damaging key major power relations, such as with Iran, China and Russia);
4. The unwillingness of Russia and China (with Russia being widely seen as the pivotal state of that pair) to endorse international intervention in Syria on the basis of R2P following their feeling that the implementation by NATO and its key members of the UN Security Council Resolution 1973 (17 March 2011) of March 2011, which by abstaining rather than vetoing it, Russia and China had allowed to pass and therefore trigger action in Libya, had exceeded what the resolution had authorised, particularly concerning the prohibition of regime change;[15] and
5. The combination of the West's reluctance to share a rule-writing role (with the Western temptation to collapse the international community into a mini-NATO coalition of the willing) with the new emerging powers, and the reticence of the latter in accepting the burden of being joint managers of the world going beyond the status quo.[16]

On the other hand, letting the situation unfold in Syria under the more or less passive gaze of the international community has not simplified these complexities, let alone brought answers to them and mitigated the risks associated with international action in the framework of R2P. In fact, the outcome has probably been worse. The humanitarian and human rights crises have not only continued but also deepened. This is especially the case since in 2013–2014 the terrorist organisation ISIL, by taking advantage of sectarian strife and the Syrian civil war, has expanded and gained territories on both sides of the Syria–Iraq border, bringing about further

[15] For more on the issue, Alex J. Bellamy, 'From Tripoli to Damascus? Lesson Learning and the Implementation of the Responsibility to Protect', *International Politics* 51:1 (2014).
[16] Ramesh Thakur, 'Syria and the Responsibility to Protect' in Robert W. Murray and Alasdair McKay, eds, *Into the Eleventh Hour: R2P, Syria and Humanitarianism in Crisis* (op. cit.).

mass crimes and instability in Syria and, beyond – in Iraq and possibly more areas in the future.

Finally, against the background of a growing geostrategic threat and the emotional commotion created by the successive video executions of prisoners and hostages, an international air strikes campaign targeting ISIL started to be conducted in September 2014 in Iraq and Syria. Interestingly, unlike for R2P, which was presumably impossible to deploy without the support of a UN Security Council resolution, the lack of UN Security Council endorsement for the air strikes has not prevented action from being undertaken. This shows that humanitarian and human rights crises, and therefore R2P, never stop, on their own, being weaker than geostrategic and national interest considerations when it comes to projecting a concrete sense of international responsibility and solidarity.

Ukraine and the hijacking of R2P

The situation in Ukraine has never been such that the R2P approach was going to be applicable. To be sure, since the crisis started in late 2013, people have died due to police brutality, clashes during protests and, since April 2014, the fighting in eastern Ukraine between Ukrainian government forces and rebels. But casualties, although tragic, have been relatively low and human rights violations have not met the standards of genocide, war crimes, ethnic cleansing and crimes against humanity to which R2P is linked, either before or after February 2014.[17] In addition, from historical, political and geostrategic standpoints, Ukraine is too close to Russia for Moscow to tolerate an international intervention encompassing the use of force in the country.[18] This would truly be a *casus belli* for Russia. Western powers and the United States in particular have known this all along. Hence the fact that in the past months, even as Crimea was separating from Ukraine and as the military confrontation worsened in the southeast of Ukraine, an international intervention was never in the cards.

It is, therefore, quite ironic that the rhetoric of R2P has in some way become part of the Ukrainian crisis. It is all the more ironic that this

---

[17] Late February 2014 saw the departure of President Yanukovych and his replacement by an interim administration.

[18] Henry Kissinger put it in the following terms in March 2014: 'The West must understand that, to Russia, Ukraine can never be just a foreign country ... Ukraine has been part of Russia for centuries, and their histories were intertwined before that ... Crimea, 60 percent of whose population is Russian, became part of Ukraine only in 1954, when Nikita Khrushchev, a Ukrainian by birth, awarded it as part of the 300th-year celebration of a Russian agreement with the Cossacks ... Ukraine has been independent for only 23 years'. 'To Settle the Ukraine Crisis, Start at the End', *The Washington Post*, 5 March 2014.

injection of R2P into the Ukrainian conflict and the debates surrounding it has taken place on the initiative of Russia. After all, Russia has never been a supporter of R2P. As we alluded to earlier, it had been its chief opponent in Syria and, before that, in the context of Kosovo in the late 1990s. And yet, without referring to R2P itself, Vladimir V. Putin has put forward R2P rhetoric to justify the involvement of and possible use of force by the Russian Federation in Ukraine. In fact, this has been his main argument, along with the principle of self-determination, to present Russia's engagement in Ukraine as conforming to respect for international law, to which, while arguably circumventing it, he says he is very much attached.[19]

In this perspective, on 4 March 2014, in a press conference that it is worth quoting at length, the president of the Russian Federation offered a vigorous justification for the Russian involvement in Ukraine. He started by indicating that, although he understood the frustrations of Ukrainians, the way in which the government was changed was illegal: 'Only constitutional means should be used in the post-Soviet space, where political structures are still very fragile, and economies are still very weak'. He insisted that 'wherever a person lives, whatever part of the country, he or she should have the right to equal participation in determining the future of the country'.[20] He then turned to the question of the use of force, clearly linking it to the rhetoric of R2P, claiming the mantle of legitimacy because Russia had been invited by the elected President Viktor Yanukovych 'to protect the lives, freedom and health of the citizens of Ukraine'. He pointed to 'the rampage of reactionary forces, nationalist and anti-Semitic forces going on in certain parts of Ukraine, including Kiev ... When we see this we understand what worries the citizens of Ukraine, both Russian and Ukrainian, and the Russian-speaking population in the eastern and southern regions of Ukraine.' In such circumstances, 'if we see such uncontrolled crime spreading to the eastern

---

[19] In September 2013, as the United States was contemplating the possibility of using force against the Syrian government after the use of chemical weapons, Vladimir Putin published an article in the *New York Times*, stressing that the Russian opposition to the use of force in Syria was based on the respect for international law: 'We are not protecting the Syrian government, but international law ... Under current international law, force is permitted only in self-defense or by decision of the Security Council. Anything else is unacceptable under the United Nations Charter and would constitute an act of aggression'. Vladimir V. Putin, 'A Plea for Caution from Russia', *New York Times*, 11 September 2013. Yet on the ground, concerning the alleged threats to Russian-speaking Ukrainians, the questions of self-determination and the referendum, or the presence of Russian troops in southeast Ukraine, the reality has been far from matching Putin's rhetoric, and the demands of international law.

[20] 'Vladimir Putin answered journalists' questions on the situation in Ukraine', President of Russia, 4 March 2014, eng.kremlin.ru.

regions of the country, and if the people ask us for help, while we already have the official request from the legitimate president, we retain the right to use all available means to protect those people ... with whom we have close historical, cultural and economic ties'. Protecting them was both 'a humanitarian mission' and in Russia's national interests.[21]

A few days later, on 18 March 2014, in his address to State Duma deputies, Federation Council members, heads of Russian regions and civil society representatives in the Kremlin on the occasion of the signature ceremony of a bill absorbing Crimea into the Russian Federation, following the referendum held on 16 March (in which, supposedly, more than 90 per cent of Crimeans voted to become part of Russia; remaining part of Ukraine was not an option on the ballot), Vladimir Putin returned to the R2P theme by referencing NATO intervention in Kosovo in 1999 as the precedent for Russian actions in the Crimea in 2014: 'Moreover, the Crimean authorities referred to the well-known Kosovo precedent – a precedent our Western colleagues created with their own hands in a very similar situation, when they agreed that the unilateral separation of Kosovo from Serbia, exactly what Crimea is doing now, was legitimate and did not require any permission from the country's central authorities'.[22]

The fact that the Ukrainian and, more specifically, Crimean populations were never really at risk, let alone under attack,[23] that the conditions under which the referendums organised by separatists in Crimea, and then in the Donetsk and Luhansk regions (May 2014), concerning self-rule vis-à-vis Ukraine were anything but satisfactory, and that despite Moscow's denial Russian troops appear to have been operating in southeast Ukraine and playing a key role in the military operations[24], have not prevented Putin from using the R2P rhetoric.[25] With the reality on the ground having been as much at odds with words as can be, this is an illustration of how the idea of Responsibility to Protect can be hijacked and be put in the service of self-interested ends.

[21] Ibid.
[22] *Address by President of the Russian Federation*, 18 March 2014, eng.kremlin.ru.
[23] Timothy Snyder, 'Ukraine: The Edge of Democracy', *New York Review of Books*, 22 May 2014.
[24] Anatol Lieven, 'Ukraine – The Way Out', *New York Reviews of Books*, 5 June 2014, and Tim Judah, 'Ukraine: A Catastrophic Defeat', *New York Review of Books*, 9 October 2014.
[25] We should add here that in Putin's Russia there is also a victim mentality strand we later refer to concerning Israelis and Palestinians. To some extent this is linked to the sense that since the end of the Cold War the policies of the West have been geared towards encircling Russia.

Gaza as off-limits for R2P

With respect to the Responsibility to Protect and the conflict that took place in the summer of 2014 in Gaza, two issues come to mind.

First, there is the question of whether or not during that time we have witnessed one, or more, of the four crimes (genocide, war crimes, ethnic cleansing or crimes against humanity) that amount to justifying international action, including the use of force, on the basis of R2P. Now, when it comes to the first crime, genocide, this is certainly what Palestinian Authority President Mahmoud Abbas accused Israel of at the beginning of his speech at the UN General Assembly on 26 September 2014, when he said that Israel was carrying out a 'new war of genocide' against the Palestinian people.[26] However, most people are likely to think that, despite the brutality of the Israeli offensive, it has not engaged in genocidal behaviour per se.[27] In the same vein, it would be difficult to argue that ethnic cleansing has taken place. Now, what about crimes against humanity? On this point, if a crime against humanity requires that certain acts – murder, enslavement, deportation, imprisonment, torture, rape – are directed against the civilian population and that they are part of a large-scale and preconceived policy, it does not appear that the treatment of the Palestinian population by Israel in the summer of 2014 meets the threshold of a crime against humanity.

We are thus left with the issue of war crime. And here it is much more possible to make the case that serious violations of the laws and customs of war, also known as international humanitarian law, have occurred during the crisis. In this regard, the intentional targeting of non-combatants has been an issue for both sides, for Hamas (in particular with the rockets that it has been firing into Israel, aimed more at civilian neighbourhoods than at military targets) and for the Israeli Defense Force (IDF) – keeping in mind that the casualties have been far greater on the Palestinian side (more than 2,000 Palestinians killed and more than 10,000 wounded, mostly civilians) than on the Israeli one (the number of killed in the dozens, and mainly soldiers).[28]

In this context, focusing on the actions of the Israeli Defense Force (IDF), the scholar Alex J. Bellamy, basing his analysis on media reporting, considers that that there are at least four principles of acceptable

[26] Full text of Palestinian Authority President Mahmoud's Address to the UN General Assembly (New York, the United Nations), reproduced in *The Times of Israel*, 27 September 2014, www.timesofisrael.com/full-text-of-abbas-speech-to-un/.
[27] That said, the dire living conditions of people in Gaza created and perpetuated by the Israeli land and sea blockade since 2007 and this summer's conflict have been devastating and are dramatically hampering the life chances of Palestinians.
[28] 'Gaza Death Toll Increases as Israeli Strikes Continue', *The Guardian*, 25 August 2014.

wartime conduct that elements of the IDF have violated: targeting (where there is any doubt as to the military nature of a potential target, that target must not be attacked); the principle of due care (it is not altogether clear what measures the IDF has taken to minimise civilian harm); the principle of proportionality (in the context of the Israeli use of force, there are serious questions to be answered as to whether specific actions resulting in civilian deaths were proportionate to their military objectives); and the use of inherently indiscriminate weapons in civilian inhabited areas (the IDF stands accused of using munitions containing metal flechettes in civilian populated areas).[29]

Second, however, there is also the fact that it is unlikely that these violations would ever be dealt with internationally within the framework of R2P, especially in the context of the UN Security Council, let alone with reference to the use of force on the part of the international community. The United States' support to Israel has led to overlooking the violations of Palestinians' humanitarian and human rights. Incidentally, as Ramesh Thakur puts it, it may be that what amounts to a virtual lack of accountability for Israel stems not only from Israel's right and duty to defend its own people, but also from the West's historical guilt over the centuries of discrimination against the Jews that culminated in the Holocaust.[30] As for the Palestinian side, if Hamas's military tactics targeting civilians have tended to attract condemnation, how Israel policies undermine Palestinians' rights has become a mitigating factor that few are really ready to overlook in the name of R2P geared towards the protection of the rights of Israeli civilians.

Ultimately, in a tragic way, their respective experience of violations of their rights, the victim mentality, if not identity[31] that both sides have developed, each in its own way, over the years, and the emotional and passionate support (for their partisans) and condemnation (for their opponents) they derive from, make it extremely difficult for the Israeli and Palestinian sides to see themselves as perpetrators when they act as perpetrators, and for the international community to frame them as perpetrators when this is needed. Their victim mentality/identity status, which oddly, and lethally, is at the same time what they share and what separates them, while making it challenging for them to be responsible

---

[29] Alex J. Bellamy, 'The Responsibility to Protect and the 2014 Conflict in Gaza', *e-International Relations*, 22 July 2014, www.e-ir.info/category/articles/page5/.

[30] Ramesh Thakur, 'Israel's Serial Gaza Offensives Are Offensive', *e-International Relations*, 24 July 2014, www.e-ir.info/2014/07/24/israels-serial-gaza-offensives-are-offensive.

[31] On this issue on the Palestinian's and, generally, Arab's side, see for instance Samir Kassir, *Considérations sur le Malheur arabe* (Arles: Actes Sud, 2004); *Being Arab* (London: Verso, 2013).

and accountable, stands in the way of the international community being able to make them responsible and accountable. On each side of the fence, beginning with themselves, there tends to be always someone willing to find excuses for the two parties and be inclined to exonerate them for the violations that occur. In these conditions, it is not surprising how challenging it has been and continues to be to find a middle ground and call upon the Israeli and Palestinian sides to fulfil their respective responsibilities vis-à-vis the civilian populations, and sanction them when they do not respect them.

Lessons and the future for R2P?

In conclusion, at least five lessons can be drawn from the preceding analysis.

First, there is what the cases of Syria, Ukraine and Gaza tell us about the relationships of compatibility, competition and hierarchy among the key principles of international law we alluded to in the first section of the chapter. From this perspective, the three cases, each in its own way, confirm the continued primacy that the principle of national sovereignty and its associated logic of national interest play in international politics for the international community and its member states. Despite the changes brought about by R2P in the international distribution of normative and political power, they remain the dominating (hierarchy) and prevailing (competition) factors. This is shown with the case of Syria: if humanitarian and human rights considerations led the international community and its progressive member states to be 'concerned', such concerns were not strong enough for them to launch force wherever and whenever it could have been useful. However, when ISIL emerged as a geostrategic threat, what had previously not been possible suddenly became a viable option with regard to the use of force in the context of air strikes. Regarding Ukraine, humanitarian and human rights considerations served as a convenient motivation, and certainly not as an end in themselves. They were instrumentalised by Russia in the service of its national interest and commitment to consolidate and expand its sense of national sovereignty. As for Gaza, the defence of the national sovereignty and national interest of Israel appears as an absolute imperative which that continues to be challenged by its opponents.

Second, and logically in light of the above, although compared to the past, R2P represents a degree of normative, policy and political progress in addressing mass human rights violations, it is still limited. As the case of Syria shows, it is not a proof against paralysis, and standing by and doing nothing remains an option.

Third, the rhetoric of R2P can be manipulated. The Russian approach to the Ukrainian crisis illustrates this state of affairs. Manipulation is all the more possible considering the dilemmas and tensions, of which R2P is at the core, that are at work in the structure and dynamics of international law and international relations. This makes it impossible to have R2P applied in an automatic, systemic and objective fashion. Hence the fact that R2P is open to interpretation and disputes, especially for its use of force component.

Fourth, the possibility of using R2P to address atrocity crimes is based on the predicament that the identity of who the victims are, or of who is a greater victim, is clear and undisputed. But when two parties in conflict both claim victim status and mobilise supporters behind them on this basis, it becomes challenging to call upon R2P. This is in part the lesson of the Gaza case.

Fifth, R2P is, on its own, not sufficient to solve the problems it seeks to address. This is true for its use of force dimension but for its other components as well. While R2P is meant to tackle major mass crimes, beyond its immediate time and area of intervention more is needed to ensure that such crimes do not occur, or reoccur, or that, after the handling of the moment of crisis, a country does not fall into further chaos, as is the case of Libya today. In addition to international action based on R2P, there are there many more measures that have to be taken in order to tackle the structural pathologies that have led to the perpetration of crimes. On the African continent, for instance, where in recent years R2P has also been called upon, like in the Central African Republic most recently,[32] short of rebuilding, or even building, the country in crisis on a sound and healthy long-term basis, the possibility of there being a new surge of mass violence at some point is more likely than unlikely.

Against this background, what needs to be done to go further in support of R2P, and what does its future hold? On the institutional side of the question, reflections are underway to facilitate a more concrete and effective use of R2P at the United Nations, especially in the context of the UN Security Council. In this perspective, France, in the wake of inaction in Syria, put forward, in October 2013, and then again in September 2014, on the occasion of the opening of the United Nations General Assembly, the idea of a 'code of conduct' for the use of veto in the Council in situations of genocide, war crimes, crimes against humanity

---

[32] See *R2P Monitor. A Bimonthly Bulletin by the Global Centre for the Responsibility to Protect*, pp. 6–7.

and ethnic cleansing.[33] That said, although in past years the support for a 'responsibility not to veto' has grown (2013 saw increasing momentum on this issue, sparked in part by the inability of the Council to respond to the catastrophic humanitarian crisis in Syria), this is still an uphill battle. After all, why would the countries using their veto now on an ad hoc basis to oppose international humanitarian intervention accept to commit themselves on a principle and more permanent basis not to use it? The fact that the French proposal excludes its applicability to cases where the vital national interests of a permanent member of the Council would be at stake makes one even more doubtful about the progress that this proposal would allow R2P to make. Indeed, is it not the national interest and its primacy over humanitarian and human rights considerations that constitute an obstacle for a greater and better use of R2P?

More generally, and on the normative side, a key point remains regarding the evolving relationship between the rights of states and the rights of individuals. As we saw earlier in the chapter, the emergence of R2P has been made possible by the enhancement of the later. This is to say that moving ahead the R2P agenda amounts to having individuals as international right-holders being taken more and more seriously. This does not necessarily go against the state. Rather, more than anything else, it is a more responsible and effective state that is needed, one ever more dedicated and able to be at the service of individuals and their empowerment, within and beyond borders.

It is all the more urgent and imperative to encourage this orientation since in recent years, beyond situations of humanitarian crisis in times of war, fundamentalist liberal economic and financial, and market society forces have had the tendency to weaken the effectiveness of the state and its sense of solidarity and responsibility, and, ultimately, its powers to engineer, nurture and oversee liveable and decent polities and policies. Allowing this tendency to shape the future would be ironic, if it were not so counter-productive: at a time when, with R2P, room has been made for a greater sense of ethical and political solidarity and responsibility vis-à-vis individuals, law and politics, both national and international, are in

---

[33] France set out a suggestion of how the code of conduct would work in practice: it would not require an amendment of the UN Charter as it would be a mutual commitment of the five permanent members of the Security Council, who would agree to suspend their right of veto in cases of mass atrocities; it would require at least 50 member states to request the UN secretary-general to determine the nature of the crimes; once the secretary-general confirmed the commission of atrocity crimes the code of conduct would apply immediately; it would exclude cases where the vital national interests of a permanent member of the Council were at stake. For more details on this, see, for example, 'UN Security Council and the Responsibility to Protect: Voluntary Restraint of the Veto in Situations of Mass Atrocity', una.org.uk.

danger of being rendered impotent and meaningless, in fact ruling less and less in the public interest, by actors and interests that are prone to be as dismissive of solidarity and responsibility, within and beyond borders, as can be.

If nothing is done to change course and stop this perilous evolution, the progress represented by R2P will have been no more than a Pyrrhic victory. Yes, it will have been a step forward, but one more or less for nothing as it will unfold in a world where the capacity of law, international and national, to be increasingly structured around individual, national and international ethics, solidarity, responsibility and accountability will have been de facto sidelined, if not annihilated, by the triumph of what seems to be the unethical, irresponsible, unaccountable and, in the end, destructive latest trends of contemporary capitalism.[34]

In other words, R2P will have a future, and a meaningful one, only if we see it not as all that is required, and only in times of humanitarian crisis, to live in a more ethical and responsible world. It will have a future, and a meaningful one, only if we see it as part of a bigger call for the ethics and politics of solidarity and responsibility, within and beyond borders – and one that requires addressing the systemic crisis in which the contemporary world appears trapped. The kind of defensive ethics of responsibility and solidarity that it is at work in and illustrated by R2P is a positive step; nevertheless, it is no longer sufficient for the future. What is now needed, against the destructive forces that appear to dominate, in times of peace as in times of war, is a systematic ethic and culture of responsibility and solidarity to resolve the current structural problems and pathologies. Now is the time to make sure that everyday life does not become like a war-zone.

---

[34] In this latest type of capitalism, playing by the rule and taking ethics, responsibility, solidarity and accountability at face value and being held to them tend to be for the ordinary, and powerless, people. As for the powerful, for the 'masters of the universe', they seem to think and act as if they were above all this. As political institutions and leaders have less and less power and are less and less able to fulfil their obligations towards society and people, and as economic and financial actors have more and more power with hardly any sense of obligation and accountability, no wonder that political legitimacy is in short supply today, and could be in even shorter supply tomorrow.

10   The Responsibility to Protect and the just war tradition

Alex J. Bellamy

The literature on the Responsibility to Protect (R2P) is suffused with references to the principle's connection to the just war tradition. Some commentators argue that R2P arose out of just war thinking, and in particular the tradition's focus on the use of force to end tyranny and promote justice.[1] Another, more critical line of argument has suggested that R2P tries to 'distinguish between grubby, ordinary wars and *just* wars intended to stop mass atrocities' – a distinction its critics say it fails to achieve.[2] This chapter examines the relationship between R2P and the just war tradition. It focuses in particular on moral judgments about decisions to use force to protect populations from genocide and mass atrocities and the question of whether the authority to take such decisions should rest with the UN Security Council or individual states.

The first part of the chapter examines the question of decision-making criteria for the use of force. After briefly charting some of the debates about the relative merits of different criteria, I focus on the meaning and scope of just war principles relating to decisions to use force (*jus ad bellum*) and the question of how these principles can be used as a form of practical moral reasoning. The principles espoused by the just war tradition and adopted in part by the International Commission on Intervention and State Sovereignty (ICISS) should not be seen as conditions that can be 'ticked off' to establish the moral credentials of an armed intervention, but rather as a holistic framework that can guide moral reasoning and debate. The second part turns to the question of authority. International law insists that only the UN Security Council is permitted to authorise the

Thanks to Ramesh Thakur for his helpful comments and assistance on this chapter.

[1] For example Joseph Nye, 'The Intervention Dilemma', *Al-Jazeera Blog*, www.aljazeera.com /indepth/opinion/2012/06/201261292523651706.html, and Sonia Rodrigues, 'Somewhere Between Civil War and Regime Transition: The Responsibility to Protect Response to Libya and Syria', *Small Wars Journal*, 12 June 2012, at www.smallwarsjournal.com/jrnl/iss/201206.

[2] Patricia de Vries, 'just wars: The Naiveté of "Responsibility to Protect"', *World Policy Blog*, 24 May 2012, http://www.worldpolicy.org/blog/2012/05/24/just-war-naivet%C3% A9-responsibility-protect.

use of force against the will of host states but some contemporary just war theorists argue that individual states retain a right to use force unilaterally for such purposes. In contrast, I argue that the UN Charter provides a robust (albeit imperfect) institutional setting that facilitates moral debate about the use of force for human protection purposes. Without the checks and balances provided by the Charter system, just war principles and the decision-making criteria proposed by ICISS could become mere modes of self-justification for interventionist states.

Morality and the decision to use force

The most obvious point of overlap between R2P and the just war tradition relates to the just cause criteria and precautionary principles advanced by ICISS to guide decision-making for the use of force. Indeed, ICISS co-chair Gareth Evans argued that the 'ultimate intellectual origins [of the just cause and precautionary principles found in ICISS] lie in the whole tradition, and vast literature, of "just war" theory'.[3] For various reasons, however, member states rejected the notion of criteria relatively early in the negotiations leading to the 2005 agreement on R2P.[4] Nevertheless, in the wake of the 2011 NATO-led intervention in Libya, the question of criteria to guide decision-making on the use of force was placed back on the international agenda as part of the 'responsibility while protecting' concept advanced by Brazil.

The debate about criteria to guide decision-making for the use of force for human protection purposes initially arose in the context of controversy about the 1999 NATO-led intervention in Kosovo and ICISS efforts to find a way of balancing sovereignty rights with the defence of fundamental human rights. Strongest support came from the developing world, lending credence to Ramesh Thakur's view that far from establishing what was effectively a 'charter for interveners', the adoption of criteria to guide decision-making would limit and control the use of force.[5] Participants at the ICISS consultation in Cairo, for example, argued that clear and universally agreed criteria were necessary to improve the Security Council's accountability.[6] Opposition to criteria was strongest in

[3] Gareth Evans, 'When Is It Right to Fight', *Survival* 46:3 (2004), at p. 75

[4] I have discussed the relative political merits of R2P criteria elsewhere and aired a degree of scepticism. See Alex J. Bellamy, *The Responsibility to Protect and Global Politics: From Words to Deeds* (London: Routledge, 2011). I will not directly address the contemporary merits of criteria here.

[5] Ramesh Thakur, 'A Shared Responsibility for a More Secure World', *Global Governance* 11:3 (2005), at p. 284.

[6] International Commission on Intervention and State Sovereignty (ICISS), *The Responsibility to Protect: Research, Bibliography, Background* (Ottawa: International Development Research Centre, 2001), p. 378.

the West. Some doubted their capacity to influence political decision-making while others argued that it would be impossible to reach a consensus on what the criteria should be.[7] Some officials worried that criteria might encourage disenchanted groups to provoke hostilities that could draw foreign intervention.[8]

This question of whether criteria would be primarily constraining or enabling of decisive action became a key part of the debate about R2P. ICISS adopted the view that armed intervention should be limited to 'extreme' cases where a 'just cause' was established by the large-scale loss of life or ethnic cleansing, 'actual or apprehended', whether deliberately caused by the state or facilitated by neglect or incapacity.[9] In addition to these 'just cause' thresholds, the Commission set out a series of 'precautionary principles' to guide decision-making. Borrowed from just war thinking, these principles included: (1) *Right intention*: 'The primary purpose of the intervention, whatever other motives intervening states may have, must be to halt or avert human suffering. Right intention is better assured with multilateral operations, clearly supported by regional opinion and the victims concerned.' (2) *Last resort*: 'Military intervention can only be justified when every non-military option for the prevention or peaceful resolution of the crisis has been explored, with reasonable grounds for believing lesser measures would not have succeeded.' (3) *Proportional means*: 'The scale, duration and intensity of the planned military intervention should be the minimum necessary to secure the defined human protection objective.' And (4) *Reasonable prospects*: 'There must be a reasonable chance of success in halting or averting the suffering which has justified the intervention, with the consequences of action not likely to be worse than the consequences of inaction.'[10]

The delineation of criteria for the use of force has a long history but has been criticised on the grounds that, absent an authoritative judge to determine when the criteria are satisfied, such an approach grants considerable latitude to political leaders to determine the justice of their own cause. As such, they are criticised for being too permissive.[11] As Robert Tucker argued, 'historically, states interpreted the principles of justice in war in such an elastic way that they have caused them to seem compatible with any act of war'.[12] But while it is true that leaders are able to draw long

---

[7] Ibid., p. 361.   [8] Ibid., p. 381.

[9] International Commission on Intervention and State Sovereignty, *The Responsibility to Protect* (Ottawa: International Development Research Centre, 2001), p. 32.

[10] Ibid., pp. 32–37.

[11] Robert J. Myers, 'Notes on the Just War Theory: Whose Justice, Which Wars?', *Ethics and International Affairs* 10:1 (1996), pp. 115–130.

[12] Robert Tucker, *The Just War: A Study on Contemporary Doctrine* (Baltimore: Johns Hopkins University Press, 1960), p. 13.

bows in their *jus ad bellum* arguments, legitimacy demands that these claims be accepted by others. History is littered with examples of states failing to persuade others of their cause and paying a heavy price as a result: Iraq when it invaded Kuwait in 1990, Germany when it invaded Poland in 1939. Of course, the latitude that the principles afford to powerful states is precisely why, in 1945, the international community made the tight regulation of the use of force the cornerstone of the new international order governed by the UN Charter. It also partly explains why states decided not to tamper with that system when it came to endorsing R2P in 2005.

There is no reason why moral reasoning within this system of legal rules cannot be shaped by the just war tradition and criteria stemming from it. Such conditions might help guide leaders in making moral judgments about whether or not to use force for protection purposes. *Jus ad bellum* comprises three types of criteria relating to the decision to use force: substantive, prudential and procedural. Some writers argue that the first two types are more important than the third in framing judgments about the legitimacy of decisions to wage war.[13] On balance, there may be cases where the first two types are satisfied but the third is not, yet where a war is nevertheless considered legitimate. Interventions to protect civilians that are not initially authorised by the UN Security Council, such as the intervention in Liberia by the Economic Community of West African States (ECOWAS) in 1991, or local armed rebellions against tyrannical or genocidal rule, such as the re-invasion of Rwanda in 1994 by the Rwandese Patriotic Front, are two possible examples. The just war tradition – like ICISS – suggests that *all* the criteria be satisfied before force is employed but in practice there is little doubt that we afford differing weights to the various criteria when making legitimacy judgments and that this reflects our moral sensitivities. As a result, the just war principles are not criteria to be checked-off, but were rather intended as guides to inform more holistic judgments about the morality of using force in particular circumstances.

Substantive criteria

There are four substantive criteria in the *jus ad bellum*. The first is right intention: individuals must wage war for the common good, not for self-aggrandisement or because of hatred of the enemy. The inclusion of right intention by ICISS was particularly welcome because this principle is

---

[13] See James Turner Johnson, *Morality and Contemporary Warfare* (New Have: Yale University Press, 1999), pp. 32–33.

seldom discussed nowadays and it has even been suggested that it should be rejected altogether.[14] Such arguments overlook the vital role that right intentions play in underpinning the whole just war way of thinking. For the earliest just war thinkers, such as Augustine, right intention stood at the very heart of the tradition. Given the strong biblical injunction against killing (found in both the 'Ten Commandments' and in the teachings of Jesus), the earliest theorists of just war were obliged to recognise a moral presumption against killing. They argued, therefore, that killing for personal gain or out of hatred or envy was wrong.[15] When a soldier kills another, therefore, he must do so only because it is necessary to right a wrong or protect order. Violence must be directed against the wrong, not the wrongdoer.

Rejecting right intention, as some contemporary ethicists have suggested, begs the question of how killing in war could be justified at all. There are three possible avenues; all of them, however, are ultimately unsatisfactory. The first would be to extrapolate upwards from a natural law right to self-defence enjoyed by all individuals. By this account, all individuals have a right to defend themselves – including their access to essential goods like food, fuel and shelter. Therefore, all political communities have a right to defend themselves. The problem with this argument, as David Rodin has demonstrated only too well, is that the individual analogy rapidly breaks down. Unless one is invaded by a genocidal state intent on killing every member of society, an invading army does not pose a direct threat to everyone. As such, individuals in the attacked state do not all enjoy an equal individual right to self-defence since they are not all literally under threat.[16] This line of argument would also, of course, rule out *prima facie* the use of violence to protect foreigners in other countries.

The second avenue would be an act-utilitarian justification. This would hold that it is legitimate to kill if doing so leads to the greatest happiness of the greatest number. The problem with this approach is that it undermines other rules. If it is permissible to kill in general to serve the greater good, why limit killing only to combatants? Why not serve the common good more quickly by killing non-combatants? Why not use nuclear weapons? Why not use genocide – exterminating one group to serve the

---

[14] Darrel Moellendorf, *Cosmopolitan Justice* (Boulder, Col: Westview Press, 2002), esp. pp. 120–158. Also see Chris Brown, *Sovereignty, Rights and Justice: International Political Theory Today* (Cambridge: Polity, 2002), pp. 108–109.

[15] Augustine, 'Contra Faustum', in M. Dods, ed, *The Work of Aurelius Augustine* (Edinburgh: T. and C. Clark, 1876), p. 74.

[16] David Rodin, *War and Self-Defence* (Oxford: Clarendon Press, 2002).

interests of other, larger, groups? Clearly, act-utilitarianism quickly runs up against our moral sensibilities.

A third proposition would be to avoid the problem altogether by arguing that killing requires no special justification. However, almost every major moral tradition and the domestic law of every state rejects this notion.

The principle of right intention therefore remains the most plausible defence of killing in war and is the bedrock of the just war tradition. In this sense it is *prior* to just cause. Thus, ICISS was surely correct to include an intention to avert or halt harm as a key condition for the use of force for human protection purposes. The central problem with right intention though is that it is very difficult to demonstrate or test and relatively easy to mask. How do we know the intentions of another? This was less a problem for Ambrose and Augustine than it is for us, because – as Christian theologians – they argued that God knew all and would sit in judgment. This is hardly a good standard for contemporary international politics. Instead, then, we might use two proxies. First, we can read intentions into actions by asking whether an intervener's deeds exhibit care for civilian life. Where the protection of civilians is made secondary to other concerns, we might question whether an intervention ostensibly for human protection purposes really was conducted with right intent. Second, we can defer to the judgements of others and suggest that if a sufficient number of states are persuaded, then we might ascribe an intervention with right intent. It is for this reason, among others, that international authority ought to be afforded moral value. However imperfect it may be, the requirement that intervention be authorised by the UN Security Council demands that a state persuade not just itself, but also its peers, of its rightful intent.

The second substantive rule is that war may only be waged for a just cause. This is usually limited to self-defence, the defence of others, restoration of the peace, the defence of legal rights and the punishment of wrongdoers. Clearly, the ICISS 'just cause' thresholds ('large scale loss of life' or 'large scale ethnic cleansing') fall under the rubric of defence of others, restoration of the peace and the punishment of wrongdoers, and it is worth stressing that in this regard ICISS thresholds were somewhat *more* stringent than those typically found in just war thinking. Just cause is often viewed in absolute terms: a combatant either has a just cause or does not. Today, this tendency is supported by legal positivism, which holds that actors either comply with the law or violate it.[17]

[17] Michael Walzer, *Just and Unjust Wars: A Moral Argument with Historical Illustrations* (New York: Basic Books, 1977), p. 59.

Things are not so simply expressed in the just war tradition. Vitoria argued that a war could not *logically* be just on both sides, but may *appear* just to both sides. This was because human interpretations were subject to fallibility and error. Only God was free from error. Humans were plagued by 'invincible ignorance'. In such cases:

where there is provable ignorance either of fact or of law, the war may be just in itself for the side that has true justice on its side, and also just for the other side, because they wage war in good faith and are hereby excused from sin. Invincible error is a valid excuse in every case.[18]

In other words, while there is 'true' justice, we humans can never be absolutely sure that we know what it is. From Vitoria onwards, the just war tradition tended to distinguish objective justice (knowable to God) from subjective justice (knowable to humans). Therefore, a war could certainly *appear* to be just on both sides. It would often be impossible for humans to know with absolute certainty. From this flowed three important implications.

First, as Vitoria himself argued, leaders should show 'due care' in their decisions to use force. They should seek advice from learned people, welcome dissenting perspectives and listen to the opponent's arguments.

Second, the just cause rule should be understood in relative terms. As David Welch has convincingly demonstrated, in modern times states tend only to wage war when they believe their cause to be just.[19] In most wars today, therefore, both sides believe that theirs is the just cause. Vitoria argued that we should recognise that in disputed cases either side *may* have justice on its side and that ultimately God would decide. It is important not to think of just cause in absolute terms but to recognise its relativity. It is not a matter of either having or not having a just cause, but of having more or less of one. Some writers label this the criteria of 'sufficient cause'.[20]

Third, if it is accepted that doubts about 'just cause' can never be fully resolved, then a significant part of the moral burden shifts to the manner in which a war is conducted. It is no coincidence that our moral sensibilities exhibit more concern for the enemy's civilian casualties – even those unintentionally caused – in so-called wars of choice to 'save strangers' from genocide and mass atrocities than in wars of national self-defence. It is also no coincidence that recognition of the ultimate fallibility of human understanding with regards to just causes accompanied a shift

[18] Francisco de Vitoria, 'On the Law of War', in Anthony Pagden and Jeremy Lawrence, eds, *Vitoria: Political Writings* (Cambridge: Cambridge University Press, 1991), p. 313.

[19] David A. Welch, *Justice and the Genesis of War* (Cambridge: Cambridge University Press, 1993).

[20] I am grateful to Cian O'Driscoll for this point.

in the emphasis of just war thinking from *jus ad bellum* to *jus in bello* (justice in the conduct of war). If we cannot be absolutely confident in the justice of our cause, we had better be sure that our conduct is scrupulously consistent with moral and legal rules. Chief among those rules is the principle of non-combatant immunity. While it did not mention non-combatant immunity by name, ICISS acknowledged the importance of compliance with International Humanitarian Law in its discussion of 'operational principles'. This issue is especially important not only because nothing is likely to damage the legitimacy of an intervention for human protection purposes more than civilian casualties, but because there must be a point at which a combatant's disregard for *jus in bello* principles can undermine the moral quality of an otherwise just war.

This leads us to the third substantive criterion: proportionality of ends. This asks whether the overall harm likely to be caused by the war is less than that caused by the wrong that is being righted. In traditional just war thinking, what ICISS referred to as proportionality – the requirement that only the minimum necessary force be used – is typically regarded as a *jus in bello* restriction. ICISS did, however, refer to the *ad bellum* proportionality rule in its conception of 'last resort'. A further complication is that, according to James Turner Johnson, proportionality of ends is a *prudential*, not substantive, consideration. 'All prudential tests', he argued, are only to be met once the substantive tests are satisfied.[21] However, writing in the sixteenth century, Vitoria had suggested that proportionality played a more significant role in judgements about the morality of war. While war was legitimate to right wrongs, not all wrongs legitimised war. Some were not sufficiently grievous or widespread to justify the inevitable evils that war entailed. On this view, proportionality is more than a prudential calculation. Proportionality in the Vitorian sense requires a calculation of *all* the likely costs.

The final substantive test is last resort: is the use of force the only, or most proportionate, way that the wrong is likely to be righted? As ICISS recognised, last resort does not require the exhaustion of all means short of force. If it did, force would never be justified because one can always continue to negotiate until the last person is dead. Instead, last resort demands that actors carefully evaluate all the different strategies that might bring about the desired end, selecting force only if it appears to be the only feasible strategy for securing those ends. The view of last resort offered by the just war tradition, and affirmed by ICISS, eased this problem by requiring evidence that decision-makers have seriously pursued the alternatives to war.

---

[21] Johnson, *Morality and Contemporary Warfare*, p. 34.

Prudential

Just war's prudential criteria impose important checks on decisions to wage what would otherwise be justifiable wars. The principal prudential check, duly noted by ICISS, is reasonable prospects of success. This criterion holds that as war always entails some degree of evil and always endangers non-combatants, it is wrong to wage war for a justifiable purpose unless those instigating it can reasonably expect to prevail. Prudence includes consideration of both the overall likelihood of success and the costs of success. This adds an important additional consideration to the criterion, one that is consistent with the prudential questions posed by political leaders when they contemplate the use of force for human protection purposes. In short, a potential intervener may calculate that it could prevail but that the cost of doing so is likely to be prohibitively high.

Procedural

The third type of constraint is procedural. These are the requirements of right authority and proper declaration. The former lies at the heart of contemporary debates about the circumstances in which force for human protection purposes might be justified; the latter is nowadays generally viewed as arcane. These requirements developed in tandem and their origins lay in attempts during the Middle Ages to limit the incidence of war by specifying which authorities could legitimately declare it, reducing the likelihood of accidental war and forcing those intending to embark on war to seek peaceful restitution. In the Middle Ages, canon lawyers and scholastic theologians resolved the first question in favour of sovereign princes. Only those leaders with no clear superior could legitimately authorise war. In the modern era this translated into sovereign states and from the eighteenth until the mid-twentieth centuries, states were effectively given a free hand to authorise war whenever they saw fit. This right was heavily restricted by the 1945 UN Charter. Nonetheless, the question of who has the right to authorise war remains controversial: positive law suggests that only states under attack and the UN Security Council have this right while theories of natural law hold that individual states and coalitions may legitimately wage war in other instances. This is a debate I will focus on in more detail in the following section.

The requirement for proper declaration had its origins in the Roman *fetial* system, which prescribed procedures for declaring war. During the Middle Ages, the declaration requirement was held to fulfil two purposes. First, it supported the right authority test because only those princes with the authority to declare war and not be removed from power had the right to wage war. Second, by forcing those about to embark on war to clearly state their case, the declaration requirement provided an opportunity for the intended enemy to make restitution before the outbreak of hostilities. The declaration can serve a third purpose: it clearly marks the transition from peace to war and hence the type of legal rules that ought to be applied.

Among other things, the just war tradition therefore comprises a body of rules that governs the decision to wage war (*jus ad bellum*). Clearly, the criteria articulated by ICISS to guide decision-making about the use of force for human protection purposes built upon that tradition. This leaves us with the question posed earlier of whether the use of force has to satisfy all of the criteria in order to be justified or whether the violation of some rules might occasionally be justifiable? It would surely be contrary to our moral intuitions to rule the use of force by Jewish militia against the Nazis or by the Nuba people against the government of Sudan to be unjust on the grounds that it would be unlikely to succeed or has questionable authority credentials. With that in mind, it is worth reminding ourselves that what the just war tradition calls for is not the application of the criteria as a 'check list', for several of them – especially last resort and proportionality – are impossible to address in simple answers. The check list approach gives rise to an instrumentalist mindset that would see the criteria deployed by protagonists simply to defend their already determined positions. Instead, the just war tradition's rules – and the criteria espoused by ICISS – are better considered together in a holistic fashion as informing practical judgments about the morality of using force. The question is not whether leaders can 'tick off the boxes' but whether, on balance, after considering all the relevant moral factors, the use of force appears to be the most justifiable course of action.

The elephant in the room for just war thinking is that it requires only that a leader persuade him/herself about the morality of the decision to use force. This problem also troubled ICISS. This is an unsatisfactory endpoint because it assumes far too much self-restraint and self-criticism on the part of leaders. The 2005 agreement on R2P settled this issue in favour of a restrictive understanding of the authority to use force, which vested that authority exclusively in the hands of the UN Security Council (excepting each state's right to defend itself) but this concession has drawn criticism from some just war writers.

The question of authority

Emerging from a context in which the UN Security Council had repeatedly failed to protect populations from genocide and mass atrocities (in

Bosnia, Rwanda and elsewhere), the question of who had the authority to authorise the use of force for human protection purposes was among the most difficult confronted by ICISS. The Commission found that there was broad agreement that the UN Security Council should play the primary role but beyond that opinions were mixed.[22] Some agreed that the Security Council had exclusive authority.[23] Others were reluctant to reject *a priori* the morality of interventions not authorised by the Security Council. This, they worried, might entail rejecting interventions by regional organisations (such as ECOWAS in Liberia, Russia in Abkhazia, the North Atlantic Treaty Organization (NATO) in Kosovo) but might also limit the options available for responding to situations such as that found in Rwanda in 1994.[24] These concerns encouraged some to be relatively comfortable with the idea of intervention not authorised by the UN Security Council in some extreme situations.[25]

The potential that R2P might be used to justify the use of force without Security Council authorisation was a major bone of contention when member states began negotiating their commitment to the principle. The Group of 77 developing countries, including China and India, expressed concern that R2P could become an 'interveners charter'.[26]

ICISS proposed that the focus be placed on developing ways of making the Security Council work better and suggested a 'code of conduct' to achieve this effect. This provided a neat link between R2P and the decision-making criteria described above: the Security Council should be encumbered with a responsibility to protect and empowered to make effective and timely decisions. The articulation of these responsibilities would create pressure for the Council to act, reducing the need for hard choices around the question of action without a Council mandate. This move allowed ICISS to adopt a compromise between the positions described above. In place of the restrictive view that demanded Council authorisation in all cases and the permissive view that placed less emphasis on the Security Council, ICISS proposed that the primary legal

---

[22] 'The report on which we have agreed does not reflect in all respects the preferred views of any one of them. In particular, some of our members preferred a wider range of threshold criteria for military intervention than those proposed in our report, and others a narrower range. Again, some Commissioners preferred more, and others less, flexibility for military intervention outside the scope of Security Council approval'; ICISS, *Responsibility to Protect*, co-chairs' 'Foreword', p. viii.

[23] Mohamed Sid-Ahmed, 'Sovereignty and Intervention', *Al-Ahram Weekly*, 7–13 June 2001.

[24] ICISS, *Responsibility to Protect: Research, Bibliography, Background*, pp. 364–365.

[25] Ibid., p. 379.

[26] Discussed in detail in Alex J. Bellamy, *Responsibility to Protect: The Global Effort to End Mass Atrocities* (Cambridge: Polity, 2009), pp. 84–85.

authority for action was vested in the Security Council. Only if the Security Council failed to approve proposals to protect populations from serious crimes should consideration be given to alternative sources of authority. In such cases, ICISS argued that potential interveners should approach the General Assembly for declaratory support and, if that failed, work through regional organisations. The Commission observed that if the Council failed to discharge its responsibility, it would be unrealistic to expect that concerned states would not take matters into their own hands. It warned that the UN's legitimacy would be challenged if this happened and if the results proved consistent with the Commission's decision-making criteria.[27]

The 2005 agreement on R2P took matters one step further by reaffirming the Security Council's exclusive authority to authorise the use of force. Although this was necessary to ensure agreement on R2P and is the most sustainable and morally defensible position, some just war writers have expressed doubts about the morality of insisting upon Security Council authorisation, especially in situations where it is unable – whether due to a lack of will or consensus – to protect populations under threat.

Primacy of just war theory

Some strands of contemporary just war thinking question the morality of the UN Charter's rules governing force on the grounds that they exclude justice considerations and do more to protect abusive governments than they do to protect abused populations. The UN Charter prohibits the use or threat of force in international relations with only two exceptions: under Article 51, all states have an inherent right to self-defence and under Article 42, the UN Security Council has the right to authorise the use of force to enforce its decisions. This restrictive understanding of the right to use force contrasts with the just war tradition's view that the sovereign's right to wage war is limited only by *jus ad bellum* considerations and not any other external rules or criteria. From a just war perspective, the Charter may inhibit just behaviour by preventing states from undertaking what would otherwise be considered just wars – as in when they want to intervene to protect innocent civilians from tyranny or genocide. From the just war tradition's perspective, when legal rules inhibit virtuous behaviour, the moral quality of those rules is called into question.

---

[27] ICISS, *Responsibility to Protect*, pp. 53–55.

Writing in 1981, James Turner Johnson argued that while the UN Charter's rules on the use of force had 'undeniable worth' in terms of restraining war, they have 'not faithfully expressed the high values of the just war tradition as a whole'.[28] According to Johnson, the UN Charter privileges order over justice by assuming, *prima facie*, that the first use of force in a given situation is always unlawful and immoral.[29] This creates what Johnson calls an 'aggressor–defender' model whereby the 'aggressor' – the state that uses force first – is thought always to be in the wrong and the defender always in the right. As such, 'the *jus ad bellum* of contemporary international law does not measure up to the moral standard of justice: rather, its coalescence around the "aggressor–defender" dichotomy has led to an erroneous stress on the first [to] resort to military force'.[30] By contrast, Johnson argued, the just war tradition requires that aggression and defence not be seen as having intrinsic moral value and that the first use of force might sometimes be justifiable to restore or establish a more just order. This means more than simply that there may be times when the use of force is procedurally unlawful but seen by some as morally legitimate, as with NATO's 1999 intervention in Kosovo. Johnson argues that the disconnection between international law and the just war tradition on *jus ad bellum* undermines the moral legitimacy of the UN Charter itself.[31] The logical corollary of this is that when the course of action dictated by just war's *jus ad bellum* collides with the UN Charter, just actors should prioritise the former over the latter. This, of course, is directly contrary to what is required by R2P and therefore deserves closer scrutiny.

Johnson sets out three main reasons to doubt the moral quality of the UN Charter's rule on the use of force. First, by negatively evaluating any first use of force, the Charter places a very high value on the maintenance of order. As such, it protects the current configuration of nation states from transcendent moral values and emergent humanitarian principles.[32] If the first use of force is always wrong, then it should be assumed that the states are obligated not to use force when a government massacres or fails to protect sections of its own population. Yet this seems to contradict the moral sensibility that states do sometimes have a duty to protect people from their own government – a sensibility displayed by the 2005 agreement on R2P. It seems clear to Johnson, therefore, that the UN Charter is out of step with our moral sensibilities and is less legitimate because of it.

---

[28] James Turner Johnson, *Just War Tradition and the Restraint of War* (Princeton: Princeton University Press, 1981), p. 328.
[29] Cian O'Driscoll, 'James Turner Johnson's Just War Idea: Commanding the Headwaters of Tradition', *Journal of International Political Theory* 4 :2 (2008), p. 198.
[30] Johnson, *Just War*, p. 328.   [31] Ibid.   [32] Ibid.

Second, Johnson argues that undue moral authority is given to the UN Security Council. The just war tradition teaches that sovereignty invests *states* with the authority to use force to create and protect a just political order.[33] Johnson argues that the UN system lacks the attributes necessary for statehood and cannot replace that state's role in protecting justice. In particular, the UN lacks cohesion (it deals inconsistently with crises), sovereignty (it is dependent on member states) and an effective chain of command for military forces. These, he argues are both necessary attributes of states and important limitations on the UN.[34] Principal among the UN's deficiencies, however, are its lack of sovereign authority and the fact that it is not accountable in the way that national governments are.[35] According to Johnson, as 'without such authority there is no entity competent to determine just cause and undertake military action on its behalf, this means that the United Nations as an institution cannot have a *jus ad bellum* in the fundamental just war sense'.[36] The absence of these attributes undermines the legitimacy of the Security Council's war-making rights while, at the same time, the UN Charter denies these basic rights to states. According to Johnson, through the 1990s customary practice developed through which the rights reserved by law for the Security Council were extended to individual states and coalitions 'to give them rights to use military force across national borders which the positive-law concept of just cause sought to deny them'.[37] All of this supports the idea that while Council approval is 'important as a statement of consensus', the absence of Council authorisation 'does not take away the right of individual states to act according to their reading of their responsibilities'.[38]

Third, Johnson argues that the Charter inhibits the use of force to protect and uphold justice. During the Cold War, the UN was simply prevented from being the world's policeman by the veto powers of the two superpowers.[39] The end of the Cold War brought about a thawing of relations in the Security Council, opening the possibility of UN activism. However, Johnson claims that failures in Somalia and the former Yugoslavia were caused precisely by the Council's lack of sovereignty attributes discussed earlier. These experiences taught that the UN cannot be relied upon to do what is necessary to uphold justice. When tyranny strikes, the just war tradition may *demand* action that is prohibited by the UN Charter and thus by the R2P agreed in 2005. For Johnson, the

[33] Ibid., p. 4.   [34] Johnson, *Morality and Contemporary Warfare*, p. 61.
[35] James Turner Johnson, *The War to Oust Saddam Hussein: Just War and the Face of New Conflict* (Lanham: Rowman and Littlefield, 2005), p. 61.
[36] Johnson, *Morality and Contemporary War*, p. 61.   [37] Ibid., p. 62.
[38] Johnson, *War to Oust Saddam*, p. 61.   [39] Ibid., p. 63.

authority to act to uphold justice everywhere is an inherent attribute of sovereignty, which needs no 'superior authority' to legitimise the use of force.[40]

Moral primacy of UN Charter law

In response to these arguments, I argue that restricting enforcement for R2P purposes to actions authorised by the UN Security Council made good moral sense. Not only did it anchor R2P's conception of rightful authority in the only international body empowered to authorise the use of force, it also provides an – albeit imperfect – institutional setting for testing the veracity of moral claims presented by states in relation to proposals for the use of force. Without this, R2P could have become a largely self-serving rhetoric employed by the powerful against the weak. It is worth remembering in this regard that Johnson and fellow American just war theorist Jean Bethke Elshtain used just war arguments to defend the US-led invasion of Iraq in 2003 – a war not authorised by the Security Council and opposed by most UN member states.[41]

Johnson's work is emblematic of much contemporary just war thinking. Sometimes the UN Charter is overlooked entirely, but often just war thinking is presented as a way of using morality to bypass the law. I argue that this approach is unsatisfactory for two main reasons: it does not portray the post-1945 international legal order accurately, and it downplays the moral considerations that influenced the establishment of that order. Overall, I argue, morality is better served by a system that subjects moral claims about the use of force to external scrutiny.

The first problem is that Johnson's position inaccurately portrays the legal order set out in the UN Charter. Most significantly, the argument that the regime revolves around the 'aggressor–defender' distinction is misplaced, primarily because it misrepresents the nature and role of the UN Security Council. The Charter permits collective enforcement through Chapter VII of the UN Charter.[42] The Security Council is a political body vested with the legal right to authorise force whenever it thinks it necessary to maintain international peace and security. The Council is entitled to determine what constitutes a breach or threat to the peace and has interpreted its mandate more widely than the simple policing of the aggressor–defender distinction. Since its establishment,

---

[40] Ibid., p. 131.

[41] Jean Bethke Elshtain, *Just War Against Terror: The Burden of American Power in a Violent World* (New York: Basic Books, 2004); Johnson, *War to Oust Saddam*.

[42] Simon Chesterman, *Just War or Just Peace? Humanitarian Intervention and International Law* (Oxford: Oxford University Press, 2001), p. 227.

the Council has authorised the use of force in relation to Korea, Iraq–Kuwait, Somalia, Rwanda, Haiti, Bosnia, Eastern Zaire/the Democratic Republic of Congo (DRC), Kosovo (KFOR), East Timor, Afghanistan, Cote d'Ivoire, Libya and Mali and more limited uses of (non-defensive) force in relation to southern Rhodesia (Zimbabwe), DRC, Albania, Liberia, the Central African Republic, Sierra Leone, Cote d'Ivoire and Sudan (Darfur).[43] Few of these cases fit the simple aggressor–defender model. They span a spectrum of peace and security issues including reversing aggression, combating terrorists, assisting states, securing the delivery of humanitarian aid, protecting civilians, defeating their tormenters, maintaining the rule of law, disarming armed groups and apprehending war criminals.

When the Council decides not to act, this is never because it lacks the authority to do so or because of fidelity to the 'aggressor–defender' paradigm.[44] Instead, it does not act in cases where there is no political agreement about what course of action justice dictates. Thus, in the case of Rwanda, there was no armed intervention only because no state wanted to intervene; in Kosovo, Russia argued (not without merit) that the situation was not sufficiently serious and that armed intervention would do more harm than good; and in relation to Iraq, France maintained (correctly) that the evidentiary basis for war was weak. More recently, the Council reached a consensus on Libya and in relation to the crisis in Syria, no Council member has advanced a case for armed intervention. The reality is that the Council has actually done a reasonably good job of reflecting the moral will of the international community on the subject of the use of force. I can think of no case in which the Council has inhibited the use of force for protection purposes in a situation where intervention was supported by a clear majority of the world's peoples and governments.

It could be argued in response that although the Council has widened its definition of international peace and security, the Charter was initially conceived in terms of the 'aggressor–defender' model and only adopted a wider role after the Cold War. There are two problems, however, with this view. First, Article 39 of the UN Charter refers to aggression only as one of three situations in which the Council might invoke its enforcement authority, the other two being threats to the peace and breaches of the peace. Second, the Council was engaged in matters other than aggression almost from day one. In 1945–1946, the Council was engaged in the

---

[43] Based on Chesterman, *Just War*, pp. 241–250; Alex J. Bellamy and Paul D. Williams, *Understanding Peacekeeping* (Cambridge: Polity, second edition 2010).

[44] This is one of the central arguments in Chesterman, *Just War*.

Indonesia/Dutch East Indies (calling for Dutch restraint), the Thailand/ Indochina border crisis (the Council arbitrated a border dispute), and the 'Corfu channel incident' (the Council referred the matter to the International Court of Justice) – none of which involved aggression.

The second problem with the just war critique of the Security Council is that it downplays the moral concerns that underpin the UN Charter. On the one hand, the 1945 system reflects basic just war principles. On the other hand, it tackles a serious moral problem inherent in the just war tradition. I will briefly set out each of these claims in turn. As Stephen Neff has shown, the basic premises underlying the Charter regime are based on fundamental principles related to the just war tradition: the idea that the normal state of world politics is the condition of peace and the idea that force may only be used in certain carefully limited circumstances.[45] In contrast to the system that preceded it, the UN system does not entrust individual states with the right to determine the justice of their own cause for the simple reason that history has taught us that self-interested states make bad moral judges of their own actions. Instead, it awarded that role to the Security Council. Because of its voting system (a resolution must have nine affirmative votes and no negative votes from a permanent member), we can be assured that when the Council chooses to authorise force, it does so in the name of genuinely shared values and concerns and not just because of the moral inclinations or self-interest of a few powerful states. As Neff argues, 'police actions by the Security Council would be just wars of the purest kind, for the countering of aggression and the upholding of community values'.[46] Nor does the UN Charter system rule out the potential for the emergence of a thicker conception of international justice because it grants the Security Council authority to authorise force whenever it thinks it necessary to maintain international peace and security. Over time, the Council has expanded its definition of international peace and security as new points of consensus have emerged. The key difference between this and the just war view is that the UN Charter system requires that conceptions of justice be predicated on consensus among states, whereas the just war position seems to assume that its own particular conception of justice is *prima facie* universalisable and trusts the capacity of powerful states to interpret and apply the demands of justice fairly and without regard for their own interests. This latter view is politically naïve in the extreme.

---

[45] Stephen C. Neff, *War and the Law of Nations: A General History* (Cambridge: Cambridge University Press, 2005), p. 279.
[46] Neff, *War and the Law*, p. 281.

This brings me to the argument that the UN Charter system actually helps close a potentially devastating loophole in just war thinking – an issue identified early in international debates about R2P. This is the problem that, placed in the hands of self-interested states, any criteria for the use of force (whether the just war tradition or ICISS criteria) can become a convenient rationale for justifying aggressive force. As I argued earlier, some of the early just war thinkers, notably Vitoria, were aware of this problem and offered their own potential solutions.[47] To prevent both the just war tradition and R2P from succumbing to this trap, it is important that individual sovereigns not be given an exclusive right to decide the legitimacy of their own cause. The system established in 1945 clearly achieved this by requiring that states that wished to use force present their case to a Council of peers (the Security Council) and receive a mandate for action (an authorising resolution). In recent times, the Council has fulfilled this duty reasonably well. When, in 2011, NATO asked for a licence to protect the people of Libya from the clear threat posed by Gaddafi's forces, the Security Council – recognising the merits of the case – passed an immediate resolution with no negative votes. The following year, the Council granted regional actors a mandate to assist the government of Mali to suppress an Islamist rebellion.

Seen in this light, the legal order established in 1945 is an extension of the ideas set forth by Vitoria in the sixteenth century. Under this system, sovereigns are legally required to present their case for war to a group of peers. The principal purpose of this system, like the one Vitoria proposed, is to ensure as far as possible that war is waged for reasons of common morality.

Conclusion

Just war thinking provides guidance about the moral questions that political leaders ought to ask when making decisions about whether to use force. It was precisely because such decisions are fraught with difficulties that ICISS utilised some of the tradition's thinking in its own recommendations about how the international community ought to respond to the problem of genocide and mass atrocities. Although world leaders ultimately decided not to adopt the criteria for the use of force that the Commission proposed, those criteria and the just war thinking that underpinned remain useful guides that can be used to evaluate moral claims about the potential use of

---

[47] Francisco de Vitoria, 'On the American Indians', in Anthony Pagden and Jeremy Lawrence eds, *Vitoria: Political Writings* (Cambridge: Cambridge University Press, 1991), p. 313.

force. In so doing, they might be used to guide both national decision-making and debates between states. However, the just war tradition did not intend that its criteria be employed in an instrumental way to justify war or that they be treated as singular conditions to be 'ticked off'. Instead, they inform part of a greater whole and provide guidance about the moral questions that ought to be considered and debated before decisions are taken to use force. One of the principal problems with this schema, however, is that it leaves the authority to use force and to determine valid from invalid moral arguments in the hands of the self-interested state itself. This presents the danger that states might use moral arguments about protecting populations from genocide as a cloak to disguise their aggressive and self-interested use of force. It is for that reason, I have argued, that political leaders were wise to insist that the Security Council should have the exclusive authority to license the use of force for R2P purposes, for while this might create short-term frustrations, it will ensure that would-be interveners are compelled to present their case to the court of world opinion and will protect the principle from abuse.

11   War is not the answer: the Responsibility to Protect and military intervention

Jonathan Graubart

> The past is never dead. It's not even past.
>
> William Faulkner

From 2005 to 2011, the bulk of scholarly commentary on the Responsibility to Protect (R2P) doctrine agreed that following the 2005 UN General Assembly World Summit, military intervention was no longer a central component.[1] Indeed, some interventionists lamented that R2P had become 'R2P-lite'; that is, stripped of its coercive authority.[2] R2P supporters, however, maintained that through jettisoning the language of 'humanitarian intervention', featuring 'sovereignty as responsibility', prioritising prevention, and imposing tight constraints, R2P made military intervention broadly acceptable as a hard edge to be used rarely.[3] They were not pleased, then, when Nicaraguan Foreign Minister Miguel d'Escoto Brockmann, as president of the General Assembly, convened a debate on R2P in 2009 and questioned the military intervention component.[4] Special Adviser to the UN secretary-general, Edward Luck, cautioned the Assembly not to 'turn back the clock, to divide the membership' by resurrecting 'the old caricature that RtoP is

---

[1] Thomas Weiss, *Humanitarian Intervention: Ideas in Action* (Malden: Polity Press, 2007); Gareth Evans, *The Responsibility to Protect: Ending Mass Atrocity Crimes Once and for All* (Washington DC: Brookings Institution Press, 2008), p. 4; Alex Bellamy, *Responsibility to Protect: The Global Effort to End Mass Atrocities* (Cambridge: Polity Press, 2009).

[2] Weiss, *Humanitarian Intervention*, p. 117. See Aidan Hehir, 'The Responsibility to Protect in International Political Discourse: Encouraging Statement of Intent or Illusory Platitudes?', *International Journal of Human Rights* 15: 8 (2011), pp. 1331–1348.

[3] Evans, *Responsibility to Protect*, p. 48; Ramesh Thakur, *The Responsibility to Protect: Norms, Laws, and the Use of Force in International Politics* (New York: Routledge, 2011), p. 177.

[4] International Coalition for the Responsibility to Protect (ICRtoP), 'Report on the General Assembly Plenary Debate on the Responsibility to Protect', 15 September 2009.

another word for military intervention'.[5] To supporters' relief, despite airing multiple concerns, the Assembly reaffirmed the 2005 consensus.

Since the UN Security Council's invoking of R2P in 2011 to justify the US–NATO (North Atlantic Treaty Organization) military operation against Muammar Gaddafi's forces in Libya, the consensus has frayed. This action brought home that military intervention is a salient and consequential feature of R2P. Moreover, the manner of intervention – where diplomatic overtures were rejected and the goal morphed into regime change – and the disastrous aftermath – with Libya turning far more deadly and unstable – undermined the claim that R2P enables effective, well-regulated operations.[6] Consequently, support in the global South has shrunk measurably. As stated by Brazil's UN Ambassador, there is 'a growing perception that the concept of the Responsibility to Protect might be misused for purposes other than protecting civilians'.[7]

R2P defenders still prefer to keep the discussion on how to improve implementation. However, precluding a more fundamental debate is a poor idea. To begin with, there continues to be significant controversy on whether to give normative validation to use force for ostensibly humanitarian reasons. In the past, delegations with trepidations put off a confrontation on the apparent belief that the 2005 World Summit formulation had bracketed military intervention to a hypothetical possibility to be worked out in future discussions.[8] The Libyan action indicates this was a poor calculation. There, the US, UK and French governments invoked R2P to countenance the use of force with few effective restrictions and persuaded the Council to oblige. Furthermore, the stakes are high given R2P's call for a profound normative transition on the acceptability of force.

This chapter aims to advance such a debate. It first reviews the central arguments in favour of R2P's treatment of military intervention and the negative reactions to the challenges posed at the 2009 debate. It then revisits d'Escoto's critical interjections at that debate. Situating them within a pluralist–anti-imperialist synthesis, I show that his comments offer a valuable interrogation of the premises underlying the R2P

---

[5] Edward C. Luck, Special Adviser to the Secretary-General, 'Remarks to the General Assembly on the Responsibility to Protect (RtoP)', New York, 23 July 2009, pp. 2–3, www.un.org/en/preventgenocide/adviser/pdf/EL%20GA%20remarks%202009.pdf.

[6] I discuss Libya below.

[7] 'Letter Dated 9 November 2011 from the Permanent Representative of Brazil to the United Nations Addressed to the Secretary General', A/66/551-S/2011/701.

[8] Bellamy, *Responsibility to Protect*, pp. 94, 195; Paul Williams and Alex Bellamy, 'Principles, Politics, and Prudence: Libya, the Responsibility to Protect, and the Use of Military Force', *Global Governance* 18 (2012), pp. 273–297, p. 289.

approach towards military intervention. Most importantly, d'Escoto reveals a fundamental analytical shortcoming of proponents: a fervent aversion to historical scrutiny of predatory interventions from leading powers and their implications for R2P. This chapter then proceeds to conduct such a scrutiny. In so doing, I argue that the combination of enduring global structural inequalities and narrow self-interest orientation in the interventionist policies of the United States and other leading powers make it unwise to legitimate another category of military intervention.

Reviewing arguments for R2P

R2P was conceived in 2001 by the International Commission on Intervention and State Sovereignty (ICISS), a global task force chaired by Gareth Evans and Mohamed Sahnoun.[9] Its mission was 'to strengthen the prospects for obtaining action, on a collective and principled basis . . . in response to conscience-shocking situations of great humanitarian need'.[10] For supporters, R2P has done so by setting forth a comprehensive conceptual framework that resonates across the globe. As Gareth Evans proudly recalls, 'We sought to turn the whole weary – and increasingly ugly – debate about "the right to intervene" on its head and recharacterise it not as an argument about the "right" of states to do anything but rather about their "responsibility" . . . to protect people at grave risk. The relevant perspective . . . was not that of prospective interveners but of those needing support.'[11] The idea is that 'humanitarian intervention' has too much negative baggage in the global South but there is a consensus that states have the responsibility to protect their residents from such atrocities (and not perpetrate them). Supporters further credit R2P with expanding the conversation beyond military intervention. Although military force remains a necessary component of international action when a state fails to meet its responsibility, R2P includes a range of other options, with the focus on prevention.[12]

Another claimed virtue of R2P is its constraints on military intervention. Originally, ICISS drafted a version of just war criteria.[13] According to the 2005 World Summit, the conditions consist of the committing of

---

[9] International Commission on Intervention and State Sovereignty (ICISS), *The Responsibility to Protect* (Ottawa: International Development Research Centre, 2001).
[10] Ibid., p. 74.   [11] Evans, *Responsibility to Protect*, pp. 39–40.
[12] Thakur, *Responsibility to Protect*, pp. 139–140. Postconflict peacebuilding is the other central plank.
[13] These are seriousness of harm, right intention, last resort, proportional means and reasonable prospect of success. ICISS, *Responsibility to Protect*, pp. 32–37. See Alex Bellamy's chapter in this volume.

crimes amounting to genocide, ethnic cleansing, crimes against humanity or war crimes, Council authorisation, the inadequacy of peaceful means and the 'manifest fail[ure]' of national authorities to protect their population.[14] For Ramesh Thakur, co-author of the original R2P, 'R2P offers ... negotiated-in-advance rules and roadmaps for when outside intervention is justified and how it may be done ... It will thus lead to the "Gulliverization" of the use of force by major global and regional powers'.[15]

Collectively, for many supporters, each of the above virtues disproves the contention that R2P is biased against developing states. Most notably, they observe, the vigorous discontent expressed across the global South led ICISS to reaffirm support for sovereignty and to substitute Responsibility to Protect for humanitarian intervention.[16] Similarly, delegations from the global South succeeded at the 2005 World Summit in emphasising R2P's prioritisation of prevention over intervention and in precluding any non-Council approved use of force.[17] Some supporters also play up the non-Western pedigree of sovereignty as responsibility, noting that the African Union Charter incorporates the idea.[18] Because of their input, so the argument goes, the states of the global South remain largely supportive of R2P, even if they remain concerned about how to incorporate military intervention.

Finally, some supporters commend R2P's pragmatic adaptation to political realities. Realising the unlikelihood of purely altruistic military interventions, ICISS made sure to accommodate the political needs of the prevailing powers, especially the United States, given that they will do the heavy lifting. As Thakur comments, 'For the foreseeable future, there is only one country [the United States] ... with the capacity to project powers around the globe ... and only one standing military defence organization with the capacity to undertake out-of area operations [NATO].'[19] To encourage a constructive US-led role, ICISS gives its approval for mixed motives whereby the intervener also has a strong self-interest.[20] Evans and other ICISS framers effectively acknowledge that this accommodation will lead to double standards because interventions will not take place in

---

[14] *World Summit Outcome*, Document A/60/L.1A (New York: United Nations, 24 October 2005), paragraph 139.
[15] Thakur, *Responsibility to Protect*, p. 140.
[16] Ramesh Thakur, 'R2P after Libya and Syria: Engaging Emerging Powers', *Washington Quarterly*, 36:2 (2013), pp. 61–76, p. 65,
[17] Bellamy, *Responsibility to Protect*, p. 94.
[18] Luke Glanville, 'In Defense of the Responsibility to Protect', *Journal of Religious Ethics*, 41:1 (2013), pp. 169–182, p. 174. In his chapter for this volume, Amitav Acharya characterises R2P as essentially African in its origins.
[19] Thakur, *Responsibility to Protect*, p. 92.   [20] ICISS, *Responsibility to Protect*, p. 36.

situations when the great powers or close allies are implicated or where self-interest is thin. But this reflects 'a fact of life with which we simply have to live in many different international contexts'.[21] The supposed pragmatic appeal of R2P is that rather than be paralysed by geopolitical hierarchies, it carves out a category of mixed-motive, status quo friendly interventions that nevertheless save lives. At least, then, some future Rwandas may be prevented.

Having formulated a comprehensive and seemingly viable policy document, supporters did not welcome the General Assembly's convening of a debate. A review of their objections is instructive for indicating the limits of their desired dialogue.

'Blatantly unhelpful': rejecting debate on the fundamentals

Opening the debate, Miguel d'Escoto cordially remarked that the 'authors and proponents of R2P ... have the best of intentions and seek to be prudent, realistic and wise in pushing for its gradual implementation and evolution ... I respect and commend the work they are doing'.[22] R2P supporters were not placated. Edward Luck warned of carrying on 'the spectacle of debate' whereby opponents cling to myths 'like so many unwanted barnacles'.[23] The International Coalition for the Responsibility to Protect (ICRtoP) derided d'Escoto's Concept Paper as 'blatantly unhelpful' and an 'insult to the Secretary General'. It further rebuked the pre-debate convening of a thematic panel that included three prominent anti-imperialist intellectuals. None had appropriate credentials, including Noam Chomsky, 'a self-proclaimed anarchist'.[24]

---

[21] Evans, *Responsibility to Protect*, p. 64.
[22] President of the 63rd Session United Nations General Assembly, 'At the Opening of the Thematic Dialogue of the General Assembly on the Responsibility to Protect', New York, 23 July 2009, pp. 1–2, www.un.org/ga/president/63/statements/open ingr2p230709.shtml.
[23] Luck, 'Remarks', p. 3.
[24] ICRtoP, 'Report', p. 4. Notwithstanding his vast intellectual influence, Chomsky's work is often summarily dismissed by Western liberal scholars, perhaps in suspicion of Chomsky's wide political following among activists. For example, Michael Barnett, *Empire of Humanity: A History of Humanitarianism* (Ithaca: Cornell University Press, 2011), p. 6. Barnett even insinuates that Chomsky regarded all reports of Pol Pot atrocities as CIA propaganda. He is apparently referring to a co-authored volume which argues that US reporting of human rights abuses tends to mirror US policy priorities. For Cambodia, it finds that the media relied on sensationalist claims rather than reliable and more nuanced reports of mass atrocities and ignored comparable atrocities in East Timor, perpetrated by Indonesia, a recipient of US military aid. Noam Chomsky and Edward Herman, *After the Cataclysm: Postwar Indochina and the Reconstruction of Imperial Ideology* (Boston: South End Press, 1979).

Interestingly, Chomsky cautiously supported the 2005 World Summit's formulation of R2P and opined that it could prove a useful platform for challenging the practices of leading powers.[25] ICRtoP was not impressed. Its problem with Chomsky and d'Escoto was twofold. One, both highlighted military intervention as a concern. Two, both brought up a history of imperialist interventions accompanied by moral rhetoric, argued that such behaviour persists in modified form by way of aggressive interventionism, and warned that R2P could further encourage such behaviour. The ICRtoP regarded such reflections as simplistic imperialist charges, meant to provoke discontent and impede progress.[26]

The sharp rebuke from leading R2P supporters is unfortunate. To begin with, it conveys a hostile tone that belies claims of inclusivity. With regard to d'Escoto, the ICRtoP and others could have acknowledged historically grounded reasons for being suspicious of a doctrine that includes military intervention. The United States had indeed invoked both security and human rights justifications to attempt the overthrow of the Nicaraguan government in the 1980s through mining the harbours, training, arming and assisting an armed resistance, and producing and disseminating a manual for perpetrating attacks on civilian targets.[27] Although Nicaragua prevailed at the International Court of Justice, d'Escoto correctly observed that the international community had no concrete means to enforce the ruling.[28] His concern, then, that R2P's formal legal restrictions will be insufficient merits respectful attention.

The hostile tone, in turn, reflects a broader shortcoming of many R2P supporters. In insisting that the time for debate has passed, they seek to preclude issues of crucial import, such as historical trends in great power intervention and the dynamics shaping the interventionist policies of leading states. Indeed, ICISS decided at the outset 'that any attempt to examine the merits, law, legitimacy and political wisdom of past interventions would be backward looking, possibly finger-pointing, judgmental and far from helpful to our task'.[29] Similarly, the ICRtoP indicated that the only appropriate participant at the thematic panel was Gareth Evans because he 'actually worked on developing the

---

[25] 'Statement by Professor Noam Chomsky to the United Nations General Assembly Thematic Dialogue on the Responsibility to Protect', United Nations, New York, 23 July 2009, www.un.org/ga/president/63/interactive/protect/noam.pdf.

[26] ICRtoP, 'Report', p. 4.

[27] International Court of Justice, *Case Concerning the Military and Paramilitary Activities In and Against Nicaragua (Nicaragua v. United States of America)*, Judgment of 27 June 1986.

[28] 'Opening of the Thematic Dialogue', p. 3.

[29] Ramesh Thakur, *The United Nations, Peace and Security: From Collective Security to the Responsibility to Protect* (New York: Cambridge University Press, 2006), p. 249.

Responsibility to Protect and had extensive practical experience in working to prevent and halt mass atrocity crimes'.[30] It is hard to see, however, how informed judgements can be made on matters of great consequences without delving into the more fundamental and contentious themes raised by Chomsky and the other panellists.

Why R2P has not resolved the fundamental debate on military intervention

R2P supporters maintain that they have put to rest disputes on humanitarian intervention by formulating a framework that features the affirmative obligations of state sovereignty rather than conflicts between intervention and sovereignty. In so doing, they argue, the focus is on protecting victims, not giving rights to interveners.[31] Yet however tactful this new formulation may be, it does not settle the underlying issue. After all, few opponents of humanitarian intervention accord states the right to commit mass atrocities. D'Escoto, for example, observes 'there is finally broad agreement that the international community can no longer remain silent in the face of genocide, ethnic cleansing, war crimes and crimes against humanity'.[32] But opponents fear the consequences of effectively instituting a new category for using force. R2P framers have not found a breakthrough approach for alleviating such fears. Rather with respect to coercive force, R2P mirrors contemporaneous humanitarian intervention proposals in terms of emphasising the victims and articulating a set of just war derived criteria that have to be met.[33] Such proposals have not satisfied the concerns of opponents. Whether framed as humanitarian intervention or the exercise of 'responsibility', the worry remains the same; the net impact in practice will be more self-serving, destabilising interventions that exacerbate rather than mitigate suffering.

It is also unpersuasive to expect concerns of military intervention to be alleviated by linking it to prevention and peacebuilding. The idea seems to be that the latter will assure wary parties that military intervention will

---

[30] ICRtoP, 'Report', p. 4. Besides Chomsky, the other panellists were Belgian professor Jean Bricmont and Kenyan writer Ngũgĩ wa Thiong'o. Apparently, an extensive collective record of influential publications and courageous human rights and antiwar activism was not considered useful. D'Escoto disagreed: 'Responsibility to Protect is too important an issue to be left to narrow specialists, and those who have made it a profession or an industry'. 'Opening of the Thematic Dialogue', p. 3.

[31] Evans, *Responsibility to Protect*, p. 40; Thakur, *Responsibility to Protect*, pp. 139–140.

[32] 'Opening of the Thematic Dialogue', p. 1.

[33] For example, Independent International Commission on Kosovo, *The Kosovo Report* (October 2000), p. 104; Nicholas Wheeler, *Saving Strangers: Humanitarian Intervention in International Society* (New York: Oxford University Press, 2000), especially p. 38.

be used responsibly and sparingly. But whatever one thinks of these policies, it is difficult to see how they would check the negative dynamics feared by humanitarian intervention opponents. After all, these policies do not reflect new commitments. Diplomatic efforts to resolve conflict have long been official policy while peacebuilding has been prominent since the 1990s.[34] Hence, post-Cold War debates on humanitarian intervention already operated in the shadow of these other policies. Moreover, R2P remains vague on what these commitments entail, especially on how they will prevent military interventions from yielding destabilising or abusive results.[35] Unsurprisingly, as Evans and Thakur acknowledge, there is little consensus on how to apply R2P at the 'sharp end' of the R2P response spectrum.[36]

For all the attempts, then, to downplay the salience of military intervention, it is the one area where R2P seeks to break new ground normatively. Curiously, supporters sometimes deny this. At the 2009 thematic panel, Luck asserted that it is a 'tired canard that RtoP offers new legal norms or would alter the Charter basis for Security Council decisions'.[37] Such a denial rests on the twin observations that R2P is not a formal legal document and that the Council has already interpreted its Chapter VII powers to authorise force for halting domestic atrocities.[38] Although both points are technically correct, the intended implication is misleading. After all, as Evans and Thakur have noted, the point of seeking repeated global endorsements of R2P is to crystallise a new norm of customary law.[39] Moreover, while the Council had incrementally expanded the meaning of Chapter VII's threats to international peace and security, it had not – at least up until 2011 – done what R2P supporters sought: categorically declare that a domestic mass atrocity is sufficient for authorising force rather than require tangible evidence of a threat to international peace and security – meaning a cross-border dimension. As

[34] Roland Paris, *At War's End: Building Peace After Civil Conflicts* (New York: Cambridge University Press, 2004).

[35] Adam Branch makes a persuasive case that the implementation of prevention and rebuilding in sub-Saharan Africa have further deteriorated human rights as well as self-determination. Adam Branch, *Displacing Human Rights: War and Intervention in Northern Uganda* (New York: Oxford University Press, 2011).

[36] Gareth Evans and Ramesh Thakur, 'Humanitarian Intervention and the Responsibility to Protect', *International Security* 37:4 (Spring 2013), pp. 199–214, p. 200.

[37] 'Remarks', p. 3. The ICRtoP expressed similar sentiments. 'Report', pp. 6–7.

[38] Some also point to the precedent of the African Union's 2000 Charter, which allows for such use of force. Yet it gives no authority to non-AU states and sets onerous criteria, making it 'slim at best' that a coercive regional intervention would occur. Bellamy, *Responsibility to Protect*, pp. 78–79.

[39] Thakur, *Responsibility to Protect*, p. 150; Gareth Evans, 'Overview: The R2P Balance Sheet After Libya', *e-International Relations* (November 2011), pp. 34–42, p. 36.

demonstrated below, the Council's 2011 invoking of R2P with respect to the murky Libyan situation suggests that this new category could be expansive. D'Escoto was correct in recognising R2P's ambitious normative agenda on military intervention and the corresponding need for full debate.

Appreciating d'Escoto's doubts and hesitations

According to Luke Glanville, d'Escoto's interjection 'was widely interpreted [among R2P advocates] as a destructive contribution'.[40] Accordingly, such advocates, such as the ICRtoP, have shown little interest in the substance of d'Escoto's comments, preferring to reduce it to an accusation of 'redecorated colonialism'.[41] This inattention is unfortunate because his comments offer rich insights for engagement. To see why, it helps to review the underlying pluralist–anti-imperialist critique that informs them.

By pluralism, I refer to the perspective associated with Hedley Bull, which posits a modest international society of states in which there is a diversity of values and traditions and a few shared primary rules based on coexistence and stability.[42] For contemporary pluralists, the UN Charter and ensuing decolonisation embody the bedrock norms by their emphasis on sovereign equality, peaceful resolution of conflict and prohibitions on aggressive uses of force.[43] Because of limits in the breadth and depth of the international society, coupled with a highly unequal order, pluralists warn against hard global institutionalisation of moral values. There may be shared global values at an abstract level, but, as Bull articulates, 'we lack a consensus in international society as to means' and 'the appropriate institutions with which to authorize action'.[44] Without such a developed consensus, warns Bull, it would be very difficult to expect states to overcome the pursuit of power politics and national interest. Accordingly, 'we court great dangers if we allow ourselves to proceed as if it were a political and social framework already in

[40] 'In Defense of the Responsibility to Protect', p. 180.
[41] ICRtoP, 'Report', p. 3. In 'Whither R2P?' *e-International Relations* (31 August, 2011), p. 711,Thomas Weiss, in his zeal to deride d'Escoto's 'Marxist dagger', wrongly attributes the phrase to the latter.
[42] Hedley Bull, *The Anarchical Society: A Study of Order in World Politics* (New York: Columbia University Press, 1977).
[43] Robert Jackson, *The Global Covenant: Human Conduct in a World of States* (New York: Oxford University Press, 2000); Mohammed Ayoob, 'Humanitarian Intervention and State Sovereignty', *International Journal of Human Rights* 6:1 ((2002), pp. 81–102.
[44] Hedley Bull, *Justice in International Relations* (Waterloo: 1983–1984 Hagey Lectures, 1983), p. 14.

place'.[45] Besides undermining reasonably effective institutions in place for maintaining order, moral-based global regimes will be skewed towards the preferences of 'the presently prevailing great powers', upon whom cooperation is most needed.[46]

The anti-imperialism orientation invoked by d'Escoto, broadly speaking, complements the pluralist critique through a historically informed probing of the leading Western powers' interventionist policies. For the dominant global power since the Second World War, an anti-imperialist framework highlights longstanding US priorities of military preeminence, control over vital natural resources, access for US companies to trade and investment and a network of allies in strategically important locations. In furtherance of these priorities, the United States has waged repeated invasions, the most extensive in Korea, Vietnam, Iraq and Afghanistan, formed close military-security relations with repressive regimes and conducted covert warfare against many states, several of which triggered massive atrocities, including in Guatemala, Indonesia and Chile.[47] Given such priorities, anti-imperialists are sceptical of professions of moral sentiments from elite policymakers. Moral goals are primarily invoked to rationalise and elicit support for traditional objectives.[48]

D'Escoto cogently applies pluralist–anti-imperialist sentiments to pose penetrating challenges to R2P's treatment of military intervention. One trajectory mirrors Bull's warning of a mismatch between moral ambition and the actual underlying consensus. D'Escoto questions whether R2P will 'guarantee that states will intervene to prevent another Rwanda?'[49] He answers no, not simply because R2P imposes no such hard obligation, but, more importantly, because the requisite degree of global solidarity for sustaining an effective operation still does not exist. In a world, then, where solidarity is shallow and stratification is pronounced, d'Escoto asks, will R2P 'be applied in practice equally to all nation-states, or ... only by the strong against the weak?'[50] 'Recent and painful memories related to the legacy of colonialism', he continues, 'give developing countries strong reasons to fear that laudable motives can end up being misused, once more, to justify arbitrary and selective interventions against the weakest states'.[51]

[45] Ibid., p. 13.   [46] Bull, *Anarchical Society*, p. 304.
[47] Thomas McCormick, *America's Half Century: United States Foreign Policy in the Cold War and After*, 2nd Edition (Baltimore: Johns Hopkins University Press, 1989); Brian Loveman, *No Higher Law: American Foreign Policy and the Western Hemisphere Since 1776* (Chapel Hill: Duke University Press, 2010).
[48] Chomsky has consistently documented the instrumental uses. For example, see Chomsky and Herman, *After the Cataclysm*.
[49] 'Opening of the Thematic Dialogue', p. 2.   [50] Ibid.   [51] Ibid.

Finally, it is worth noting d'Escoto's interrogation of R2P's formal constraints on intervention. Pointing to the 2003 US invasion of Iraq and the 1980s efforts to overthrow Nicaragua's government, he observes that we lack 'the capacity to enforce accountability upon those who might abuse the right that R2P would give nation-states to resort to the use of force against other states'.[52] The net result, therefore, is that while R2P will be ill-equipped to reduce mass atrocities, it could very well be destabilising by subverting 'the consecrated cornerstone values ... of sovereignty and non-intervention'.[53]

Expanding upon the argument to eliminate military intervention from R2P

Consistent with the critical pluralist–anti-imperialist approach of d'Escoto, I press the challenge further, looking not at R2P's stated aspirations but its likely impact in the world 'we have, rather than the one we want'.[54]

Perhaps the most relevant global feature is the enduring hierarchical global order identified by Bull in terms of power, resources and influence. This is not to diminish the notable past and present efforts of developing states to exert their collective voice, especially at the UN General Assembly, such as mobilising unanimous support for the Declaration on the Granting of Independence to Colonial Countries and Peoples.[55] Nevertheless, on matters implicating hard global policies, such as trade, international criminal prosecution and, especially, coercive force, there is a decided tilt.[56] Thakur would seem to agree: 'The UN's political agenda is controlled largely by the Western states who are its most powerful and wealthy members.'[57] This tilt is easily discernible in R2P, notwithstanding the outreach to developing states. Consider ICISS's diagnosis of mass atrocities. Missing, observes Richard Falk, is 'any kind of critical bite that might offend those in power. There is a reluctance to name names ... and an unwillingness to address the distorting selectivity of geopolitics or to discuss the hidden motivations and incentives of the parties.'[58] The focus, instead, is on indigenous factors, particularly repressive regimes, ethnic conflicts and a

---

[52] Ibid., p. 3.   [53] Ibid., p. 1.   [54] Ibid., p. 2.
[55] Chris Alden, Sally Morphet, and Marco Antonia Vieira, *The South in World Politics* (Houndmills: Palgrave MacMillan, 2010); A/RES/1514 (XV), 14 December, 1960.
[56] See Jonathan Graubart, 'Rendering Global Criminal Law an Instrument of Power: Pragmatic Legalism and Global Tribunals', *Journal of Human Rights* 35 (2010), pp. 69–90.
[57] Thakur, *Responsibility to Protect*, p. 195.
[58] Richard Falk, *The Costs of War: International Law, the UN, and World Order after Iraq* (New York: Routledge, 2008), pp. 158–159.

deficient or failed state.[59] This assessment comports well with the US–Western view that they do not commit mass atrocities.[60] As a result, recurring practices by the United States and other Western states in arming repressive regimes, such as those in Guatemala from the 1960s to the 1980s and Indonesia from the 1970s to the 1990s, or in waging wars that inflict many casualties and trigger or exacerbate deadly internal conflicts, are conveniently omitted.[61]

Like the diagnosis bias, the envisioned intervention is similarly one-sided. As Thakur concedes, the 'only likely sites and targets of intervention . . . will be developing countries' while the approved intervener will be the United States and its allies or a US-supported regional power or bloc.[62] An R2P supporter might respond that even if one-directional, R2P enables a criteria-governed process on halting atrocities where the dispositive factors are severity of harm and operational feasibility. Such assurance, however, is not persuasive. To begin with, as Thakur observes, interveners have long based their selection on 'material self-interest' and 'discrimination between friends/allies . . . versus adversaries and rogue states'.[63] Moreover, the 2005 World Summit's formulation of R2P, in deference to the United States, lacks a set of criteria or a transparent process that could even in theory change the calculations. D'Escoto's concern, then, of R2P only being applied by the strong against the weak is well-founded. Appropriate targets for military intervention are confined to those regimes in the global periphery which are disfavoured in the West – but not close to Russia or China – and whose location offers a sizable geostrategic-economic benefit. Such an application reinforces the hierarchical global order and signals the subordinate role of moral-based policies.

Moreover, even if one is willing to tolerate such politicised selectivity, the question arises as to whether such interventions will have the desired effect. A careful answer considers how R2P will interact with longstanding military engagement policies of those expected to take the lead, especially the United States. Supporters maintain that R2P will facilitate

---

[59] See Evans, *Responsibility to Protect*, pp. 74–75, which sets forth his 'watch list criteria'. ICISS makes a passing reference to the 'rich world' being implicated through arms and monetary transfers but provides no plan for addressing this. *Responsibility to Protect*, p. 5.

[60] When asked whether the International Criminal Court might ever prosecute UK officials for its conduct in Iraq or Afghanistan, UK Foreign Minister Robin Cook replied, 'this is not a court set up to bring to book Prime Ministers of the United Kingdom or Presidents of the United States'. Quoted in Jonathan Graubart and Latha Varadarajan, 'Taking Milosevic Seriously: Imperialism, Law, and the Politics of Global Justice', *International Relations* 27:4 (2013), pp. 439–460, p. 439.

[61] John Tirman, *The Deaths of Others: The Fate of Civilians in America's Wars* (New York: Oxford University Press, 2011).

[62] Thakur, 'R2P After Libya and Syria', p. 63.

[63] Thakur, *Responsibility to Protect*, p. 194.

a benign interaction between conventional self-interest and moral impulses. A close look at the United States' record gives much reason for doubt.

There is first the matter of what is meant by the self-interest aspect. ICISS offers amorphous and relatively innocuous examples of preserving stability, increasing trade and economic growth and stemming the tide of refugees.[64] These notably understate US foreign policy interests. Much more illuminating is a document produced by a bipartisan, Pentagon-sponsored task force from 2000. This defines the preeminent interests as solidifying overwhelming military superiority, preventing the emergence of any rival regional hegemon or coalition, securing access to vital resources and extending global economic integration along neoliberal lines receptive to US economic actors.[65] True to this spirit, recent US military engagement has comprised 'full spectrum threat dominance', expansion of military bases and security partnerships with strategically useful regimes and reinterpretation of laws of war to widen the permissible scope of targets.[66] To expect these enduring interest-based policies to be reconstituted into a benign, principled direction is highly naïve considering that they are supported by influential constituencies and are institutionally entrenched. Accordingly, appeals to employ force for moral reasons will have to be vetted through the dominant military-security institutions to ensure sufficient focus on national interests. Some moral arguments may survive but there is little reason to expect desirable net consequences from the ensuing implementation.

Instructive in this regard is the R2P-approved 2011 US–NATO intervention in Libya. Appropriately, Gaddafi's Libya was a periphery, oil-rich state, had a history of tension with US–Western states and lacked influential allies. R2P supporters hail the intervention as a triumph for R2P in mobilising a robust operation that halted an imminent massacre by Gaddafi.[67] For them, the motives of morality and conventional national interest happily aligned whereby the goal of stopping a slaughter was central while the US–NATO interest in stability in the Middle East–North African region ensured a sustained military

---

[64] ICISS, *Responsibility to Protect*, p. 72.

[65] Hart–Rudman Commission, *Seeking a National Strategy: A Concert for Preserving Security and Promoting Freedom* (US Commission on National Security/21st Century, 15 April 2000).

[66] Loveman, *No Higher Law*, p. 351; Bruce Cronin, 'Reckless Endangerment Warfare: Civilian Casualties and the Collateral Damage Exception in International Humanitarian Law', *Journal of Peace Research*, 50:2 (2013), pp. 175–187.

[67] Williams and Bellamy, 'Principles, Politics, and Prudence'; Evans, 'Overview', p. 41; Thakur, 'R2P After Libya and Syria', pp. 69–70. Thakur concedes that NATO did not respect Resolution 1973's restricted scope.

commitment.[68] Further evidence of the merits of this action is the Arab League's endorsement of a no-fly zone in March shortly before the intervention.[69]

A number of factors, however, complicate this appealing narrative. To begin with, the moral situation cannot be reduced to NATO rescuing innocent civilians in Benghazi and elsewhere facing imminent massacre. Although Gaddafi's regime was brutal and ruthless in suppressing challenges, it had committed no large-scale massacres of civilians in response to the armed uprising.[70] The various rebel forces of the National Transitional Council (NTC), meanwhile, had also perpetrated abuses, including lynching of suspected 'African mercenaries'.[71] Moreover, moral indignation of the United States and its closest Arab allies was highly selective in the region, as indicated by events in Bahrain, host to the US Fifth Fleet. While the Saudi-led Gulf Co-operation Council (GCC) spearheaded an Arab League endorsement of intervention in Libya, it reacted very differently that same month to Bahrain's crackdown of democracy protesters.[72] Led by close US ally Saudi Arabia, GCC states sent over a thousand soldiers along with tanks to assist the crackdown.

The diplomatic record and humanitarian outcome are similarly problematic. Both NATO and the NTC peremptorily rejected proposals for ceasefires offered directly by Gaddafi and through the African Union's mediation.[73] Instead, NATO extended its intervention to regime change. During the offensive, Gaddafi's forces, the militias and NATO all committed multiple war crimes.[74] Following the overthrow and execution of Gaddafi, the insurgency engaged in revenge killings of presumed Gaddafi supporters and forcibly displaced many more, including 30,000 residents in Tawergha.[75] The

[68] Thakur, 'R2P, Libya and International Politics as the Struggle for Competing Normative Architectures', e-International Relations (November, 2011), pp. 12–14, p. 13.
[69] Evans, 'Overview', p. 41.
[70] Hugh Roberts, 'Who Said Gaddafi Had to Go?', London Review of Books 33:22 (2011), pp. 8–18.
[71] International Crisis Group (ICG), Popular Protest in North Africa and the Middle East (V): Making Sense of Libya, (6 June 2011), p. 4; Amnesty International, The Battle for Libya: Killings, Disappearances and Torture (September 2011), pp. 70–79.
[72] The GCC provided six of the nine votes for the Arab League resolution. Horace Campbell, NATO's Failure in Libya: Lessons for Africa (Pretoria: African Institute of South Africa, 2012), p. 79.
[73] Roberts, 'Who Said Gaddafi Had to Go?'; ICG, Popular Protest in North Africa, p. 28.
[74] Amnesty International, The Battle for Libya; C.J. Chivers and Eric Schmitt, 'In Strikes on Libya by NATO, an Unspoken Civilian Toll', New York Times, 17 December 2011.
[75] Human Rights Watch, 'Libya: Apparent Execution of 53 Gaddafi Supporters' (24 October 2011), www.hrw.org/news/2011/10/24/libya-apparent-execution-53-gaddafi -supporters; Human Rights Watch, 'Libya: Militias Terrorizing Residents of "Loyalist"

various militias persist to the present, inflicting great violence and unrest in much of the country.[76]

Overall, the record strongly suggests that conventional interests played the preeminent role rather than simply complementing moral concerns for Libyan civilians. If humanitarian goals had been paramount, it is difficult to explain NATO's refusal to pursue diplomatic offers that may have reduced the immediate threat faced by civilians of attacks from either Gaddafi or insurgent forces while making possible a more peaceful political transition.[77] Conversely, if the goals involved gaining a close ally and corresponding investment opportunities in an oil-rich state, extending US military-security contacts in Northern Africa and exerting influence on the political and economic directions of the broader Arab Spring, a full-scale intervention makes sense, even if the aims have not been fully realised.[78] National interests also explain well the diametrically divergent US response to the crackdown in Bahrain, where the United States did nothing while its closest regional allies intervened on behalf of the repression. To be sure, one can argue that the intervention may have averted a brutal crackdown in Benghazi, although there is reason to question some of the alarmist warnings.[79] Yet the death toll sharply accelerated after NATO's intervention with Benghazi subject to far more violence now while a former CIA asset, Khalifa Hifter, has led a military counter-offensive that may amount to an attempted coup.[80] More disturbing is the long-term boost to US military-security and neoliberal economic objectives in the region, a development hardly conducive to sustainable justice.

Tellingly, the Libyan intervention foreshadows what to expect from R2P's formal constraints and invites us to consider d'Escoto's observation that the world lacks effective means for holding dominant powers to institutional constraints. Recent history indicates good reason for doubting the effectiveness of the 2005 World Summit's two principal constraints on military intervention: the imminence of one of the specified international crimes and Council approval.

The Council is designed to privilege the interests of great powers and its decision-making process is mostly shaped by political negotiations.[81] The

---

Town', (30 October 2011), www.hrw.org/news/2011/10/30/libya-militias-terrorizing-residents-loyalist-town.

[76] Patrick Markey, 'Heavy Shelling, Clashes Spread in Libya's Tripoli', Reuters, 31 July 2014.

[77] ICG, *Popular Protest in North Africa*, pp. 28–30.

[78] Roberts, 'Who Said Gaddafi Had to Go?', Steve Niva, 'The "Matrix" comes to Libya', *Middle East Research and Information Project*, 2 November 2012.

[79] Ibid., pp. 4–5.

[80] Ethan Chorine, 'The New Danger in Benghazi', *New York Times*, 27 May 2014.

[81] David Bosco, *Five to Rule Them All: The UN Security Council and the Making of the Modern World* (New York: Oxford University Press, 2009).

United States has not always prevailed at the Council and is often challenged by Russia and China. Nevertheless, in the post-Cold War era, it has employed its abundant military power, economic resources and geostrategic influence to shape the Council to its liking. For approval of the 1991 invasion of Iraq, the US offered debt forgiveness to Council members Zaire and Egypt and halted aid to Yemen after its no vote, with Secretary of State James Baker remarking, 'Yemen's permanent representative just enjoyed about $200 to $250 million dollars' worth of applause for that [vote]'.[82] Overall, the United States has been the 'principal driver of the Council's agenda and decision', earning it the moniker the 'Permanent One'.[83] It has secured multiple resolutions authorising peacekeeping and peacebuilding operations, including in Iraq, which have advanced its geostrategic interests and facilitated the reconstruction of states along US-friendly economic and security directions.[84] As seen with Libya, the United States has heavily influenced which trouble spots become serious candidates for R2P intervention.[85]

Given the Council's considerable politicisation, it is understandable that d'Escoto would find distressing R2P's widening of the permissible circumstances for authorising force. To begin with, R2P gives the United States an added tool for validating the use of force. Hence, in 2011, the United States, United Kingdom and France simply relied on the imminent mass atrocity claim rather than make a case for a cross-border threat to international peace or security. Compare this to 2002 and Iraq, where the United States and United Kingdom had to put forward a dubious weapons of mass destruction (WMD) argument. If R2P had already attained salience, the two states would have given it at least equal billing in Council negotiations. The tactic may not have worked but it would have at least mobilised additional pressure on resistant governments.[86] As the Libyan case illustrates, one should not be all that confident of the

---

[82] Ibid., pp. 160–161.

[83] David Malone, 'Introduction', in David Malone, ed, *The UN Security Council: From the Cold War to the 21st Century* (Boulder: Lynne Rienner, 2008), pp. 1–15, p. 8.

[84] Paris, *At War's End*.

[85] Council Resolution 1970 demonstrates US influence as well on who attracts serious ICC attention. The resolution refers the Libyan situation to the ICC but conveniently excludes any actions prior to February, 2011, when Gaddafi cooperated in the US rendition programme. Human Rights Watch, 'US/UK: Documents Reveal Libya Rendition Details', (9 September 2011), www.hrw.org/news/2011/09/08/usuk-documents-reveal-libya-rendition-details.

[86] Granted, both Evans and Thakur rejected the moral argument for the war. Gareth Evans, 'Humanity Did Not Justify This War', *Financial Times*, 15 May 2003; Ramesh Thakur, 'Chrétien Was Right: It's Time to Redefine a "just war"', *Globe and Mail* (Toronto), 22 July 2003. Yet a number of prominent Western liberal voices did raise such moral arguments, including a co-author of the original R2P, Michael Ignatieff. 'On Second Thought: Arguing Iraq – Ten Years Later', *The New Republic*, 20 March 2013.

restraining power of R2P's requirement of an imminent mass atrocity. Instead of careful deliberation, one can expect that when the United States and allies wish to use force, they will issue dramatic claims of the enemy's record and warn of horrors to follow from inaction. For Libya, President Barack Obama warned that 'if we waited one more day', a vast massacre would occur that would 'stain the conscience of the world' while Libya's deputy ambassador to the UN, who had just defected, proclaimed that Gaddafi had 'already started the genocide against the Libyan people'.[87] These exaggerated narratives, including a likely fabricated report of aerial slaughters by Gaddafi of peaceful demonstrators on 21 February 2011, were widely reported upon in the West with little critical scrutiny.[88] Similarly, the Charter's demand of last resort proved equally malleable with NATO ignoring diplomatic overtures.

Lastly, there is the distinct possibility that the United States will unpack R2P's moral justification for using force from the requirement of Council approval. It has acted similarly in the past. For Kosovo in 1999 and Iraq in 2003, the United States intervened without Council approval, proclaiming the right to determine unilaterally what presents a threat to international peace and security. In 1994, US Ambassador to the United Nations Madeline Albright announced, 'we will behave, with others, multilaterally when we can and unilaterally when we must'.[89] In 2007, Susan Rice, now President Obama's national security adviser, extended this perspective to R2P. With Andrew Loomis, she argued that where the moral circumstances are compelling, it is acceptable for the United States to find alternative means of legitimation when Council approval is not forthcoming.[90]

In sum, a sober assessment of global realities and of US interventionist policy dynamics finds that a deepening of R2P's norm on military intervention will, on the one hand, present a powerful and malleable rationale for justifying the use of force while, on the other, present limited

---

[87] Barack Obama, 'Remarks by the President in Address to the Nation on Libya', (28 March 2011), www.whitehouse.gov/the-press-office/2011/03/28/remarks-president-address-nation-libya; Colin Moynihan, 'Libya's U.N. Diplomats Break with Gaddafi', *New York Times*, 21 February 2011. For a review of a similar pattern regarding NATO's intervention in Serbia-Kosovo, see Jonathan Graubart, 'R2P and Pragmatic Liberal Interventionism: Values in the Service of Interests', *Human Rights Quarterly* 35:1 (2013), pp. 69–90, p. 85.

[88] Roberts, 'Who Said Gaddafi Had to Go?', pp. 20–22.

[89] Steven Greenhouse, 'U.S. Says Iraq Appears to Resume Pullback from Kuwait Border', *New York Times*, 17 October 1994.

[90] Susan Rice and Andrew Loomis, 'The Evolution of Humanitarian Intervention and the Responsibility to Protect', in Ivo Daalder, ed, *Beyond Preemption: Force and Legitimacy in a Changing World* (Washington DC: Brookings Institute, 2007), pp. 59–95, p. 91. This view was shared by most US foreign policy experts interviewed by Brookings, pp. 85–86.

operational constraints. This development is no small concern. As even interventionist Thomas Weiss acknowledges, the United States has been part of a great power tradition of raising the 'rhetoric of humanitarianism ... most stridently in cases where the humanitarian motive was weakest'.[91] Oddly, he later remarks that the danger facing the globe now 'is not too much [US intervention] but rather too little humanitarian intervention'.[92] Given how assertive the United States has been in employing military force (Iraq – repeatedly – Afghanistan-Pakistan, Libya, Yemen, Somalia), in reserving the right to act unilaterally, in relaxing the scope of constraints demanded by laws of war, and in invoking moral claims, the danger is the opposite.

Conclusion: why abolition is preferable to reform

It is helpful to consider two likely responses to this chapter's case for the abolition of the military intervention component. First, as seen in Syria, has not US–Western zeal for intervention faded as a concern? But the concern is not that R2P makes leading states more eager to intervene militarily. As always, they will be guided by strategic cost-benefit calculations. President Obama, so far, has concluded that direct military force in Syria is unwise. Rather, the fear is that the United States and other leading states will find it easier to articulate an acceptable justification when it does perceive force to be strategically useful. Indeed, influential, interventionist voices have already cited R2P as authority for intervening even without Council approval.[93] Hence, while a US military invasion of Syria seems unlikely, R2P provides complementary rhetorical support – in addition to counterterrorism – for pursuing a range of interventions, from arming favoured rebel groups to air strikes. Indeed, the United States has launched air strikes on Islamic State forces in Iraq and indicated it may extend such strikes to Syria without seeking international (or Syrian) authorisation.[94] In short, the external normative constraints have substantially diminished.

Second is Thakur's argument on the merits of reform over abolition. The idea is that it is too late to return to an era that categorically prohibits interventions to stop atrocities. It is far better, then, to develop an effective rule-based system rather than have powerful states exercise

---

[91] Weiss, *Humanitarian Intervention*, p. 37.   [92] Ibid., p. 134.
[93] Paul R. Williams, J. Trevor Ulbrick and Jonathan Worboys, 'Preventing Atrocity Crimes in Syria: The Responsibility to Protect', Atlantic Council, 10 September 2012, www.acus.org/new_atlanticist/preventing-atrocity-crimes-syria-responsibility-protect.
[94] Toby Helm and Martin Chulov, 'US "set to launch air strikes" on Senior Isis Leaders in Syria', *The Observer*, 23 August 2014.

unconstrained, ad hoc interventions.[95] Accordingly, Thakur commends Brazil's proposal for redressing the flaws exposed by the Libyan intervention. In a paper entitled 'Responsibility While Protecting', Brazil calls for specific criteria for determining when force is warranted and what the limits will be and a process for monitoring and holding accountable the interveners. For Thakur, this approach could make a real difference as opposed to simply advocating prohibition, which will be ignored.

Although tempting on the surface, this approach is too optimistic on the prospects for reform and too pessimistic on what a formal repudiation of force can accomplish. On the former, the United States has zealously guarded its exclusive right to decide when and how to use force. Efforts since the 2005 World Summit to place specific operational constraints, even as declaratory language, have gone nowhere. Furthermore, as reiterated in Libya, the United States typically refuses to conduct investigations of US-inflicted civilian deaths or cooperate in such efforts.[96] Hence, the chances of securing enforceable operational and monitoring criteria appear fanciful.

One might enquire as to what good it would do to close the door categorically to R2P-based interventions given the United States' attitude. Yet there are reasons for qualified optimism. First, the Libyan intervention has wrecked what was already thin global South support.[97] Thus, the prospects are promising for gaining General Assembly declarations that delink R2P from military intervention and demand stricter interpretation of the threat to international peace and security thresholds. Granted, such an action will not exert a seismic impact on US interventionist policies or that of other leading states; they will still be primarily shaped by geostrategic and economic objectives. But by being deprived of the R2P justification, these states will face greater normative hurdles for employing force. Similarly, eliminating R2P's military intervention component will modestly affect internal debates – both in policy circles and among the broader public – by giving one less rhetorical lever for interventionists.

Assuming R2P can be stripped of its dangerous military component, its value remains to be seen. It may, as d'Escoto and Chomsky suggest, provide an aspirational document to mobilise grass roots activism against the depredations of states, including the most powerful. But for that to happen, there are no quick fixes. At the intergovernmental level, the best hope is invigorated diplomacy coupled with forceful reiterations of Charter norms against aggressive force. Long-term hopes for solidarity,

---

[95] Thakur, *Responsibility to Protect*, p. 158.
[96] Chivers and Schmitt, 'An Unseen Civilian Toll'; Tirman, *Deaths of Others*.
[97] Peter Beaumont, 'Yes, the UN Has a Duty to Intervene. But, When, Where, and How?', *The Observer*, 4 March 2013.

however, lie outside the corridors of power in ways that confront – rather than obscure – the practices and comforting narratives of the powerful.[98] What ICISS commissioners found 'backward looking' and 'finger pointing' is, in fact, essential for instilling an informed global citizenry that can move us to a better world.

---

[98] I discuss counterhegemonic solidarity-human rights approaches in 'R2P and Pragmatic Liberal Interventionism', pp. 88–90.

Part III

The Responsibility to Protect
and international social purposes

12   United Nations peacekeeping and the Responsibility to Protect

Mats Berdal

The relationship between the history and evolution of United Nations (UN) peacekeeping on the one hand, and the emergence of the doctrine of a Responsibility to Protect (R2P) on the other, is intimate, complex and paradoxical.

The element of intimacy is most obvious in relation to the immediate origins of R2P. The central idea underlying it – that individual states and, should they fail, the 'international community, through the UN', have a 'responsibility to protect populations from genocide, war crimes, ethnic cleansing, and crimes against humanity'[1] – is very closely connected to the traumatic experiences of UN peacekeeping in the early post-Cold War period. The impotence of UN peacekeepers in the face of genocide in Rwanda in 1994, and the cruel irony of a 'UN Protection Force' unable to protect civilians in the 'safe area' of Srebrenica in 1995, powerfully stimulated a normative shift, already encouraged by the passing of the Cold War, in favour of the justice-related provisions of the Charter.[2] R2P, to which member states committed themselves in principle at the UN World Summit in 2005, remains the most notable expression of that shift.

The complexity of the relationship derives from the fact that the normative force which R2P idea has acquired, notwithstanding the continuing and inevitable controversies to which its 'operationalisation' remains subject, has itself influenced the evolution of UN peacekeeping and the debate about its purposes. This is evident, above all, in the now widely held presumption that one of the chief tasks of UN peacekeepers is to 'protect civilians under imminent threat of physical violence'.[3] Indeed, it

I am most grateful for the comments provided on an earlier draft of this chapter by Nicholas Morris and Alvaro de Soto.

[1] *World Summit Outcome*, Document A/RES/60/1 (New York: United Nations, 24 October 2005), paragraph 139.
[2] For the distinction between the 'justice' and 'order'-related provisions of the Charter, see Adam Roberts, 'Order/Justice Issues at the UN', in Rosemary Foot, John Lewis Gaddis and Andrew Hurrell, eds, *Order and Justice in International Relations* (Oxford: OUP, 2003).
[3] United Nations Document S/RES/1701, 11 August 2006, paragraph 12.

is a task explicitly envisaged for nearly all of the peacekeeping operations authorised by the Security Council since 1999.

The mandate to protect civilians, however, even though it is now routinely inserted in Council resolutions, has created expectations which UN peacekeepers have manifestly found very difficult to meet. And it is this reality that has given rise to the paradoxical aspect of the relationship between peacekeeping and R2P: by raising expectations yet failing to deliver on the promise of protection, situations have been created in which, perversely, mass atrocity crimes of the kind that R2P is fundamentally concerned to prevent have not only been allowed to occur but, in some cases, have become more likely to occur.

This chapter explores these relationships in greater detail. It is premised on the conviction that this cannot be done merely through an abstract examination of the conceptual evolution of R2P and its possible implications for the future of UN peacekeeping. Any discussion of the relationship between R2P and peacekeeping must be placed within the context of a wider awareness of the actual experience, the underlying political character and the hard realities of UN peacekeeping itself. To this end, the chapter proceeds in three, partly overlapping, parts.

The first examines the evolution of UN peacekeeping from its 'classical' phase through to the period of retrenchment and stocktaking that followed the horrors in Rwanda and Bosnia. It focuses specifically on the question of protection and protection responsibilities for UN peacekeepers, and on the lessons drawn in this regard from the experiences of 1992–1995. Special attention here is given to the UN mission in Bosnia where the challenge of protecting civilians in the midst of ongoing conflict was at the very centre of the controversies that plagued the mission. While the UN's experiences in Rwanda, Bosnia and parts of Africa in the first half of the 1990s all fed a powerful sentiment of 'never again', thus helping to lay the normative ground for the emergence of R2P in the following decade, the record of operations since 1999, when UN peacekeeping picked up again, raises some disturbing questions about the kinds of lessons that have in fact been learned. The record suggests, depressingly, that the chief lesson of the early post-Cold War years – the need, when embarking on peacekeeping in complex, non-permissive environments, to align means with ends, aspirations with resources, in support of an overall political strategy – was never internalised by member states.

The second part examines the emergence of civilian protection as an explicit mandate entrusted to UN peacekeepers. It examines the context and reasons for this and, crucially, looks at the attempt to interpret and implement the mandate in the field, focusing on the UN Mission in the

Democratic Republic of Congo (MONUC).[4] In spite of MONUC's presence, the eastern part of the DRC has been the scene of continuing violence, mass atrocity crimes and recurring 'protection crises' for well over a decade. This has contributed to a conflation of the 'civilian protection in peacekeeping' agenda with that of R2P. While this conflation is both understandable and in some sense inevitable, it has also proved problematic.

The third and final part of the chapter considers the consequences and paradoxes resulting from this conflation. It argues that the history of UN peacekeeping provides much evidence of creative adaption to changing geopolitical and normative circumstances. That same history, however, also points to certain fundamental limitations of UN peacekeeping as an instrument at the disposal of member states. It is these limitations that are now most urgently in need of recognition. In terms of the future of R2P, this suggests that there may well be a role for peacekeepers in so-called Pillar Two activities, that is, in 'helping States to build capacity to protect'.[5] UN peacekeepers engaging in enforcement action in the absence of overall strategic and political direction, however, is certain only to reproduce protection crises.

The evolution of UN peacekeeping and the question of protection

From Suez to Sarajevo

United Nations peacekeeping did not evolve out of a specific Charter mandate. It emerged instead from the search, in Secretary-General Dag Hammarskjöld's words, for 'possibilities of substantive action by the UN in a split world'.[6] As a form of non-coercive, third-party intervention resting on the linked principles of host state consent, impartiality as the determinant of operational activity and the prohibition against the use of force except in self-defence, peacekeeping represented a functional adaption by the UN to the geopolitical realities of the Cold War. Hammarskjöld's priority in the late 1950s was to localise conflict 'with potentially wide international repercussions'.[7] To this end, lightly

---

[4] MONUC was renamed MONUSCO (UN Stabilisation Mission in the DRC) in July 2010.

[5] *Implementing the Responsibility to Protect*, United Nations Document A/63/677, 12 January 2009, paragraph 28.

[6] *Introduction to the Annual Report of the Secretary-General, June-1959-June 1960*, United Nations Document A/4390/Add.1, p. 4.

[7] Ibid., p. 5.

equipped peacekeepers, as early experiences in the Middle East had shown, might usefully be deployed to defuse tensions and help prevent any 'widening of the geographical and political area covered' by the East–West confrontation.[8] Their deployment would explicitly not aim 'to enforce any specific political solution of pending problems or to influence the political balance to such a solution'.[9]

In October 1973, Secretary-General Kurt Waldheim issued a set of guidelines for the Second UN Emergency Force in the Middle East (UNEF II), amounting in effect to a codification of the essential features of UN peacekeeping. These reiterated the importance of the principles of consent, the non-use of force except in self-defence, impartiality and, generally, the avoidance of any actions that might 'prejudice the rights, claims or positions of the parties concerned'.[10] Less often cited, but critical to the effective functioning of any UN peacekeeping force, were three other conditions: political support and continuous backing from a united Security Council as the mandating authority; readiness on the part of member states to provide personnel along with the necessary financial and logistical support required to sustain operations; and, closely connected, an acceptance by troop contributing countries of the established UN chain of command so that a peacekeeping force 'can function as an integrated and effective military unit'.[11] The extent to which these conditions have been met has historically played a key role in determining the comparative success of individual UN field operations.

For most of the Cold War period Waldheim's guidelines provided the basis for the deployment of lightly equipped military units to calm and defuse tensions between parties, usually involving some form of interposition between adversaries in the wake of active hostilities. Comprised mainly of infantry units, UN forces invariably deployed without reserves and usually with limited logistic support, factors that necessarily restricted their mobility.

Until the late 1980s, UN peacekeepers were also deployed overwhelmingly in conflicts between states, usually at the boundary of two jurisdictions. The exceptions to this rule, however, form a vitally important, though on the whole also a neglected, part of the history of UN peacekeeping. Not only were the UN operations in Cyprus, southern Lebanon and, above all, Congo in the early 1960s, major operations in their own right, but these experiences of internal peacekeeping are also deeply

---

[8] Ibid., pp. 4–5.
[9] *Summary Study of the Experience Derived from the Establishment and Operations of the Force (UNEF)*, United Nations Document A/3943, 9 October 1958, paragraph 167.
[10] United Nations Document 42/22.10.73, 26 October 1973, paragraph 3.   [11] Ibid.

relevant to the concerns of the present chapter. In this context, two additional observations need to be made.

First, the physical protection of civilians was never an explicit, let alone a primary, concern of traditional UN peacekeeping. Insofar as peacekeepers were able to provide protection from violence, it was an ancillary function, reliant on the goodwill and self-interest of the parties to the conflict or, simply, an indirect consequence of the politically calming and stabilising effect of the UN's presence on the ground. In particular, peacekeepers were neither mandated nor expected to take 'the initiative in the use of armed force'[12] in order to protect civilians under the threat of violence. It is true that Dag Hammarskjöld, in what now appears a rather striking message, informed Katanga's secessionist leader, Moïse Tshombe, in 1960 that it was 'the duty of the United Nations Force to protect the civilian populations and [that] this duty is … in no way restricted by the rule of non-intervention applied by the Force in relation to domestic conflicts'.[13] Even so, ONUC itself did not have a specific mandate to protect civilians and when military force was used it was to prevent the secession of Katanga. The protection of civilians afforded by peacekeepers remained a secondary or derivative function of UN peacekeeping throughout the Cold War period.

Nor was the provision of humanitarian relief to victims during conflict, as distinct from active protection measures, ever a major task of peacekeeping. Even so, when the UN High Commission for Refugees (UNHCR) was later thrust into the role of providing relief in the midst of ongoing conflict, an internal background paper perceptively drew attention to the significance of earlier exceptions to this general rule. 'It is interesting to note', it commented, that

for the peace-keepers in Congo, Cyprus and Lebanon, the provision of relief to civilians during internal conflict raised many of the same problems and dilemmas that are confronting modern peace-keepers … Having to preserve peace in a situation of civil strife, inevitably lead[s] to friction with one or more of the political groups.[14]

This touches directly on the second observation alluded to above and it concerns the attitude of member states towards risk. 'At least until the mid-1990s', Alan James observed in 1994, 'peacekeeping has always been

---

[12] United Nations Document A/3943, 9 October 1958, paragraph 179.
[13] Dag Hammarskjöld, quoted in Alan Doss, 'In the Footsteps of Dr Bunche: the Congo, UN Peacekeeping and the Use of Force', Paper for King's College London CSDRG project on 'The Use of Force in Peacekeeping Operations', 2012.
[14] *Protecting Humanitarian Mandates of UN Operations in Complex Emergency Situations Involving Peace-Keeping*, UNHCR Draft Report, 2 July 1993, UNHCR.

thought of as a low-risk activity. States provide personnel on that basis'.[15] The experiences of ONUC, in the course of which some 250 peace-keepers lost their lives, came to be seen as an exception and one that had to be avoided. The assumption on which states made troops available for UN duty continued to be that of a generally permissive and benign environment. But this had another consequence: the expectation that peacekeeping was risk-free meant that the requirements for a properly 'integrated and effective' military force – most notably unity of command, attention to force protection, better logistics and tactical mobility – could be, and typically were, ignored. When the operational environment began to change, troop contributors responded not by addressing the requirements of military effectiveness but by finding other ways of reducing risk to themselves, either by resisting deployments or, indeed, by withdrawing and refusing to contribute altogether. In writings on peacekeeping, especially its deficiencies and the sources of its travails, too little attention has been given to the attitude of troop contributors towards risk, a subject which, as will be argued more fully, is directly relevant to the relationship between peacekeeping and R2P.

The crisis of UN peacekeeping, 1992–1995

Because the emergence and character of UN peacekeeping during the Cold War were so closely linked to the geopolitical realities of the day, it was perhaps inevitable that the diminution of East–West tensions would also lead to calls for more 'proactive' action on the part of UN troops in the field, something which it was felt might require a modification, if not the abandonment, of established principles of peacekeeping, most notably those pertaining to the use of force. Optimism about new possibilities was evident in *An Agenda for Peace* where 'peace-keeping' was now defined as 'the deployment of a United Nations presence in the field, *hitherto* with the consent of all the parties concerned'.[16] The comparative success of several, mostly small-scale, UN operations at the tail end of the Cold War – the UN Iran–Iraq Military Observe Group (UNIIMOG), UN Good Offices in Afghanistan and Pakistan (UNGOMAP), the UN Verification Mission in Angola (UNAVEM I), the UN Observer Group in Central America (ONUCA) and, above all, the UN Transition Assistance Group in Namibia (UNTAG) – nourished still further optimism about the possibilities of peacekeeping in a new era.

---

[15] Alan James, 'The Congo Controversies', *International Peacekeeping* 1:1 (1994), p. 48.
[16] United Nations Documents A/47/277 – S/24111, 17 June 1992, paragraph 20.

By early 1992, however, optimism was beginning to give way to gloom as discussions about the future of UN peacekeeping were increasingly framed by the manifest difficulties that 'blue helmets', from Somalia to the former Yugoslavia, were encountering in internal or civil war-like settings. A number of overlapping features distinguished these settings from those to which risk-averse troop contributors had become accustomed: the presence of irregular, often numerous and poorly controlled armed groups; large concentrations of internally displaced populations; the absence of clear front lines; the deliberate targeting of civilians and ongoing, violent contests over control of territory, populations and the location of governmental authority. Against these realities it became common to talk of the 'crisis of peacekeeping'.[17]

In these circumstances, many commentators and a growing body of academic writings displayed impatience, even a half-mocking disregard, for those who, they argued, continued to draw undue attention to the earlier lessons and limits of UN peacekeeping. Doing so, it was argued, was to be stuck in the past, unwilling to see that the world had changed and that UN peacekeeping practices had to change accordingly, specifically by becoming more 'robust' and 'muscular'. 'The international community', as one oft-quoted paper insisted, 'must define the new domain of collective military activity that lies between peacekeeping and enforcement' and devise new doctrines accordingly.[18]

Now, insofar as anyone was implying that 'traditional peacekeeping' was suitable to conditions of ongoing civil war, such impatience was plainly justified. But that was not really the point; very few suggested they were appropriate to conditions of civil war. On the contrary, careful consideration of the historical experience of peacekeeping only served to show *why* operations in Somalia,[19] Rwanda and the former Yugoslavia were likely to meet with catastrophe. In other words, appreciating the lessons offered by the history of UN peacekeeping was to appreciate its limitations and their sources (including the fundamentally risk-averse mindset of troop-contributors). As such it was also to warn against the dangers of placing too great a burden of expectations on peacekeeping, or – amounting to the same – to use it as a substitute for meaningful political action to deal with the underlying causes and drivers of conflict. As for the question of the use of force, the point at issue was not so much whether or not circumstances might arise (or had already arisen) that

[17] Adam Roberts, 'The Crisis in Peacekeeping', *Forsvarsstudier* 2, (1994).
[18] John Ruggie, 'Wandering in the Void', *Foreign Affairs* 72:5 (1993), p. 27.
[19] Ramesh Thakur, 'From Peacekeeping to Peace Enforcement: The UN Operation in Somalia', *Journal of Modern African Studies* 32:3 (1994), pp. 387–410.

justified forceful military action, but rather whether the conditions, in terms of clarity of political objectives and military preparedness, needed for force to be applied effectively were in place. It was to this latter issue that the secretary-general spoke, rightly, in his *Supplement to An Agenda for Peace*:

In reality, nothing is more dangerous for a peace-keeping operation than to ask it to use force when its existing composition, armament, logistic support and deployment deny it the capacity to do so. The logic of peace-keeping flows from political and military premises that are quite distinct from those of enforcement; and the dynamics of the latter are incompatible with the political process that peace-keeping is intended to facilitate.[20]

When written, in January 1995, these conclusions reflected the frustrations and disappointments of peacekeeping over the past three years, above all in the former Yugoslavia. They contained important, indeed essential, truths that needed restating. But there was, of course, a rub and it lay in the word 'intended'. As the three previous years had also shown, the real difficulty arises when there is no political process to facilitate and peacekeeping becomes, in effect, a substitute for it. That too, as events in Srebrenica were to show some six months after the report was issued, is not only dangerous but a potential recipe for humanitarian disaster and mass atrocity crimes.

The lessons from Bosnia and the origins of R2P

The UN peacekeeping operation in Bosnia forms an indelible part of the background to the emergence of R2P. The lessons that member states chose to draw from the mission and the sense of guilt that the fall of Srebrenica, along with the still greater horror of the Rwanda genocide, induced in the liberal conscience powerfully influenced subsequent efforts to reform UN peacekeeping and fed a strong and laudable sentiment of 'never again'. More specifically, they prompted calls for UN peacekeepers to be entrusted, as a matter of course, with explicit responsibilities for the protection of civilians in armed conflict.

UN peacekeepers deployed to Bosnia in 1992. For the next three years they were resourced, configured and instructed by the Council to operate on the basis of 'normal peace-keeping rules of engagement'.[21] Until the fall of Srebrenica in mid-July 1995, the activities of UN peacekeepers were geared towards the pursuit of three overarching objectives: relieving the humanitarian consequences of the war; containing the war and

[20] United Nations Document A/50/60, S/1995/1, 25 January 1995, paragraph 35.
[21] United Nations Document S/24540, 10 September 1992, paragraph 9.

preventing its spread within and outside Bosnia; and facilitating the efforts of the parties themselves to reach a negotiated settlement to their political differences. These were the objectives around which the Security Council – otherwise divided on the origins, nature and best way of handling the war – could find common ground. They were also the objectives in support of which member states were prepared to offer personnel for UN duty. In the first of these areas, the UN's achievements were considerable and have often been underplayed.[22] Still, none of these objectives defined a clear-cut political end-state for Bosnia and, as such, failed to provide the UN's complex and multifaceted engagement in the conflict with a clear sense of strategic direction. This became an ever-more critical problem as the war wore on. One aspect of the problem, as UNHCR's first Special Envoy in former Yugoslavia, José-Maria Mendiluce, observed in October 1993, was that the UN's presence generated 'false expectations among civilian population [sic] who initially believed in UNPROFOR's capacity to stop the atrocities, to stop the crimes, to stop ethnic cleansing and provide some sort of protection for the civilians'.[23]

It is true, and it is frequently pointed out by those most critical of the peacekeepers' performance on the ground, that by 1995 a large number of Council resolutions dealing with Bosnia had been adopted under Chapter VII of the Charter. These resolutions, however, also reaffirmed all previous resolutions by the Council and their implementation, especially those relating to the delivery of humanitarian relief, depended on the consent and cooperation of the parties. Added to this was the critical fact that UNPROFOR remained, again until the late summer of 1995, configured for traditional peacekeeping tasks and troop contributors remained not only wary but extremely reluctant to place their soldiers in harm's way.[24]

This reluctance, taking the form of a determination to minimise risks to one's own nationals in the field, has been under-emphasised in writings and commentary on UN peacekeeping generally. In part, this no doubt stems from a natural disinclination by states publicly to advertise the caveats they frequently attach to the release of national contingents for

---

[22] The raw statistics alone are impressive. According to UNPROFOR's own immediate *End of Mission Report*, the UNHCR delivered over 853,000 tonnes of aid by road convoys while a further 159,000 were airlifted. *Force Commander's End of Mission Report*, HQ UN Peace Forces, Zagreb, 31 January 1996.

[23] José-Maria Mendiluce, 'The Limits of Humanitarian Action: The Case of Former Yugoslavia', IPA Conference on Conflict and Humanitarian Action, October 1993, p. 11.

[24] Kofi Annan, 'Talking Points for UNPROFOR Troop Contributing Meeting 1 October 1993', Department of Peacekeeping Operations (DPKO), United Nations.

peacekeeping duty. If they were to advertise these, the resulting mismatch between professed concern and actual commitment would, more often than not, prove uncomfortable.[25] Still, interference in the UN chain of command – through specific restrictions on employment of troops and/or through the maintenance of direct communications between capitals and contingent commanders – has always been an aspect of UN peacekeeping. In permissive environments such interference can be kept at tolerable levels and is unlikely fatally to undermine the Force's ability to carry out its tasks. The intensity of interference, however, has always been closely connected to the perception of risk: the greater the risk, the more troop contributors have tended to intervene, all the more so if no compelling national interest is perceived to be at stake and public opinion is divided or uncertain about the rationale for involvement. 'Under these circumstances', as Kofi Annan, then in charge of UN peacekeeping, informed the Special Committee on Peacekeeping in March 1994, 'if an operation runs into difficulties – and especially if it takes causalities – public support is rapidly undermined. Troop contributing countries are then tempted to withdraw their contingents or to direct them to take a risk-averse approach, even though this may further jeopardise the mission.'[26]

In Bosnia the limits of peacekeeping were only fully acknowledged by key troop contributors and the Council after the massacre of some 8,000 men following the fall of Srebrenica in July 1995. In the wake of the disaster, a number of developments were exploited to prepare the stage for decisive military action in early September 1995, actions that would eventually force the Bosnian Serb political leadership to the negotiating table and help bring the conflict to an end. Chief among these were: the withdrawal of peacekeepers from exposed and vulnerable positions throughout Bosnia; the reinforcement of UNPROFOR; the change in command and control arrangements governing the use of NATO air power in support of UN forces; and, not least, the weakening of the Bosnian Serb position following the success of Croat military offensives in the Krajina.

In terms of lessons for the prevention of mass atrocity crimes and the challenges of protection, two observations need to be made here. First,

---

[25] The Dutch troops deployed in Srebrenica in 1995 have received much criticism for their response to the Bosnian Serb onslaught in July 1995, much of it justified (even with the luxury of hindsight). Rather less attention, however, has been given to other troop contributors who, when asked, refused to rotate into the exposed and vulnerable enclave. These included Nordic troops, long-standing and committed supporters of UN peacekeeping, who insisted on staying in government-controlled Tuzla, thus minimising the risk to their troops.

[26] 'Draft Statement to 113th Meeting of Special Committee on Peacekeeping', DPKO, 28 March 1994.

the actions in the summer of 1995, culminating in *Operation Deliberate Force*, involved a shift from peacekeeping to war-fighting or enforcement; not a ratcheting up of the former or a blurring of the two. It is important to be clear about this: the shift required a change in UNPROFOR's force posture and rules of engagement, as well as in the attitude of troop-contributing countries towards risk. It was not, as is sometimes suggested, an instance of 'robust' or more 'muscular' peacekeeping in action.

Second, the decision to go to war also involved actively siding with one or more parties to the conflict, notably, in this case, the Croatian military in its Krajina offensive. For risk-averse members of Council and troop contributors, this had one obvious advantage: it left the fighting on the ground to others, thus minimising risk to UN peacekeepers. But, as has been the case elsewhere, enlisting the support of local allies – whether in order to compensate for manpower shortages and/or to reduce the exposure of one's own troops – carries its own risks and will often raise moral issues that are far from straightforward or unambiguous. Operation Storm undoubtedly saw mass atrocity crimes committed by Croatian forces against the Serb population in Krajina. The risks and dilemmas for UN peacekeepers, even though over-stretched and under international pressure to protect civilians, in allying themselves with national authorities, would resurface in a different form in Cote d'Ivoire, Sierra Leone and especially in the Congo over the following decade.

The rise of civilian protection in peacekeeping mandates

The protection of civilians in peacekeeping and R2P

When UN peacekeeping, after a hiatus following the traumas of the early 1990s, began to pick up again towards the end of the decade, the subject of protection of civilians was, unavoidably, at the centre of discussions about the future direction of UN field operations. In the Srebrenica Report – an impressive and meticulous dissection of the events leading up to the fall of Srebrenica, released in November 1999 – the UN Secretariat accepted that it had 'failed to do [its] part to help save the people of Srebrenica'.[27] The following month, the independent inquiry into UN actions during the Rwanda genocide was released, listing among its recommendations that 'specific provisions related to the protection of civilian populations should be included in mandates of peacekeeping operations'.[28] Both reports, long anticipated, appeared shortly after the

---

[27] *The Fall of Srebrenica*, United Nations Document A/54/549, 15 November 1999.
[28] *The Carlson Report*, United Nations Document S/1999/1257, 16 December 1999, p. 57.

secretary-general's first report on the 'Protection of Civilians in Armed Conflict', which had recommended a series of measures, many of them distinctly vague on detail and largely aspirational in nature, to 'strengthen physical protection'.[29] Responding to the report in September 1999, the Security Council expressed 'its willingness to consider how peace-keeping mandates might better address the negative impact of armed conflict on civilians'.[30] Since then, the protection of civilians has been the subject of frequent debates by the Council. More significantly, start-ing with the establishment of the United Nations Mission in Sierra Leone in October 1999, peacekeeping missions have routinely and expressly been mandated under Chapter VII of the Charter 'to afford protection to civilians under imminent threat of physical violence'.[31] Since 1999 and until early 2013, 12 missions have been explicitly mandated to protect civilians.

While the experience of peacekeeping in the early half of the decade does much to explain the prominence that civilian protection has assumed since the late 1990s, no systematic attempt was made early on to spell out the possible implications of adopting such mandates for peacekeepers in the field. The secretary-general's initial report discussed 'measures to strengthen physical protection' under various headings, one of which was 'peacekeeping'. The actual measures proposed were hardly new, however, and, more significantly, no attempt was made to address the thornier issues raised by asking peacekeepers to assume protection responsibilities in the midst of ongoing internal conflict.

The extent to which the protection of civilians by UN peacekeepers was nonetheless firmly on the agenda was also clear from the Brahimi Report of 2000. That report, however, at least provided a much more systematic and thoughtful attempt to distil lessons from the past decade than did the secretary-general's first report on the protection of civilians in armed conflict. This was evident in the panel's notable words of caution about the possible implications – and dangers – of placing the protection of civilians at the centre of peacekeeping operations. While recognising the importance of addressing the plight of civilians in armed conflict, the panel expressed its concern 'about the credibility and achievability of a blanket mandate in this area'. It perceptively added: 'Promising to extend such protection establishes a very high threshold of expectation. The potentially large mismatch between desired objective and resources

[29] United Nations Document S/1999/957, 8 September 1999.
[30] United Nations Document S/RES/1265, 17 December 1999, paragraph 10.
[31] United Nations Document S/RES/1270, 22 October 1999, paragraph 14.

available to meet it raises the prospect of continuing disappointment with United Nations follow-through in this area.'[32]

Those expectations were further heightened by the emergence of R2P, resulting in a conflation of two sets of overlapping but also, in important ways, distinct debates. In order to appreciate this more clearly, it is necessary to turn to the experiences of peacekeeping operations entrusted with civilian protection responsibilities after 1999. And here the history of MONUC in the DRC, whose experiences have been echoed in West Africa (Cote d'Ivoire and Sierra Leone) and the Horn (Sudan), merits special attention.

MONUC, mass atrocities and the protection crises in the DRC

The UN's peacekeeping involvement in the DRC began in 1999 with the deployment of a small observer and monitoring mission following the signing of the Lusaka Ceasefire Agreement in July that year. In theory, the agreement marked the end of the Second Congo War. In reality, fighting and predation against civilians never ended in the eastern part of the country: the provinces of South Kivu, North Kivu and Province Orientale.[33] Further agreements, notably the Pretoria Accord of July 2002, facilitated the withdrawal of foreign forces from the region but did not put an end to the fighting in eastern Congo, where continuing violence was fuelled, increasingly, by powerful local and regional economic agendas developed around the control and exploitation of the area's natural resources.[34] The first multiparty elections held in the country in over forty years, in 2006, did not fundamentally alter the logic of violence and the exploitative and predatory political economy underlying it. All too often that violence has taken the form of mass atrocities.

Against this backdrop, MONUC has not only expanded in size, eventually reaching an authorised strength of some 22,000 uniformed personnel, but has also been entrusted with an ever more ambitious and complex mandate. In particular, the centrality of MONUC's protection responsibilities has increased steadily over time, and has done so in response to a series of 'protection crises' – Kisangani in 2002, Ituri and Bukavu in 2003 and the Goma crisis of 2008. From 2003 onwards, in the wake of the Ituri crisis, an increasingly 'robust' stance was taken over the use of force by

---

[32] *Brahimi Panel Report*, United Nations Document S/2000/809, 21 August 2000, paragraph 63.
[33] See Gérard Prunier, *Africa's World War – Congo, the Rwanda Genocide and the Making of a Continental Catastrophe* (Oxford: OUP, 2009), pp. 223–227.
[34] Ibid., p. 277.

UN peacekeepers, underlined by a further expansion of troop numbers and a mandate change authorising it 'to use all necessary means to fulfil its mandate'.[35] The change was especially notable from 2005 onwards when, increasingly, UN peacekeepers also came to provide 'direct operational support'[36] to the new Congolese National Army (FARDC), supposedly an integrated force created following the peace accord of 2003. In December 2008, the Security Council placed protection of civilians at the very heart of its mandate, making it clear that it 'must be given priority in decisions about the use of available capacity and resources, over any of the other tasks'.[37]

While the ever-growing centrality of civilian protection to MONUC's mission was plainly a response to failures and events on the ground, there was also an obvious connection to the parallel emergence of the R2P doctrine. While the R2P commitment in the 'Outcome document' of 2005 was silent on how the doctrine might be operationalised – a subject that has divided member states sharply since – it certainly spawned debate and, crucially, placed the issue of protection against mass atrocity crimes firmly on the international agenda. Given the frequency of such crimes in eastern Congo, the protection issue naturally migrated to the top of MONUC's list of operational priorities. In order to appreciate the precise difficulties this came to pose for MONUC, and by extension the wider issues it raises regarding the relationship between R2P and UN peacekeeping, a more detailed consideration of key developments on the ground following the formal end of the war, agreed in December 2002, is required.

In early May 2003, fighting intensified between rival Lendu and Hema militia groups in Ituri for control of the regional capital, Bunia, resulting in widespread killings, atrocities and large-scale displacement. The UN peacekeepers present – a battalion of less than 700 Uruguayan soldiers that had been hastily redeployed from elsewhere in the DRC – found themselves under-resourced, ill-equipped, eager to withdraw and unable to do more than statically guard the UN compound. On 9 May, the secretary-general was also informed that the '700 Congolese national police who were sent to Bunia by President Kabile (for the most part without vehicles and communications) [had] virtually disintegrated as a formed unit'.[38] By early June, more than 5,000 people were

---

[35] United Nations Document S/RES/1493, 28 July 2003, paragraph 26.

[36] Doss, 'In the footsteps of Dr Bunche', p. 15.

[37] United Nations Document S/RES/1856, 22 December 2008, paragraphs 3 and 14.

[38] United Nations Document S/2003/566, 27 May 2003; 'Statement on the Situation in Ituri', DPKO, 9 May 2003.

sheltering in a 'camp literally pressed up against the wall'[39] of the MONUC HQ compound, while another 7,000 were huddled together at the airport. MONUC, as the secretariat repeatedly informed the Council, 'did not have the capacity to restore order in the town or, should circumstances further deteriorate, to protect civilians under threat'.[40] Against this backdrop, the UN secretary-general asked the Security Council for a 'well-equipped multinational force, under the lead of a Member State' to be deployed to Bunia in order provide security and to protect civilians.[41] With France agreeing to act as the 'framework nation' for an EU force, the Council authorised the deployment of an Interim Emergency Multinational Force (IEMF) to Bunia on 30 May 2003.[42] Codenamed Operation *Artemis*, the IEMF deployed to Bunia in early June 2003 and remained strictly confined to that town for the duration of its deployment. The force, totalling some 1,500 well-equipped troops, had an immediate impact on the local balance of power. Although the IEMF made no attempt to demilitarise the town, as far as shoring up the UN's precarious position was concerned, the secretary-general would later acknowledge that the 'presence of a robustly equipped force in Bunia, under Chapter VII of the Charter, helped to stave off an impending humanitarian crisis'.[43]

While this was no doubt true in relation to the immediate crisis in Bunia, both the medium- to long-term strategic impact of Artemis and, crucially, its impact on the situation for civilians outside the immediate area of deployment proved far less clear-cut. Indeed, for many it proved catastrophic. The central difficulty, as an assessment produced for the UN Secretariat correctly identified, was 'the strict insistence on the very limited area of operations', which 'merely pushed the problem of violent aggression against civilians beyond the environs of the town, where atrocities continued'.[44] In fact, Artemis never covered more than a 15 × 15 km area in and around Bunia, even though the DPKO and MONUC on several occasions urged the French Government to take a flexible approach vis-à-vis the deployment and duration of the IEMF.[45] As the

---

[39] 'Briefing by Carolyn McAskie to the Security Council – The Situation in the DRC, 4 June 2003, 11:00 hrs', p. 3.

[40] 'Press Statement attributable to the Spokesperson of the Secretary-General', 9 May 2003.

[41] United Nations Document S/2003/574, 15 May 2003.

[42] United Nations Document S/RES/1484, 30 May 2003.

[43] United Nations Document S/2003, 17 November 2003, pp. 18–19.

[44] 'Operation Artemis: The Lessons of the IEMF', Best Practices Unit, DPKO, 2004, p. 14.

[45] Jan-Gunnar Isberg and Lotta Tillberg, *By All Necessary Means: Brigadier General Jan-Gunnar Isberg's Experience from Service in the Congo, 2003–2005* (Stockholm: Swedish National Defence College, 2012), p. 22; private communication with UN staff.

head of MONUC's office in Bunia at the time, Alpha Sow, would later write: 'While Bunia may be enjoying relative security, the names of towns such as Drodro, Largo, Nizi, and Fataki have become sadly famous for the atrocities committed there against civilians'.[46] Significantly, it was *not* as if the Council had not been explicitly warned by the Secretariat precisely of this possibility beforehand. On 4 June, Carolyn McAskie, the UN's deputy emergency relief coordinator, appearing before the Council together with the head of DPKO, Jean-Marie Guéhenno, welcomed the Council's authorisation of the IEMF, though she added:

> I believe that the force can have its greatest impact if it extends its influence outside Bunia, for example, by patrolling on the main axis of Bunia to Mahagi, Bunia to Komanda and Eringeti, and Bunia to Kasenyi. This will improve the protection afforded to civilians in this area and facilitate humanitarian assistance outside Bunia. Without these steps, I fear that the conflict could be displaced to locations outside Bunia, and Bunia could become a magnet for people from surrounding villages.[47]

The fear, repeatedly communicated by the Secretariat to the Council in June 2003, that IEMF's self-imposed geographical and time limitations might result in a 'relocation' of fighting and massacres elsewhere in Ituri, proved well grounded. Still, the Council, and specifically France as the lead nation, repeatedly resisted the Secretariat's entreaties to 'take a flexible approach vis-à-vis the IEMF'.[48] Indeed, on the very day the IEMF began its deployment, Jean Marie Guéhenno, who had just returned from a visit to the region and to Paris, reported to the secretary-general that the French government was very clear on two things: the IEMF's mandate would not be expanded beyond Bunia, and the limited timeframe set for withdrawal, 1 September, was not negotiable.

McAskie's briefing to the Council, while focused on the immediate crisis in Ituri, also drew attention to the situation elsewhere in eastern Congo, stressing that it too was 'extremely poor, particularly in North and South Kivu'.[49] This fact, along with the sobering effect of recent events, prompted the Security Council to strengthen MONUC in late July 2003. By Security Council Resolution 1493 the authorised strength of the force was increased to 10,800, and this included provisions for an 'Ituri brigade' to fill the vacuum when the IEMF departed. At the same time, MONUC was explicitly authorised 'to use all necessary means to fulfil its

---

[46] Alpha Sow, 'Achievements of the IEMF and Future Scenarios', in Mark Malan and João Gomes Porto, eds, *Challenges of Peace Implementation: The UN Mission in the DRC* (Pretoria: ISS, 2004), p. 211.

[47] 'McAskie to the Security Council', p. 3.

[48] 'Note on Meeting, DPKO/DPA on DRC', 9 June 2003.

[49] 'McAskie to the Security Council', p. 3.

mandate in the Ituri district and, as it deems it within its capabilities, in North and South Kivu'.[50] This was intended to give the UN peacekeepers greater scope for proactive action, allowing it to exercise the kind of force that the IEMF had displayed on a smaller scale and within strictly defined geographical limitations. The change in mandate and the expansion of MONUC did, notably from 2005 onwards, lead to a far more 'robust' stance.

If anything, however, the protection crisis and operational strain on MONUC deepened. There are two closely connected reasons for this. In the first place, the expansion of MONUC force levels has not overcome problems inherent to all UN peacekeeping operations; problems whose debilitating impact on force cohesion are invariably magnified in conditions of civil war. In face of the logistical and operational challenges presented by eastern Congo at war, MONUC has remained an ill-equipped, poorly and unevenly trained force, lacking in unity of command. The IEMF force in 2003 had underscored the value of specialist capabilities and greater mobility, but that force had been rapidly and unceremoniously withdrawn and its effects highly localised. The UN Ituri Brigade, consisting of some 5,000 troops and established to take over from IEMF, was consciously conceived by troop-contributors as a force capable of more 'robust' action. And yet, as its first commander, Jan-Gunnar Isberg, has written, it still 'lacked essential equipment for intelligence, communications, protracted operations away from. . . camps and barracks, night operations and operations in the Eastern lakes'.[51] These deficiencies alone severely compromised the ambition to protect civilians.

Secondly, the inability to provide effective protection – brought home by repeated crises at a time when the emergence of R2P focused local, international and non-governmental organisation (NGO) attention on the subject of mass atrocity crimes – did not lead to any diminution of expectations. If anything, civilian expectations only increased as the 'protection of civilians' became ever more central to MONUC's mandate.[52] In these circumstances, the only possible response to the 'protection deficit' was to intensify collaboration with 'national authorities', that is, with FARDC. The latter had been created out of the merger and supposed integration of numerous armed factions and rebel

---

[50] United Nations Document S/RES/1493, 28 July 2003, paragraph 26.

[51] Isberg and Tillberg, *By All Necessary Means*, p. 31.

[52] For an excellent analysis of how and why expectations of MONUC among civilians became 'prodigiously high', see Emily Padden, *Taking Sides – Impartiality, Norm Contestation and the Politics of UN Peacekeeping*, D.Phil. Dissertation, Oxford University, April 2013, pp.185–187.

groups following the peace accord of 2003, several of which were known to have committed mass atrocity crimes. In theory, MONUC might have played an important role in what would later be categorised as Pillar Two assistance under R2P, that is, active and targeted assistance (including, inter alia, through capacity building, training and norm diffusion) aimed at 'helping states to exercise their responsibility to protect'.[53] In practice, however, limited resources, limited political commitment and, above all, the reality of on-going conflict and a persistent 'protection deficit', ensured that little meaningful security sector reform was undertaken. Although the Security Council did call on MONUC to help reform the security sector in the DRC, 'no financial provisions were made to support this ambition'.[54] Reflecting on his experience as under-secretary-general of humanitarian affairs between 2007 and 2010, John Holmes described the 'official armed forces' in the DRC as 'badly equipped, badly trained, badly paid, badly housed, badly disciplined and, as an inevitable result, bad in all senses of the word'.[55] Unsurprisingly, he added, 'they often prey on the population as much as any illegal militia'.[56]The consequences of all this were doubly damaging.

On the one hand, by aligning itself with and working alongside the new Congolese army, MONUC's legitimacy was compromised and weakened. According to Joshua Marks, 'during anti-militia operations in Ituri in 2005–2006, FARDC abuses were especially corrosive to MONUC's image and local support' as it 'systematically pillaged homes and abused citizens under the pretext of hunting for rebels'.[57] Again, when the FARDC in 2009, in close collaboration with MONUC, launched a series of campaigns against the FDLR[58] and other rebel groups in eastern Congo, 'credible evidence' soon emerged of FARDC soldiers carrying out 'large-scale targeted massacres of civilians in the Kivus',[59] still further tarnishing MONUC's and the UN's image.

---

[53] 'Implementing the Responsibility to Protect', A/63/677, 12 January 2009.

[54] Doss, 'In the footsteps of Dr Bunche', p. 15. See also Henri Boshoff, 'Completing the DDR process of armed groups in the DRC and the link to security sector reform of FARDC,' Pretoria: ISS, 23 November 2010.

[55] John Holmes, *The Politics of Humanity – The Reality of Relief Aid* (London: Head of Zeus, 2013), p. 136.

[56] Ibid.

[57] Joshua Marks, 'The Pitfalls of Action and Inaction: Civilian Protection in MONUC's Operations', *Africa Security Review* 16:3 (2007), p. 77.

[58] The FDLR (Forces Démocratiques de Libération du Rwanda) remains one of the largest armed groups in the Kivus and includes remnants of the old Rwandan Army (ex-FAR) and Interahamwe militia members that fled to eastern Congo after the 1994 genocide.

[59] *Report of the Special Rapporteur on Extra-Judicial, Summary or Arbitrary Executions*, United Nations Document A/HRC/14/24/Add.3, 1 June 2010, paragraph 26.

On the other hand, militias responded to more aggressive operations by MONUC and FARDC by stepping up their own predatory activity against vulnerable civilian populations. Thus, in response to the MONUC-supported operations by the Congolese army in 2009 (notably during Operation Kimia II), the FDLR embarked upon what the UN's special rapporteur, Philip Alston, described as a strategy of 'systematic large-scale revenge killings', involving summary executions, rape and the torching of villages.[60] In Alston's assessment, these 'attacks were foreseeable and perhaps even inevitable in the absence of an adequate protection presence'.[61] Alston was highly critical of MONUC's inability to offer more effective protection and especially to exercise due diligence vis-à-vis its local allies in 2009. While some of his criticisms were no doubt justified, he failed, at a much more fundamental level, to link MONUC's predicament to the Security Council's overall handling of the Congo crisis. As Alan Doss, special representative of the secretary-general and head of MONUC from 2007 to 2010, would later write:

In reality, MONUC engaged in band-aid protection, usually responding to the symptoms of violence not the causes. And because the Mission simply did not have the resources to physically ring-fence civilians against all possible threats, some form of MONUC–FARDC collaboration was unavoidable if not always desirable.[62]

There is a final consideration here. The band-aid approach in the DRC is comparable to the lack of strategic direction and decisive political action from which UNPROFOR suffered between 1992 and 1995. In the absence of such direction, MONUC, faced with a multiplicity of over-lapping, often highly localised, conflicts and with a force that remains – notwithstanding the enlargements that have taken place – ill-equipped for the tasks confronting it, has been drawn ever more deeply into the ongoing conflicts in DRC's eastern provinces. This has only detracted further from a permanent solution to the protection crisis and the lasting removal of conditions that are encouraging production and re-production of R2P crimes. While there have been 'tactical successes' and innovation by peacekeepers on the ground, it is only right to ask whether the long-term trend in eastern Congo is one of steady improvement. Sadly, every indication is that it is not and that, instead, it has sunk into what is more akin to a 'permanent state of emergency'.[63] Indeed, in late 2012, OXFAM, in its sixth protection assessment since 2007, covering the three

---

[60] Ibid., paragraphs 10–16.   [61] Ibid., paragraph 21.

[62] Doss, 'In the Footsteps of Dr Bunche', pp. 37–38.

[63] Timothy Raeymaekers, 'Why History Repeats Itself in Eastern DR Congo' p. 4. www.e-ir.info/2012/12/20/why-history-repeats-itself-in-eastern-dr-congo/.

eastern provinces of South Kivu, North Kivu and Orientale, concluded that 'overall, the security situation has deteriorated significantly in many areas'.[64] Responding to the deteriorating situation and signs of growing instability, the Security Council, in March 2013, decided to establish a new Intervention Brigade under the command of the MONUSCO Force Commander, with 'responsibility of neutralising armed groups ... and reducing the threat posed by armed groups to state authority and civilian security in eastern DRC'.[65] On the basis of the evidence presented here, there are good reasons for believing that the Intervention Brigade, while it may well score tactical victories, will only reinforce strategic failure *unless* the underlying political issues at the heart of conflict and the complex political economy that drives much of the violence are not addressed. Early assessments of FIB's performance bear this out. Briefing the Council in March 2014 after the apparent defeat of one of the larger rebel groups operating in eastern Congo, the *Mouvement du 23 mars* (M-23), the head of MONUSCO, Martin Kobler, noted how the brigade had contributed to 'the restoration of pockets of stability' in eastern Congo.[66] Bunia after the IEMF intervention in 2003 was also, for a while, a 'pocket of stability'. More significantly, the defeat of M-23, while itself a welcome development, has done little to improve 'the overall security situation ... as over fifty different armed groups ranging from neatly structured militias [including the FDLR] to ragtag bandit gangs continue to operate across eastern DRC'.[67] It was against this reality that the secretary-general, reporting to the Council in mid-2014, observed that while 'some progress' had been made in tackling 'the recurring cycles of violence in eastern Congo', it was 'still too slow and remain[ed] extremely fragile'.[68]

The conflation of R2P and civilian protection in peacekeeping

On the occasion of the tenth anniversary of the first report on the protection of civilians in armed conflict, the UN secretary-general found, when all was said and done, few grounds for celebration. 'For all the reports,

[64] *Commodities of War*, 164 OXFAM Briefing Paper, November 2012. See also *Report of the Group of Experts on the DRC*, United Nations Document S/2012/843, 12 November 2012.
[65] United Nations Document S/RES/2098, 28 March 2013, paragraph 9.
[66] Security Council 7137th Meeting, 14 March 2014, S/PV.7137,p.2.
[67] Christoph Vogel, 'Islands of Stability or Swamps of Insecurity?', *Africa Policy Brief*, No.9, 2014, EGMONT, pp.1.–2.
[68] United Nations Document S/2014/450, 30 June 2014, paragraph 86.

resolutions and actions of the last decade', he concluded, 'the situation that confronts civilians in current conflicts is depressingly similar to that which prevailed in 1999'.[69] The observation raises some obvious questions. How should the gulf between aspiration and actual results be overcome? How, in particular, can one ensure that protection crises in peacekeeping do not generate and reproduce conditions resulting in R2P mass atrocity crimes?

The answers offered to these questions – especially those provided by a number of 'lessons learned' studies and by the Secretariat itself – have tended to be of a practical and managerial kind. They have sought to identify weaknesses in existing missions and proposed specific measures to rectify them: better integration of civilians and military components in missions charged with protection; better and more effective use of intelligence resources in order to improve situational awareness; efforts to increase the mobility and tactical responsiveness of peacekeepers on the ground; greater readiness to use force.[70] Other studies have focused on enhancing co-ordination – the holy grail of so many reports into the workings of the UN system – among different mission components charged with protection responsibilities.[71] Many of these reports have drawn on elements of best practice, learning and innovation that have taken place within missions, often against the heaviest of odds. Undoubtedly, the kinds of actions recommended would, if adopted more broadly, strengthen the capacity to provide protection and prevent mass atrocity crimes.

The question remains, however, why progress has been so modest. It is a question that has not always been addressed head-on by the minor industry now devoted to proposing solutions, however innovative, to the UN's 'protection crisis'. In the end, the central difficulty does not lie in identifying the deficiencies in existing missions. Studies that focus narrowly on how to improve the UN's capacity to protect civilians, while valuable within their own restricted terms of reference, have not adequately confronted four fundamental problems; problems that emerge not just from an assessment of ongoing or recent missions but from the history of UN peacekeeping since its inception.

---

[69] United Nations Document S/2009/277, 29 May 2009, paragraph 23.

[70] These are some of the recommendations put forward in one thoughtful report; see Stian Kjeksrud and Jacob Aasland Ravndal, *Protection of Civilians in Practice – Emerging Lessons from the UN Mission in the DRC*, Norwegian Defence Research Establishment (FFI) Report No. 2010/02378, 15 December 2010.

[71] 'Protection of Civilians: Coordinating Mechanisms in UN Peacekeeping Missions', DPKO/DFS Comparative Study and Toolkit, 2012.

The first of these concerns the ability of UN-mounted peacekeeping operations to take on protection tasks in non-permissive environments. The operational challenges involved in effectively protecting civilians in the context of a peacekeeping operation are formidable and, notwithstanding the many peacekeeping reforms introduced and partially implemented since 2000, UN missions have proved unable to overcome built-in weaknesses that have been a feature of peacekeeping since its earliest days: the absence of unity of command; uneven quality troops offered for peacekeeping service; deficiencies in logistics, intelligence and tactical mobility; and the lack of strategic reserves. Where the operational environment has been generally stable and benign, it has in the past been possible to live with such weaknesses. The particular demands of civilian protection in the context of internal conflicts or civil wars, however, pose challenges that are of a qualitatively different kind. Not the least of these is the inescapable fact that a UN force, however much it may try to avoid it, will be drawn into the politics of the conflict and of the country in which it is deployed.

Complicating this is an insufficiently acknowledged reality: the deep reluctance of UN troop contributors to expose their soldiers to risk, an attitude reflected in the adoption, spoken or unspoken, of national caveats and the penchant for interfering in the UN chain of command. This remains the default position of states providing troops for UN peacekeeping: states still provide personnel to the UN on the assumption that peacekeeping is a 'low-risk activity'.[72] When the risk is deemed too high they choose either not to provide troops under a UN flag or to place national forces outside the UN chain of command, as during Operation Palliser in Sierra Leone in 2000 or Artemis in the DRC in 2001. It is worth reminding oneself here that the mass atrocity crimes in Rwanda and Srebrenica, crimes which provided such an impetus to the emergence of the R2P idea, did not change the fundamentally risk-averse and conditional attitude of troop contributors to UN missions. For all the post-genocide professions of guilt and acknowledgement of failure to act on the part of member states, the reality is that out of 19 countries that by 1994 had made a commitment in principle to provide troops on stand-by for the UN, not a single one of them offered to send troops to Rwanda in May 1994.[73] The date here is significant: the genocide was by this stage an accomplished and acknowledged fact. Moreover, when some six months later, the secretary-general, faced with a major protection emergency in the eastern Congo, approached 39 member states about the possibility of

---

[72] United Nations Documents A/47/277 – S/24111, 17 June 1992.
[73] 'Supplement to an Agenda for Peace', paragraph 43.

putting together a multinational force to disarm militarised refugee camps, he received only *one* positive response.[74]

Second, civilian protection mandates raise expectations among local populations and within the 'international community' (including what may loosely be called international public opinion), which end up presenting under-resourced and ill-equipped missions with often irreconcilable pressures for action. Changes in normative climate, of which R2P is an expression, have added both to expectations and pressures. Responding to them, the attempts by mission leaderships and peacekeepers to meet 'protection deficits' can, and have had, perverse consequences, resulting in increased predation and violence against civilian populations and, ultimately, in mass atrocity crimes. This has come about in a combination of different ways. On the one hand, the prospect that protection will be extended to civilians under threat from a particular group may cause that group to step up attacks, especially if doing so forms part of a deliberate strategy of cleansing territory of an opponent. The prospect of protection may also encourage the threatened group to congregate and seek refuge in large numbers where small and ill-equipped contingents of UN troops are located, thus providing a tempting target for attack given the likelihood that UN forces in situ will be incapable of providing protection. Finally, faced with these kinds of challenges the UN has often had little choice but to enter into some form of partnership with national authorities and local security forces, especially if those authorities actually represent the nominally legitimate power in the land. Such reliance, however, has created its own set of problems as local allies have themselves, all too often, proved deeply abusive in pursuit of their own political and military agendas (from Vietnam to Afghanistan, the risks inherent in forming alliances with local security partners is hardly new). Efforts by UN peacekeepers to engage in Pillar Two activities to address the problems of local security partners have proved woefully inadequate.

The third problem is inextricably linked to those discussed above. It concerns the mandate given to UN peacekeepers and the 'intentions' of the Security Council and troop contributors when authorising missions and providing troops. In their otherwise excellent and carefully researched report on the record of civilian protection between 1999 and 2009, Holt and Taylor provide one curious and potentially confusing conclusion: 'Despite enduring consistency in mandate *language* regarding physical protection of civilians, there is no consistent perception of Council *intent* amongst senior UN mission staff, either within the UN

---

[74] Sadako Ogata, *The Turbulent Decade* (New York: W.W. Norton & Co, 2005) pp. 203–204.

Secretariat or UN peacekeeping missions'.[75] The first part of the sentence is unproblematic. The second is less so for it appears to suggest that the problem is one of 'perception of intent' rather than a much more basic one: the Council has consistently and wilfully ignored questions about what it would take to translate high-sounding intentions into meaningful and realisable objectives on the ground.

In the same vein, it has avoided confronting questions raised by the reliance on local allies or 'security partners'. Security Council resolution 1856 (2008), for example, which elevated civilian protection to the highest priority for MONUC, stressed the need for MONUC to work in 'close cooperation with the Government of the Democratic Republic of the Congo'.[76] As Holt and Taylor rightly emphasise, however, the resolution did not 'directly acknowledge the fundamental tension between the imperative to protect civilians on the one hand, and the requirement to work closely with the Congolese government – and particularly the FARDC, which remains one of the chief threats to civilians – on the other'.[77] In these circumstances, it is hardly surprising that mission leaderships and contingent commanders have had to make their own judgements on the basis of the resources actually at their disposal. There is a depressing parallel here to the experience of missions in the early 1990s, including in the former Yugoslavia. And member states cannot here, as they are wont to do, place all of the blame on the Secretariat for failing to tell the Council – as the Brahimi Panel urged it to do back in 2000 – 'what it needs to know, not what it wants to hear, when formulating or changing mission mandates'.[78] In the case of MONUC, the secretary-general's report on the implementation of Resolution 1291 made it perfectly clear that MONUC 'would not have the capacity to protect the civilian population from armed attack'.[79]

If, for a moment, we were to treat the Security Council as an effectively functioning decision-making entity - leaving aside, that is, the divisions and tensions among member states that usually shape and influence its decision-making processes - it is impossible to escape the conclusion that it has acted with gross irresponsibility by repeatedly and unashamedly holding out the promise of effective protection while consistently

[75] Victoria Holt and Glyn Taylor with Max Kelly, *Protecting Civilians in the Context of UN Peacekeeping Operations: Successes, Setbacks and Remaining Challenges*, Independent Study Commissioned by the DPKO and DPA, 2009, p. 7 (emphasis in original).
[76] United Nations Document S/RES/1856, paragraph 3.
[77] Holt and Taylor, *Protecting Civilians*, p. 284
[78] *Brahimi Panel Report*, paragraph 64 (d).
[79] United Nations Document S/2000/30, 17 January 2000, paragraph 67.

avoiding, when tested, the kinds of actions that would offer a meaningful chance of delivering on that promise. The Council is not, of course, a unitary actor and this explains why actual policy outcomes often fall so far short of the noble and high-sounding rhetoric that always accompanies Council decisions. Even so, in the particular case of the DRC at least, the source of the UN's malaise cannot be put down merely to paralysing divisions among Council members. It was John Holmes' sense, after three years as under-secretary-general for humanitarian affairs, that the DRC, even though it frequently appeared on the Council's agenda, 'was, in fact, something of a diplomatic orphan'.[80] In the final analysis, the UN's agonised and deeply troubled mission in Congo reflects a fundamental lack of political commitment on the part of the Council to address the conflict and its regional dimensions, and all that flows from this: an absence of strategic direction, no sustained focus on the dynamics of the conflict, ad hocery and limited resources.

And this brings us to the fourth and arguably most serious problem with the managerial, or try-harder, approach to civilian protection alluded to above: it runs the risk of detracting both focus and effort away from the underlying political causes, local and regional, of protection crises and mass atrocity crimes. In the words of Alan Doss:

> The Lusaka and Pretoria agreements, while providing the basis for the political reunification of the country, did not end the violence in the eastern Congo and no alternative strategy was developed at a political level to deal with the growing protection crisis. As a result, MONUC was progressively pulled into a robust protection role in a piecemeal fashion. Although the Congolese government was regularly reminded of its protection responsibilities, the international community increasingly turned towards MONUC as the 'quick-fix' to fill the protection vacuum.[81]

Where does all this leave the problematic, but probably inevitable, conflation of peacekeeping and R2P?

This chapter suggests that there is a strong case, once again, for recognising the limitations of UN peacekeeping as an instrument to deal with certain categories of problems. The blurring of the distinction between peacekeeping and enforcement, the ever-growing number of tasks entrusted to peacekeepers and the very language of Council resolutions, reinforced by a normative climate that saw the adoption of R2P commitment in 2005, have all generated expectations that peacekeepers are not in a position to fulfil. This is true above all in relation to ongoing internal conflicts. To recognise these limitations is far from suggesting that there is

---

[80] Holmes, *The Politics of Humanity*, p.139.
[81] Doss, 'In the Footsteps of Dr Bunche', p. 42.

no role for peacekeepers. As hinted elsewhere in the chapter, the most promising such role is likely to be in the consent-based provision of Pillar Two support. But this too requires resources – resources beyond those granted for these tasks in most of the missions established since 1999. Nor, it should be added, does recognising the limitations of peacekeeping suggest there is no place for the use of force in responding to mass atrocity crimes. That, clearly, is not the conclusion to draw from the UN's experience in Rwanda and former Yugoslavia. This does not, however, undermine the central contention of this chapter, to wit that clarity with respect to the limitations as well as the possibilities of UN-mounted field operations is, paradoxically, also the first step to identifying where the true contribution of UN peacekeeping to preventing mass atrocity crimes and building support for R2P lies.

13 Humanitarian law, refugee protection and the Responsibility to Protect

William Maley

The development since 2001 of the doctrine of the Responsibility to Protect (R2P) has been one of the most important normative developments in international relations in the last century. At a truly remarkable pace, it has moved from being an idea articulated by the International Commission on Intervention and State Sovereignty to a principle endorsed by leaders of United Nations member states at the World Summit in 2005, and given further substance by its employment to justify protective action for the population of Libya at the time of the overthrow of the Gaddafi regime, although the precise import of this particular case remains open for debate.[1]

Nonetheless, it is but one of a range of norms that have appeared in the last century and a half with a view to offering some kind of protection to people in vulnerable situations. The establishment in 1863 of the International Committee of the Red Cross (ICRC) was one event of fundamental importance in highlighting the need for protection of the vulnerable: the stimulus for the ICRC's establishment was the carnage on the battlefield of Solferino that had been witnessed by Jean-Henry Dunant when by chance he found himself in the vicinity of combat, and which he documented in a famous memoir.[2] The corpus of international humanitarian law, also known as the law of armed conflict, that has developed since then provides critical protections for those in the firing line in armed combat. Another kind of protective regime is that which exists for the benefit of those forced to flight by a well-founded fear of being persecuted. The 1951 Convention Relating to the Status of Refugees is an important source of normative obligation in this respect, but it is only one part of a wider regime augmented by other instruments, and by institutions such as the Office of the United Nations High Commissioner for Refugees.

---

[1] See Marie-Eve Loiselle, 'The Normative Status of the Responsibility to Protect after Libya', *Global Responsibility to Protect* 5:3 (2013), pp. 317–341.

[2] Henry Dunant, *A Memory of Solferino* (Geneva: International Committee of the Red Cross, 1992).

This chapter is concerned with a particular theoretical problem, namely how parallel but *distinct* norms can come into conflict with each other. It is easy to assume that norms with a broadly similar humanitarian impetus will prove complementary, but that need not be the case. The reason for this is that norms are implemented in a highly political environment in which considerations of domestic politics may dispose rulers to seek ways of avoiding responsibilities that their predecessors may have voluntarily accepted. The area of greatest risk is with respect to refugees: here, the emerging R2P norm may be exploited by states seeking to free themselves of responsibilities under existing refugee norms. This chapter is directed at identifying how this risk might arise, and how it can be minimised. It is divided into six sections. The first addresses the question of how norms arise. The second discusses the key dimensions of R2P as a nascent or embryonic norm. The third is concerned with the development and enforcement of norms embodied in international humanitarian law. The fourth examines refugee norms and their rather different enforcement mechanisms, while the fifth turns to the difficulties that may arise in giving effect to norms in an intrinsically political environment. The sixth offers some brief conclusions.

Norms: force, development, scope

The R2P doctrine represents one of the most important embryonic norms of the last hundred years. If it becomes widely accepted, it will have a transformative effect on relations between states. In order, however, to understand why this would be the case, it is important to elaborate on what we mean by 'norms', and to clarify how they can come into existence and shape the behaviour of political actors. At its most basic, according to James S. Coleman, 'a norm concerning a specific action exists when the socially defined right to control the action is held not by the actor but by others'.[3] Social norms 'specify what actions are regarded by a set of persons as proper or correct, or improper or incorrect. They are purposively generated, in that those persons who initiate or help maintain a norm see themselves as benefiting from its being observed or harmed by being violated.'[4] Norms are therefore grounded in *normative expectations of behaviour*, which provide secondary reasons for action going beyond the mere self-interest of actors. Norms differ in this respect from social conventions. Conventions, at least in the initial phase, may have no

[3] James S. Coleman, *Foundations of Social Theory* (Cambridge: Harvard University Press, 1990), p. 243
[4] Ibid., p. 242.

particular normative dimension, although with the passage of time a convention may be 'internalised' by the actors following it so that it does come to have normative force. A pure convention of behaviour provides an equilibrium solution to a coordination problem, but is sustained by the self-interest of actors.[5] That said, the mechanisms that can support norms are many and varied. In a path-breaking study, Robert Axelrod pointed particularly to *metanorms* – norms that one must punish those who do not punish departures from first-order norms. However, he identified a number of other mechanisms as well. These included, most notably: (1) the *dominance* of one group over another; (2) *internalisation*, a situation in which 'violating an established norm is psychologically painful even if the direct material benefits are positive'; (3) *deterrence*, where 'even if punishing a defection is costly now it might have long-term gains by discouraging other defections later'; (4) *social proof*, when the actions of an individual are in response to the actions of others whose behaviour he or she can observe; (5) *membership*, where an individual is a voluntary member of a 'group working together for a common end'; (6) *law*, which may support, maintain and extend pre-existing norms; and (7) *reputation*, which is relevant because violating a norm 'would provide a signal about the type of person you are'.[6]

Norms have a complex history in writings about international relations, but in recent decades they have attracted attention in the context of both regime theory and constructivist ideas about world affairs. In his discussion of regimes, Krasner depicted regimes as 'implicit or explicit principles, norms, rules, and decision-making procedures around which actors' expectations converge in a given area of international relations'. Norms he saw as 'standards of behaviour defined in terms of rights and obligations'.[7] While the processes by which norms take shape are complex and varied,[8] Constructivist scholars have illuminated the importance of norm entrepreneurship. Norm entrepreneurs, Finnemore and Sikkink have argued, 'are critical for norm emergence because they call attention to issues or even "create" issues by using language that names, interprets,

---

[5] David Lewis, *Convention: A Philosophical Study* (Cambridge: Harvard University Press, 1969), p. 78.
[6] Robert Axelrod, 'An Evolutionary Approach to Norms', *American Political Science Review* 80:4 (1986), pp. 1095–1111 at pp. 1104–1107.
[7] Stephen D. Krasner, 'Structural Causes and Regime Consequences: Regimes as Intervening Variables', in Stephen D. Krasner, ed, *International Regimes* (Ithaca: Cornell University Press, 1983), pp. 1–21 at p. 2.
[8] See Ramesh Thakur, *The Responsibility to Protect: Norms, Laws and the Use of Force in International Politics* (London: Routledge, 2011), pp. 1–13; Amitav Acharya, 'The R2P and Norm Diffusion: Towards a Framework of Norm Circulation', *Global Responsibility to Protect* 5:4 (2013), pp. 466–479.

and dramatizes them'.[9] In a strict sense, norm entrepreneurs may be dispensable. One can imagine a situation in which norms emerge through the internalisation of conventions without an entrepreneur playing a significant role. Nonetheless, in many cases, norm entrepreneurs have indeed proved significant, whether one speaks of individuals such as Raphael Lemkin, who devoted his later life to promoting the norm against genocide, or bodies such as the International Commission on Intervention and State Sovereignty which gave rise to the notion of a responsibility to protect.

Where the idea of norm entrepreneurship is particularly useful is in helping to explain the emergence of what one might call 'instant norms'. Some approaches to the emergence of norms see the creation of norms as a learning process in which actors engaging with each other in an iterated rather than one-off fashion adjust their behaviours so that they match the expectations of other actors in ways that prove mutually beneficial.[10] Norms that emerge in this way may take quite some time to crystallise, and there may be room for considerable debate over whether norms have emerged, and if so, what their precise content might be. Where, however, norm entrepreneurs are active, the whole process of norm generation may be speeded up. This is particularly the case if the objective of the norm entrepreneur is to produce a new rule of international law, since the process of crafting a new treaty can move as quickly as the potential parties to the treaty are prepared to permit. Almost the classic example was the campaign promoted by Canadian Foreign Minister Lloyd Axworthy to procure a ban on anti-personnel landmines. Embodied in the 1997 Ottawa Treaty which came into effect in 1999, it produced in short order a very effective norm that rapidly choked off a problem that through much of the 1990s had looked likely to leave a hideous legacy well into the twenty-first century.[11] As an exercise in norm creation, the promotion of the notion of a global responsibility to protect had some striking similarities to Axworthy's earlier exercise, with the support of the Canadian government being a critical element. Where it differed was in the engagement of the mass public. Axworthy's landmines campaign sought to generate a groundswell of public opinion in favour of a new norm, and was very successful in doing so. The norm entrepreneurship

---

[9] Martha Finnemore and Kathryn Sikkink, 'International Norm Dynamics and Political Change', *International Organization* 52:4 (1998), pp. 887–917 at p. 897.

[10] See Edna Ullmann-Margalit, *The Emergence of Norms* (Oxford: Oxford University Press, 1977).

[11] See Ramesh Thakur and William Maley, 'The Ottawa Convention on Landmines: A Landmark Humanitarian Treaty in Arms Control?', *Global Governance* 5:3 (1999), pp. 273–302.

surrounding the Responsibility to Protect was a much more cerebral exercise, although the International Commission held consultations with civil society groups and experts in Ottawa, Geneva, London, Maputo, Washington DC, Santiago, Cairo, Paris, New Delhi, Beijing and St Petersburg.[12]

One other important difference needs to be noted. Many norms are formulated in such a way as to prohibit forms of destructive behaviour, and embody sanctions that can be directed against those who behave destructively. The Ottawa Treaty held out the prospect that those who continued to manufacture, transfer, stockpile or use anti-personnel mines would be anathematised. A Responsibility to Protect norm does not fit this particular pattern. The mass atrocity crimes with which R2P is concerned are already anathematised in a range of different instruments. An R2P norm is rather concerned with finding more effective ways of promoting responses to such atrocities. Given commitments to the sovereignty of states in the international system, it is exceedingly difficult actually to *sanction* any single state for not becoming involved in efforts to deal with mass atrocity crimes. Therefore, if the R2P norm is to become effective, it is unlikely to be because any sanction is in place to bolster it; rather, its effectiveness will be measured by the extent to which it is internalised – that is, so accepted by key states as *the* way in which to approach the problem of mass atrocity crime that it is unthinkable that it not be applied when circumstances demand.

R2P as a norm

Barely a decade has passed since the International Commission on Intervention and State Sovereignty introduced the vocabulary of a 'responsibility to protect'. This is a very short time span indeed when compared to the centuries it took for the idea of state sovereignty to be refined following the Peace of Westphalia.[13] In addition, the terrorist attacks of 11 September 2001, coming only three months before the release of the International Commission's report, focused a great deal of attention on counterterrorism rather than the kinds of mass atrocity crime

---

[12] See International Commission on Intervention and State Sovereignty (ICISS), *The Responsibility to Protect: Report of the International Commission on Intervention and State Sovereignty* (Ottawa: International Development Research Centre, 2001), p. 83. The present author was a participant in the New Delhi consultation.

[13] On the evolution of ideas of sovereignty, see Stephen D. Krasner, *Sovereignty: Organized Hypocrisy* (Princeton: Princeton University Press, 1999); Daniel Philpott, *Revolutions in Sovereignty* (Princeton: Princeton University Press, 2001); Luke Glanville, *Sovereignty and the Responsibility to Protect: A New History* (Chicago: University of Chicago Press, 2013).

with which the report was concerned. This makes it all the more remarkable that the report did not fall dead from the press, something that can be attributed in part to the energy devoted by some of the commissioners to ensuring that its message would not be lost in the wider clamour of those times. That said, it is only to be expected that many issues relating to R2P remain contested, as they will surely do for quite some time to come.

The International Commission report's impact was undoubtedly a product in part of its clarity and rigour. In perhaps its most quoted passage, it stated that 'where population is suffering serious harm, as a result of internal war, insurgency, repression or state failure, and the state in question is unwilling or unable to halt or avert it, the principle of non-intervention yields to the international responsibility to protect'. It went on to argue that the Responsibility to Protect embraced three specific responsibilities – the responsibility to prevent, the responsibility to react, and the responsibility to rebuild. Affirming the central role of the United Nations Security Council as a source of right authority, it argued that 'the Security Council should take into account in all its deliberations that, if it fails to discharge its responsibility to protect in conscience-shocking situations crying out for action, concerned states may not rule out other means to meet the gravity and urgency of that situation – and that the stature and credibility of the United Nations may suffer thereby'.[14]

The idea of a responsibility to protect has since undergone considerable refinement.[15] Most importantly, the 2005 World Summit, recognising the potential for disputes over the meaning of 'serious harm', sharpened the focus of R2P to four specific crimes to act as its trigger: genocide, war crimes, ethnic cleansing, and crimes against humanity.[16] It also voiced a commitment on behalf of participating leaders to react to these affronts, stating 'we are prepared to take collective action, in a timely and decisive manner, through the Security Council, in accordance with the Charter, including Chapter VII, on a case-by-case basis and in cooperation with relevant regional organizations as appropriate, should peaceful means be inadequate and national authorities manifestly fail to protect their populations from genocide, war crimes, ethnic cleansing and crimes against humanity'.[17] But that said, until it is buttressed by considerable state

[14] ICISS, *The Responsibility to Protect*, pp. xi, xiii.
[15] See Alex J. Bellamy, *Global Politics and the Responsibility to Protect: From Words to Deeds* (London: Routledge, 2011), pp. 26–50; Elizabeth G. Ferris, *The Politics of Protection: The Limits of Humanitarian Action* (Washington DC: Brookings Institution Press, 2011), pp. 162–173.
[16] See Gareth Evans and Ramesh Thakur, 'Humanitarian Intervention and the Responsibility to Protect', *International Security* 37:4 (2013), pp. 199–207 at p. 201.
[17] *World Summit Outcome*, Document A/RES/60/1, 24 (New York: United Nations, 2005), paragraph 139.

practice, it will remain a subject of debate exactly how R2P should shape the wider normative space that it inhabits. This is in no small measure because the United Nations system is not geared up to respond consistently to threats to international peace and security. The veto power of the permanent members of the Security Council ensures that this is the case: no matter what atrocities might be committed by a permanent member or one of its close allies, authorisation from the Security Council for action is most unlikely to be forthcoming. Nevertheless, while these limitations might be cause for some disgust, they should not be cause for despair. The mere fact that one cannot stop all atrocities is no basis for abandoning the effort to prevent at least some.

The emphasis on the authority of the Security Council provides some protection against abuse of the doctrine. (Hitler, after all, claimed to be acting on behalf of suffering co-ethnics when he pursued his plans for expansion in Europe in the 1930s.) Perhaps the greatest challenge for R2P is to secure action when it is needed. As one scholar has recently pointed out, 'the Council's role in *authorizing* actions designed to fulfil international responsibilities (particularly those involving the use of military force) cannot and should not be confused with the role of actually *fulfilling* such responsibilities'.[18] When a genocide breaks out in a country such as Rwanda, very few countries will be motivated by direct and immediate *interests* to do anything about it. Indeed, a crime that is widely known to be occurring may go unaddressed because each observer expects some other observer to take the lead in responding.[19] If action is to be taken, it will need to be because the R2P norm has been internalised to the point that it provides an additional reason for action.

Norms rarely emerge in virginal form. They arise in the context of concerns that have often long preoccupied those who seek to promote norms as solutions to political problems, and often take shape alongside other norms and rules that may have something to offer. It may be quite important that new protective norms not undermine existing normative structures, since in their embryonic phase at least, their protective force may be limited. Some normative structures are more fragile than others. To demonstrate this, it is useful to discuss two important sets of norms, namely international humanitarian law and refugee protection norms.

[18] Jennifer M. Welsh, 'Who Should Act? Collective responsibility and the Responsibility to Protect', in W. Andy Knight and Frazer Egerton, eds, *The Routledge Handbook of the Responsibility to Protect* (London: Routledge, 2012), pp. 103–114 at p. 109.

[19] See Geoffrey Brennan and Loren Lomasky, *Democracy and Decision: The Pure Theory of Electoral Preference* (Cambridge: Cambridge University Press, 1993), pp. 125–126.

International humanitarian law

Humanitarian protection largely dates from the nineteenth century, and paralleled an increasing focus on the rights and concerns of those beyond the realm of political elites. For members of political elites, norms of course have a venerable history. Customary diplomatic law encoded a range of norms of behaviour with respect to representatives of states, underpinned by an understanding of reciprocity: that if a state mistreated the representatives of another state, it could hardly complain if its own ambassadors were mistreated as well. It is not at all surprising that one of the most ferocious conflicts in Europe, the Thirty Years War, was triggered by the 1618 'Defenestration of Prague', in which three representatives of the King of Bohemia were ejected from a third storey window in the Bohemian chancellery. It was only much later, however, that humanitarian norms began to take shape to protect those outside the level of political elites. Yet once this process began, it was remarkable how relatively quickly it moved. In part this reflected the growth of individualism and humanitarian ideas in the aftermath of the Enlightenment; in part it reflected a growing significance of thinking about individual rights, which have a longer pedigree than is often conceded.[20] However, of great significance in bringing about these changes was the entrepreneurship of Jean-Henry Dunant, and the activism of both those who fell under his influence and of the Red Cross movement that he played a critical role in founding.

A mere quirk of circumstance, noted earlier, accounted for this: Dunant happened to witness the mayhem at the Battle of Solferino, and was motivated by the spectacle to do something about the horrors of war that he had witnessed. The ICRC was the organisational manifestation of the concerns that Dunant felt. More broadly, however, the Red Cross was able to tap into growing concerns about the costs of war for both combatants and civilians. By the second half of the nineteenth century, the development of photography had brought images of war in a more realistic fashion into the vision of large numbers of people for whom it would otherwise have been a remote phenomenon. There was thus a certain amount of fertile soil in which new ideas could be planted. The ultimate consequence was the development of two very important streams of international law, sometimes called the Law of The Hague and the Law of Geneva, that sought to give effect to new norms of conduct in the context of military operations.[21]

---

[20] See Christian Reus–Smit, *Individual Rights and the Making of the International System* (Cambridge: Cambridge University Press, 2013).

[21] For an overview, see Frits Kalshoven and Liesbeth Zegveld, *Constraints on the Waging of War: An Introduction to International Humanitarian Law* (Cambridge: Cambridge University Press, 2011).

These two streams of law are central to modern understandings of what constitutes a war crime. The Law of The Hague (embodied mainly in The Hague Conventions of 1899 and 1907) is broadly concerned with protections for combatants, while the Law of Geneva (comprising the four 1949 Geneva Conventions and the two 1977 Additional Protocols to those Conventions) is much more directly concerned with civilians and non-combatant personnel who might be at risk in the context of armed conflict.[22]

A distinctive feature of the laws of armed conflict is how widely they have come to be accepted. One reason, beyond any doubt, is reciprocity. A military that does not meticulously observe its obligations under international humanitarian law is poorly placed to demand that its soldiers be properly treated if they become prisoners of some other force, or that the status of its civilian population be respected. Two other factors, however, also come into play. One is that certain standards of behaviour seem, at least at the doctrinal level, to be shared across a range of different societies and cultures. Even the Taliban in Afghanistan sought to convey the impression that they respected some restraints on the waging of war.[23] The other has been the development of enforcement mechanisms through which criminal prosecutions can occur. The most striking examples of these were to be found in the International Military Tribunals in Nuremberg and Tokyo that tried and convicted German and Japanese war criminals at the end of the Second World War, along with a range of national judicial processes which dealt with war crimes committed by figures less prominent than those who were arraigned in the major trials. In a number of these trials, the perpetrators of war crimes were handed capital sentences that were then carried out.[24] Of course, in other conflicts, a much gentler approach was taken: US Lieutenant William Calley, for example, served a far lighter sentence than the March 1968 My Lai massacre in South Vietnam might have justified, not least because of popular agitation in his favour.[25] It remains to be seen what difference

---

[22] For relevant texts, see Adam Roberts and Richard Guelff, eds, *Documents on the Laws of War* (Oxford: Oxford University Press, 2000).

[23] See Muhammad Munir, 'The Layha for the Mujahideen: An Analysis of the Code of Conduct for Taliban Fighters under Islamic Law', *International Review of the Red Cross* 93:881 (2011), pp. 81–102.

[24] For background, see Telford Taylor, *The Anatomy of the Nuremberg Trials* (New York: Alfred A. Knopf, 1993); Donald Bloxham, *Genocide on Trial: War Crimes Trials and the Formation of Holocaust History and Memory* (Oxford: Oxford University Press, 2001); Neil Boister and Robert Cryer, *The Tokyo International Military Tribunal: A Reappraisal* (Oxford: Oxford University Press, 2008).

[25] Claude Cookman, 'An American Atrocity: The My Lai Massacre Concretized in a Victim's Face', *Journal of American History* 94:1 (2007), pp. 154–162 at p. 161.

the 2002 establishment of the International Criminal Court, pursuant to the Rome Statute of 1998, will make in this respect.[26]

There is very significant overlap between the war crimes with which international humanitarian law is concerned, and the mass atrocity crimes that are the focus of the Responsibility to Protect doctrine. They are not, however, identical. At the Nuremberg Trial, it proved necessary, as well as entirely appropriate, to include in the indictment of the accused not just war crimes in the strict sense of the term, but also crimes against humanity. The reason for this was that not all mass atrocity crimes were covered by the laws of armed conflict. A mass atrocity crime might occur entirely within the boundaries of a single state, without any interstate or even intrastate conflict occurring. Systematic persecution of a particular minority, for example, could be carried out by the government of the state against its own people, and historically this has been all too common a phenomenon.[27] Furthermore, criminal law exists to punish people for proven crimes, and – hopefully – to deter the commission of crimes in the first place. Once, however, a genocide or exercise of mass ethnic cleansing is underway, to warn the perpetrators that they may be criminally liable is not necessarily an effective way of dealing with the problem. They will have already crossed their Rubicon. One of the key factors leading to the genesis of R2P was that existing norms had proved *un*equal to the task that the international community confronted when faced with appalling events such as the Rwandan genocide of 1994.[28] That may not always be the case, but one Rwanda is one horror too many.

Refugee norms

All too often when people find themselves in desperate need, representatives of states are nowhere to be found. The renowned economist Albert O. Hirschman wrote an insightful book entitled *Exit, Voice and Loyalty* which rightly put *exit* at the top of the list of options that one might choose in such circumstances.[29] Hirschman himself had experienced the situation. Of Jewish background, he found himself in Marseilles following the

---

[26] See William A. Schabas, *An Introduction to the International Criminal Court* (Cambridge: Cambridge University Press, 2011).

[27] See R.J. Rummel, *Death by Government* (New Brunswick: Transaction Publishers, 1994).

[28] On these events, see, for example, Samantha Power, *'A Problem from Hell': America and the Age of Genocide* (New York: Basic Books, 2002), pp. 329–389; Michael Barnett, *Eyewitness to a Genocide: The United Nations and Rwanda* (Ithaca: Cornell University Press, 2002); Roméo Dallaire, *Shake Hands with the Devil: The Failure of Humanity in Rwanda* (Toronto: Random House, 2003).

[29] Albert O. Hirschman, *Exit, Voice and Loyalty: Responses to Decline in Firms, Organizations, and States* (Cambridge: Harvard University Press, 1970).

fall of France in June 1940, and, in alliance with the dynamic young American journalist Varian Fry, he helped organise the escape through Spain to America of a range of eminent Europeans who were under threat from the Nazis and their Vichy collaborators,[30] including figures such as Hannah Arendt, Marc Chagall, Heinrich Mann, Franz Werfel and Lion Feuchtwanger. What is remarkable about this case, however, is that Fry and Hirschman received no support of any significance from US authorities. The United States had recognised the Vichy regime and located its embassy to France in Vichy. Maintaining cordial relations with the puppet regime headed by Marshal Pétain was given unambiguously higher priority than assisting in the rescue of those who were vulnerable to the racist ideologies of the Nazis. Here one finds an ominous warning – that the needs of individuals can easily be subordinated by political processes to what are seen as higher political objectives.

The Westphalian political order is premised on the centrality of states, and more broadly on the supposition that protection for individuals is to be obtained from the state of which they are citizens. Equally, however, there has developed a recognition that not all states are alike, that some states will prove unequal to the task of protecting their citizens, while in the worst of cases, predatory forces in control of the state may turn directly against their own. The phenomenon of the 'refugee' can thus be seen as reflecting a failure of the states system properly to perform its tasks, and under those circumstances one can argue that those states which are happy to harvest the benefits of the system owe duties towards those whom the system has failed.[31] Given the vast scale that refugee flows can take,[32] one can certainly argue that more lives have been saved through such people acting on their own initiative than have ever been saved through rescue operations consciously mounted by the international community.

Specific norms for the protection of refugees are now embodied in the 1951 Convention Relating to the Status of Refugees and its 1967 Protocol, as well as texts such as the 1969 Organization of African Unity's (OAU) Convention on the Specific Aspects of Refugee Problems in Africa and the 1984 Cartagena Declaration on Refugees. The 1951 Convention classes as a refugee a person who 'owing to well-founded fear of being persecuted for

---

[30] See Carla Killough McClafferty, *In Defiance of Hitler: The Secret Mission of Varian Fry* (New York: Farrar, Straus and Giroux, 2008).

[31] See Emma Haddad, *The Refugee in International Society: Between Sovereigns* (Cambridge: Cambridge University Press, 2008); Anne McNevin, *Contesting Citizenship: Irregular Migrants and New Frontiers of the Political* (New York: Columbia University Press, 2011).

[32] See Peter Gatrell, *The Making of the Modern Refugee* (Oxford: Oxford University Press, 2013).

reasons of race, religion, nationality, membership of a particular social group or political opinion, is outside the country of his nationality and is unable or, owing to such fear, is unwilling to avail himself of the protection of that country'. The 1951 Convention outlines a range of refugee rights,[33] of which arguably the most important is that of non-refoulement in Article 33.1 – 'No contracting State shall expel or return ("refouler") a refugee in any manner whatsoever to the frontiers of territories where his life or freedom would be threatened on account of his race, religion, nationality, membership of a particular social group or political opinion.'

Does this mean that refugees are adequately protected in contemporary international society? Hardly. For a considerable period of time, it has been clear that many states are more interested in paying lip-service to refugee protection than in carrying a significant burden. The enforcement mechanisms for refugee rights are inherently weak, as are the incentives for burden sharing. Many refugees, when they flee persecution, find themselves in territories that are nearly as stressed and unstable as those which they have fled, and which lack the wherewithal to provide assistance even to their own populations, let alone a substantial influx of forced migrants. Yet asymmetries of power in the international system mean that these states of first asylum may have limited leverage in procuring cooperation from richer, more remote states, which often prefer the option of 'cherry-picking' refugee populations by resettling the more highly educated and skilled and leaving developing countries with responsibility for the poor, the non-literate and the disabled.[34] One consequence, ironically, has been the growth of protracted refugee situations in which refugees are 'warehoused' with little prospect of encountering a durable solution to their problem in the form of safe repatriation, or integration in their country of first asylum, or resettlement to a more nurturing environment.[35] The danger of such situations is that they can

[33] James C. Hathaway, *The Rights of Refugees under International Law* (Cambridge: Cambridge University Press, 2005).

[34] For discussion of these asymmetries, see Astri Suhrke, 'Burden–Sharing During Refugee Emergencies: The Logic of Collective versus National Action', *Journal of Refugee Studies* 11:4 (1998), pp. 396–415; Alexander Betts, *Protection by Persuasion: International Cooperation in the Refugee Regime* (Ithaca: Cornell University Press, 2009); William Maley, 'Refugee Diplomacy', in Andrew F. Cooper, Jorge Heine and Ramesh Thakur, eds, *The Oxford Handbook of Modern Diplomacy* (Oxford: Oxford University Press, 2013), pp. 675–690; Martin Gottwald, 'Burden Sharing and Refugee Protection', in Elena Fiddian-Qasmiyeh, Gil Loescher, Katy Long and Nando Sigona, eds, *The Oxford Handbook of Refugee and Forced Migration Studies* (Oxford: Oxford University Press, 2014) pp. 525–537.

[35] See Gil Loescher, James Milner, Edward Newman and Gary G. Troeller, eds, *Protracted Refugee Situations: Political, Human Rights and Security Implications* (Tokyo: United Nations University Press, 2008); Howard Adelman, ed, *Protracted Displacement in Asia: No Place to Call Home* (Aldershot: Ashgate, 2008).

become breeding grounds for extremism as people detached from normal life and without hope succumb to simple messages to the effect that violence offers a legitimate means for escaping from the plight in which people find themselves. They can also provide fodder for host-country agendas.[36]

Ultimately, the protections available for refugee rights are very fragile. While the office of the United Nations High Commissioner for Refugees has protective responsibilities under its Statute, in practice the UNHCR is so heavily burdened with responsibilities for relief delivery that its capacity to provide individualised assistance to people in danger is often compromised.[37] In contrast to the case of norms embodied in the law of armed conflict, reciprocity does little to promote good-faith implementation of refugee protection norms. Furthermore, there is no international tribunal to which refugees can have recourse in order to enforce the rights that the 1951 Convention grants to them. Refugees depend on the benevolence or goodwill of states for the protection of their rights, and this protection is often not forthcoming. One reason why this is the case is that refugee protection often becomes entangled in the toxic domestic politics of democratic states. Refugees are strangers, and not everyone wants to help them. They can readily be blamed by populists for all the ills that voters resent, ranging from unemployment and urban sprawl to traffic congestion and amorphous unease that the character of a community is beginning to change. In July 1938, a conference at Evian was held at the instigation of US President Franklin D. Roosevelt to address the terrible plight of Jews fleeing Nazi Germany. In his address to the conference, the Australian delegate remarked that 'as we have no racial problem, we are not desirous of importing one'.[38] This kind of mindset has by no means disappeared.

Reconciling norms

It is useful at this point to draw together some of the elements of the previous discussion. At least where the norms embodied in international humanitarian law are concerned, the story is a relatively happy one. In key

---

[36] See, for example, Farnaz Fassihi, 'Iran Recruiting Afghan Refugees to Fight for Regime in Syria', *The Wall Street Journal*, 15 May 2014.

[37] See William Maley, 'A New Tower of Babel? Reappraising the Architecture of Refugee Protection', in Edward Newman and Joanne Van Selm, eds, *Refugees and Forced Displacement: International Security, Human Vulnerability, and the State* (Tokyo: United Nations University Press, 2003), pp. 306–329.

[38] Quoted in Martin Gilbert, *The Holocaust: The Jewish Tragedy* (London: William Collins, 1986), p. 64.

respects, international humanitarian law provides the micro foundations for the macro response that R2P involves. There is no real risk that dissemination and wider acceptance of an R2P norm will be at the expense of protections under international humanitarian law; on the contrary, to the extent that those making the case for action under R2P point to war crimes as support for their argument, they reduce the risk that war crimes may be swept under the carpet, as on occasion has happened. Furthermore, in democratic polities, it is relatively rare to encounter strong domestic pressure groups opposed to the prosecution of war crimes per se. What one more frequently encounters are attempts to exculpate specific individuals such as Lieutenant Calley, who may be seen by some of their fellow citizens as scapegoats for guiltier people higher up the chain of command.

Where refugee protection is concerned, however, the story is rather different. R2P can potentially underpin preventive action that may avert the need for exit.[39] Yet at the same time, it is important to note that protective norms are fundamentally concerned with those who are seeking *asylum*. While UNHCR welcomes the contributions of states that are prepared to resettle refugees in need from countries of first asylum, this is essentially an act of benevolence rather than something that is required of states by virtue of some evolved norm. Japan, for example, certainly has the economic capacity to resettle a significant number of refugees, but it has not become a significant country of resettlement, because in exercise of its sovereign rights it has opted not to do so. It is the appearance at a country's border of a person claiming the protections of the 1951 Convention (or some like instrument) that activates the obligations that arise from the normative framework of refugee protection. Yet there is no doubt whatsoever that in many wealthy developed countries, the disposition to welcome such approaches has been shrinking, and in some cases shrinking dramatically. Some states have sought to frame those seeking asylum in this way as somehow illegitimate or even criminal.[40] Others have sought to use various control mechanisms to prevent those in need of protection from reaching the point where they can actually lodge a protection claim.[41] Still others have attempted to deter such approaches by

---

[39] See Angus Francis, 'The Responsibility to Protect and the International Refugee Regime', in Angus Francis, Vesselin Popovski and Charles Sampford, eds, *Norms of Protection: Responsibility to Protect, Protection of Civilians and Their Interaction* (Tokyo: United Nations University Press, 2012), pp. 215–233,

[40] See Sharon Pickering, *Refugees and State Crime* (Sydney: The Federation Press, 2005); Catherine Dauvergne, *Making People Illegal: What Globalization Means for Migration and Law* (Cambridge: Cambridge University Press, 2008), pp. 50–68.

[41] Thomas Gammeltoft-Hansen, *Access to Asylum: International Refugee Law and the Globalisation of Migration Control* (Cambridge: Cambridge University Press, 2011).

providing for detention without trial of asylum seekers often beyond the reach of judicial oversight.[42] In dangerous ways, refugees have found themselves 'securitised', with claims of 'security risk' and the need to protect 'sovereignty' being cited as a basis for attempts by states to wash their hands of responsibilities that they had freely accepted in exercise of their sovereign capacities.[43] Part of the problem arises from a tension between international norms and democratic or populist politics. Perhaps in most societies, one should expect to find voters who are not enthusiastic about the prospect of having to interact with people who are different from themselves, and who therefore respond to promises to maintain the homogeneity of populations. At the same time, a number of countries have witnessed the rise of parties of the far right for which agitation against refugees has proved an electorally rewarding strategy: party leaders such as Jean-Marie Le Pen of the Front National in France, Jörg Haider of the Freiheitliche Partei Österreichs in Austria and Pauline Hanson of the One Nation Party in Australia come to mind. The risk that these figures pose is not that they will gain power themselves, but rather that elements of their platforms will be adopted by more mainstream parties seeking to win back some of the extremists' supporters.

Plainly many different factors have contributed to these developments. Nonetheless, there is a risk that some actors with no desire to discharge their responsibilities towards refugees may see intervention in refugee-producing areas as a device for limiting refugee flows. Gibney, for example, has noted that 'the Clinton Administration in the US, faced with criticism over its policy of summarily interdicting asylum seekers on boats heading for Florida, launched a military intervention into the island nation of Haiti, largely to restore a regime less likely to produce refugees'.[44] But beyond this, there is a risk that states may also seek to cite the activation of the Responsibility to Protect as a basis for deferring the processing of refugee claims or even rejecting them altogether. The claim that there is no need to offer protection to people 'here' because they are in the process of being protected 'there' could prove extremely insidious, especially given than it may take years before one can plausibly conclude that international action has made it safe for

---

[42] Daniel Wilsher, *Immigration Detention: Law, History, Politics* (Cambridge: Cambridge University Press, 2012).

[43] See Danièle Joly, *Haven or Hell? Asylum Policies and Refugees in Europe* (London: Macmillan, 1996); Vicki Squire, *The Exclusionary Politics of Asylum* (London: Palgrave Macmillan, 2009); Jeremy Harding, *Border Vigils: Keeping Migrants Out of the Rich World* (London: Verso, 2012).

[44] Matthew J. Gibney, *The Ethics and Politics of Asylum: Liberal Democracy and the Response to Refugees* (Cambridge: Cambridge University Press, 2004), p. 1.

vulnerable people to return to a particular country.[45] It is hard as yet to point to a specific example of this kind of misuse of the R2P norm, but since the norm is still in its adolescence, if not exactly its infancy, it pays to be wary even at this stage about ways in which it could be misappropriated by political actors whose ultimate objectives may be anything but humanitarian.

Conclusion

In a contribution to the deliberations of the International Commission on Intervention and State Sovereignty in 2001, this author adopted the language of Montesquieu in cautioning that intervention, if it were to be attempted, should be attempted with a trembling hand.[46] So much can easily go wrong in the aftermath of an intervention – a point strikingly illustrated by US experience in Iraq after 2003[47] – that the International Commission was extremely wise in setting a high threshold before the R2P doctrine would be in engaged. What this chapter has done is identify another kind of problem that could flow as an unintended consequence of the acceptance of R2P. There is a concrete risk that political leaders seeking to ingratiate themselves with domestic audiences may seize on the notion of a Responsibility to Protect as a means of washing their hands of other normative obligations that they have voluntarily assumed. This would doubtless be a cynical exercise on their part, but such things have been known to happen. In no sense does this provide a basis for walking away from mass atrocity crimes. On occasion the only effective way to deal with them will be robust action, of the kind that was tragically absent in Rwanda, and for that matter during the Cambodian genocide of 1975–1978. But it does mean that there is a problem that needs to be addressed: that the consolidation of the R2P norm may end up undermining other protective norms that it was never designed to weaken.

How might this problem be addressed? It is hardly likely that political leaders will pay it much attention, but fortunately they are by no means the only relevant contributors to this discussion. Scholarly commentators

---

[45] See William Maley, 'Political Transitions and the Cessation of Refugee Status: Some Lessons from Afghanistan and Iraq', *Law in Context* 22:2 (2005), pp. 156–186.

[46] See William Maley, 'Twelve Theses on the Impact of Humanitarian Intervention', *Security Dialogue* 33:3 (2002), pp. 265–278.

[47] See David L. Phillips, *Losing Iraq: Inside the Postwar Reconstruction Fiasco* (Boulder: Westview Press, 2005); George Packer, *The Assassins' Gate: America in Iraq* (New York: Farrar, Straus and Giroux, 2005); Ahmed S. Hashim, *Insurgency and Counter-Insurgency in Iraq* (Ithaca: Cornell University Press, 2006). The US invasion of Iraq was not in any sense an exercise in the responsibility to protect, but it remains a potent example of the limitations of force as a tool for overcoming complex problems.

and norm entrepreneurs are well placed to address the issue more directly. To the extent that the promotion of R2P is underpinned by humanitarian impulses, those impulses equally support attention being paid to the needs of refugees to flee from the scene of mass atrocity episodes. In particular, there is no harm in reiterating that the honouring of R2P principles should never be at the expense of other protective norms that have developed in response to critical needs. Rather than being seen as in conflict with each other, the norms embodied in international humanitarian law and in refugee law and practice should be seen as *complements* to the Responsibility to Protect, members of a family of principles directed at preventing, ameliorating and confronting lethal practices that degrade our common humanity. Yet they are not to be taken for granted. Against the example of great humanitarian figures such as Dunant, one can all too easily point to a Hitler, a Stalin or a Pol Pot. Sustaining protective norms requires constant vigilance.

14   Is the Responsibility to Protect doctrine gender-neutral?

Susan Harris Rimmer

Introduction

On Monday [20 May 2013], terrified women and children who arrived, seeking sanctuary again, were battered away from the safety of the SANDF-Munigi base in the Congo while mortars were exploding nearby. Simone Schlindwein, of the German *Tageszeitung*, was 'shocked by the remorseless way in which South African soldiers were keeping terrified refugees away from their compound' while the fighting raged on.

Censorbugbear, online blogger[1]

Is the Responsibility to Protect (R2P) doctrine gender-neutral? Is this the right question? Instead, should we measure if this doctrine contributes materially or theoretically to the feminist goal of gender equality; or is the doctrine flawed in its design and could its implementation cause or exacerbate harm to women and girls involved in conflict? What would the R2P doctrine mean to the terrified women and girls seeking refuge at the UN compound as described above?

In 2010, Australian jurist Hilary Charlesworth published a seminal article entitled 'Feminist Reflections on the Responsibility to Protect' in the lead journal *Global Responsibility to Protect*.[2] At that juncture, she found that it was 'worth engaging with concepts such as the Responsibility to Protect because they can unsettle the standard boundaries of the discipline and increase the possibility of its transformation' but that the design of the R2P doctrine has been 'influenced by men's lives and the dominance of masculine modes of reasoning'.[3] In 2010, this

---

[1] Blogpost 20 May 2013, available at www.censorbugbear.org/genocide/sa–national –defence–force–soldiers–refuse–to–protect–terrified–civilians–fleeing–from–drc–civil –war–fighting–may20–2#uwBmV7fCdOGX06QO.99, accessed 20 May 2013.

[2] Hilary Charlesworth, 'Feminist Reflections on the Responsibility to Protect', *Global Responsibility to Protect* 2:3 (2010), pp. 232–249.

[3] Charlesworth, 'Feminist Reflections on the Responsibility to Protect', at p. 249.

article was one of very few examples of feminist engagement with the R2P doctrine, with almost no engagement in the reverse direction from R2P scholars. It built in turn upon a pivotal UN INSTRAW report in 2006.[4] I review international developments from 2009 to 2014 to re-examine this proposition and view R2P through a variety of feminist reactions.

Based on this analysis, I argue that the experience of armed and societal conflict is gendered, which has been plainly accepted by the Security Council in relation to the women, peace and security agenda. Therefore, R2P cannot claim nor should it pretend gender-neutrality in its response to conflict, and if it does, or simply ignores gender issues or continually relegates women to the category of 'vulnerable populations', its proponents risk losing credibility. In 2010, Charlesworth's analysis was that the doctrine in fact offers 'gendered and racialised accounts of peace and conflict and the capacity of intervention to defuse violence'.[5] I argue that this remains the case based on my reading of contemporary conflicts before the Council such as those in Mali, the Democratic Republic of Congo (DRC) and Afghanistan, and may have indeed become more entrenched. However, there has undoubtedly been recognition of this critique and more movement around the protection agenda of R2P advocates in the area of the prevention of, and increased accountability for, sexual and gender-based violence (SGBV). This could be interpreted as a sign of engagement with a feminist agenda of women's empowerment and participation, but also interpreted as a sign of the paternalist and essentialist gender politics observed in the founding documents of R2P as a concept.

In 2010, Charlesworth concluded that[6]:

For the doctrine to offer support for women's equality, it would need to take into account a broader set of factors that impinge on women's lives, including women's economic marginalisation, the effect of militarisation and systemic discrimination against women. It would need to engage with the private subordination of women and the widespread violence against them outside the formal structures of the state. It would need to problematise the idea of intervention, recognising that it can exacerbate injustices by reinforcing particular forms of

---

[4] Jennifer Bond and Laurel Sherret, 'A Sight for Sore Eyes: Bringing Gender Vision to the Responsibility to Protect Framework', INSTRAW, March 2006. This in turn was based on Marilou McPhedran, Laurel Sherret and Jennifer Bond, 'R2P Missing Women – Canada's Responsibility to Perceive', a discussion paper for Fragile States Conference, 27 November 2005. See also Eli Stamnes, *The Responsibility to Protect: Integrating Gender Perspectives into Policies and Practices* (Oslo: Norwegian Institute of International Affairs, 2010).
[5] Charlesworth, 'Feminist Reflections on the Responsibility to Protect', at p. 249.
[6] Ibid.

world order. The Responsibility to Protect principle would also need to be framed more modestly, not as a single solution to atrocities, but as one strand of a complex response that draws inspiration and ideas from everyone affected by violence.

I assess current R2P claims against a spectrum of feminist reactions since 2009. R2P advocates seem to have largely ignored explicit gender issues, which have been taken up instead by the women, peace and security (WPS) agenda in a different UN Security Council silo focusing on thematic agendas. However, as noted, there is some alignment around the goal of accountability for sexual violence in conflict. This alignment rests on a presumption that the gender aspects of the four mass atrocity crimes that make up R2P are settled in law and in practice, which requires further interrogation. In return, feminists tend to have largely ignored R2P as a doctrine other than to express concerns about paternalism or imperialism in relation to the intervention pillar. I offer several ideas with which R2P advocates should engage in order to increase the possibility of wider support for the emerging norm.

About R2P: what's bred in the bone

The R2P had important antecedents that developed over a fairly short time frame (by UN standards), beginning with the December 2001 report of the International Commission on Intervention and State Sovereignty (ICISS), convened by the Canadian Government with only one female representative.[7] The R2P doctrine is essentially derived from three paragraphs of the 2005 World Summit Outcome outlining the responsibility of each state to protect its populations from genocide, war crimes, ethnic cleansing and crimes against humanity.[8]

This chapter focuses mainly on developments from January 2009 to May 2014, beginning with the release by the secretary-general of the report *Implementing the Responsibility to Protect*, followed by the

---

[7] International Commission on Intervention and State Sovereignty (ICISS), *The Responsibility to Protect: Research, Bibliography, and Background* (Ottawa: International Development Research Centre, 2001). Subsequent reports showed strong UN interest and slightly different iterations of the concept of the R2P, including Secretary-General's High-Level Panel on Threats, Challenges and Change, *A More Secure World: Our Shared Responsibility* (New York: United Nations, 2004); Secretary-General of the United Nations, *In Larger Freedom: Towards Development, Security and Human Rights for All* (New York: United Nations, 2005); as well as United Nations Security Council Resolutions 1674 (April 2006) and 1706 (August 2006) on Darfur.

[8] *World Summit Outcome*, Document A/RES/60/1 (New York: United Nations, 24 October 2005), paragraphs 138–140.

consideration of the report by the General Assembly in July 2009.[9] On 14 September 2009, the General Assembly adopted by consensus its first resolution on R2P, agreeing to hold further discussions on the international understanding to intervene to stop atrocities from taking place.[10] Since then, the secretary-general and the General Assembly have sought to 'operationalise' the doctrine but also debate the concept in order to allay concerns and misconceptions.[11] R2P can be best understood in this new implementation phase as 'three pillars and four crimes',[12] to be implemented in a way that is 'narrow but deep'.[13] Pillar One represents the primacy of state responsibility, Pillar Two refers to the duty of the international community to provide assistance, and Pillar Three is that the international community will react to violations such as genocide and mass atrocity in a timely and decisive manner.[14] The emphasis of the R2P doctrine in its implementation phase has been on the prevention of genocide and mass atrocities.

With apologies to Homer, these three World Summit paragraphs have launched one thousand interpretations, with the academy split between prophets[15] and blasphemers,[16] operationalists and comparators.[17] The doctrine has also generated a plethora of toolkits, protection pyramids and military doctrines. The most challenging proposition is whether R2P can be of worth when only weaker states will ever be the recipients of intervention due to the operation of the Security Council. There have often been allegations that R2P has a post-colonial or imperialist tang about it.[18] As Jose Alvarez puts it, there may be black marks 'built into the very soul' of R2P, which the implementation debate brings to light.[19]

---

[9] Ban Ki-moon, *Implementing the Responsibility to Protect*, Document A/63/67 (New York: United Nations, 17 January 2009).

[10] General Assembly Resolution 63/308 (2009).

[11] Ban Ki-moon, *Implementing the Responsibility to Protect*, at p. 1.

[12] Heraldo Muñoz, *The Responsibility to Protect: Three Pillars and Four Crimes* (Working Paper no. 53, *Human Rights and Human Welfare*, 1 August 2009).

[13] Ban Ki-moon, *Implementing the Responsibility to Protect*, at p. 2

[14] Ban Ki-moon, *Implementing the Responsibility to Protect*.

[15] See generally the writings of Alex J. Bellamy and Gareth Evans.

[16] See generally Jose Alvarez and Anne Orford.

[17] See further Joshua G. Smith, 'The Responsibility to Reflect: Learning Lessons from Past Humanitarian Military Interventions', *Journal of Humanitarian Assistance* (March 2006).

[18] Mark Busser, 'Interrogating the Ethics of the Responsibility to Protect', Paper presented at the International Studies Association 49th Annual Convention, San Francisco, 26 March 2008.

[19] Jose Alvarez, 'The schizophrenias of R2P', Hague Joint Conference on 100 years of international law, 30 June 2007, at p. 6.

These issues were aired at length in the 2011–2013 debates[20] about whether the Libya intervention had overreached its mandate to protect civilians and instead moved into regime change,[21] and about the Security Council's failure to respond to widespread violations and civilian deaths in Syria and Iraq.[22] The debates about R2P continue in 2014, but they are very rarely centred on questions of gender, not even questions of violations of the rights of women and girls in Libya, Iraq, DRC and Syria.[23] R2P debates are centred squarely on country contexts, as can be seen by the format of the Global Center for R2P Updates – unlike WPS debates which are global and focus on structural inequalities across nations and conflicts. WPS advocates often find it difficult to influence current crisis talks about gender issues in a country under discussion, for example Syria.[24] There are few debates in either practitioner or academic forums about whether and how the international community would respond to the protection needs of marginalised sections of the population, such as women in the Democratic Republic of Congo, as opposed to weaker states generally. The two communities are beginning to converge and debate.

About the women, peace and security agenda: agency and participation

A cluster of UN Security Council Resolutions (UNSCR) comprise the WPS agenda. Those resolutions are UNSCR 1325 (2000), UNSCR 1820 (2008), UNSCR 1888 (2009), UNSCR 1889 (2009), UNSCR 1960 (2010), UNSCR 2106 (2013) and UNSCR 2122 (2103).[25] In July 2013, a new Resolution, 2106, was passed during the United Kingdom's presidency, the fourth to focus on conflict-related sexual violence. This resolution adds greater operational detail and a focus on women protection advisers, and reiterates that all actors, including not only the Security Council and parties to armed conflict, but all

---

[20] See, for example, the robust exchange between Gareth Evans and Ramesh Thakur, and Robert A. Pape, in 'Correspondence: Humanitarian Intervention and the Responsibility to Protect', *International Security* 37:4 (2013), pp. 199–214.

[21] See further Alex J. Bellamy, 'Libya and the Responsibility to Protect: The Exception and the Norm', *Ethics and International Affairs* 25:3 (2011), pp. 263–269.

[22] Spencer Zifcak, 'The Responsibility to Protect after Libya and Syria', *Melbourne Journal of International Law* 13:1 (2012), pp. 1–35.

[23] The Responsibility to Protect has been reaffirmed by the Security Council in its Resolutions 1674 (2006), 1894 (2009), 2117 (2013) and 2150 (2014).

[24] Hibaaq Osman, 'Where Are the Syrian Women in the Geneva Peace Talks?', *The Guardian*, 23 January 2014.

[25] The full texts of the WPS core resolutions are available under their year of adoption from www.un.org/documents/scres.htm.

member states and United Nations entities, must do more to implement previous mandates and combat impunity for these crimes.[26] In October 2013, after an open debate on 'women, the rule of law and transitional justice in conflict affected situations', Resolution 2122 was adopted to request more regular briefings from relevant UN agencies, more attention to WPS issues when issuing or renewing mandates of UN missions, and committing to a High Level Review of implementation of WPS in 2015.[27]

In essence, the 1325 agenda states that women and girls experience conflict differently from men and boys.[28] Women have an essential role in conflict prevention, peace building and post-conflict reconstruction, and states are required to ensure women are represented in all decision-making.[29] The later resolutions focus on ending impunity for sexual violence in conflict and increasing the participation of women in the UN's own 'good offices' roles in mediating conflict and negotiating peace. Resolution 1325 was ground-breaking and the agenda led to the appointment of a new special rapporteur on sexual violence in conflict, Margot Wallström, in 2010 (currently Zainab Bangura holds this position), as well as annual reporting by the secretary-general.[30] One of the key actions is for states to design and implement National Action Plans. Thus far, only around forty countries have implemented National Action Plans, few are funded, and there are few or no baseline data for many of the actions.[31] This has led to claims that the institutional commitment is more rhetorical than real.

Even the rhetoric has proven controversial. In the last three years, debates on the thematic agendas have been criticised for extending beyond the Security Council's mandate (such as the focus on sexual

---

[26] United Nations Document S/RES/2106 (2013), Adopted by the Security Council at its 6984th meeting, 24 June 2013.

[27] Susan Harris Rimmer, 'When WPS met CEDAW (and Broke Up with R2P?), *E-International Relations*, 13 March 2014, available at www.e-ir.info/2014/03/13/when-wps-met-cedaw-and-broke-up-with-r2p.

[28] See further Special Issue: Australia on the UN Security Council: Progressing the Women, Peace and Security Agenda, *Australian Journal of International Affairs* 68:3 (2014).

[29] Louise Olsson and Theodora–Ismene Gizelis, 'An Introduction to UNSCR 1325', *International Interactions: Empirical and Theoretical Research in International Relations* 39:4 (2013), pp. 425–434.

[30] Christine Bell, *Women and Peace Processes, Negotiations, and Agreements: Operational Opportunities and Challenges* (Oslo: Policy Brief, The Norwegian Peacebuilding Resource Centre, 13 March 2013).

[31] Aisling Swaine, *National Implementation of the UN Security Council's Women, Peace and Security Resolutions* (Oslo: Policy Brief, The Norwegian Peacebuilding Resource Centre, 14 March 2013).

violence during election violence).[32] But there is some evidence that WPS issues are being considered more routinely in debates, affecting mandate design and adding weight to the 'zero tolerance' policy for UN peace-keeping forces[33] Other commentators argue that the resolutions and resulting actions have focused too much on the protection of civilians agenda or sexual violence, and not enough on participation and conflict prevention; in other words, 'women's agency'.[34] There are critiques that WPS has struggled with gender mainstreaming, the gendered nature of peace and security institutions[35] and the lack of sex-disaggregated data required to underpin policy.[36]

As a piece of polylateral diplomacy,[37] linked to both regional and global social movements, the women, peace and security agenda is strong, despite wide acknowledgement of its flaws.[38] Advocates argue that the core premise of the WPS agenda remains being attentive to the security needs of half the world's population, and thereby builds the legitimacy of the Security Council as a normative actor. So how have these two

---

[32] United Nations Security Council, 'Third Cross–Cutting Report on the Women, Peace and Security Agenda' (2013), available at www.securitycouncilreport.org/cross–cutting–report /women–peace–and–security–sexual–violence–in–conflict–and–sanctions.php, accessed 13 March 2013, at p. 9.

[33] Op cit.

[34] Inger Skjelsbaek, 'Responsibility to Protect or Prevent? Victims and Perpetrators of Sexual Violence Crimes in Armed Conflicts', *Global Responsibility to Protect* 4:2 (2012), pp. 154–171 at p. 163.

[35] For example, Charlesworth cites a UNIFEM study in 2009 found that only 2.4 per cent of signatories to peace agreements since 1992 had been women and that no woman had ever been designated as a 'chief mediator' by the United Nations: Charlesworth, 'Feminist Reflections on the Responsibility to Protect', at p. 245. See further Christine Bell and Catherine O'Rourke, 'Peace Agreements or "Pieces of Paper"? The Impact of UNSC Resolution 1325 on Peace Processes and their Agreements', *International and Comparative Law Quarterly* 59 (2010), pp. 941–980.

[36] Chantal de Jonge Oudraat, 'UNSCR 1325—Conundrums and Opportunities', *International Interactions: Empirical and Theoretical Research in International Relations* 39:4 (2013), pp. 612–619.

[37] Geoffrey Wiseman, *'Polylateralism' and New Modes of Global Dialogue* (Leicester: Discussion Papers No. 59, Leicester Diplomatic Studies Programme, 1999), at p. 41: 'My working definition of this concept is: "the conduct of relations between official entities (such as a state, several states acting together, or a state–based international organisation) and at least one unofficial, non–state entity in which there is a reasonable expectation of systematic relationships, involving some form of reporting, communication, negotiation, and representation, but not involving mutual recognition as sovereign, equivalent entities"'.

[38] For example, see the websites of the NGO Working Group on WPS at www.women peacesecurity.org/about/ and the Women's International League of Peace and Freedom (WILPF) at www.peacewomen.org/, as well as a wide array of academic and activist groups. For similar R2P groups, see The International Coalition for the Responsibility to Protect (ICRtoP) at icrtopblog.org/ and the Global Center for R2P, www.globalr2p.org/.

communities of practice revolving around the Security Council interacted with each other?

Initial feminist reactions to R2P

How have various groupings of women leaders, organisations and academics responded to R2P, and has this response changed or developed? The response of many grass-roots civil society organisations has been generally positive, if muted, since the ICISS report, mostly because their attention has focused on the possibility of links between R2P and Security Council Resolution 1325, which, as explained above, focuses on the wider agenda of inclusion of women in decision-making around peace and peacebuilding.

Principle and pragmatism

By and large, female leaders of international humanitarian agencies have been positive about R2P, but less interested in the fine print. In some ways, this shows acceptance of the principle and reflects self-interests. As the secretary-general says, 'there is a common element in these diverse efforts to help States help themselves: they largely depend on civilian, not military, expertise and presence'.[39] Even where humanitarian experts such as Roberta Cohen have had weighty criticisms of the doctrine, they have still come down in support.[40] Mostly this is because of the appeal of the principle expressed in the doctrine. Erika Feller, from UNHCR, expressed the hope in 2006 that the international adoption of R2P would enable states to move beyond issues of sovereignty and security in order to respond in a more pure sense to human suffering:[41]

The significance of the concept of a responsibility to protect is that it does not rest on mandates, or indeed on international conventions. Rather, it comes into play in response to needs … The protection situation may be equally acute for an earthquake victim in Pakistan, for an IDP in the Sudan, or for a victim of trafficking in Eastern Europe.

---

[39] Ban Ki-moon, *Implementing the Responsibility to Protect*, at p. 18.

[40] Roberta Cohen, 'The Responsibility to Protect: The Human Rights and Humanitarian Dimensions', *Harvard Human Rights Journal Annual Symposium*, February. Available at www.reliefweb.int/rw/rwb.nsf/db900SID/VDUX-7PTTLY?OpenDocument, accessed 12 March 2013.

[41] Erika Feller, 'The Responsibility to Protect – Closing the Gaps in the International Protection Regime and the New EXCOM Conclusion on Complementary Forms of Protection', Speech delivered at 'Moving on: Forced Migration and Human Rights', Conference, New South Wales Parliament House, Sydney, 22 November 2005.

The second reason is because many field-based civil society groups and agencies feel that the root of many of their problems in attempting to protect civilians lies in being unable to engage political will from key states in a timely manner, and then converting this will into practical assistance. For example, in Syria in 2012–2014, humanitarian agencies were advocating strongly for humanitarian access to civilians caught up in the conflict and prevention of further harm. The R2P doctrine holds such promise, over time, although possibly not yet if the recent Security Council debates on Syria and Iraq (or lack thereof) are any guide. As the then High Commissioner for Human Rights Navi Pillay said in 2009, 'we should all undertake an honest assessment of our ability to save lives in extraordinary situations'.[42] Much depends, therefore, on how the R2P doctrine is implemented. If invocations of R2P lead to humanitarian access, the doctrine receives support.

Female political leaders have also been supportive. For example, the International Women Leaders Global Security Summit was held on 15–17 November 2007 in New York City, co-hosted by H.E. Mary Robinson, president of Ireland (1990–1997), and the Rt. Hon. Kim Campbell, prime minister of Canada (1993). This Summit brought together sixty-eight women leaders from thirty-six countries, and the subsequent report shows that there is firm support for the R2P doctrine, as is clear from the following extract:[43]

Women leaders have been particularly effective in mediating complex conflicts and are acutely aware of the social, economic and political effects of mass atrocity and armed conflict. The collective experience of women leaders uniquely positions them to articulate the priorities of the emerging R2P norm ... The responsibility to protect strongly complements existing commitments to protect women's human rights and security and should be incorporated into existing work programmes and advocacy efforts. There is a pressing need for more champions worldwide and in particular for women leaders to add their voices and efforts to those who and in particular for women leaders to add their voices and efforts to those who believe in and advocate for the protection of civilians from genocide and crimes against humanity.

The working group did acknowledge that the R2P doctrine requires more clarification as to scope, prevention and implementation. There is significant conflation with the WPS agenda. It stated that 'monitoring and early warning systems do not yet exist with appropriate mechanisms to trigger action. When action is a real possibility, then scope of mandate

---

[42] 'Assembly President warns on doctrine to intervene on war crimes, atrocities', UN News Centre, 23 July 2009.

[43] Antonia Potter and Jaime Peters, *International Women Leaders Global Security Summit Report* (February 2008), at p. 6.

and provision of resources become problematic'.[44] The recommendations from the women leaders emphasised political leadership, non-
violent resolution of conflict, humanitarian values, a consistent and
agreed threshold for intervention, and female participation and agency.[45]

Ambivalence and exclusion

There was early discontent expressed by many civil society organisations
about the lack of gender analysis in the ICISS report and the lack of
representation on the ICISS (one woman, eleven men) and the high-level
panels (four women, twelve men). Ambassador Swanee Hunt stated in
2009: 'So it's tragic that R2P is not rising to the standard of inclusion
mandated by the UN itself. Tragic, but understandable, since the traditional security paradigm was created by men for men.'[46]

This is more a reaction to the proponents of R2P than the doctrine
itself, the perception that R2P advocacy was a 'boys' club' or an exclusive
community of distinguished international civil servants and academics.[47]
Some pacifist women's organisations such as the Women's International

---

[44] Potter and Peters, *International Women Leaders Global Security Summit Report*, at p. 9.

[45] "To fulfill the responsibility to protect, we must:

Actively reinforce the global consensus that all nations bear collective responsibility to
protect civilian populations from genocide, war crimes, ethnic cleansing and crimes
against humanity.

Clearly and consistently articulate the international community's responsibility to
first take action through diplomatic and other non-violent means when states fail to
prevent or respond effectively to the above mentioned crimes, even when committed by
non-state actors.

Press government representatives at the United Nations to articulate a clear threshold
for taking military action to prevent these crimes, and to press the UN Security Council
to authorize decisive and timely action when this threshold is crossed.

Insist that women's views are sought and women leaders are included in all peace and
security initiatives, including Track I and II negotiations.

End impunity for violence against women and promote gender awareness in all stages
of peace processes by mandating training for civilian and military personnel on the
various ways insecurity manifests for women, including rape, murder, sexual harassment,
unfair treatment and unequal power relations between men and women.

Call on world leaders to protect the impartial and independent space of humanitarian
actors working alongside military forces in areas of crisis".

Extracted from Potter and Peters, *International Women Leaders Global Security Summit
Report*, at p. 9.

[46] Swanee Hunt, 'The UN's R2P Report Is Missing Out by Half', *Huffington Post*, available
at www.huffingtonpost.com/swanee–hunt/the–uns–r2p–report–is–mis_b_171198.html,
2 March 2009, accessed April 2009.

[47] Caritas, University of Sydney, and Global Action to Prevent War, New York, *Right to
Protection: Whose Responsibility and How?*, available at www.sydney.edu.au/arts/peace
_conflict/research/AH_Conference%20report%202.pdf, September 2008, accessed 18
February 2013, at p. 3.

League of Peace and Freedom reject the concept of armed intervention outright and the general air of paternalism in the intervention pillar.

There has been a split reaction from many feminists to this idea of R2P as an elitist edifice, linked to the criticism that R2P is dangerously interventionist. Karen Engle has argued cogently against forcing those who want to redress a major problem to present it 'in terms of a crisis that only immediate military intervention can resolve'.[48] But despite these reactions, there has been limited sustained academic feminist analysis of the R2P doctrine as noted.

The responsibility to be gender-sensitive

R2P agents have taken on board and begun to address some of the critiques offered by gender advocates, but also to increase support through a potentially powerful alliance with the WPS supporter group and take advantage of their legitimacy.

At the UN, these links were made much earlier. The secretary-general has attempted to incorporate some gender analysis and linkages between R2P and the WPS agenda in his annual reports. In his 2009 report *Implementing the Responsibility to Protect*, Ban Ki-moon confirmed that rape and other forms of sexual violence could constitute crimes against humanity, war crimes or constitutive acts with respect to genocide, which constitute the foundational crimes which trigger R2P.[49] He also stated (somewhat obliquely) that gender-based violence could be an early warning indicator of mass atrocities, reiterated in the 2013 report on prevention.[50] This was reaffirmed more clearly in the secretary-general's 2010 R2P report[51] and his 2011 report on regional arrangements and R2P.[52] His 2012 report on timely and decisive responses does not contain

---

[48] Karen Engle, '"Calling in the Troops": The Uneasy Relationship among Women's Rights, Human Rights, and Humanitarian Intervention', *Harvard Human Rights Journal* 20 (2007), pp. 189–226 at p. 190.

[49] Ban Ki-moon, *Implementing the Responsibility to Protect*, at paragraph 34.

[50] Ban Ki-moon, *Implementing the Responsibility to Protect*, paragraph 3, at p. 31.

[51] UN Secretary-General, *Early Warning, Assessment and the Responsibility to Protect*, Document A/64/864 (New York: United Nations, 14 July 2010), paragraph 12 at p. 5. 'Such groups may be among the first to detect an upsurge in the persecution or demonization of minorities, in patterns of sexual and gender-based violence, in the recruitment of child soldiers, in forced internal displacement or in the employment of hateful and dangerous speech to spur violence against targeted groups within a society'. UN Secretary-General, *Responsibility to Protect: State Responsibility and Prevention*, Document A/67/929-S/2013/399 (New York: United Nations, 2013) at paragraph 32.

[52] UN Secretary-General, *Role of Regional and Sub-Regional Arrangements in Implementing Responsibility to Protect*, Document A/65/877–S/2011/393 (New York: United Nations, 27 June 2011), at paragraph 26, p. 8: 'The danger of mass atrocity crimes, particularly

any gender analysis per se.[53] His 2014 report encourages any measure, noting the 1325 agenda, that protects 'vulnerable populations'.[54]

The secretary-general did, however, release a report in January 2012 entitled *Conflict-Related Sexual Violence* in response to WPS resolutions, including country situations on the UNSC agenda. The issue was not linked to R2P explicitly, but certainly considered within the protection of civilians frame. It stated that 'security forces are mandated to protect, not prey upon, the civilian population. The uniform should symbolize security, discipline and public service, rather than rape, pillage and terror.'[55] These reports are now released annually and debated by the UNSC in March, with an annexed 'List of parties credibly suspected of committing or being responsible for patterns of rape and other forms of sexual violence in situations of armed conflict on the agenda of the Security Council'.[56]

The International Coalition for R2P, one of the leading organisations advocating for R2P, also released a report and an opinion piece on International Women's Day 2012, stating that[57]

women must be included as equal players in the international community who can contribute to preventing mass atrocities, assisting in protection, resolving conflict, and securing lasting peace and justice. To date, however, gaps remain as steps have not been taken to truly engender RtoP [...]

the role of women in the prevention of mass atrocities has yet to be formally recognized in the context of RtoP, and is reflective of a broader gap in the number of women participating in prevention, protection, and rebuilding in a conflict setting.

In 2012 a Special Issue of the *Global Responsibility to Protect* journal was released on 'R2P and Sexual and Gender Based violence'. It was based on an Australian workshop on women, peace and security and opportunities for alignment with Responsibility to Protect, and represents the most

---

involving sexual and gender-based violence, is most acute where the rule of law is weak and the security sector is in need of substantial reform.'

[53] UN Secretary-General, *The Responsibility to Protect: Timely and Decisive Response*, Document A/66/874–S/2012/578 (New York: United Nations, 5 September 2012), followed by an informal interactive dialogue hosted by the General Assembly.

[54] UN Secretary-General, *Fulfilling Our Collective Responsibility: International Assistance and the Responsibility to Protect*, Document A/68/947-S/2014/449 (New York, UN, September 2014).

[55] UN Secretary-General, *Conflict–Related Sexual Violence* Documents A/67/792-S/2013/149 (New York: United Nations, 11 March 2013) and S/2014/181 (13 March 2014).

[56] UN Secretary-General, *Conflict–Related Sexual Violence*, paragraph 5.

[57] ICRtoP, 'Women and the Responsibility to Protect', blog post 9 March 2012, available at www.icrtopblog.org/2012/03/09/women-and-the-responsibility-to-protect; 'The Role of Women in the RtoP Framework' (undated), available at www.responsibilityto protect.org/index.php/women-and-conflict.

thorough academic investigation of the idea of whether R2P is gender-neutral conducted thus far. The dialogue focused on three central themes: (1) What states should do to realise the goals set out in UN Security Council Resolution 1325; (2) The advantages and disadvantages associated with the alignment of R2P with WPS in the fields of international policing and peacekeeping, conflict resolution, peacebuilding and transitional justice; and (3) The extent to which the structural prevention ambitions of WPS can be assisted by association with early warning and assessment mechanisms relating to genocide, war crimes, ethnic cleansing and crimes against humanity.[58] The participants focused on strengths and weaknesses of both the WPS and R2P agendas.

For WPS, the problems were perceived to be the lack of implementation and resourcing of National Action Plans; the small number of women engaged in conflict prevention, resolution and rebuilding and in senior positions in peacekeeping, policing and special political missions; and the concern that the WPS agenda has been too focused on protection of women from sexual violence and not on 'establishing awareness of the link between armed conflict and women's daily lived experience, often characterised by domestic violence, inequality before the law, lack of access to education and constrained economic opportunities'.[59] It further stated that[60]

the failure thus far to draw links between WPS and R2P raises the likelihood that states and international organisations will continue to fail to prevent sexual and gender based violence, in part because gender-specific considerations have not been built into early warning and assessment mechanisms relating to the 'R2P crimes' (genocide, war crimes, ethnic cleansing and crimes against humanity). Indeed, it was noted that the academic literature on early warning tended to overlook the role of gender, gender inequality and gendered violence.

In relation to R2P, three 'worries' were set out, some strategic, some conceptual. R2P was seen by some participants as a 'controversial concept', which therefore might undermine political support for WPS. Some felt the R2P principle 'effectively reduced women to the status of passive victims in need of protection. By reinforcing state sovereignty, some suggested, R2P might actually give fresh legitimacy to systems of domination that endanger and marginalize women.' This concern correlates to Charlesworth's observation that R2P, whether in its prevention, reaction or rebuilding phases, 'requires the importation of expertise; it

[58] Sara Davies, 'Preventing, Protecting and Empowering: Women, Peace and Security and R2P' (blog), available at www.protectiongateway.com/2012/10/30/r2pandwps/, 30 October 2012.
[59] Davies, 'Preventing, Protecting and Empowering: Women, Peace and Security and R2P'.
[60] Ibid.

involves top-down intervention, with little emphasis on empowering local people, particularly women'.[61] Finally, participants felt that R2P ignored the idea women might also be perpetrators of crimes and sidelined the measures that women adopt to protect themselves.[62]

In the special issue that followed the workshop, a high-quality and wide range of views about R2P were aired, primarily from WPS scholars approaching R2P. Bond and Sherret argue that even though R2P has been developed in parallel to WPS, the achievement of peace and security for women is crucial to its goals, and the evidence is increasing that gender equality measures reduce the risk of violent conflict.[63] Furthermore, 'sovereigns cannot realize their protection responsibilities unless they have established the framework, policies and environment that protect the groups at highest risk and most vulnerable to the R2P four crimes'.[64]

Bond and Sherret are persuasive as to why R2P should take on board more gender analysis to its own benefit. Sara E. Davies and Sarah Teitt focus more on the 'how', recommending early warning, engaging the Security Council to adopt measures to curb the widespread or systematic commission of violence against women, building national capacity to prevent such abuse and identifying obstacles to the prevention of mass sexual violence.[65] They admit that the history of R2P has not included language that deliberately evokes the protection of women and the promotion of gender in preventing genocide and mass atrocities, but state that this does not preclude the R2P and WPS agendas becoming mutually reinforcing.[66] And yet this logical interaction has not in fact occurred. Framing the links between the doctrines only in terms of SGBV means that some of the most difficult issues to resolve are left out, relating to wider women's participation and agency.

Davies and Teitt also put forward the view that 'the omission of specific references to women and gender in R2P texts does not mean women are "missing" or "ignored" because protection of women is embedded within

---

[61] Charlesworth, 'Feminist Reflections on the Responsibility to Protect', at p. 244.

[62] Ibid.

[63] Jennifer Bond and Laurel Sherret, 'Mapping Gender and the Responsibility to Protect: Seeking Intersections, Finding Parallels', *Global Responsibility to Protect* 4:2 (2012), pp. 133–153.

[64] Bond and Sherret, 'Mapping Gender and the Responsibility to Protect', summarised by Sara E. Davies and Eli Stamnes, 'Introduction', *Global Responsibility to Protect* 4:2 (2012), at p. 129.

[65] Sara E Davies and Sarah Teitt, 'Engendering the Responsibility to Protect: Women and the Prevention of Mass Atrocities', *Global Responsibility to Protect* 4:2 (2012), pp. 198–222 at p. 200.

[66] Davies and Teitt, 'Engendering the Responsibility to Protect', at p. 198.

the principle's scope via the four crimes to which it applies'.[67] This view runs counter to the analysis of many feminist international lawyers that the SGBV categories under international criminal law are not yet closed, and their investigation and prosecution are still tenuous or absent in many international contexts. For example, forced maternity outside the context of genocide or rape is not itself a war crime.[68]

R2P and WPS: uneasy convergence

Taking Charlesworth's 2010 reflections as a starting point, we can trace gender developments and offer a preliminary assessment.[69]

Have R2P debates taken into account a broader set of factors that impinge on women's lives, including women's economic marginalisation, the effect of militarisation and systemic discrimination against women? Have R2P advocates engaged with the private subordination of women and the widespread violence against them outside the formal structures of the state?

Not yet, but the WPS agenda also needs to go deeper in this regard. The 'narrow but deep' approach to preventing and responding to the four R2P crimes does not naturally draw the eye to wider patterns of systemic inequality within a state, and there is no consideration of issues of religion, culture or political economy. This in turn makes the construction of gender-sensitive early warning systems less likely to be achieved successfully to prevent the four crimes occurring against women and girls. Also, the focus on battle deaths in the intervention debates in Libya and Syria can obfuscate the narrative of what is happening to women and girls in terms of non-battle deaths due to maternal mortality or other health issues, economic hardship, changes in religious laws (such as virginity tests) and the experience of displacement.

R2P advocates have not brought enough gender awareness generally to the responsibility to rebuild. Women's rights are indeed often at risk of being traded for the support of political factions in post-conflict situations; for example, in attempts to engage with the Taliban in Afghanistan. Moreover, the R2P principle currently marginalises women's experiences through the prominence it accords to ex-combatants in the context of peace-making and rebuilding after conflict.[70]

---

[67] Davies and Teitt, 'Engendering the Responsibility to Protect', at p. 204. See further Sara E. Davies, Zim Nwokora, Eli Stamnes and Sara Teitt, eds, *Responsibility to Protect and Women Peace and Security: Aligning the Protection Agendas* (Leiden: Martinus Nijhoff, 2013).

[68] Susan Harris Rimmer, *Gender and Transitional Justice: The Women of Timor Leste* (London: Routledge, 2010), at pp. 120–123.

[69] Charlesworth, 'Feminist Reflections on the Responsibility to Protect', at p. 249.

[70] Ibid., at p. 244.

Have R2P advocates problematised the idea of intervention, recognising that it can exacerbate injustices by reinforcing particular forms of world order?

There has certainly been more analysis of the threshold and evolution of intervention mandates under R2P in the wake of the Libyan intervention and the lack of ability to gain traction to address the conflict in Syria, as can be seen in the 2012 report of the secretary-general. But even so, evidence of mass rape within Syria did not gain political attention in the manner that the possible use of chemical weapons did. A report released in January 2012 by the International Rescue Committee identified rape as the first reason why Syrians were leaving as refugees – up to 600,000 had left at that point; the figure now stands at 3.2 million.[71] Marcos Méndez has noted that the countries that make up the Group of 8 are able to agree on a *Declaration on Preventing Sexual Violence in Conflict* but are at the same time completely paralysed regarding the Syrian war.[72]

In 27 April 2010, when the then special rapporteur called the DRC the 'rape capital of the world',[73] the UN had not made significant investments or had significant success in the prevention of sexual violence in that territory. But there has been some progress on another conflict which has had truly awful consequences for women and girls but received little accountability or political attention, as noted in the secretary-general's report on *Conflict-Related Sexual Violence*. He named the 23 March Movement (M23, also known as the Congolese Revolutionary Army) as a key perpetrator.[74] On 28 March 2013, weeks before the shameful manner in which women and girls were treated in the incident recalled at the opening of this chapter, the UN Security Council authorised the establishment of an 'Intervention Brigade' to counter rebel groups in North Kivu province in the eastern part of the Democratic Republic of Congo, bordering Rwanda (Security Council Resolution 2098). The brigade (roughly 3,000 troops) is to operate within the UN Organization Stabilization Mission in the Democratic Republic of the Congo (MONUSCO) and has been established for 12 months. The brigade is headquartered in Goma. MONUSCO's mandate has been extended until 31 March 2015.[75]

---

[71] International Rescue Committee, *Syria: A Regional Crisis* (New York: International Rescue Committee, January 2013.

[72] Marcos Méndez, 'Male War, Male Peace' (Blog) OpenDemocracy, 25 July 2013, available at www.opendemocracy.net/opensecurity/marcos-m%C3%A9ndez/male-war-male-peace.

[73] UN News Centre, 'Tackling sexual violence must include prevention, ending impunity – UN official', 27 April 2010.

[74] UN Secretary-General, *Conflict-Related Sexual Violence*.

[75] United Nations Security Council, *Special Report of the Secretary-General on the Democratic Republic of the Congo and the Great Lakes Region*, Document S/2013/119, February, 27,

Resolution 2098 creates the first combat force with a mandate to carry out targeted operations to 'neutralize and disarm' a range of armed groups. Specified groups include the M23, the Lord's Resistance Army (LRA) and the Democratic Forces for the Liberation of Rwanda (FDLR). Resolution 2098 mandates the intervention brigade to carry out offensive operations both unilaterally and jointly with the Congolese army 'in a robust, highly mobile and versatile manner' in order to combat armed groups (paragraph 9). The resolution states that the Intervention Brigade must operate 'in strict compliance with international law, including international humanitarian law and with the human rights due diligence policy on UN-support to non-UN forces' (paragraph 12 (b)). The Brigade has not yet had a measurable impact on the diminution of violence against women in the DRC, with the secretary-general noting a 14 per cent increase in sexual violence in his 2014 report.

A more positive move was the appointment of former President of Ireland and UN High Commissioner for Human Rights Mary Robinson as special envoy for the Great Lakes Region on 18 March 2013, her term ending on 17 July 2014. Robinson deployed considerable energy and political capital in bringing the suffering and the potential contribution of the women of DRC to international attention. As Charlesworth notes: 'it is all too rare that women are appointed to such positions and it brings some substance to the Security Council's urging of the UN Secretary-General in SCR 1325 (2000) "to appoint more women as special representatives and envoys to pursue good offices on his behalf"'.[76]

Has the Responsibility to Protect principle been framed more modestly, not as a single solution to atrocities, but as one strand of a complex response that draws inspiration and ideas from everyone affected by violence?

A certain modesty has infused R2P debates since the backlash against the Libyan intervention. Gareth Evans and Ramesh Thakur hold fast that the intervention saved 'tens of thousands of lives, in Benghazi and elsewhere', but that they are 'not so sure that the NATO-led operation in Libya remained a textbook case for its duration'.[77] The secretary-general's reports and subsequent debates, as well as the burgeoning academic writing on R2P, have gone some way to considering a wider range of issues than military responses to atrocities that can be framed as a crisis. However, several

---

2013; United Nations Security Council, *'Intervention Brigade' Authorized as Security Council Grants Mandate Renewal for United Nations Mission in Democratic Republic of Congo*, Document SC/10964, Security Council 6943rd Meeting, 28 March 2013.

[76] Charlesworth, 'New Forms of Peacekeeping', available at asiapacific.anu.edu.au/regarding-rights/2013/04/12/new-forms-of-peacekeeping/.

[77] Gareth Evans and Ramesh Thakur, 'Correspondence: Humanitarian Intervention and the Responsibility to Protect', pp. 205–206.

initiatives have not gone forward, such as Edward Luck's recommendation to form a working group on women and R2P. The areas identified by Davies and Teitt for collaboration are a very good start for further engagement.

Conclusion

R2P is not gender-neutral, but it may have a gender blind spot.[78] Some of this could be cured by inclusion strategies and a more deliberate gender lens, working against the idea of an 'elite' group and seeking to actively support the WPS agenda where it overlaps with R2P aims. Some of the flaws are not within R2P itself as a concept but in the current paradigm of the Security Council in which both doctrines try to influence state actors unwilling to embrace wider ideas of how to maintain peace and security.

Those huddled women and children outside the SANDF-Munigi compound would likely not find much comfort in the UN's performance in DRC, even with the 'Intervention Brigade'. Current reports by the secretary-general[79] or UNSC Resolution 2147 (2014) are unlikely to reassure or inspire them to feel included or protected.[80] On 28 October 2014, the UN Security Council marked the 14th anniversary of the adoption of resolution 1325 (2000) by holding an Open Debate on 'Women and peace and security', with a particular focus on forced displacement. Some 6.3 million people from the DRC, of whom an estimated 2.6 million were internally displaced, were still in need of assistance as of September 2014, but only 35 per cent of the US$839 million required for the humanitarian response had been received.[81] However, the Military Gender Field Advisory section of MONUSCO finally began work on 1 October 2014 in Goma.

This consideration of the gender status of R2P has raised many larger questions. Can the role the Security Council plays in R2P interventions be a more modest one – promoting norms in resolutions, shaping the mandates of peacekeeping operations (PKO), referring cases to the

---

[78] Eli Stamnes, *The Responsibility to Protect: Integrating Gender Perspectives into Policies and Practices* (Oslo: Norwegian Institute of International Affairs, 2010), at p. 9.

[79] United Nations Security Council, *Report of the Secretary-General on the Implementation of the Peace, Security and Cooperation Framework for the Democratic Republic of the Congo and the Region*, Document S/2014/697, 24 September 2014.

[80] At paragraph 27: 'Requests MONUSCO to take fully into account gender considerations as a cross cutting issue throughout its mandate and to assist the Government of DRC in ensuring the participation, involvement and representation of women at all levels, including in stabilization activities, security sector reform and disarmament, demobilization and reintegration processes, as well as in the national political dialogue and electoral processes, through, inter alia, the provision of gender advisers.'

[81] UNSC, *Report of the Secretary-General on the Implementation of the Peace, Security and Cooperation Framework for the Democratic Republic of Congo and the Region*.

International Criminal Court? Should the Security Council focus more
on the R2P prevention pillar of peace-making and post-conflict peace
building? What would need to happen for the prevention pillar to gain
more traction in international debates? Does the culture of militarism and
crisis undermine the neutrality of humanitarian assistance and the promotion of women's rights? What will be the interplay between R2P and
the new gender architecture at the UN?

Generally, this analysis has found that the relationship of R2P to the
women, peace and security agenda at the Security Council is usually
overlooked or undercooked, despite direct relevance to at least two R2P
pillars. The WPS agenda lacks consistent implementation by UN members; in fact, women's rights are often traded for the support of political
factions in post-conflict situations. If the Security Council cannot follow
its own rules, what hope should women have that R2P would be applied
in their interests in an intervention? Military intervention to protect
women's rights uses a volatile and risky technique to support women's
equality, one that is easily misused and indeed capable of exacerbating
violence against women. R2P advocates need to build trust, make some
gains for women within the other R2P pillars and deliberately include the
participation of more and diverse women in shaping its ambitious vision
for the future.

15   The Responsibility to Protect: a Western idea?

Jacinta O'Hagan

Introduction

The Responsibility to Protect has been hailed as one of the most significant normative developments in world politics since 1945, a 'normative breakthrough that lays the foundation for a new international politics of mass atrocities'.[1] Its endorsement at the 2005 United Nations World Summit provided an unprecedented acknowledgement by the global community that such responsibilities exist. This endorsement of R2P represents a quintessential cosmopolitan moment in world politics – it demonstrated recognition that there is an obligation to respond to harms visited upon others, and that this obligation is not confined by the political boundaries of the state.

At the same time, eddying around R2P since its inception has been the question of whether it represents a genuine universal consensus on how to respond to mass atrocity crimes. R2P remains dogged by accusations that it does not in fact represent a universal doctrine; rather it is but another iteration of the interests of the powerful over the weak cloaked in the language of universals, a means for the projection of the values and interests of the West. The backlash generated by NATO's action in Libya and the subsequent inability of the international community to reach a consensus to implement an R2P mandate in Syria added grist to the mill of such critiques. These differing interpretations of the purposes of R2P speak to a critical question that is central to any theoretical analysis of R2P: is it an innately Western idea?

This question can be addressed at an empirical level: who formulated, promoted and has supported R2P? To what extent has the development

I am grateful to Luke Glanville, Andrew Garwood-Gowers and William Maley for their very useful insights and comments in relation to preliminary drafts of this chapter.
[1] Alex Bellamy, *Global Politics and the Responsibility to Protect: From Words to Deeds* (London and New York: Routledge, 2011), p. 6.

of R2P been driven by the West? However, the question can also be posed at a deeper level: can we say that the ethical premises that lie at the heart of R2P reflect the moral and political values of a particular society, that of the West? These questions bring to the fore the issue of the cultural politics of R2P. Despite the copious materials produced in recent years on R2P, this is an aspect of R2P which had been somewhat neglected;[2] and yet the evolution of R2P is deeply embedded in the cultural politics of the international system. An important aspect of this is the degree to which the modern system was shaped by the expansion of the West and resistance to it. This story of expansion and resistance forms the crucial context within which R2P has evolved. This chapter argues that as a framework for responding to mass atrocity crimes, R2P is not in itself a Western idea. However, the institution that it promotes as the principal vehicle to prevent the eventuation of such atrocities – sovereignty – is an innately Western idea in so far as it is derived from Western political theory and historical experiences. Even those who critique or reject R2P do so in the name of protecting sovereignty. Sovereignty therefore is both a site of contest in the debate surrounding R2P but also the mechanism being used to build consensus on how to respond to mass atrocity crimes.

There are inherent risks in invoking grand cultural identities such as the West. Principal among these are the dangers of essentialisation and homogenisation of complex societies and processes. The West is an amorphous and fluid concept, invoked to mean a multitude of things in different contexts. Yet at the same time, to invoke the West is to invoke a range of critical reference points, which can be used to locate oneself or others in broader structures of history, power and politics. Similarly there is a risk of generating homogenised and essentialised conceptions of non-Western societies. While alert to the risk of essentialisation and wary of falling into its pitfalls, I would argue that the power of the West as a signifier of identity of power relationships makes the discourse of the West and non-West a factor we cannot ignore in theorising R2P.[3]

This chapter proceeds in two sections. It first discusses the roots of concepts of sovereignty, responsibility and protection, and their reso-nances in non-Western societies. It then examines cultural politics of the empirical development of R2P. In both sections it reflects on the importance of the legacies of the cultural politics of the international system for understanding non-Western attitudes towards R2P.

---

[2] An important contribution to this field is Rama Mani and Thomas. G. Weiss, *The Responsibility to Protect: Cultural Perspectives in the Global South* (London and New York: Routledge, 2011).

[3] The terms non-West and global South are often treated as synonymous in the literature and are used interchangeably in this chapter.

The cultural politics of sovereignty and responsibility

Thinking theoretically about R2P means thinking about the genres of responsibilities it entails. In the first instance R2P is a doctrine that focuses on accountability: who or what can be held accountable for the protection of populations from egregious harms? It expresses both a positive and a negative conception: there is a responsibility both to afford protection as well as not to violate the most basic right of populations: the right to life. It is a doctrine that focuses on responsibility as a set of prospective duties. In the first instance it is the duty to prevent. Only when prevention has failed is the responsibility to act invoked. It both invokes a legal responsibility to conform with existing bodies of international humanitarian and human rights law, but also a strong sense of moral responsibility; and it seeks to embed this as a powerful international norm. R2P speaks to specific responsibilities of authorities to protect their own peoples from harm, but also more extensive responsibilities of the international community to provide support and protection where the state fails to do this.

The core puzzle that lies at the heart of R2P is the relationship between sovereignty, responsibility and protection. Asking whether R2P is an innately Western idea entails asking to what extent approaches to these concepts and this relationship are innately Western. There are powerful links between Western history and political thought, and conceptions of sovereign responsibility. Sovereignty is defined in this chapter as 'legitimated claims to political authority'.[4] It is a fluid rather than a static concept, the social construction of which varies across time and context.[5] The predominant conception of sovereignty in the modern international system is one of 'supreme authority within a territory' that emerges from the Westphalian moment in European history. A further 'revolution' in sovereignty came with the American and French Revolutions, which shifted the locus of sovereignty from the divinely ordained ruler to the people.[6] This is a concept of sovereignty premised on conceptions of natural liberty and the fundamental right to self-determination. Sovereignty as we envisage it today, therefore, has deep roots in Western political thought and history. However, this conception of sovereignty became embedded into the

---

[4] Luke Glanville, 'The Antecedents of "sovereignty as responsibility"', *European Journal of International Relations* 17:2 (2010), pp. 233–255, at p. 236.

[5] Christian Reus-Smit, 'Human Rights and the Social Construction of Sovereignty', *Review of International Studies* 27:4 (2001), pp. 519–538; Jens Bartleson, *A Genealogy of Sovereignty* (Cambridge: Cambridge University Press, 1995).

[6] Daniel Philpott, *Revolutions in Sovereignty: How Ideas Shaped Modern International Relations* (Princeton: Princeton University Press, 2001).

foundations of modern international system through the processes of deco-lonisation and the UN Charter. Through this, the rights of formerly colo-nised peoples to self-determination and non-interference were recognised. The 'globalisation' of sovereignty addressed the inequalities in the interna-tional political structures between Western and non-Western societies that had characterised the international system of European empires.

A key component of R2P as a concept and a doctrine, however, is that states have responsibilities as well as rights. There is nothing new in the idea that responsibility is an innate component of sovereignty, but ideas about how responsibilities are constituted have been reconfigured in different iterations of sovereignty. Luke Glanville identifies three key constructs of sovereign responsibility. The first of these is the concep-tion of sovereign responsibilities premised on a social contract, which is closely associated with Jean Bodin and Thomas Hobbes. The subjects' submission to the authority of the sovereign was conditioned by the sovereign's responsibility for the safety of the people.[7] The second is responsibility premised on protection of fundamental rights, which emerged in the wake of the French and American Revolutions. This concept of sovereign responsibility encompassed protection of the rights of individuals but also of the collective right of the people to liberty, or to self-determination.[8] Glanville's third conception of sovereignty as responsibility is premised on the idea of trusteeship: that stronger and more advanced 'civilised' societies have a responsibility to protect those perceived as lacking the capacity to govern themselves in accordance with the 'standards of civilisation'. This now contentious concept of sovereign responsibility was expressed in concepts such as the 'sacred trust of civilisation' and the civilising mission, which helped to justify the expansion of European imperial sovereignty over non-European peoples.

Each of these three constructs of sovereignty as responsibility and protection is closely linked to Western historical and political develop-ment. In asking whether R2P is innately a Western idea, however, it is also important to consider whether or not concepts of sovereign responsibility and protection resonate in non-Western societies. As noted above, it is neither possible nor desirable to seek to identify a homogenous non-Western response to this question. What we can say, however, is that there exist powerful examples of concepts of responsibility and protection

---

[7] Glanville, 'The Antecedents of "sovereignty as responsibility"', p. 239. See also Luke Glanville, *Sovereignty and the Responsibility to Protect: A New History* (Chicago: The University of Chicago Press, 2013).

[8] Glanville, 'The Antecedents of "sovereignty as responsibility"', p. 242; Bellamy, *Responsibility to Protect*.

in non-Western traditions, values and philosophies. This is in relation both to conceptions of responsibilities within domestic political communities, but also more extensive conceptions of obligations to aid those outside one's immediate political community.

The idea that those who hold political authority have a responsibility to protect their subjects or citizens spans many societies and cultures. One of the most prominent and widely cited of these is within the Confucian traditions within China. As Yeophantong notes, Chinese ideas of responsibility are intimately connected to notions of both social and political order. In Imperial China, order was premised on the maintenance of duties and obligation within a complex hierarchical relationship. The ruler, who was mandated by heaven, was charged with the maintenance of order through rightful conduct and government by example. This took the form of the ruler assuming the responsibility for the protection of both the spiritual and material welfare of his or her subjects. 'How well a ruler was able to cater for the interests of the people ... became a tangible measure of the ruler's legitimacy.'[9] Glanville further argues that the philosopher Mencius suggested that a punitive war could be waged on a tyrant by other benevolent rulers who might both punish tyranny 'and bring comfort to the people'.[10] Similar examples of the legitimacy of a ruler's authority being linked to responsibility can be found elsewhere in Asia, such as the Mauryan Emperor Ashoka's (269–232 BC) acknowledgment that he ruled 'according to the law, ratification of my subjects under the law, and protection through the law'. 'Asia', argues Thakur, 'has its own rich tradition that vests sovereignty with responsibility for the lives and welfare of subjects while circumscribing the exercise of power with the majesty of law that stands above the agents.'[11] Further illustrations of the idea that the authority of rulers is premised on obligations both to protect and act justly towards their subjects can also be found in Islamic, Hebrew and Buddhist texts.[12] Religion can often play a

---

[9] Pichamon Yeophantong, 'Governing the World: China's Evolving Conceptions of Responsibility', *The Chinese Journal of International Politics* 6 (2013), pp. 324–364, at pp. 336–337.

[10] Luke Glanville, 'Retaining the Mandate of Heaven: Sovereign Accountability in Ancient China', *Millennium* 39:2 (2010), pp. 323–343, at p. 334.

[11] Ramesh Thakur, 'Libya and the Responsibility to Protect: Between Opportunistic Humanitarianism and Value-Free Pragmatism', *Security Challenges* 7:4 (2011), pp. 13–25, at p. 17.

[12] The Qu'ran maintains that all rulers are obligated to act justly towards their subjects; Hebrew scripture inveighs the king's responsibility to judge God's people justly and to champion and assist the needy and the poor; Buddhist texts affirm the duty of the king to maintain law and order for the benefit of people and to look after their economic welfare: Brian D. Lepard, *Rethinking Humanitarian Intervention* (University Park: Penn State University Press, 2003), pp. 60–61.

significant role in this conditioning of sovereignty by responsibility. As Nkulu-N'Sengha notes, a powerful dimension of many faiths is the idea that sovereignty rests with God, who stands above earthly rulers and state power. The ruler is therefore ultimately accountable to God for the treatment of God's people.[13] There are then powerful examples from different societies and cultures of the responsibility of a ruler to protect the people being linked to the legitimacy of the ruler.

R2P, however, concerns not only internal responsibilities, but also the more extensive responsibilities to protect those beyond one's immediate community. This speaks to humanitarian traditions, which can be found across the globe and across the ages. As Ephraim Isaacs notes, humanitarian codes can be found across cultures in ancient texts as well as in the strictures of contemporary religions and philosophies.[14] They are often premised on conceptions of benevolence, and compassion expressed as charity or philanthropy towards those in need, but can also be premised on the idea that helping those in need is a matter of justice. In Judaic and Islamic traditions, for instance, providing assistance to those in need, such as orphans, widows, refugees, strangers or the poor, is an obligation of the faithful.[15]

Similarly, Paul Gordon Lauren's discussion of the evolution of international human rights observes that all the world's major religious traditions address the issue of human responsibilities to others. All 'share a universal interest in addressing the integrity, worth and dignity of all persons and, consequently, the duty toward other people who suffer without distinction.'[16] The tenets of Islam, for instance, are deeply

---

[13] Mutumbo Nkulu-N'Sengha, 'Religion, Spirituality, and R2P', in Rama Mani and Thomas G. Weiss, eds, *Responsibility to Protect: Cultural Perspectives in the Global South* (London and New York: Routledge, 2011), pp. 25–61, at pp. 44–5.

[14] Ephraim Isaacs, 'Humanitarianism across Religions and Cultures', in Thomas G. Weiss and Larry Minear, eds, *Humanitarianism Across Borders: Sustaining Civilians in Times of War* (Boulder: Lynne Rienner, 1993), pp. 13–22, at p. 13.

[15] Jamal Krafess, 'The Influence of the Muslim Religion on Humanitarian Aid', *International Review of the Red Cross* 87:858 (2005), pp. 327–342. There is debate within Islamic scholarship as to whether these obligations are confined to fellow Muslims or extend to fellow human beings more broadly. Recent trends within key transnational Islamic humanitarian organisations such as Muslim Aid and Islamic Relief suggest there is a strong community of practitioners who support the latter position. Ahmad Al Noorbala, 'Interview with Ahmad Al Noorbala (President of Red Crescent Iran)', *International Review of the Red Cross* 87: 858 (2005), pp. 243–251.

[16] Paul Gordon Lauren, *The Evolution of International Humans Rights* (Philadelphia: University of Pennsylvania Press, 1998), pp. 5, 7. The Hindu texts articulate a vision of the sacredness of all human life that compels believers to practise compassion and charity towards those in need. The Judaic tradition commences with the legend of the shared fatherhood of God to all people and the fundamental importance of the creation of human beings 'as members of one family and as individuals endowed with worth'. Buddhist teachings eschew the caste system and advocate practices of universal

imbued with concepts of the obligation to the other, particularly to those who are suffering, and articulate a belief in the innate equality among men. Taken together, the work of Isaacs and Lauren suggests there are strong foundations for arguing that in many cultures and societies, conceptions of responsibilities towards those in need are not necessarily bounded by the limits of one's social or political community. What remains controversial in relation to R2P, however, is the extent of these responsibilities and the degree to which it is viewed as legitimate to use force in pursuit of them.

The conditions under which the use of force is legitimate, and the laws that govern it, are encompassed in conceptions of international humanitarian law. I do not propose to survey the broad array of non-Western perspectives on this vast topic, except to note that conventions and codes that govern when war is legitimate and how it should be fought can be found in most of the world's religious and philosophical traditions.[17] However, the concern that military intervention will be used by the West to undermine the norms of self-determinations and non-interference, which are fundamental to former colonial and small states, and to once again 'police' or control non-Western societies, significantly influence perceptions of R2P. In this respect, perceptions of R2P continue to be shaped and even compromised by the cultural politics of the international system. These were further aggravated by the post '9/11' international environment of interventionism into which R2P was launched.[18]

The cultural politics of R2P

The development of R2P as a form of response to mass atrocity crimes was in no small part a response to the tensions that surrounded humanitarian intervention. Four aspects of the debate surrounding humanitarian intervention are particularly salient. The first is that humanitarian intervention is really a mask or vector for the promotion of a Western dominated international order. Underpinning this position is the pluralist argument that the norm of non-intervention protects the weak from the strong in a world of unequal power and is fundamental to the

---

brotherhood. Confucian texts also articulate the idea that 'within the four seas, all men are brothers'.

[17] Alex Bellamy, *Just War: From Cicero to Iraq* (Cambridge: Polity, 2006), p. 4; Lepard, *Rethinking Humanitarian Intervention*.

[18] Amitav Acharya, 'Refining the Dilemmas of Humanitarian Intervention', *Australian Journal of International Affairs* 56:3 (2002), pp. 373–381, at p. 380. This was an environment in which, argues Acharya, there was a reversal of the trend towards principled as opposed to geopolitical intervention.

maintenance of an egalitarian international order. Second is the perception that it is a revival of liberal imperialism, with human rights becoming the new 'standard of civilisation'.[19] As in the era of European empires, this standard was being employed to assess states' capacities to exercise 'effective' sovereignty. The third point of contention is selectivity. Perceptions that powerful Western actors and coalitions have only intervened in crises in which they either have strategic interests, or which do not clash with their broader interests, fuelled suspicion of Western instrumentalism and double standards.[20] The fourth point of contention concerns the issue of right authority in endorsing humanitarian interventions. Non-Western states typically view UN Security Council sanction as essential to the legitimacy of international intervention. At the same time, however, the global South has been critical of the dominance of the UN Security Council by the five permanent members of which only one – China – can lay claim to representing the global South. Taken together, these four points of tension contribute to arguments that humanitarian intervention is both a Western discourse and a practice that promotes and sustains the interests of Western actors.

R2P represented a conscious effort by its proponents to move beyond the cultural politics of humanitarian intervention in two important ways. First, it deliberately sought to reframe the language of response to mass atrocities, detaching it from the language of humanitarian intervention. In shifting from a discourse of the rights and duties of intervention to that of responsibility and protection of populations, R2P represented an effort to frame responses to mass atrocities in a language which resonated transculturally. It was also one that invoked a more egalitarian discourse entailing a mutual recognition of common responsibilities.[21] The International Commission on Intervention and State Sovereignty (ICISS) itself drew upon a multicultural range of commentators and contributors. It was co-chaired by Australia's Gareth Evans and Algeria's Mohamed Sahnoun and included members from across the globe. It travelled and consulted widely in a range of regional conferences.

Second, proponents of R2P sought to address issues of process that had fuelled concerns that humanitarian intervention was a mask for the powerful. In its development of a set of criteria for intervention, ICISS

---

[19] Mohammed Ayoob, 'Third World Perspectives on Humanitarian Intervention and International Administration', *Global Governance* 10:1 (2004), pp. 99–118.

[20] Ayoob, 'Third World Perspectives'.

[21] International Commission on Intervention and State Sovereignty (ICISS), *The Responsibility to Protect: Report of the International Commission on Intervention and State Sovereignty* (Ottawa: International Development Research Centre, 2000), p. 16.

sought to provide a decision-making framework that could address the fraught issues of selectivity and right authority, and specify and bind intervention on human rights grounds;[22] for instance, the criteria suggested by the 2001 ICISS report limit intervention to the protection of communities at risk of harm from their government. It did not sanction the outright overthrowing of a regime. This then, argues Amitav Acharya, provided a definition of intervention that 'can be usefully separated from the West's ideologically-charged democratic enlargement.'[23]

Third, as supporters of R2P have argued, it encapsulates and is built upon existing commitments to international institutions and norms that have been widely endorsed by both Western and non-Western states. It is anchored, 'in existing international law, in institutions and in lessons learned from practice'. These include human rights and international humanitarian law.[24] 'There is nothing added ... to existing international law', argues Ann Orford 'by the secretary-general's claim that 'the primary raison d'être and duty' of every state is to protect those within its territory'. Similarly, Edward Luck has argued that the role of R2P is to amplify and multiply the voices calling for the implementation of human rights, humanitarian and refugee norms, not to replace them.[25]

The empirical development of R2P as a doctrine also strongly supports the argument that it is not simply a Western idea or doctrine. As has been widely noted, the roots of the doctrine lie in Africa. This is clearly articulated by Edward Luck's observation that 'the concept emerged, quite literally, from the soil and soul of Africa'; the horrors of the Rwandan genocide played a catalytic role in convincing the world's peoples and governments that 'everything possible must be done' to prevent the reoccurrence of such mass atrocities.[26] It was also an African UN secretary-general, Kofi Annan, who challenged the international community to

---

[22] Acharya, 'Refining the Dilemmas of Humanitarian Intervention'.   [23] Ibid, p. 75.

[24] Louise Arbour, 'The Responsibility to Protect as a Duty of Care in International Law', *Review of International Studies* 34:3 (2008), pp. 445–458 at p. 448; *The Responsibility to Protect*, p. 6.

[25] Anne Orford, *International Authority and the Responsibility to Protect* (Cambridge: Cambridge University Press, 2011), p. 23; Edward C. Luck, 'Building a Norm: The Responsibility to Protect Experience', in Robert I. Rotberg, ed, *Mass Atrocity Crimes: Preventing Future Outrages* (Washington DC: Brookings Institution Press, 2010), pp. 108–127 at p. 109.

[26] Luck cited in Paul D. Williams, 'The "Responsibility to Protect", Norm Localisation and African International Society', *Global Responsibility to Protect* 1:3 (2009), pp. 392–416, at p. 397. This echoed the secretary-general's statement that R2P 'emerged from the soil, spirit, experience and institutions of Africa' 'Upcoming Debate on Responsibility to Protect Not About History', But Charter of the United Nations; Secretary General Tells General Assembly, UN Document SG/SM/12374 (21 July 2009).

formulate a meaningful and effective response to mass atrocity crimes. It was a senior African diplomat, Sudan's Francis Deng, who first clearly articulated the concept of 'sovereignty as responsibility' in his work on the challenges to peace and security in post-Cold War Africa.[27] The idea was expanded and honed in the work of Deng and Roberta Cohen on internally displaced persons (IDPs), a study commissioned by Egyptian UN Secretary-General Boutros Boutros-Ghali. As Paul Williams further notes, the ideas set out in R2P relate closely to those intrinsic to the peace and security architecture being developed in Africa first within the OAU and subsequently in the new African Union.[28] The experiences of conflict and instability contributing to mass atrocity crimes in the continent provided a strong impetus for the call from a shift from 'non-interference to non-indifference'.[29]

Perhaps one of the most powerful arguments used to counter the suggestion that R2P is a Western idea is the broad, indeed almost universal endorsement of the idea by the international community. The acceptance of paragraphs 138 and 139 of the UN 2005 World Summit Document by both Western and non-Western states signalled a basic consensus that states and the international community bore some form of responsibility to protect peoples from mass atrocity crimes. 'The mandate', argued UN Special Representative Edward Luck, 'could not be clearer or come from a higher authority'.[30] The UN General Assembly's acceptance of the secretary-general's 2009 report further supports the argument that R2P not only has non-Western roots but also non-Western support. Only a handful of states maintained positions of strong opposition to endorsement of R2P as a doctrine. Even these states have not completely rejected conceptions of responsibility and protection. Sudan, for instance, acknowledged that duties of protection were conferred on a government by the social contract.[31]

---

[27] Francis M. Deng, Sadikiel Kimaro, Terrence Lyons, Donald Rothschild and I. William Zartman, *Sovereignty as Responsibility: Conflict Management in Africa* (Washington DC: The Brookings Institution, 1996).

[28] Paul D. Williams, 'The "Responsibility to Protect", Norm Localisation and African International Society', pp. 399–400; Kwesi Aning and Samuel Atuobi. 'Responsibility to Protect in Africa: An analysis of the African Union's Peace and Stability Architecture', *Global Responsibility to Protect*, 1:1 (2009), pp. 90–113.

[29] Paul D. Williams, 'From Non-Intervention to Non-Indifference: The Origins and Development of the African Union's Security Culture', *African Affairs* 106:423 (2007), pp. 253–279.

[30] Edward C. Luck, 'Remarks to the General Assembly on the Responsibility to Protect (R2P), New York, 23 July, 2009' (New York: United Nations, 2009).

[31] A/63/PV.101, 2009, p.10; Global Centre for the Responsibility to Protect, *Implementing the Responsibility to Protect: The 2009 General Assembly Debate: An Assessment* (New York: Global Centre for the Responsibility to Protect, 2009).

Achieving this consensus, it must be acknowledged, was not a smooth process. Complex negotiations underpinned the adoption of paragraphs 138 and 139 of the 2005 UN World Summit Declaration, during which several significant elements of the original ICISS report were put to one side.[32] One of the most notable of these was the set of criteria for judging if intervention was warranted. Furthermore, in the period following the 2005 Summit (2006–2007) there was some retreat from the 2005 endorsement, or what Bellamy has called a 'revolt' against R2P, spearheaded by Arab and Asian states.[33] This revolt came in the form of resistance to the Security Council's affirmation of the concept, and a strongly negative reaction to utilisation of the concept by the Human Rights Council's High-Level Mission commissioned to investigate the role of the Sudanese government in Darfur. The UN Security Council finally affirmed the responsibility to protect in Resolution 1674 after six months of negotiations. In the case of Darfur, the key concerns related closely to those already expressed about humanitarian intervention. First, there was concern that R2P could be used to justify coercive interference in the domestic affairs of states. Second, there was concern about right authority. This related to a perceived lack of clarity in identifying which bodies were authorised to employ R2P. At the heart of the 'revolt' were suspicions that R2P was creeping beyond the limits defined in the 2005 Declaration.[34]

This 'revolt' generated, however, careful efforts by Ban Ki-moon to rebuild consensus on R2P. Working closely with the special representative for R2P and genocide, and through the development of a consultative process, the secretary-general sought to re-establish support for the concept and doctrine.[35] The emphasis was placed on framing the doctrine as one that resonated with the global community as a whole, and addressing the concerns that had been expressed about both the definition and implementation of R2P. Luck has argued that what was required was

---

[32] Russia and China expressed 'deep reservations'. India's permanent representative to the UN even challenged the legal and moral status of R2P. The reservations were not solely held by non-Western powers, however. The United States was also circumspect about endorsing the concept of R2P. See Bellamy, *Global Politics and the Responsibility to Protect*, pp. 22–25, and Bellamy, *Responsibility to Protect*, pp. 66–67 for an outline of the key developments in the negotiation process.

[33] Bellamy, *Global Politics and the Responsibility to Protect*, p. 30; Luck, 'From Promise to Practice'. A 2007 report from the Human Rights Center at the University of California at Berkeley listed eleven 'backsliding countries', which included China, India and Brazil. Cited in Oliver Stuenkel, 'The BRICS and the Future of R2P: Was Syria or Libya the Exception?', *Global Responsibility to Protect* 6:1 (2014), pp. 3–28.

[34] Bellamy, *Global Politics and the Responsibility to Protect*, p. 31; Luck, cited in Stuenkel 'The BRICS and the Future of R2P: Was Syria or Libya the Exception?', p. 99.

[35] Luck, cited ibid, pp. 100–102.

'clarification and cohesion' of the doctrine. This included affirmation that implementation of R2P would be based on what had been already agreed to in 2005, and greater specificity as to what types of crises would trigger the implementation of R2P.[36] A second important element of the secretary-general's approach was the prioritisation of engagement and consultation with the UN General Assembly on R2P. This spoke to the need for a greater sense of inclusiveness in both the development and implementation of R2P as a doctrine.

The UN secretary-general's 2009 major report to the General Assembly entitled *Implementing the Responsibility to Protect* was a significant marker in this process of reframing R2P. It was based on extensive consultation with member states. Its ordering of the existing commitments into 'three pillars' it subtly reaffirmed the authority and sovereignty of states; highlighted the role of prevention and the duty of the international community to assist in this respect; and emphasised that recourse to forceful intervention is a last resort and an action governed by the UN Charter. It emphasised the roots of the doctrine in Africa, and in so doing thus highlighted that this was not simply a Western concept. In addition, the report, and indeed subsequent reports, acknowledged the importance of regional and sub-regional organisations in all phases of R2P and particularly in Pillar Two, prevention. Once again this enhanced a sense of the broader ownership of R2P.

The subsequent General Assembly debate also provided all member states with an opportunity to articulate their response to this report clearly. This move towards enhanced consultation was further indicated by the institution of the annual informal interactive dialogue at the General Assembly. Each of these has discussed a report by the secretary-general on an aspect of the implementation of R2P.[37] Each report is based on extensive consultation with member states, signalling a willingness to broaden the processes of consultation and debate on R2P beyond the UN Security Council to the body that was representative of the international community as a whole. These measures were clearly intended to recognise and address the concerns of non-Western states. They aimed both to defuse perceptions that R2P was being largely shaped by the great powers and the powerful Western states, and to confirm the

---

[36] Luck, 'Remarks to the General Assembly'; Global Centre for the Responsibility to Protect, *Implementing the Responsibility to Protect*, p. 1.

[37] At time of writing, these have included: *Early Warning Assessment and R2P* (2010); *The Role of Regional and Sub-Regional Arrangements in implementing R2P* (2011); *Timely and Decisive Response* (2012); *Responsibility to Protect: State Responsibility and Prevention* (2013); and; *Fulfilling Our Collective Responsibility: International Assistance and the Responsibility to Protect* (2014).

centrality of the UN Charter as the foundation of the concept and principal platform for the implementation of R2P.[38] They further aimed to counter perceptions that R2P was simply another expression of the 'unwanted barnacle' of humanitarian intervention[39] and, in so doing, reaffirm that R2P was a method of enhancing rather than undermining sovereignty.

To some extent, these measures succeeded. Within the General Assembly debates, there has been widespread acceptance – even among detractors of R2P – of the principle that states do have a responsibility to protect their citizens from the mass atrocity crimes specified. The General Assembly's acceptance of the UN secretary-general's 2009 report and subsequent reports is a measure of success in this consensus-building process and engagement. The referencing of R2P in UN Security Council resolutions on Darfur and Cote D'Ivoire and, most significantly, the framing of intervention in Libya in terms of R2P, marked significant progress in achieving consensus on R2P as a doctrine that should and could be implemented in the international system.[40] There have also been several references to R2P in Security Council resolutions since the landmark Resolution 1973.[41] What is now being debated is not *if* there is a responsibility, but *how* this should be implemented. But it is in *this* respect that the endorsement of R2P by a number of non-Western states has been somewhat circumspect.

Non-Western approaches to, and endorsements of, R2P have not been homogeneous.[42] Some of the concept's strongest supporters are non-Western states that have themselves been the victims of mass atrocities, such as Rwanda, Sierra Leone, Timor Leste and, in the 2012 Dialogue, Libya and Cote d'Ivoire. The Philippines and Singapore are members of the informal 'Group of Friends' of R2P. Other non-Western states have been far more strategic and cautious in their support. Among these are emerging non-Western powers such as China, Brazil and India. India, for instance, has been vociferous in its criticism of R2P as an instrument of

---

[38] Luck, 'Building a Norm'.   [39] Luck, 'Remarks to the General Assembly', p. 3.

[40] See Bellamy, *Global Politics and the Responsibility to Protect* and Luck, 'Building a Norm', on the rebuilding of consensus from 2007 onward in the wake of a backlash against R2P in the 2006–2007 period.

[41] Alex Bellamy, 'Lesson Learning from the Implementation of the Responsibility to Protect', *International Politics* 51:1 (2014), pp. 23–44. Bellamy notes seven such resolutions, including two further on Libya.

[42] For instance, while the Non Aligned Movement presented a statement on behalf of its membership to the 2009 UNGA debate, a number of members of the movement also chose to make their own statements. Some of these were at odds with that of the NAM. Global Centre for the Responsibility to Protect, *Implementing the Responsibility to Protect*, p. 4.

Western interventionism. However, it grudgingly supported the endorsement of R2P in the 2005 World Summit; voted for Resolution 1970 on
Libya; and abstained in the Security Council on Resolution 1973. In so
doing India has sought to balance its objections to R2P with concerns for
maintaining perceptions of its capacity to act as a responsible great
power.[43] China's position on R2P has been described as 'dichotomous'.[44]
China endorsed the 2005 World Summit document and the 'prudent
description' of R2P it contained.[45] Despite playing an important role in
facilitating UN Security Council Resolution 1674 endorsing R2P, it went
on to express concerns about the expansion or misuse of the concept,
abstaining from a 2006 resolution on Darfur, and vetoing draft Security
Council resolutions sanctioning the governments of Myanmar and
Zimbabwe in 2007 and 2008. It supported Resolution 1970 on Libya
and abstained from Resolution 1973, facilitating its passage. However,
it joined Russia in vetoing three draft Security Council resolutions
pressing the Syrian government to ensure the protection of its citizens.
China thus navigates a shifting strategic path through its expressed
concerns for civilian protection with those about non-consensual military intervention. Patrick Quinton-Brown differentiates such 'cautious
supporters' of R2P such as India and China, who agree with the concept
but remain sceptical of its implementation, from rejectionist states. This
latter category refers to a small number of non-Western states who have
been strongly critical of R2P, arguing that it is fundamentally flawed or
requires renegotiation.[46]

Just as the positions adopted by non-Western states on R2P have not
been homogenous, neither have they been static: some states have shifted
their position over time. Bellamy notes, for instance, that a number of
Asian states such as Indonesia have moved from the 'revolt' against R2P
in 2006 towards a more accommodating and supportive attitude in the
2009 debate.[47] The motivations that underlie states' endorsement of R2P

[43] Ian Hall, 'Tilting at Windmills: The Indian Debate over the Responsibility to Protect
after UNSC Resolution 1973', *Global Responsibility to Protect* 5:1 (2013), pp. 84–108.
[44] Sarah Teitt, 'Assessing Polemic, Principles and Practices; China and the Responsibility
to Protect', *Global Responsibility to Protect* 1:2 (2009), pp. 208–236; Andrew Garwood-
Gowers, 'China's "Responsible Protection" Concept', *Asian Journal of International
Law*, forthcoming.
[45] Liu Tiewa, 'China and the Responsibility to Protect: Maintenance and Change of Its
Policy for Intervention', *The Pacific Review* 25:1 (2012), pp. 153–173.
[46] Patrick Quinton-Brown, 'Mapping Dissent: The Responsibility to Protect and Its State
Critics', *Global Responsibility to Protect* 5:3 (2013), pp. 260–282. Among the thirteen
rejectionist states, Quinton-Brown includes, for instance, Venezuela, Syria, Algeria,
Sudan, Iran, Cuba and North Korea.
[47] Alex Bellamy and Mark Beeson, 'The Responsibility to Protect in Southeast Asia: Can
ASEAN Reconcile Humanitarianism and Sovereignty', *Asian Security* 6:3 (2010),

can vary greatly. However, they serve to reinforce perceptions of R2P as a universal concept and doctrine. At the same time, the qualified nature of the endorsements by a number of non-Western states, and its rejection by some, continue to demonstrate that, in certain important respects, R2P remains a contested concept.

The key issues of contention for many non-Western states lie not with Pillars One and Two of the doctrine, which concern recognising states' sovereign responsibilities to protect their citizens and assisting them to build their capacity to fulfil these. This is consistent with the argument in the first section of this paper, that acceptance of the idea that states do have responsibilities to protect their populations is widespread among Western and non-Western countries. The key issues of contest continue to be with the implementation of Pillar Three: the responsibility of international community to act to prevent and halt mass atrocity crimes when a state manifestly fails to protect its populations; and with consistency in the invocation and application of R2P as a doctrine.[48] These are less issues of the recognition of sovereign responsibilities than of the implementation of the international community's responsibilities when sovereign responsibilities are not met. For instance, while the majority of speakers in the 2009 debate affirmed that the Security Council should be ready to take timely and decisive action to protect populations from mass atrocity crimes, and twenty-seven speakers affirmed the *obligation* to take such measures, a number of non-Western speakers expressed concerns about the potential misuse of coercive power. A further important aspect of this debate concerned right authority; that is, the importance of retaining the UN Security Council as the sole body that may authorise intervention. At the same time, the unrepresentative nature of the Security Council remained a central concern of many non-Western states.[49]

Further recurrent issues in this debate and in the subsequent informal dialogues are concerns that any use of force if sanctioned would be proportionate; and that intervening forces would limit their actions to the mandate provided, focusing on the protection of civilians rather than the pursuit of broader political goals such as regime change. Another core

pp. 262–279 at p. 267; Luck, 'Building a Norm: The Responsibility to Protect Experience', p. 122.

[48] It should be noted, however that concerns regarding implementation also extend to Pillars One and Two. The debates and Dialogues at the UN General Assembly have demonstrated a concern with how these should be implemented in ways that support states, but do not compromise other support processes, such as development assistance, nor interfere unduly in domestic affairs: Nicole Deller, 'Challenges and Controversies', in Jared Genser and Irwin Cotler, eds, *The Responsiblity to Protect: The Promise of Stopping Mass Atrocities in Our Time* (Oxford: Oxford University Press, 2012), pp. 62–84.

[49] Global Centre for the Responsibility to Protect, *Implementing the Responsibility to Protect.*

concern has been selectivity: for instance, several speakers in the 2009 debate pointed to the absence of an international response to the bombardment of Gaza that year as an illustration of the inconsistent application of R2P.[50] These concerns were further fuelled by the outcome of the NATO-led Libyan intervention which resulted in the eventual removal of the Gaddafi regime. This rejuvenated suspicion that the West was prepared to use R2P as an instrument to pursue its own political and strategic interests, including forcible regime change. The 'blowback' of the Libyan intervention in turn coloured the debate surrounding the international response to the crisis that then erupted in Syria, and the vetoing by China and Russia of three draft UN Security Council resolutions which invoked the Syrian government's responsibility to protect its population.[51]

The concerns expressed about Pillar Three of R2P clearly echo those held about humanitarian intervention, suggesting R2P as a concept has not managed to totally evade the legacy of that concept, nor of the cultural politics surrounding its evolution.[52] In 2009, the then UN General Assembly President Miguel d'Escoto Brockmann invoked the legacy of Western imperial dominance of the non-West, arguing that 'colonialism and interventionism used responsibility to protect arguments'.[53] Critics of R2P argue that it continues to reflect the Western dominance and is simply a reiteration of humanitarian intervention. Sudan, for instance, argued in the 2009 General Assembly debate that R2P and humanitarian intervention are 'two sides of the same coin'.[54] A number of others – including Iran, North Korea and Pakistan – expressed scepticism that R2P was a licence for unilateral intervention by the powerful in other countries.[55] These comments built upon wariness and suspicion generated by the use of language of humanitarian protection to justify US-led interventions in Afghanistan and Iraq, and Russia's invocation of R2P to justify its intervention in Georgia in 2008. The invocation of R2P by

---

[50] Quinton-Brown usefully clarifies these concerns as relating to six core themes: politicisation; misuse and abuse of R2P; traditional sovereignty and non-interference; aversion to the use of force; post-colonial ideology; Security Council illegitimacy; and early warning deficiencies. See Quinton-Brown, 'Mapping Dissent', p. 265.

[51] Alex Bellamy has questioned this assumption, arguing that the factors contributing to the failure of these resolutions may be case-specific rather than signalling a broader rejection of R2P in the wake of Libya. See Alex Bellamy, 'Lesson learning'.

[52] See, for example, Aidan Hehir, 'The Permanence of Inconsistency: Libya, the Security Council, and the Responsibility to Protect', *International Security* 38:1 (2013), pp. 137–159.

[53] Statement by H.E. Miguel d'Escoto Brockmann, president of the UN General Assembly at the opening of the 97th Session of the General Assembly on Agenda Item 44 and 107, UN General Assembly, New York, 23 July, 2009.

[54] Deller, 'Challenges and Controversies', p. 63.

[55] Global Centre for the Responsibility to Protect, *Implementing the Responsibility to Protect*, p. 7.

French Foreign Minister Bernard Kouchner in the wake of Cyclone Nargis in Myanmar in 2008 further raised the spectre of the expansion of R2P beyond the narrowly defined limits of mass atrocity crimes to natural disasters, and of coercive interference in domestic affairs.[56] As noted above, concerns about the West's willingness to instrumentalise R2P for purposes beyond civilian protection were fuelled by the fallout from the Libyan intervention.

These events suggest that, as Amitav Acharya has observed, R2P refines but does not resolve the dilemma of humanitarian intervention.[57] The dilemma of humanitarian intervention revolves around how best to protect civilian populations from mass atrocity crimes without undermining the sovereign rights of states. These sovereign rights are understood themselves as an important form of protection from external interference and thus of their of peoples' self-determination. From this perspective, one could argue therefore that criticisms by non-Western states of Pillar Three of R2P do not necessarily constitute a rejection of sovereign responsibility. Rather they are a re-affirmation of sovereignty as the locus of responsibility and mechanism for the protection of the rights of the weaker in the international order from the strong. Pillars One and Two, however, are more easily accepted as measures that enhance recognition of sovereign responsibility. What is significant here is the centrality of the concept of sovereignty to the discourse of both the critics and the supporters of R2P. It is a conception of sovereignty that encompasses conceptions of territorial authority and rights that have strong roots in the West but have been widely embraced by the non-West.

On balance there is a strong case to argue that the non-West has not rejected the concept or doctrine of R2P. Only a few states have stood staunchly by outright condemnation of R2P. In the 2009 UN General Assembly debate only four of the ninety-four speakers – Venezuela, Cuba, Sudan and Nicaragua – sought to 'roll back' the commitments of the 2005 World Summit Declaration on R2P.[58] In the 2012 informal dialogue, only two speakers – Cuba and Venezuela – remained outright opponents of the norm.[59] Rather than rejection of R2P, there has been wariness about how the concept might be implemented and advocacy of the need to ensure that its implementation reflects the perspectives and values of non-Western states. For instance, the General Assembly debate of 2009

---

[56] Bellamy and Mark Beeson, 'The Responsibility to Protect in Southeast Asia'.
[57] Acharya, 'Mapping the Dilemmas'.
[58] Global Centre for the Responsibility to Protect, *Implementing the Responsibility to Protect*, p. 4.
[59] Global Centre for the Responsibility to Protect, '*Timely and Decisive Response*'.

and subsequent dialogues have seen many states focus on the need for R2P to be lodged within a broader conception of vulnerabilities and protection that encompassed issues of prevention in the form of early warning systems and capacity building.[60]

The participation of non-Western states in the UN General Assembly debates and subsequent dialogues signals a desire of many non-Western states to influence the development of the concept and implementation of R2P, and a willingness to exercise some control over the discourse of R2P itself. Further evidence of this came in the wake of the 2011 Libya intervention where, rather than outright rejection of Pillar Three, we saw calls for stricter control and greater accountability in interventions. Brazil's 2012 proposal of the idea of 'responsibility while protecting' (RWP) sought to address growing perceptions of the misuse of the concept for purposes other than protecting civilians, arguing that 'the international community must show a great deal of responsibility while protecting'. To this end Brazil proposed a series of guidelines that should be enacted to ensure that any use of force is legitimate, judicious, proportionate 'and limited to the objectives established by the Security Council'.[61] It proposed that compliance with Security Council resolutions should be monitored and evaluated on an ongoing basis.[62] In a similar vein, in 2012, Ruan Zongze, vice-president of the key Chinese think-tank the China Institute for International Studies, put forward the idea of 'responsible protection' (RP). Responsible protection was also framed in terms of concerns with the conduct of the Libyan intervention, and that R2P could be used by the West as a pretext for interventionism. It also articulates guidelines for decision-making on military interventions, and for the monitoring and supervising of such interventions to reduce the potential for R2P to be used 'as cover for other strategic objectives unrelated to civilian protection'.[63] Undoubtedly there are strong resemblances between the justificatory criteria proposed RWP and RP, and those in the original ICISS report.[64] However, it is significant that both RWP and RP are measures being proposed by leading voices from the non-West. Both suggest an interest by important

---

[60] Global Centre for the Responsibility to Protect, *Implementing the Responsibility to Protect*, p. 5. See also Quinton-Brown, 'Mapping Dissent'.

[61] United Nations Document A/66/551–S/2011/701, 2011.   [62] Ibid, p. 4.

[63] Garwood-Gowers, 'China's "Responsible Protection" Concept', 3; Ruan Zongze, 'Responsible Protection: Building a Safer World', China Institute for International Studies, 15 June 2012. Garwood-Gowers further notes that responsible protection was subsequently the subject of an international conference hosted in October 2013 by the CIIS. I am extremely grateful to Andrew Garwood-Gowers for introducing me to this development and for sharing with me his work and insights on R2P.

[64] See Garwood-Gowers (ibid.) for a comparison of these frameworks.

non-Western actors not only in ongoing engagement with R2P, but furthermore an interest in exercising influence over the direction and discourse of R2P.

Conclusion

It would be mistaken and indeed arrogant to assume that conceptions of responsibility and protection are distinctively or uniquely Western. The idea that those in authority owe some form of responsibility to protect those whom they govern is innate to many relationships of authority. The transcultural resonance of the concepts is one of the reasons why these were chosen as ways to frame responses to mass atrocity crimes. R2P has been carefully nurtured as a universal idea. Its evolution has been shaped by a conscious effort by proponents to frame it both as a concept and a doctrine that are not innately Western, either in origin or in terms of its support base in the broader global community. This has been prompted in no small part by an effort to escape the legacy of the cultural politics of the international system that have dogged R2Ps precursor, humanitarian intervention.

There are strong grounds for arguing that R2P is an idea that has strong philosophical, cultural and political roots in the non-West. In addition, the concept and doctrine has been widely endorsed by non-Western states, albeit cautiously by many. It is the implementation, the process rather than the idea, which has been the site of contest and debate. The issues do not concern whether those in authority should be responsible and even accountable for the protection they afford their subjects and citizens, nor even whether or not some of these responsibilities fall to the broader international community: they concern the mechanisms and processes through which these should be afforded and – in particular – how and when the responsibilities of the international community should be enacted to provide protection to populations in need.

One of the most significant elements of the debate surrounding R2P is the degree of consensus there is on these questions in the contemporary international system. All parties to the debate – even R2Ps detractors – agree that responsibility for the protection of peoples lies with the sovereign state. There is also consensus that sovereignty is the best mechanism through which protection can be afforded. Even those who reject the concept of R2P do so in the name of protecting sovereignty. What is intriguing here is that sovereignty – or perhaps more accurately the modern sovereign state – *is* a distinctively Western idea. It is in this respect, rather than in the conceptions of responsibility or protection, that R2P is grounded in Western history, philosophy and political thought. On the one hand sovereignty is a site of contest in debates over how we should prevent and respond to mass atrocity crimes – but it is also the chosen means through which to build consensus on the nature and scope of responsibilities.

The debate surrounding R2P is not about whether this concept should be embraced but how it should be interpreted. Here one could argue that much consensus has been achieved. However, the debate is itself deeply embedded in the cultural politics of the evolving international system. Suspicions remain that R2P can be a vehicle for the projection of Western interests and values on weaker states. It is here that the debate continues to be informed by resentment and fear of structural inequalities in the international system that are a legacy of the history of interaction between Western and non-Western societies.

16   Colonialism and the Responsibility to Protect

Siddharth Mallavarapu

Introduction

The Responsibility to Protect (R2P) is a relatively recent entrant in the burgeoning lexicon of contemporary international relations. It was only in 2001 that the International Commission on Intervention and State Sovereignty (ICISS) articulated and developed the idea of R2P. The attempt was made consciously to depart from the doctrine of humanitarian intervention and its prior instantiations which had lent it a fairly dubious international reputation. As a follow-up to the 2001 report assembled by Gareth Evans, Mohamed Sahnoun and their team, the UN Secretary-General Kofi Anan in 2004 inaugurated a High-Level Panel on Threats, Challenges, and Change. This latter effort culminated in the Report titled *A More Secure World: Our Shared Responsibility.*[1] The R2P was characterised here as an 'emerging norm'. Subsequently, in 2005 at the UN General Assembly World Summit, the R2P was invoked again in the context of 'helping States build capacity to protect their populations from genocide, war crimes, ethnic cleansing and crimes against humanity and to assisting those which are under stress before crises and conflicts break out'.[2]

There are several important facets pertaining to the evolution of R2P and where we stand currently in relation to both the doctrine and its applicability. First, it is important not to equate R2P with 'formal international law'.[3] Second, the phraseology of an 'emerging norm' implies that it is 'a norm situated in limbo halfway between existence and

The author would like to place on record his deep gratitude to Himadeep Muppidi, Rajen Harshe, the co-editors of this volume and scholars at the Centre for Global Cooperation, Duisburg, Germany for insightful comments on a draft version of this piece. The usual disclaimer applies.

[1] The R2P Coalition, 'History and Timeline of R2P'. Accessed on 23 November 2013 at www.r2pcoalition.org/content/view/22/.

[2] *World Summit Outcome*, Document A/RES/60/1 (New York: United Nations, 24 October 2005). Accessed on March 1, 2013 at www.un.org/summit2005/documents.html.

[3] Jean-Marc Coicaud, 'International Law, the Responsibility to Protect and International Crises', Chapter 9 of this volume.

non-existence'.[4] Third, in terms of the broader politics surrounding R2P, notwithstanding claims to impartial applicability, I argue that there is sufficient reason to be wary of the 'fiction of neutrality'.[5] Fourth, it is apparent that there exist unresolved grey areas both in doctrinal and operational terms as far as R2P is concerned and the attendant 'ambiguity' undermines its overall reputation.[6] Finally, I concur with the view that R2P has not been able to circumvent in any fashion the more generic 'paternalism' of the powerful that has long characterised the dominant framings of contemporary international relations practice.[7] It has been rather unsuccessful in assuaging deeper and well-founded historical suspicions, especially among decolonised states, about the motivations of major Western powers in the international system. Arguably, then, R2P represents 'old wine in a new bottle', cosmetic in its effort to remedy both the legacy and perils of humanitarian intervention.[8]

Interventionism has had a long history. My intent in this piece is at least partially to historicise its usage while attempting to peel layers of its make-up to reveal its intimate association with modalities of colonial rule. I do this by engaging different registers – chronicling the contending bases of intervention, the links between race and international law and the multifaceted motivations of international humanitarianism, and by exploring the grammar of 'non-territorial forms of sovereign rule' as exercised during the times of Empire.[9] Further, I also seek to examine the imposition of new 'technologies of rule' through epistemic manoeuvres, the pervasiveness of non-inclusivity in global governance architectures alongside the re-insertion of old frames of colonial rule now recast in sync with the sensibilities of the prevailing *Zeitgeist*.[10] I argue that the doctrine of Responsibility to Protect continues to bear the weight of these legacies. While it appears to transform the external façade, it continues to embody colonial path-dependencies. Currently,

[4] Carlo Focarelli, 'The Responsibility to Protect Doctrine and Humanitarian Intervention: Too Many Ambiguities for a Working Doctrine', *Journal of Conflict and Security Law* 13:2 (2008), pp. 192–193.
[5] Makau Mutua, 'Savages, Victims, and Saviors: The Metaphor of Human Rights', *Harvard International Law Journal* 42:1 (2001), pp. 201–245.
[6] Focarelli, 'The Responsibility to Protect Doctrine and Humanitarian Intervention', pp. 191–213.
[7] Philip Cunliffe, 'Dangerous Duties: Power, Paternalism and the "Responsibility to Protect"', *Review of International Studies* 36: S1 (2010), pp. 79–96.
[8] Stephen P. Marks and Nicholas Cooper, 'The Responsibility to Protect: Watershed or Old Wine in a New Bottle?', *Jindal Global Law Review* 2:1 (2010), pp. 86–130.
[9] Anne Orford, 'Jurisdiction without Territory: From the Holy Roman Empire to the Responsibility to Protect', *Michigan Journal of International Law* 30:3 (2009), pp. 981–1015.
[10] Nikolas Rose, 'Governing "Advanced" Liberal Democracies', in Aradhana Sharma and Akhil Gupta, eds, *The Anthropology of the State: A Reader* (Malden: Blackwell, 2006), pp. 144–162.

it does not inspire much confidence either as doctrine or as policy, especially among those in the global South, often touted as the principal beneficiaries of this largesse.

It is not implausible to acknowledge that states are capable of butchering their own citizens. Nor can we remain casual observers from the sidelines when such grave transgressions occur.[11] However, when the exception to intervene becomes a normalised expectation, as in the R2P premised in practice on a fundamentally 'asymmetrical valuing of human life' and on flexible interpretations of split international mandates, suspect motivations are often concealed behind claims of Good Samaritanism.[12] A telling instance of both the doctrinal and operational complexities of R2P was recently reflected in Libya (2011), while the unfolding Syrian political theatre (2013 onwards) quite evidently poses renewed and substantial challenges to the doctrine and its applicability.

Contending logics of intervention

External political intervention is by no means a novel feature of the contemporary international landscape. The threat of intervention for reasons other than plain humanitarianism has always been present in the air, particularly for political subjects who have been at the receiving end of colonialism. The problem is further augmented in post-colonial states which continue to possess precious resources viewed as invaluable to major powers. Even prior to formal colonial rule there had been several instances of aggression by larger political entities against smaller or weaker political entities. Colonial rule is the most easily recallable of these recent histories where interventions by external powers were intended to secure further markets for imperial expansion as well as re-configuring polities, economies and societies fundamentally in keeping with the interests of the coloniser.

Any discussion of intervention inevitably nudges us in the direction of a basic question – how do we conceive of sovereignty? In the modern world, states are regarded as sovereign when they come to be internationally recognised as such and are able at least minimally to fulfil their basic

---

[11] Jean-Hervé Bradol, 'The Sacrificial International Order and Humanitarian Action', in Fabrice Weissman, ed, *In the Shadow of 'Just Wars'* (Ithaca: Cornell University Press), pp.1–22

[12] Orford, 'Jurisdiction without Territory', pp. 981–1015; Pratap Bhanu Mehta, 'From State Sovereignty to Human Security (via Institutions?)', in Terry Nardin and Melissa S. Williams, eds, *Humanitarian Intervention* (New York: New York University Press, 2005), pp. 259–285.

obligations towards their citizenry. However, notwithstanding the principle of sovereign equality, we live in a world inhabited by various grada-
tions within the state system. Some states tend to be perceived as more
significant than others and as a consequence have higher stakes in preserving a particular status quo that retains comparative advantage and
denies a level playing field to the rest. Picture this: Rwanda did not
qualify for humanitarian intervention when scores of Tutsis were being
brutally massacred by the Hutus, while intervention in Iraq was carried
out irrespective of the fact that weapons of mass destruction (WMDs)
were not found, and in the absence of UN Security Council authorisation.
Much of international relations history is a litany of similar double standards when it comes to the application of apparently universal norms.

The justificatory grounds for intervention have varied, but implicit
assumptions about race, the inherent superiority of some powers over
others to order international affairs, the rhetoric of altruism, lithe interpretations of sovereignty and deeper epistemic prejudices of one kind or
another appear to surface continually in one form or another. In the
course of this chapter, I rely primarily on representative (rather than
exhaustive) strands of scholarship to advance my case that we need to
be wary of moves such as R2P, embed them in wider narratives involving
master–client power relations and ask why there is often more than what
meets the eye in apparently innocent semantic shifts of emphasis.

Race and international politics

In a seminal piece dwelling on the links between colonialism and international law, Antony Anghie asserts that 'the concept of race is inextricably
connected with one of the defining characteristics of international law – its
universality'.[13] Conventional accounts of international law present it as a
technical and neutral domain where certain standards are mutually agreed
on by diverse international actors. However, what is often overlooked is
'the enduring role that race plays in shaping the character of contemporary
international relations and international law'.[14]

The lineage of contemporary international law reveals the employment
of strong distinctions between the 'civilised' and the 'uncivilised', con-
cretely between Europeans and non-Europeans in the international system. While the European state was seen as the gold standard in terms
of modern sovereign statehood, especially in the nineteenth century,

---

[13] Antony Anghie, 'Civilization and Commerce: The Concept of Governance in Historical
Perspective', *Villanova Law Review* 45:5 (2000), pp. 887–911 at p. 888.
[14] Ibid., p. 890.

non-Europeans were largely viewed through the prism of 'backwardness' and 'inferiority'. As Anghie claims in this context, 'the paradox is that the deployment of language of the uncivilized, the barbarian, the backward, enabled the construction of contemporary international law – both by justifying the practices of colonialism, and further, by ostensibly providing some measure of theoretical coherence to the events that occurred in the nineteenth century'.[15]

The two principal logics of colonisation were 'trade' and the 'civilizing mission'.[16] Neither of these facets has fallen off the contemporary map in terms of the persistent asymmetries that obtain between the global North and South and the implicit rationales for the superiority of one over the other. Global capitalism generates a steamrolling logic calling for harmonisation of laws in the service of global capital while liberal democracy is viewed as the single most hegemonic model in terms of organising polities around the world.[17] Democracy promotion, the spread of human rights and the opening of markets are all seen as values of which large territorial chunks of the global South always falls woefully short. It is in this context that Anghie suggests that 'what may be required is the telling of alternative histories – histories of resistance to colonial power, histories from the vantage point of the people who were subjected to international law, and which are sensitive to the tendencies within such conventional histories to assimilate the specific, unique histories of non-European peoples within the broader concepts and controlling structures of such conventional histories'.[18]

Consider a history of the mandate system as viewed by those subject to it.[19] This account of the history of the mandate system is likely to depart from history as written by those imposing the mandate. Mandates represented a form of tutelage over former colonies, again premised on the continued need for a superior power to guide an inferior one, usually a formerly colonised power. The subjects of the former mandate system now take umbrage at terms like 'good governance'. It would not be inaccurate to argue that 'the concept of good governance, particularly because of its reliance on universal international human rights norms, may appear to be a neutral concept that is potentially applicable to all states. However, the political crises and corruption that afflict advanced industrial states, are rarely if ever discussed in terms of internationally articulated norms of global governance. In practice, then, good

---

[15] Ibid., p.889.   [16] Ibid., passim.
[17] B.S. Chimni, 'International Institutions Today: An Imperial Global State in the Making', *European Journal of International Law* 15:1 (2004) pp. 1–37.
[18] Anghie, 'Civilization and Commerce', p. 891.   [19] Ibid., p. 904.

governance is a concept which is largely developed in relation to and is principally applied to, Third World States'.[20]

In the contemporary international system, the 'technologies of rule' to sustain these distinctions between the global North and the global South have only proliferated. The brute language of the 'civilizing mission' now has been replaced by a 'patronizing benevolence' of a different kind although it basically continues to preserve the privilege and order erected on prior gross colonial injustices.[21] It is not far-fetched in this context to ask if the R2P represents an element in this continuum of colonial power relations. What is the unstated etiology of R2P, viewed against the backdrop of a broader international ecology of power relations? Who are its principal protagonists? Who is it principally directed against and how does it lodge itself as a 'neutral' and impartial mechanism to render global justice while in reality being driven by much more narrowly constructed geopolitical interests? Does it factor in, even in a minimal way, any of the fundamental structural inequalities that result in vastly unequal life chances for people around the world as well as focus on broader structural remedies to quell responses that culminate in objectionable violence? The R2P debate cannot avoid squarely confronting questions such as these if it is to be rendered legitimate and widely acceptable. It is perhaps not unfair to ask whether 'the basic task is that of reproducing in the non-Western world a set of principles and institutions which are seen as having been perfected in the Western world and which the non-Western world must adopt if it is to make progress and achieve stability'.[22] I think these concerns cannot be avoided, especially given the tardy history of intervention by major powers in the erstwhile colonised world. Even today, when a crisis erupts in Mali, the political reflex of the dominant powers is to turn to France, the former colonial power in Mali, to offer a resolution for the country. What explains the continued persistence of this expectation in an international system which otherwise claims to be cured of colonial mindsets?

[20] Ibid., pp. 893–894.

[21] B.S. Chimni, 'For Epistemological and Prudent Internationalism', *Harvard Law School Human Rights Journal* November 28, 2012. Accessed online on 1 March, 2013, at www.harvardhrj.com/2012/11/for-epistemological-and-prudent-internationalism/; Anghie, 'Civilization and Commerce', p. 910; Louise Arbour, 'The Responsibility to Protect as a Duty of Care in International Law and Practice', *Review of International Studies* 34:3 (2008), pp.445–458; Kok-chor Tan, 'The Duty to Protect', in Terry Nardin and Melissa S. Williams, eds, *Humanitarian Intervention* (New York and London: New York University Press, 2006).

[22] Anghie, 'Civilization and Commerce', p. 894.

The complex map of altruism

Much of what has been said about the connections between race and international relations also spills over in accounts of the global history of humanitarianism. Michael Barnett eloquently captures this sentiment when he claims that 'when humanitarians dream of changing the world, they do so in their own language. In the nineteenth century, humanitarians favoured the language of civilization, believing that commerce, Christianity, and colonialism would save lives and societies. Today many humanitarians (and others) aspire to create the conditions of positive liberty, to enable individuals to live a life of dignity and realize their aspirations, but they often assume that the holy trinity of democracy, markets, and the rule of law will enable individuals to do so.'[23]

When distinguishing between different species of humanitarianism, mention is made of an imperial phase, a subsequent era of 'neo-humanitarianism' and the ongoing era of 'liberal humanitarianism'. Each phase reflects different time periods as well. For Barnett, the period from the 'late eighteenth century to World War II' represented the first phase of humanitarianism. This was followed by the period beginning at the commencement of the 'end of World War II to the end of the Cold War' and the third phase is where we stand now globally.[24] Further, each of these phases had certain traits that marked them off from other phases and typified them in one idiom or the other. Neatly stated, 'for Imperial Humanitarianism it was colonialism, commerce and civilizing missions; for Neo-Humanitarianism the Cold War and nationalism, development and sovereignty; and for Liberal Humanitarianism the liberal peace, globalization and human rights'.[25]

Humanitarianism in one sense could be viewed as an overarching package bringing to bear a diverse repertoire of underlying ideas and beliefs that inform particular trajectories of political proselytisation.[26] The broader context of humanitarianism is important to appreciate to help us disentangle diverse features of humanitarianism.[27] The first and most crucial facet of humanitarianism is that it is intimately tied to the world of politics.[28] We must resist the temptation to treat it as a more

---

[23] Michael Barnett, *Empire of Humanity: A History of Humanitarianism* (Ithaca: Cornell University Press, 2011), p. 231.

[24] Ibid., p. 7.   [25] Ibid, p. 9.

[26] Anne Orford, 'Muscular Humanitarianism: Reading the Narratives of the New Interventionism', *European Journal of International Law* 10:4 (1999), pp. 679–711.

[27] Barnett, *Empire of Humanity*, p. 12.

[28] Bradol, 'The Sacrificial International Order and Humanitarian Action', pp.1–22; Michael Barnett, 'Humanitarianism Transformed', *Perspectives on Politics* 3:4 (2005), pp. 723–740.

sanitised discourse bereft of all the compulsions of political expediency. Second, it appears clear from existing accounts that there is no single version of humanitarianism. It therefore makes eminent sense to refer to it in the plural rather than in the singular.[29] Third, humanitarianism speaks both to the generic and the specific. Humanitarianism is sometimes fused with millennial visions and often endowed with claims of universality while simultaneously seeking anchorage in specific local milieus.[30] A particularly important aspect of humanitarianisms then is their promise of emancipation combined with a Nietzschean 'will to power'.[31] There is an inescapable eschatological dimension to humanitarianism in its claims to universalism and to move beyond purely cosmetic fixes to political quandaries.[32] However, the emancipatory potential coexists with prevalent modalities of power. This is further complicated when the idea of 'moral progress' seems intrinsic to humanitarian endeavour.[33]

A more troubling aspect relates to the moral topography of the 'ethics of care' argument which is always implicit in all stripes of humanitarian endeavour.[34] There is a patronising dimension that is cast sometimes as neutral political involvement but in reality is generically partisan, and privileges certain values over others. Barnett argues that 'humanitarianism is partly paternalism – the belief that some people can and should act in ways that are intended to improve the welfare of those who might not be in a position to help themselves'. There might, however, also be some redeeming features of paternalism as well. While not denying the claustrophobic elements of paternalism, it has been suggested that 'a world without paternalism might be a world without an ethics of care'.[35] Is it true that some form of paternalism is inevitable to generate care? Can we think of achieving empathy with our fellow citizens beyond our national boundaries without setting up simple binaries of superiority and inferiority? Is there a way out of the standard-operating-procedures logic to establishing conditions of care? These questions must engage our attention when we think about doctrines like R2P. It is quite evident that R2P casts itself as an 'ethic of care' intervention. However, it is

---

[29] Costas Douzinas, 'The Many Faces of Humanitarianism', *Parrhesia* 2 (2007), pp. 1–28. Last accessed on 25 November, 2013 at www.parrhesiajournal.org/parrhesia02/parrhesia02_douzinas.pdf.

[30] Anna Lowenhaupt Tsing, *Friction: An Ethnography of Global Connection* (Princeton: Princeton University Press, 2005); Liisa H. Malkki, 'Speechless Emissaries: Refugees, Humanitarianism and Dehistoricization', *Cultural Anthropology* 11:3 (1996), pp. 377–404.

[31] Larry Minear, *The Humanitarian Enterprise: Dilemmas and Discoveries* (Bloomfield: Kumarian Press, 2002).

[32] David Kennedy, *The Dark Sides of Virtue: Reassessing International Humanitarianism* (Princeton: Princeton University Press, 2004).

[33] Barnett, *Empire of Humanity*, p. 12.   [34] Ibid.   [35] Ibid.

encoded with more than a generous dollop of 'paternalism' fused with specific national interests in the manner in which it is eventually administered and applied while claiming emancipatory potential.[36] It is important to recognise that what is more problematic is how it changes our understanding of sovereignty, with serious implications especially for weaker and less influential actors in the international system. R2P can also be embedded in a larger discourse about 'good governance'. Without denying partial culpability to post-colonial states in the manner in which their states are administered today, it is quite clear that ideologies like 'good governance' echo 'complex and ongoing sets of power relations between the European and non-European worlds'.[37]

R2P has been approached from several perspectives, including that of just war theory. Terry Nardin, drawing on Michael Walzer, suggests that it is important to consider the 'duty to protect' beyond merely the 'right to intervene'.[38] Philip Cunliffe argues that 'of all the varied iterations of the "responsibility to protect", not a single formulation of the doctrine to date is able succinctly to express and logically demonstrate that there is a single, identifiable agent formally obliged to act or intervene in a particular situation. There is no "automacity" in the doctrine – no governmental machinery or legislation that spontaneously comes into effect once the "duty" is breached.'[39] The 'duty to care' claim of Louise Arbour remains an abstraction bereft of real commitments to 'concrete people' in Cunliffe's account of the workings of R2P.[40] He is equally scathing in his indictment of the manner in which R2P evades the issue of being responsive to local populations. He observes that 'the responsibility to protect does not merely ensconce coercion in relations between states; it also has the potential to distort the structure of representative government within states'.[41]

In recent years, it has been argued that R2P also encourages back door unilateralism. Oliver Corten and Vaios Koutroulis observe that 'unilateralism may operate in disguise. As the Libyan precedent has shown, even in the context of an operation authorized through proper "multilateral" channels, unilateral tendencies creep back into the picture through the interpretation of the mandate and the definition of the limits to the authorization.'[42] Anne Orford examines the several invocatory lives

---

[36] Ibid., pp. 223–224.   [37] Anghie, 'Civilization and Commerce', p. 910.

[38] Terry Nardin, 'From Right to Intervene to Duty to Protect: Michael Walzer on Humanitarian Intervention', *European Journal of International Law* 24:1 (2013), pp. 67–82.

[39] Cunliffe, 'Dangerous duties', p. 84.   [40] Ibid., p. 93.   [41] Ibid., p. 96.

[42] Oliver Corten and Vaois Koutroulis, 'The Illegality of Military Support to Rebels in the Libyan War: Aspects of jus contra bellum and jus in bello', *Journal of Conflict and Security Law* 18: 1 (2013), p.91

of 'moral internationalism' with implications that take us beyond standardised dichotomies of realism and moralism in the conduct of international relations.[43] Jean-Marc Coicaud in this volume points to a lack of consensus on R2P and argues that it is likely to be effective only if it successfully opens up a fresh normative space capable of addressing 'the systemic crisis in which the contemporary world appears trapped'.[44] Jonathan Graubart also within the folds of this book observes that 'however tactful this new formulation may be, it does not settle the underlying issue'.[45]

It is clichéd to suggest that the road to hell is paved with good intentions. Clichés sometimes help us encapsulate a gut sense of politics. Researching and writing about the seamier facets of human rights advocacy, David Kennedy some years ago coined the phrase the 'dark sides of virtue' and laid bare why it was problematic to attribute a simple benignness to those claiming human rights as panacea to all our political ills.[46] My overall sense is that much of R2P activism also falls into many similar crevices and therefore needs to be far more cautiously interpreted as a remedy to unacceptable human violence in polities, economies and societies outside our immediate domestic confines. Such a reading would invite far closer scrutiny of the 'emancipatory' claims of advocates of R2P and the pitfalls of leaving unaddressed more basic structural inequities in the international system, as well as an examination of the many pretences of universalism along with the suspect claim of furthering 'good governance'.

Rethinking sovereignty

Sovereignty is at the crux of the matter when we debate the doctrine and practice of R2P. There is a fundamental distinction some scholars draw between humanitarian intervention and R2P. In the earlier understanding, 'humanitarian intervention was largely conceived of as an exceptional measure undertaken in situations of emergency and extreme human suffering brought somewhat uneasily under an international jurisdiction to protect peace and security, or more controversially, to represent universal values'.[47] In the new understanding, instead of treating

---

[43] Anne Orford, 'Moral Internationalism and the Responsibility to Protect', *European Journal of International Law* 24:1 (2013), pp. 83–108.

[44] Coicaud, 'Responsibility to Protect: Logics of Power and Rights of International Law', Chapter 9 of this volume.

[45] Jonathan Graubart, 'War Is Not the Answer: R2P and Military Intervention', Chapter 11 of this volume.

[46] Kennedy, *The Dark Sides of Virtue*, pp. 3–35.

[47] Orford, 'Jurisdiction without Territory', p. 996.

intervention as an exception, what R2P achieves is a normalisation of 'international presence as authorized, and indeed mandated, by international legal obligations'.[48] Sovereignty in this new rendering is not an exception but a responsibility which implies that the international community must respond to specific crises. The international community here frequently turns out to be a euphemism for a select few major powers. Thus 'the terms in which international jurisdiction is formulated still envisage an expansive role for the international community in policing the action of governments'.[49] Such a move also departs from conventional territorial framings of sovereignty. As Anne Orford asserts, 'we might understand the emergence of the responsibility to protect concept as signalling the intensification of a non-territorial form of jurisdiction that applies to the world as a whole. International jurisdiction understood in such terms, and from the perspective of those claiming to represent the universal, would necessarily take priority over merely particular authority.'[50] Thus the overall attempt is 'to fashion the international community into something resembling a really big State'.[51]

The other apprehensions relating to R2P are expressed by Edward Luck (special adviser to the UN secretary-general in 2008) in a decade-long audit of the doctrine and its empirical record. While generally upbeat about the possibilities that R2P offers in the years ahead, Luck concedes that 'selectivity' and potential abuses of 'sovereignty' are some key challenges on which the future success or failure of R2P hinge.[52]

Further, it is important to raise the other question which is intimately linked to sovereignty fortunes particularly of states that invite the application of R2P – what criteria or 'methodology of assessment' identify a case as a particularly apt case for a 'measure of last resort' (intervention) in the calibrated R2P arsenal?[53] In the absence of general agreement on these criteria there appears to be a fair degree of latitude for major powers to manipulate brewing political situations in states where there is a keen desire to overhaul from the outside when a suitable conjuncture or political contingency provides itself. Luck himself argues that 'though its political clout stems from moral angst, challenging moral rectitude into effective policy remedies is a formidable challenge'.[54]

While it is clear that absolute sovereignty is no longer possible, it does not derogate from the 'paradox that humanitarian intervention is always an action of strong states with respect to relatively weaker states'.[55]

---

[48] Ibid., p. 999.   [49] Ibid., p. 1007.   [50] Ibid., p. 1010.   [51] Ibid., p. 1011.

[52] Edward, Luck, 'The Responsibility to Protect: The First Decade', *Global Responsibility to Protect* 3:1 (2011), pp. 1–13.

[53] Ibid.   [54] Ibid., p. 9.

[55] Mehta, 'From State Sovereignty to Human Security (via Institutions?)', p. 260.

Further, what has been raised in relation to humanitarian intervention also finds renewal in the context of R2P. We need to ask 'under what conditions can the claims of sovereignty be abrogated? If sovereignty is seen as a conditional grant, the challenge is specifying the conditions under which the claims of sovereignty may be forfeited.'[56]

An inflection point in the move from humanitarian intervention came post-Rwanda. Kofi Annan's enunciation of 'two concepts of sovereignty' is of special pertinence here. He observes that 'just as we have learnt that the world cannot stand aside when gross and systematic violations of human rights are taking place, we have also learnt that, if it is to enjoy the sustained support of the world's peoples, intervention must be based on legitimate and universal principles. We need to adapt our international system better to a world with new actors, new responsibilities, and new possibilities for peace and progress.' Annan argued that while Rwanda demonstrated the price of indifference, Kosovo 'raised equally important questions about the consequences of action without international consensus and clear legal authority'.[57]

There are four facets which Annan recognises as crucial to the concept of intervention. First, it must be premised on genuine universality. This is consistent with what liberals such as Pratap Bhanu Mehta in India also observe in this context: that 'to construe the debate between those who appear to be stricter noninterventionists and those who defend humanitarian intervention as a debate between those who defend cosmopolitan law or universal values, on the one hand, and those who defend the claims of particularity, on the other, can be misleading. Even noninterventionists are concerned about universal values such as peace and protecting weak states.'[58] Second, Annan makes a plea for a departure from the conventional reading of national interests. In his own words, 'a new, broader definition of national interest is needed in the new century, which would induce states to find greater unity in the pursuit of common goals and values. In the context of many of the challenges facing humanity today, the collective interest is the national interest.'[59] Third, a significant part of the onus also rests on bodies such as the United Nations Security Council which need to be sufficiently nimble-footed both to comprehend and respond to challenges as and when they arise. Finally, Annan emphasises the need for sustained effort if a durable peace has to be achieved. He points out in this connection that 'just as our commitment to humanitarian action must be universal if it is to be

---

[56] Ibid., p. 263.
[57] Kofi Annan, 'Two Concepts of Sovereignty', *The Economist*, 16 September 1999.
[58] Mehta, 'From State Sovereignty to Human Security (via Institutions?)', p. 263.
[59] Annan, 'Two Concepts of Sovereignty'.

legitimate, so our commitment to peace cannot end as soon as there is a ceasefire'.[60]

I am not persuaded that R2P as envisaged in its current form actually resolves the issues to which Annan gestures in no uncertain terms. Its legitimacy continues to be suspect (especially post-Libya). Its universality is contested and it continues to be unsuccessful in assuaging anxieties regarding a conflation of strategic national interests with collective interests while its empirical record of commitment to durable peace remains tenuous at best. It is not that these problems are not capable of being resolved. However, it takes a great deal of political ingenuity to craft an arrangement which at least substantially addresses these issues persuasively and comes to be perceived as sincere, inclusive and workable.

Hypocrisy might well be an inescapable dimension of politics. Both Stephen Krasner and Martha Finnemore, coming from diverse IR theoretical vantage points, identify this in their own assessments as an important trope to understand facets of world politics.[61] Notwithstanding this, for any political arrangement not to flounder, 'it has to pay attention to three complementary considerations. First, it must work hard to not be limited to a zero-sum game. Second, inequalities in the international distribution of power must be balanced by an exchange of rights and duties that is mindful of the interest of the various actors; this is especially important in a democratic environment. Third, agreement must be sought after regarding community membership, the identity of right holders, the hierarchy among them, what it means in terms of rightful conduct, and international authority.'[62] This appears to be a tall order but again is not an impossible institutional design to accomplish if it is broadly multilateral and genuinely accommodating of plurality in an otherwise imperfect world.

Epistemic biases and prejudices

An important aspect of power relates to the broader politics surrounding knowledge formations. How do we define categories? What lenses frame our dominant understandings of particular issues? Who are cast

---

[60] Ibid.

[61] Stephen D. Krasner, *Sovereignty: Organized Hypocrisy* (Princeton: Princeton University Press, 1999); Martha Finnemore, 'Legitimacy, Hypocrisy, and the Social Structure of Unipolarity: Why Being a Unipole Isn't All It's Cracked Up to Be', *World Politics* 61:1 (2009), pp. 58–85.

[62] Jean-Marc Coicaud, 'The Evolution of International Order and the Fault Lines of Legitimacy', in Hilary Charlesworth and Jean-Marc Coicaud, eds, *Fault Lines of International Legitimacy* (Cambridge: Cambridge University Press, 2010), pp. 87–114, at p. 99.

as the protagonists and villains in particular conceptions of world order? What exclusions characterise our assessment of particular human circumstances, and how do these exclusions and workings of power have a direct impact on larger political outcomes and the real lives of people?

It is against this backdrop that I turn to the idea of 'epistemological internationalism'. According to B.S. Chimni, the concept intends to 'correct the Eurocentric bias that characterizes information and knowledge produced by agencies of Western civil society and States of cultures, societies and histories of non-western nations by taking into account their self-understandings as a basis for expression of international solidarity, including suggesting different modes of intervention in the international community'.[63] A part of the lament relates to the selective dissemination of information which results in poor political judgements. Powerful Western media conglomerates beam images bereft of the larger overall context and tend to be opportunely used by governments to up the ante for particular ends. Governments could end up relying on 'a grossly exaggerated picture of ground realities' that does not contribute meaningfully to form intelligent, rigorous and fair political judgements. A part of the objective of inserting categories such as 'epistemological internationalism' into this debate is to acknowledge a dire need 'for the decolonization and democratization of information and knowledge networks'.[64] Earlier movements such as the plea for a New International Economic Order (NIEO) emerging from the global South were never really allowed to translate into tangible realities and it turns out that our principal sources of information continue to be the few powerful though limited set of big corporate media houses. Civil society understood in simplistic terms further complicates the scenario. In a scathing indictment of this problem, Chimni argues that 'there is an unfortunate tendency of western civil society to represent the domain of human rights violations as simply a relationship between predator and post-colonial states, and its weird leaders, and suffering populations. Removed from the scene is the role of dominant global social forces, international institutions and powerful States in embedding and sustaining economic and political structures that lead to gross violations of human rights.'[65] The irony is that this 'allows precisely those social forces, institutions, and States that are complicit in human rights violations to turn up on the scene as saviors'.[66]

The implication of these distorted bases for autonomous political judgement is that it also truncates a serious discussion of 'options' in a

[63] B.S. Chimni, 'For Epistemological and Prudent Internationalism', *Harvard Law School Human Rights Journal*, (2012); Last accessed online on 1 March 2013 at www.harvardhrj.com/2012/11/for-epistemological-and-prudent-internationalism.
[64] Ibid.   [65] Ibid.   [66] Ibid.

crisis situation. In contrast, 'prudent internationalism essentially means leaving non-western societies to deal with their own social and political problems. It calls for a degree of empathy to be shown towards internal explanations of the social and political crisis. After all, non-western people are not without history, including a history of resistance to local elites and foreign occupations. The strength and spirit of ordinary people in opposing vicious regimes in non-western societies should not be underestimated.'[67]

The 'asymmetrical valuing of human life' strikes scholars across diverse theoretical persuasions – critical IR theorists, neo-Marxists, post-colonial theorists and liberals as well.[68] More worrying is the fact that 'intervention exemplifies rather than overcomes the asymmetrical valuing of life on which the moral valences of sovereignty depend'.[69] To cut a long story short, it is important to ensure that greater agency be attributed to local populations.[70] Agency also needs to be understood here as crediting them with intelligence to figure out what might work best for their own political systems in crisis situations. Western intervention or doctrines like R2P cannot serve as a panacea to deeper structural problems which an unequal international order itself has in various ways perpetuated. The reliance on the employment of force from the outside is often misplaced and only worsens the plight of the local population as they are caught in the crossfire of their own government's army and armed military forces from the outside. Domestic governments which pummel their own citizens lose credibility and are likely to be overthrown by their own people who care deeply about their dignity and well-being. External actors underestimate this dimension and immerse themselves in the act of 'empowering' local citizenry against their governments, not always due to some altruistic motive but to also make inroads into other polities and societies and too often to safeguard more sectarian foreign policy interests. This has unfortunately proved to be the norm rather than the exception.

Conclusion

My central contention in this chapter is that R2P needs to be treated as part of an older and much wider global history of interventionism. While we may quibble or even fundamentally disagree about the diverse species

---

[67] Ibid.
[68] Mehta, 'From State Sovereignty to Human Security (via Institutions?)', p. 279.
[69] Ibid, p. 279.
[70] Frédéric Mégret, 'Beyond the "Salvation" Paradigm: Responsibility to Protect (Others) vs the Power of Protecting Oneself', *Security Dialogue* 40:6 (2009), pp. 575–595.

of interventionism, it would be fallacious to disregard this lineage when it comes to R2P. Blandly stated, R2P cannot be neatly disassociated from the prior modalities of colonial rule. Both in terms of its accent and actual operationalisation, it is burdened by the past, much as it tries unsuccessfully to tug in another direction. The world is no *tabula rasa* and although we may inhabit a different era today, the underlying premise that the West (used as shorthand here to refer to the traditional major powers) knows best remains essentially unaltered, though increasingly contested. It may not be stated explicitly on each occasion but it still latently informs much of the thinking when it comes to dealing especially with contentious issues pertaining to traditional 'high politics' in the international system.

During the course of this chapter, I have sought to assemble over-lapping sensibilities while looking at how we may conceive of the diverse logics of intervention, the motivations for humanitarianism, the reinven-tion of sovereignty and the epistemic implications and strategies pursued for the exercise of international power, or, to use a stronger word, the retention of Northern 'hegemony'. With regard to intervention, there have been several justificatory moves that have served as a pretext in the past to argue that there are exceptions to the general principle of non-intervention in the internal affairs of other states. If anything, states that have undergone colonial experiences continue to be extremely wary of external powers setting their houses in order, and with good reason.

What also emerges from our account is that we cannot sidestep the question of the links between race and international relations. Racial assumptions continue to hide behind seemingly benign assessments of the international situation. The connections between race and interna-tional law have been most clearly fleshed out in the work of scholars such as Anghie, but a tradition of robust Third World Approaches to International Law (TWAIL) scholarship continues to showcase its resi-lience and workings across diverse issue areas and policy arenas in contemporary international relations.[71] If anything, the history of

---

[71] Makau Mutua and Antony Anghie, 'What Is TWAIL?', *Proceedings of the Annual Meeting of the American Society of International Law* 94 (5–8 April 2000), pp. 31–40; James Thuro Gathii, 'TWAIL: A Brief History of Its Origins, Its Decentralized Network, and a Tentative Bibliography', *Trade, Law and Development* 3:1 (2011) pp. 26–64; Obiora Chinnendu Okafor, 'Critical Approaches to International Law (TWAIL): Theory, Methodology or Both?', *International Community Law Review*, 10:4 (2008), pp.371–378; Boaventura de Sousa Santos, 'Beyond Abyssal Thinking: From Global Lines to Ecologies of Knowledges', *REVIEW*, 30:1 (2007), pp. 45–89; B.S. Chimni, 'Third World Approaches to International Law: A Manifesto', *International Community Law Review* 8:1 (2006), pp. 3–27; Luis Eslava and Sundhya Pahuja, 'Between Resistance and Reform: TWAIL and the Universality of International Law', *Trade, Law and Development* 3:1 (2011), pp. 103–130.

colonialism reminds us of the need to be suspicious of moves that cement certain forms of domination that lodge themselves as a natural part of the furniture of the international system.

The modalities of power operate far more insidiously today in contrast to the naked exploitation and plunder of resources during the era of colonialism.[72] It takes the form of sustaining vast unevenness in the international system and naturalising this inequity.[73] Who would in principle be opposed to an idea like R2P that on the face of it is intended to save the lives of fellow human beings elsewhere? What objection could be raised to the idea that democracy needs to travel to different corners of the world and it might need a nudge on the way by those better placed? Who would argue today that human rights are not desirable wherever we inhabit the planet? In reality, we know that none of these ideas is as simple as it appears. Quotidian politics in the global South, both at home and internationally, increasingly require us to contend with the grotesqueness of power and its many lives in different political theatres. There is considerable inconsistency when it comes to the application of principles, not all human lives seem to count the same in practice, and we witness a fair amount of political dithering in instances when no real stakes appear on the horizon of the major powers.

The invocation of the 'human' figure also reveals a fascinating lineage.[74] Humanitarianism, we learn from Barnett's account, has had a convoluted global history. What we continue to witness are the echoes of the imperial presence in some liberal variants of the 'paternalism' of today. This is not entirely to rule out the possibility of human altruism but to acknowledge that much of its not-so-distant history has been imbued with Orientalist signatures of good and evil, right and wrong.

The most crucial site of struggle (though not always conspicuous) has been to do with the re-definitions of sovereignty. States today cannot claim absolute sovereign rights, and rightfully so. It has indeed been a sustained struggle to get to the point where our expectation is that states are to be more responsive to their peoples. However, this does not also translate into an untrammelled right of outside powers to intervene in the affairs of other states. From the work of Orford and Chimni, it is not hard to discern that doctrines like R2P, by casting 'sovereignty' as

---

[72] Gayatri Chakravorty Spivak, 'Neocolonialism and the Secret Agent of Knowledge', *Oxford Literary Review* 13:1 (1991), pp. 220–251.

[73] David Kennedy, 'The Mystery of Global Governance', *Ohio Northern University Law Review*, Kormendy Lecture, Ohio Northern University, Pettit College of Law, 25 January 2008. Accessed on 25 November 2013 at www.law.harvard.edu/faculty/dkennedy/pub lications/Kennedy_GlobalGovernance.pdf.

[74] Jenny Edkins, 'Humanitarianism, Humanity, Human', *Journal of Human Rights* 2:2 (2003), pp. 253–258.

'responsibility', seek to normalise the possibility for external powers intervening, stripping away the exception while remaining deeply imbricated with traditional geopolitical agendas.

Is R2P redeemable? Is it worth salvaging? I am not sure that either of these is possible or desirable given its current status and viability. The Libyan invocation has confirmed our worst fears about the R2P. All the checks and balances prior to military resort were not followed through with any diligence, arms were supplied to rebels and regime change was never mandated to begin with. Was this an accidental breach, or rather accidental breaches? From my perspective, there is nothing in the praxis of R2P that inspires confidence that it is going to be vastly different the next time. If anything, the prior history of interventionism, the hubris of material power and the myopia of a geopolitics that cannot wait do not augur well for serious international redress when warranted, least of all in the garb of 'responsibility'.

Index